I dedicate this book to the memory
of Natalia Bologovskaya,
a Russian seamstress and the first to see me in Paris,
who gave me the idea for this book.

BEAUTY IN EXILE

The Artists, Models, and Nobility Who Fled the Russian Revolution and Influenced the World of Fashion

ALEXANDRE VASSILIEV

Translated from the Russian by
Antonina W. Bouis and
Anya Kucharev

Harry N. Abrams, Inc., Publishers

Page 2: *Genya Gorlenko, a Russian model famous in Paris in the 1930s, in an evening dress from Maggy Rouff, Paris, 1936.*

Editor, English-language edition: Ellen Nidy
Design Coordinator, English-language edition: Tina Thompson

Library of Congress Cataloging-in-Publication Data

Vasil'ev, Aleksandr, 1958-
    [Krasota v izgnanii. English]
    Beauty in exile : the artists, models, and nobility who fled
the Russian Revolution and influenced the world of fashion /
by Alexandre Vassiliev ; translated from the Russian by
Antonina W. Bouis and Anya Kucharev
        p. cm.
    Includes bibliographical references and index.
    ISBN 0–8109–5701–9
    1. Fashion designers—Russia (Federation)—Biography.
2. Russians—Foreign countries—Biography. 3. Russians—
Foreign countries—History—20th century. 4. Costume design—
Russia (Federation)—History—20th century. I. Title.

TT505.A1 V3713 2000
746.9'2'092247—dc21

                                            00-38973

Printed and bound in Italy

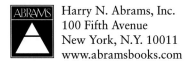
Harry N. Abrams, Inc.
100 Fifth Avenue
New York, N.Y. 10011
www.abramsbooks.com

CONTENTS

AUTHOR'S NOTE

This book is the fruit of many years' work, and the author is obliged to many people who lived and live in the most varied countries and who were willing to share their reminiscences. Their help was also invaluable in the selection of illustrations. I thank everyone who helped bring this book to life with their personal documents and photo archives. I am very grateful to all those who, even though we could not meet personally, gave me priceless information by letter, fax, and telephone interview, without which the book would have been incomplete.

I thank the following for their contributions to my work:

Lady Iya Abdy, Sir Valentin Abdy, Galina Achair-Dobrotvorskaya, Countess Lisha von Adlerberg, Kerem Ayan, Countess Lillian d'Ahlefeld-Laurwig, Prince Nikolas Andronikoff, Countess Carmen Apraxine, Countess Mira Apraxine, Count Nikolas Apraxine, Sonya Ardashinkova, Alexandre Arbatt, Natalie Auberjonois, Mona Averino, Prince Teïmouraz Bagration-Moukhransky, Michel Baibabaeff, Irina Baronova, Irina Balina-Vasilieva, Nikolai Beriozoff, Count Lennart Bernadott, Billy Boy, Ekaterina Bobrikova-Bonnet, Irina Borodaevskaya, Countess Jacqueline de Beaugourdon, Natalia Bologovskaya, William Brui, Nikolai Briansky, Helen Boulatzel, Dmitri Bouchéne, Princess de Caraman-Chimay, Leslie Caron, Anna Christoforoff, Alexandra Danilevskaya, Alexandra Danilova, Jacques Deleon, Baroness Galina Delwig-Gorlenko, Natalia Derfelden, Rostislav Doboujinsky, Halinka Dorsovna, Mine Erbek, Erté, Alexei Fedoseev, Jacques Ferrand, Hélène Gaudin de Villaine, Alexandra Gayard, Tamara Geva, Igor Glier, Princess Irène Galitzine, Maria Grekova, Kirill Grigoriev, Tamara Grigorieva, Prince Azamat Guirey, Valéry Guillaume, Mary Gurevich-Bloch, Georgi Hagondokoff, Ismail Hagondokoff, Irina Holman de Koby, Alla Ilchun, Tamara Ilchun, Michel Jellatchitch, Countess Veronique Kapnist, Valentina Kachouba, Yevgenia Kholodnaya-Laniken, Miquel Kireeff, Nina Kirsanova, Baroness Julia von Klodt-Jurgensburg, Olga Koreneva, Elen Korniloff, Natalie Krassovska-Leslie, Countess Olga von Kreutz, Nikolai Kulikovsky-Romanov, Tatyana Leskova, Jean Noel Liaut, Elinka Lizina, Prince Andrei Lobanov-Rostovsky, Count du Luart, Marvin Lyons, Gray McCartney, Princess Maria Magaloff, Carol Mann, Vicente Garcia Marquez, Maria Mertsalova, Sulamif Messerer, Princess Tatyana Metternich, Anna Miasoedova, Inna Mishchenko, Olga Morozova, Olga Morozova de Basil, Countess Vera Moussine-Pouchkine, Florence Muller, Maria Nenarokova, Nadezhda Nilus, Baroness Anastasia Nolken-Margoulis, Princess Alexandra Obolenskaya, Prince Nikolai Obolensky, Princess Janina Obolenskaya, Irina Odoevtseva, Natalie Offenstadt, Galina Panova, Felix Pissarsky, Zenaide de Plagny, Irina Pleve, Maya Plisetskaya, Vera Pokrovskaya-Lazuk, Nina Prikhnenko, André Prokovsky, Vera Pyatakova, Barbara Rapponet, Prince Mikhail Romanov, Prince Nikolai Romanov, Lidia Rotwand, Vladimir Reine, Tatyana Riabouchinska, Svetlana Samsonova, Galina Samtsova, Countess Praskovya Brun de Saint-Hippolyte, Princess Xenia Scherbatoff, Countess Alexandra Schouvaloff, Alexander Serebriakoff, Ekaterina Serebriakoff, Baroness Kira von Medem Sereda, Lev Skorokhodov, Nina Smirnova-Bieger, Princess Irina Strozzi, Barbara Santos-Shaw, Nina Shik, Baroness Irina von Shlippe, Elena Shreter, Varvara Shoupinskaya, Countess Natalia Soumarokova-Elston, Xenia Sfiris, Olga Stark-Kononovich, Aida Sycheva, Nina Tverdaya, Maria Ter-Markarian, Countess Emilia Tatishcheva, Nina Tikhanova, Count Peter Tolstoy, Count Sergei Tolstoy, Baroness Elena von Tiesenhausen, Francoise Taynac-Siu, Prince Sergei Trubetskoy, Pincess Olga Trubetskaya, Xenia Trippolitoff, Prince Cyrill Toumanoff, Tamara Toumanova, Natalie Trjezak, Tatiana Varshavskaya, Anastasia Vertinskaya, Lydia Vinokourova, Igor Volkov, Alice Vronska, Natalia Zamtchalova, Countess Zarnekau, and Faina Zelinskaya.

I also want to thank the newspapers from various Russian émigré communities that carried my advertisements seeking Russian models and people from the world of fashion while I was researching this book: *Nasha Strana* in Buenos Aires, *Predtechenskii Listok* in Canberra, *Russkaya Zhizn'* in San Francisco, and *Russkaya Mysl'* in Paris.

I am endlessly grateful to the archives and libraries that gave me access to photographs and rare newspapers and magazines that helped me in my work. In Paris that is the Bibliothèque National de France, the Bibliothèque de l'Opéra, the Bibliothèque des Arts Décoratifs, and the Bibliothèque Tourgeneff; in Harbin, the library of Harbin University; in Santiago, the National Library of Chile; in Hong Kong, the library of the Academy of Visual Arts; in Glasgow, the library of the Glasgow School of Arts; in Ankara, the National Library of Turkey; in Brussels, the Library La Cambre; and in Moscow, the library of the Russian Theater Union.

I am profoundly grateful to the museums that showed me rare dresses and accessories from their collections: in Paris, the Musée de la Mode et du Textile and the Musée de la Mode et du Costume; in London, the Victoria and Albert Museum; in New York, the Metropolitan Museum; and in Santiago, the National Historical Museum.

I am sincerely grateful to my mother, Tatyana Vassilieva-Gulewicz, and my sister, Natalia Tolkunova, for editing my early drafts and for their moral support over the long years of work on this book.

I would like to thank Antonina W. Bouis and Anya Kucharev for the excellent translation of my Russian text in a very true and poetic manner, and my American editor, Ellen Nidy, for the marvelous work she has done with the book.

This new English edition has been enlarged and updated with facts that I discovered only after the Russian-language edition published by Slovo was printed. I would be very grateful to my esteemed readers if they would help me continue my research in this field, which is largely unknown to the general public, by sending me new details and any corrections for future editions of *Beauty in Exile*.

In reading *Beauty in Exile* I learned many things about which I had known nothing, even though I had lived in the émigré community myself. . . . This book shows how Russian émigrés tried to survive while waiting for what many believed was the inevitable return to their homeland. Young men and not-at-all young ones found jobs as taxi drivers or salesmen of electrical appliances, typewriters, books and newspaper subscriptions, and so on. They took on whatever gave them the means to live until they could return. And not only men, but the women took jobs, as Alexandre Vassiliev tells us, describing the initiatives of several of my close relatives—including Princess Irina Alexandrovna and Princess Maria Pavlovna. The Russian émigrés did not give up, even when a return to the homeland went from inevitable to mirage. The Russian reader will find an entertaining description of the life of the émigrés, who were saddened less by the loss of their wealth and once-high position in Russia than by the gradual realization that they would probably never see their homeland again.

Prince Nikolai Romanovich Romanov

1
THE BALLETS RUSSES AND RUSSIAN FASHION

The Russian influence on twentieth-century fashion began in the 1900s. For the first two decades of the century—the years leading up to World War I, throughout it, and immediately following it until the 1920s—Russian performers and actors had an enormous influence on the development of fashion. Even before the mass exodus of émigrés from Russia as a result of the 1917 revolution and ensuing civil war, Europe was acquainted with Russian culture from Sergei Diaghilev's Ballets Russes and other, even earlier, examples of Russian art abroad, particularly exhibits organized by the patron of the arts Princess Maria Klavdievna Tenisheva.

The Russian art that influenced Western culture and fashion in the first two decades of the twentieth century can be divided into two main categories: native Russian, or Slavic, forms and colors; and themes or motifs that were not Russian in origin, but which were taken up by artists. Diaghilev's Ballets Russes, which popularized themes from the East and antiquity, fell into the latter category. Fin-de-siècle Europe, with its friability of social standards and the gradual changes in the institution of the family as a result of female emancipation, was fertile ground for the new fashionable styles introduced by Diaghilev.

The Russian influence on culture and fashion in Paris began during the period when Art Nouveau, called Art Moderne in Russia, was at its height. This movement, which flourished all over Europe, appeared as a reaction against the indus-

trial revolution with its mechanical production and against Victorian art with its retrospective and eclectic approach. Art Nouveau was a collective child of European artists during this marvelous era when fluid lines were still valued in art and strict rules of composition and balanced relationships of color still existed. Attempting to achieve a unified aesthetic of both arts and crafts, the creators of Art Nouveau rehabilitated folk art in many countries, including Russia. Fin-de-siècle artists, interested in creating new technologies in applied arts while also resurrecting old ones, tried to do everything to unite the natural and artificial in metal, glass, and wood. Art Nouveau works are characterized by organic forms, fluid, pastel colors, and a contrasting variety of surfaces and

Opposite: *Olga Stark-Kononovich in a Cambodian dance at the Folies Bergères, Paris, in a costume created in the style of Bakst, 1930.*

Above: *Alexandre Benois, Exchange of Odalisques, 1910.*

textures combined with melancholy and mysterious subjects and images.

National romanticism was one aspect of Art Nouveau. The search for the original sources of folk art led many Russian artists deep into their country's traditions and history, creating a heightened interest in folk epics, called *byliny*, and legends and sagas.

National romanticism existed in architecture, painting, applied art, and, naturally, fashion. In the first decade of the century, national romanticism was widespread throughout Europe and was highly developed in the art of Scandinavia and the Baltic countries. In Russia it led to what became known as the neo-Russian style, which adopted the forms of Art Moderne. It was this fin-de-siècle neo-Russian style that influenced European fashion.

The neo-Russian style was elevated to semiofficial art in Russia, where the spread of Art Nouveau was undoubtedly aided by the Empress Alexandra Feodorovna, wife of Tsar Nicholas II. Née Alice, Princess of Hesse, the empress was raised in Darmstadt, Germany, later one of the major centers of European Moderne, and famed for its artistic colony and regular art exhibits. The empress liked *Jugendstil*, the German variety of Moderne, and, naturally, supported the development of analogous forms in Russia. The ball at the Winter Palace in 1903, with costumes designed by the artist Sergei Solomko is one of the most vivid examples of the court's acceptance of the neo-Russian style.

The studios in the artists' colonies of Abramtsevo, the estate outside Moscow belonging to Savva Mamontov, the owner of a private opera company, and Talashkino, the estate in Smolensk belonging to Princess Tenisheva, were the best-known and most significant centers of neo-Russian arts-and-crafts production.

Diaghilev's magazine, *World of Art (Mir iskusstva)*, often published reproductions of works in the neo-Russian style. With the rise of interest in crafts, this style moved into fashion, not changing the fashionable silhouette popular in Russia in the 1900s, but influencing the ornamentation. Thanks to the successful work in Tenisheva's workshops

Above: *Ida Rubinstein. Paris, 1920s.*

Above right: *Jacques-Emile Blanche, Tamara Karsavina in the costume of the Firebird, 1915.*

Below right: *Georges Stein, Place du Châtelet, Paris, 1908.*

Opposite above: *Diaghilev with members of his troupe: on his left, the ballerina Olga Khokhlova, behind her, artist Mikhail Larionov, 1916. Photo by Valentina Kachouba.*

Opposite below: *Vaslav Nijinsky in front of poster for Diaghilev's Ballets Russes, the United States, 1917. Photo by Valentina Kachouba.*

Архив Валентины Кашубы, Мадрид

in Smolensk and Polenova's in Abramtsevo, as well as a series of crafts exhibits in the capital and the outlying regions, fashionable outfits included elements of "folk" costumes. Russian lace, more severe than Belgian or French, became more fashionable than the imports. The ruffles and detailing of unbleached linen lace went wonderfully well with the summer dresses worn at the dacha, Russians' country home, during the Chekhovian period of the turn of the century.

Lace makers from Vologda and Eletsk finally achieved national recognition and their handiwork was highly valued in the fashionable circles of St. Petersburg and Moscow. Stylized Ukrainian and Russian cross-stitching embroidery also appeared in fashionable stores in the cities. Embroidery was used not only on everyday summer blouses, but on dressier outfits, such as dresses for walking and receiving guests. But however popular these neo-Russian styles may have been in Russia, they were not what became

part of the arsenal of the fin-de-siècle Parisian fashion plates.

The first items borrowed from Russia by Parisian trendsetters were Siberian furs, sable in particular. The visit by Tsar Nicholas II to Paris in 1897 gave rise to French interest in the Russian empire, and fur trim and linings "*à la Russe*" became very prestigious. The celebrated fashion houses of Worth, Doucet, and Drecoll used fur to trim their models.

In 1905 the patriotically inclined Maria Tenisheva organized an exhibit in Paris of crafts from Talashkino. She hired a hall in the Société des artistes modernes on rue Caumartin, decorating it with paintings by artists Nikolai Roerich and Ivan Bilibin and with drawings of churches built by Roerich and Pokrovsky, a background that set off brilliantly the embroidery by the peasant women of Talashkino. The princess's own account of the influence of Russian crafts on Paris fashion is important: "Both my Paris shows had a strong effect

11

on fashion and accessories for women. A year later I noticed a clear influence of our embroidery, our Russian dresses, *sarafans* [peasant women's dresses], shirts, tea dresses, *zipuns* [homespun peasant coats], in fact the term 'blouse russe' appeared, and so on. Jewelry was also affected by our Russian artistry, which pleased me and was a reward for all my efforts and expense. It was clear that everything they saw had a powerful effect on French artists and tailors."[1]

Tenisheva took part in creating the costumes for the opera *Snow Maiden* (*Snegurochka*) by Rimsky-Korsakov at the Paris Opéra Comique. She wrote in

her memoirs: "I was given unlimited credit. Since it was impossible to get the right fabrics for the costumes, I made all the *sarafans* embroidered from top to bottom, and that, naturally, was not cheap. The *kokoshniki* [women's headdresses], necklaces, *shugai*, and men's costumes—all passed through my hands, and I made the crown of Tsar Berendei personally in my studio, since the one made by the theater's jeweler was unsatisfactory."[2]

Princess Tenisheva's activity undoubtedly helped Russian style enter western Europe. She wrote: "I am happy and proud that it befell me to intro-

Фонд Картье, Париж

Библиотека «Ла Канбр», Брюссель

Opposite left: *Members of the Russian choir, Agrenev Slavyansky, appearing in Vienna, 1907.*

Opposite above: *The actress Maria Verdinskaya in a blouse in the Russian style, St. Petersburg, 1908. Photo by K. A. Fisher.*

Opposite center: *Linen blouse embroidered in the neo-Russian style, Russia, 1910s.*

Opposite below: *The perfume Scheherazade by Charles Fax, Paris, 1910.*

Left: *Grand Duchess Vladimir in a Russian costume at a ball at the Winter Palace, 1903. The headdress and shoulder cape is a precious parure of diamonds and emeralds from Cartier and the brooch has a 107-carat emerald.*

Right: *Tsar Nicholas II at a ball at the Winter Palace dressed as Tsar Alexei Mikhailovich, 1903.*

duce the West to our antiquity, our art, to show them that our past had been touching and marvelous."[3]

However, the most significant Russian influence on European fashion came through the genius Sergei Pavlovich Diaghilev. Paris first came to know Diaghilev at the Autumn Salon of 1906, when he opened the exhibit of Russian visual art, which spanned the period from Vladimir Borovikovsky, a painter of the late eighteenth century, to Mikhail Vrubel, one of the founders of the Russian Art Moderne. At the festive opening ceremonies a special section was devoted to Russian icons. The show's success is described in the biography *Diaghilev* by Serge Lifar, a loyal friend of the great impresario: "The exhibit of paintings was a brilliant success, Russian artists were understood and appreciated, and many former associates of *Mir iskusstva* were invited to join the Autumn Salon.

They wanted to give Diaghilev the Legion of Honor but he declined it in favor of Bakst—could the manifestation of yet another Russian art unknown to Paris be as successful—Russian music?"[4]

At the time, France was very friendly with Russia, and Diaghilev's events were supported by society. One of the most elegant ladies of the Belle Époque, Comtesse de Greffulhe, helped organize the financial support for Diaghilev's projects. In 1907, with the brilliant performances of Felia Litvin and Feodor Chaliapin, Diaghilev gave spoiled Paris the masterpieces of Russian classical and opera music.

Diaghilev's role in attracting European interest in Russian art served different goals, much greater in scope, than the work of Princess Tenisheva, who was a passionate devotee of the neo-Russian style. In the early twentieth century there existed two currents of Russian influence on the West: one, according to Lifar, introduced Paris to "faux Berendeys and Stenka Razins,"[5] and the other gave freedom to artistic experimentation of unsurpassed magnificence, by the name of the Ballets Russes, which went on to become a milestone in twentieth-century culture.

In 1909 Diaghilev presented Paris with Mussorgsky's *Boris Godunov.*

Diaghilev had prepared this production for a long time: he wanted to show the authentic Russia of the late sixteenth and early seventeenth centuries, and to that purpose he scoured Russian villages collecting real Russian peasant dresses and Russian pearls and embroidery of the period.[6]

The result of the scrupulous preparation of costumes and scenery, based on the sketches of Bilibin, Konstantin Yuon, and Alexander Benois, executed at the Hermitage Theater in St. Petersburg, was stunning. The magnificent Russian pre-Petrine garments overwhelmed the Parisians. The critic Arnold Haskell wrote about it in 1935 in his book *Diaghileff: His Artistic and Private Life*: "This operatic realism was entirely new to the French, and that, together with the beauty of the choral singing and Chaliapin's double triumph, subsequently occupied the chief attention of the press."[7]

Архив Валентины Кашубы. Мадрид

Above: *Nikolai Zverev and Lyubov Chernysheva in the leading roles of the ballet* Scheherazade *at the Alhambra, Paris, in costumes from sketches by Bakst, 1916. Photo by Valentina Kachouba.*

Below: *A sketch by Leon Bakst for the sets of* Scheherazade, *1910.*

Above right: *Vera Fokine in the costume of Zobeide from* Scheherazade, *from a sketch by Bakst, Stockholm, early 1920s.*

Below right: *Dancers from the Diaghilev troupe in costumes designed by Bakst for* Scheherazade *at the Alhambra, 1916.*

Архив Валентин за Кашубы. Мадрид

Previous page: *Ballet dancers Efremova, Zamukhovskaya, and Kachouba performing an Oriental dance, Paris, 1921. Their costumes of brocade lampshade skirts, pearls, and egrets were created under the influence of Bakst's designs and executed by Valentina Kachouba.*

Left: *Denise, the wife of Paul Poiret, in the dress "Sorbet" created by the house of Poiret, Paris, 1913.*

Right: *Paul Poiret, the great reformer in women's fashion, Paris, around 1914.*

Below: *The 1002 Nights Ball given by Poiret on July 24, 1911, in his Paris house.*

16

Above: *Georges Lepape,* Souvenir of the 1002 Nights Ball, *1911. A drawing of Denise Poiret in the "Minaret" dress, designed by Paul Poiret.*

Below: *Lampshade dress of emerald green muslin, harem pants of orange crepe, Paris, 1913.*

Right: *Mata Hari with an Oriental egret feather in her hair, Paris, 1913.*

The three seasons from 1906 to 1908 determined the future success of Diaghilev's Ballet Russes, which lasted until the impresario's death in 1929. Thanks to their artistic influence on the social and cultural life of Paris, Russian artists and performers were embraced with delight, and the world of fashion was quite interested in the new Russian colors and forms.

With the help of people close to him—Princess Polignac, Misia Sert, Prince Argutinsky-Dolgoruky, and, certainly, his faithful colleagues Benois and Bakst—Diaghilev presented the first season of the Ballets Russes in Paris in 1909. He managed to bring to Paris a troupe of talented artists headed by the innovative choreographer Mikhail Fokine, and on the memorable day of May 19, 1909, the Ballets Russes opened with Fokine's ballet *Le Pavillion d'Armide,* featuring sets by Benois. The troupe performed at the old Paris

17

Châtelet theatre, which Diaghilev re-modeled. Among the performers were the incomparable Anna Pavlova, the beautiful Vera Karalli, the "Moscow Hercules" Mikhail Mordkin, the talented Adolf Bolm, the adorable Tamara Karsavina, and the genius Vaslav Nijinsky. That same evening two other ballets were presented as well—*Polovtsian Dances* from the Alexander Borodin opera *Prince Igor* and *Le Festin*, a suite consisting of individual duets and dances, including *lezghinkas*, czardas, *hopaks*, mazurkas, *trepaks*, and other Hungarian dances.

The second program of the first ballet season, presented on June 2, 1909, at the same theater, included two other productions by Fokine, *Les Sylphides* and *Cleopatra*, in which the rare gifts of Fokine's student Ida Rubinstein were seen for the first time in Paris. Diaghilev's first ballet season was a smashing success. Lifar wrote down Diaghilev's assessment: "Success? Triumph? These words mean nothing and cannot convey the enthusiasm, that sacred fire and sacred madness that engulfed the entire audience."[8]

The most popular ballets of the first season were *Polovtsian Dances* and *Cleopatra*, which had not only Fokine's innovative choreography in common, but also exotic oriental subjects. The *Polovtsian Dances* enchanted with their steppe wildness, while the appearance of Ida Rubinstein as Cleopatra was very impressive in the setting created by Bakst—she was carried out by six enormous slaves.

European fashion in 1909 was under the influence of the neo-classical style: a silhouette with elevated waist featuring straight lines. Wide-brimmed hats were in vogue and the most fashionable pattern was stripes. It was only during

An unknown woman in Oriental garb in the style of Poiret and Bakst, Paris, 1913.

the second season of the Russians' siege of Paris that the fashion world gave in to the pressure of Fokine's and Bakst's Oriental exotica. The 1910 Paris season of Diaghilev's Ballets Russes opened on June 4 at the Grand Opera with Fokine's one-act ballet, *Carnival*, to Schumann's music. This production had been seen before—in February of that year in St. Petersburg and in May at the Berlin Westens Theater. Overshadowed by the triumphant success of Fokine's *Scheherazade*, *Carnival* is often overlooked by fashion historians. Yet the costumes for this ballet were harbingers of women's fashion during World War I. The sketches created by Bakst showed the silhouette that became popular in the years 1915 and 1916, with shorter skirts and Spanish ruffles and a predilection for polka dots and whites.

Above: *An evening dress with kimono sleeves, designed by the Drecoll House, Berlin, 1913. Photo by Talbot.*

Right: *An evening manteau with fur collar, from the fur atelier Falensky, Paris, 1913. Photo by Talbot.*

19

The Fokine–Bakst *Scheherazade* played another unexpected role—it anticipated many artistic forms that later became component parts of Art Deco. *Scheherazade* showed sophisticated Western audiences Bakst's version of Persian, which consisted of Ottoman costumes and interiors. Arnold Haskell wrote, "*Scheherazade* set the tone in fashion, shedding bright colors into store windows and women's dresses, illuminating the tones of all subsequent theater sets. It moved to the stage of revues and music halls, until Diaghilev himself had to hide from it."[9]

Yes, this production, whose bloody and erotic plot was also invented by

Above left: *The artist Konstantin Somov in Oriental costume, St. Petersburg, 1910s.*

Above right: *The ballerina Natalya Truhanova in costume with an Empire raised waistline, Paris, 1912.*

Right: *A box with motifs from Scheherazade, Argentina, 1910s.*

20

Музей искусств, Индианаполис

Bakst, was for many years the symbol of Russian ballet abroad. The passionate love of Sultaness Zobeide, danced by Ida Rubinstein, for her ebony slave, Vaslav Nijinsky, excited the feelings of the delighted Parisian women. The sheer harem pants of the odalisques, the colorful garments of the eunuchs, the turbans of Sultan Sharir and his beloved but unfaithful Zobeide, the drapes of Oriental palaces, carpets and brocade pillows, lampshades, egrets, and strings of pearls astonished the audience. The characteristic Parisian desire to possess the latest and most unusual came to the fore, and the exotic Oriental winds blew into the ateliers of the Parisian creators of fashion and design.

Beyond fashion, the plot of *Scheherazade* influenced the morals and mores of the period. The sensual delights of semiclad harem girls with half-naked, black, muscular slaves on the palace's pillows was simultaneously shocking and attractive. Fokine was the first choreographer to bring an element of pure sexuality onto the stage, thereby emancipating the views of men and women in the sphere of the theater. The violation of this taboo brought on the wrath of moralizing critics. Bakst was called an erotomaniac and Diaghilev's Ballets Russes a degenerate enterprise. *Scheherazade*'s notoriety only added to its success, and audiences demanded tickets. Everyone expected to see indescribable harem orgies on stage.

The colors and combinations of the costumes and sets created by Bakst had an enormous influence on twentieth-century fashion. Seemingly incompatible colors combined on stage: purple and blue, yellow and red, green and orange. These types of contrasts were

William MacGregor Paxton,
Russian Woman, *1909. The portrait depicts an unknown woman in fashionable dress with a raised Empire waistline.*

21

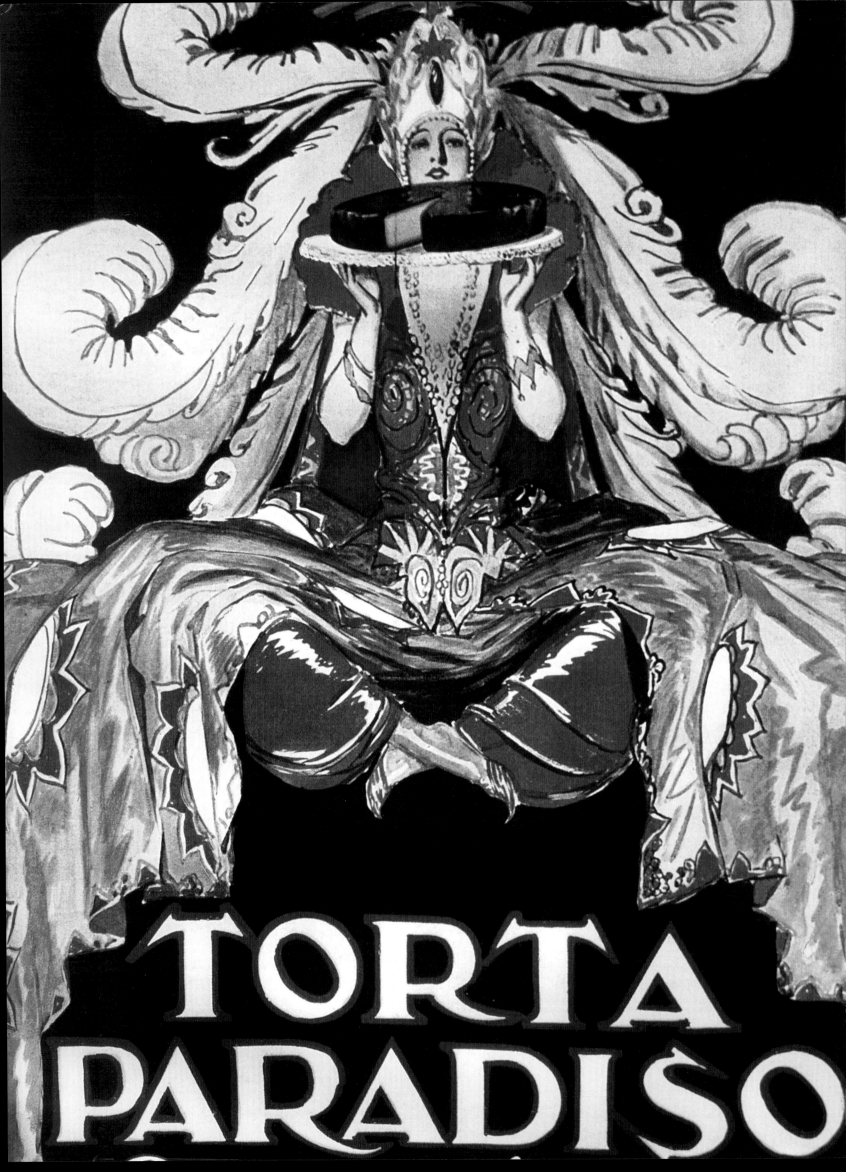

contrary to the concepts of beauty that had long been inculcated in the civilized world by Art Nouveau artists. Only combinations of pale pink with delicate lilac, watery blue or pistachio green were considered in good taste. The vivid colors of Diaghilev's Ballets Russes forced people to look at the world through a prism of bright sensations, to come to love color in its original form. For instance, the combination of orange and green, offered by Bakst, was accepted

with delight and lasted a long time. Moving from the stage to the world of fashion and interior decoration, it was extremely popular in the 1920s.

Other productions by the Diaghilev troupe from the 1910 season—*Giselle* with Nijinsky and Karsavina, *The Firebird* with music by Stravinsky, and the divertissement *Orientalia*—drew mixed reactions. The romantic *Gisèlle* was considered old-fashioned by many, but *The Firebird*, with sets by Alexander Golovin

and costumes by Bakst, delighted them. In any case, after two triumphant seasons Russian ballet became a permanent fixture of Parisian artistic life.

The productions of subsequent years—*Petrouchka, Le Spectre de la Rose, Narcissus, Le Dieu Bleu, Swan Lake, Thamar,* and *L'Après-midi d'un Faun*—were milestones in the history of European culture. Expressing the opinion of many contemporaries, the French writer Louis Fillet remarked, "This was

Opposite: *An advertisement for Torta Paradiso, made by Terrabusi and Co., Argentina, 1920s.*

Above: *Alexander Filister Proktor, sketch for a fan,* Souvenir of the Russian Ballet "Carnival," *1910.*

Left: *Demetr Chiparus,* At a Masquerade, *statuette of bronze and ivory, 1920s.*

Right: *An illustration by Mikhail Bobyshev of Vera and Mikhail Fokine in the ballet* Carnival, *from the magazine* Solntse Rossii, *Russia, 1916.*

23

an event, unexpected, a storm, a kind of shock, *Scheherazade, Prince Igor, The Firebird, Swan Lake, Le Spectre de la Rose*. In other words, I can say without exaggeration that my life is divided into two parts: before and after the Russian ballets. All our ideas, our perceptions were transformed. The scales fell from our eyes."[10]

One of the first to succumb to the charms of the Ballets Russes was the

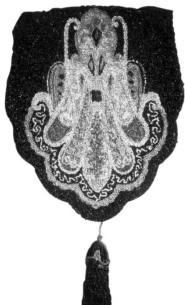

fashion setter of the period, Paul Poiret. The great reformer of women's clothing was seven years younger than Diaghilev and belonged to the same generation of people born in the 1870s. In 1898 he began working for the famous fashion house Raudnitz & Cie, directed by Madame Cheruit. The next year he joined one of the most talented creators of fashion of the Art Nouveau era, Jacques Doucet, and in 1901 he moved

№ 4711. *Loción* **Troica**

Above top: *A fragment of a three-quarter-length evening gown, embroidered beads on tulle, from a drawing by Bakst. From the workshop of Nadezhda Lamanova, Moscow, 1913.*

Above bottom: *A beaded reticule, Russia, 1910s.*

Left: *An advertisement for the German eau-de-cologne "Troica" in the Argentine magazine* El Hogar.

Right: *Parisian women at the races at Longchamps, 1913.*

24

to the oldest and most prestigious Paris fashion house, Worth. It was there that Poiret first encountered Russian taste and a few Russian clients. Worth, founded by the Englishman Charles Frederick Worth in 1857, dressed all the brilliant courts of Europe in the era of the Second Empire. Numerous Russian aristocrats who ordered the fabulously expensive gowns from Worth are captured in their finery by the brush of the brilliant François Xavier Winterhalter. During the reign of Nicholas II, the house of Worth—which, after the death of its founder, was now being run by his sons, Jean-Philippe and Gaston-Lucien—dressed Empress Alexandra Feodorovna and some of the ladies at her court.

In his memoirs, *En habillant l'époque* [Dressing an Era], Poiret, who had worked for Worth while Worth was still alive, gives a lively description of a titled Russian client, Princess Bariatinsky: "Once Mr. Worth was looking out the window at the lively rue de la Paix. He liked watching the bustle of the carriages bringing celebrities from around the world to his house. Suddenly he turned quickly and cried out, 'Ladies, ladies, it's Princess Bariatinsky!' I thought his heart was beating harder. All the saleswomen jumped up simultaneously and in the blink of an eye they had set up chairs along the walls, preparing for a

Below: *A box of "Powder of the Harem" talcum powder manufactured by Riegel and Co., Valparaiso, Chile, 1910–20s. The influence of the Ballets Russes affected even the names of cosmetics, such as perfumes, creams, powders.*

Right: *A summer dress of silk muslin and satin, Russia, early 1910s.*

Коллекция автора, Париж

Коллекция автора, Париж

25

show. They turned to the elevator doors. Hearing the noise, the servants came. Mr. Worth himself during this was trying to clamp shut the mouth of his little dog, also excited by the general turmoil.

"I stood at the end of this animated line impatiently awaiting a glimpse of the beautiful princess, the cause of this excitement. When the cab finally reached our floor, I was astonished to see in it a lady in black, resembling a fat priest with a red face, leaning on two canes and smoking a large cigar. All the staff gave her a servile, low bow. Worth himself bent in two. Princess Boryatinskaya announced, with a marked Russian accent, 'Worth, show me your latest,' using the familiar *tu* with him. The princess wished him to start with coats. Worth suggested that the princess take several chairs. The mannequins scurried, and I had the honor of showing a coat we had just completed, an innovation. Now it would be considered banal, even old-fashioned, but back then nothing like it existed. It was a black wool kimono, trimmed with black satin. The sleeves reached almost to the ground, ending in embroidered stripes, resembling the garments of the Chinese mandarins. I don't know whether the princess did not like the Chinese in general or whether she recalled the siege of Port Arthur or something else. But she shouted: 'How horrible! It looks like a sack!' I was terribly upset, embarrassed, and worried that I would never be able to please Russian princesses."[11]

Opposite: *Vera Fokine wearing the costume of the Firebird, Paris, 1926.*

Above left: *Vera Kholodnaya in an Oriental costume in the style of Bakst, Moscow, c. 1915.*

Above right: *Ivan Mosjoukine in Epstein's film* Lion of the Moguls, *Paris, 1924.*

Center: *A still from a French silent film with an Oriental theme, 1910s.*

Below: *A cartoon from* Punch, *London, 1924. "Dear, maybe we could move from Chelsea and go back to sitting on chairs again?" A joke about the trend introduced by Bakst of sitting on harem pillows.*

Poiret opened his first small store in 1903 on the rue Auber and then expanded the business. His designs, with their unprecedentedly clear lines and simple forms, attracted Parisian women. He was the first couturier to raise the waist in women's dresses, recalling Empire lines and thereby creating an elongated silhouette, like a cue stick. In the 1906 model called "Lola Montez," Poiret freed women from corsets, and in the spring of 1910 he introduced harem pants and pants-skirts into their wardrobes. The height of Poiret's creativity coincided with the height of the Ballets Russes. While in 1908–09 Poiret was interested in the severe forms of neo-classicism with elements of Empire in the details and drape of dresses, in 1910 his collection became lit up with the brightest Oriental fantasy.

In museum circles of Paris, the question of whether Poiret was influenced by the Ballets Russes is still discussed. Poiret himself wrote: "Like many other French artists, I was delighted by the Ballets Russes, and I would not be surprised if it had a certain influence on me. But I must stress that my reputation was created much earlier than that of Mr. Bakst." [12] There are definite notes of jealousy in that statement. Bakst and Poiret had never worked together; how-

Above: *An advertisement for "Cream of the Harem" with a photograph of Anna Pavlova, from the Chilean magazine* Family, *February, 1924.*

Below: *Delia Franciscus (Norka Russkaya), a violinist, in Oriental garb, 1917. Photo by Franz von Reil.*

Opposite: *Anna Pavlova and Hubert Stowitte in* Peri, *a short ballet, Buenos Aires, 1919. Photo by James Abbe.*

ever, let us note that contacts between Diaghilev and Poiret existed as early as autumn 1910 when, several months after the premiere of *Scheherazade*, Poiret invited Diaghilev and Nijinsky to his

salon to show them his latest models.

One thing is indisputable: Poiret's collections in the 1910s are filled with Oriental exotica. He created semisheer harem pants, introduced turbans with egrets, pearl necklaces, and lampshade-like skirts. The colors of his models echoed the fiery tones characteristic of Bakst, with carmine accompanying ultramarine, orange with emerald, and pink with gold. Using "theatrical" trims of fur and fringe and embroidery of beads, jet, and stone, Poiret achieved unusual effects and great commercial success. He could not admit to being an imitator of Bakst, of course, but the influence of the Ballets Russes on Paris fashion in the 1910s was quite obvious to contemporaries.

Prince Peter Lieven in his book, *The Birth of the Ballets-Russes*, wrote: "The influence of this style was felt far beyond the confines of the theatre. The dress designers of Paris incorporated it in their fashions. Poiret and Callot began to model gowns inspired by Bakst's painting. "Ballets-Russes" turbans and cushions came into fashion; dress material, even, began to be manufactured in the same style." [13]

Yielding to the general fascination, some Parisian, and then London and Berlin, fashion houses in the 1910s pre-

pared collections *à la Ballets Russes*. The most successful in this trend was the famous Callot Soeurs, founded in 1888 by Marie Callot, one of four sisters. It was among the first to introduce saffron yellow in their models, part of Bakst's palette, and to popularize harem skirt-pants.

The house of Paquin, founded in 1891, one of the most respected fashion houses of France, hired Bakst in the early 1910s, and he created a series of sketches of evening and day dresses for Madame Paquin. The house carried models in the Bakst–Diaghilev manner throughout the 1911–13 seasons. One such exotic outfit of the period is described in detail in the memoirs of the Diaghilev ballerina, Natalya Vladimirovna Truhanova, a Parisian fashion plate and great flirt: "My arsenal—I mean my toilette—that evening was outstanding: a dress the color of raspberry geranium with a flower frisson stitched on muslin velvet: the shape of the dress is empire, with a corsage trimmed in pearls and gold embroidery, with short sleeves and a long train that is tossed over the arm. . . . A wide diamond band shone on my head, a diamond necklace on my neck, drop pearl earrings and pearl bracelets. Gold slippers with matching stockings completed the ensemble. The mirror reflected my vision, which even I found astonishing."[14]

Outside France, the Viennese–Berlin house of Christoffe von Drecoll, founded in Vienna in 1894, and the first-rate Lucile, founded in London in 1895 by Lady Duff Gordon, were fans of the new forms. After the Diaghilev troupe performed in London, Orientalism filled the salons of British society, and aristocratic women tried to look like harem girls. The London newspaper *Queen* on July 1, 1911, described one such fashion plate: "We noticed a lady in the parterre who must have come straight from the seraglio. Her dress of rich silk with embroidery was shapeless, her head was wrapped in a round turban."[15]

A major triumph for Oriental motifs was the 1002 Nights Ball, given by Poiret in his Paris townhouse on June 24, 1911. The occasion, an homage to Russian ballet, was a distinctive quotation from *Scheherazade*. All the guests at the masked ball were dressed as Persian ambassadors, Ottoman eunuchs, Indian *bayadères*, or Arabian odalisques. Poiret in a turban and luxurious caftan was a sultan and his wife, Denise, his favorite harem wife, whose prototype was Zobeide. Most of costumes for the ball had been prepared by Poiret himself, and he had not skimped. Precious Persian rugs were spread right in the courtyard of Poiret's fabulous house, the wine flowed like water, Eastern melodies played all night—the unforgettable theatrical evening was a great success.

After that, Oriental balls became the fashion. Countess Klein Michel held something similar in St. Petersburg, and Countesse de Clermont-Tonnerre in Paris. The primary garment that the fashionable ladies adopted from the endless celebration of Oriental luxury and voluptuousness was the lampshade skirt. Denise Poiret wore one of the first at the 1002 Nights Ball. It consisted of semisheer muslin harem pants and a short skirt with a hoop, like a lampshade. Georges Lepape, the great fashion illustrator, depicted her in it. European women suddenly all wanted to see themselves as slave girls or concubines of a sultan.

In the fall and winter of 1911–12, Poiret took a group of runway models on a long tour of eastern Europe, visiting Warsaw, Krakow, Moscow, St. Petersburg, Bucharest, Budapest, and Vienna. In Moscow and St. Petersburg he lectured and showed his latest designs and also met with the Russian designer Nadezhda Petrovna Lamanova. In his memoirs, Poiret wrote: "Lamanova was an outstanding seamstress and at that time became my dear friend. It was she who revealed the charms of Moscow, that precious gateway to Asia. Even

Opposite: Anna Pavlova in the costume of the Firebird, 1928. Photo by James Abbe.

now I see her against the background of the icons of the Kremlin, the cupolas of St. Basil's Cathedral, and the marvelous collection of modern art belonging to Mr. Shchukin."[16]

Thus, in a roundabout way, Diaghilev's exotica, not without the help of Poiret, reached Russia, thereby closing the circle of the metamorphosis of prewar fashion. It should be noted that Lamanova's exquisite models of those years had an echo of the harem theme. A few of her dresses, from the museum of Baron Stieglitz and the closet of the actress Karakhan, are now in the collections of the State Hermitage Museum in St. Petersburg. The author's collection contains two rare pieces combining the creativity of Lamanova and Bakst: muslin three-quarter-length evening dresses beaded and embroidered at Lamanova's studio after a drawing by Bakst for the Bolshoi Theater ballerina Ekaterina Geltser. She received the sketch from Bakst in 1910 when she danced with the Diaghilev troupe.

Among the St. Petersburg fashion houses under the strong influence of Oriental trends were Gindus and Bresac. The first belonged to Anna Grigoryevna Gindus, who studied in Paris at Paquin and then opened her own establishment in St. Petersburg at 45 Mokhovaya Street. The house of the Frenchman Auguste Bresac was on the Moika Canal, number 42, and, since 1865, made elegant designs for St. Petersburg society.

It must be said that all these mind-boggling Baghdad toilettes of the 1912–13 season were not taken seriously by Russian high society, the aristocracy, who had more severe, English tastes. In Russia, it was the stars of stage and screen who were the passionate fans of this style. National and provincial actresses including the operetta prima donna Irina Orlova, and the dramatic actresses V. A. Mironova, E. V. Stefanovich, A. P. Milich, E. T. Zhikhareva, B. I. Rutkovskaya, and Maria Verdinskaya had themselves photographed dressed *à la Ballets Russes*.

But the most fertile soil in Russia for Diaghilev's exotic style was in silent film. One striking example is the in-

Архив автора. Париж

than the rest, created a decorator's studio called Martine, named after one of his daughters. This salon, which opened in April 1911 on the rue St. Honoré, created pillows, wallpaper, fabrics, carpets, and ceramics. Under the direction of Madame Sérusier, teenage girls from poor families drew designs for fabrics and embroidery. Thanks to Bakst and Poiret, harem pillows became a fixture for thirty years.

Another element in the Oriental transformation of homes and apartments was the silk, often painted, lampshade with fringe. It was intended to create intimate coziness in the domestic hearth. Additions to the interiors were narrow minaret windows, low, carved Constantinople tables, and soft rugs. The ballerina Natalya Truhanova describes such a fashionable interior of the early 1910s: "There was no chandelier. It was replaced by a tall *lampadaire*—a lamp on a pole topped by a brilliant alabaster chalice, from which poured a soft and yet bright light. The floor was covered by a multitude of various-sized rugs. Small, low tables with flowers and smoldering scents were everywhere. Simple, woven armchairs covered with gold-embroidered fabrics. Finally, a long and narrow divan-bed, smothered in furs and bright pillows, among which sat our host."[17] The house belonged to Gabrielle D'Annunzio, the famous Italian poet. The ballet *Scheherazade* made sitting on the floor or receiving guests while lounging on a divan very popular:

comparable film beauty Vera Kholodnaya, the first Russian vamp. Other film stars who liked Oriental fashions were Nathalie Lissenko, Zoya Barantsevich, Lydia Ryndina, and Zoe Karabanova. These stars, most of whom later emigrated to Europe, excited hearts and muddled minds, creating the first images of the femme fatale on the screen. Makeup from the Diaghilev ballets was also introduced to film—heavy-lidded, weary eyes, the rustle of long lashes, perfidious lips, and deathly pale skin. The look eventually moved from the screen to fashion, and the femme fatale

became the symbol of female beauty in the 1920s.

The Ballets Russes changed tastes in interior decoration, as well. Bright colors and shimmering tones became fashionable, and the tiniest details in bedrooms and living rooms were transformed by the taste for the exotic. Draperies with large Persian patterns became popular; they were used as overhangs on beds, lambrequins, and drapes. Another mania was for carpets and pillows, which created an air of the seraglio. Poiret, who discovered the commercial aspect of this style earlier

Tamara Karsavina, Berlin, 1920s.

32

this fashion lasted through the late 1920s.

Poiret opened his perfume shop Rosine, named after another daughter, at 39 rue de Colisée—the first attempt to create a line of perfumes under a fashionable brand name. Other couturiers followed suit. Poiret's Oriental flair was obvious in the names for his perfumes and cosmetics: "Maharaja," "Chinese Night," "Forbidden Fruit," and "Golden Chalice." Other perfume firms created spicy scents like "Sacuntala" and "Nirvana." Even the magazine advertisements for the famous German cologne "Troica" began using scenes from *Scheherazade.*

Poiret's rivalry with Bakst did not end his contacts with Russians; they had just begun. On January 3, 1913, Poiret met a

Above: *Tamara Karsavina in the film* Road to Power and Beauty, *directed by Wilhelm Prager, 1920s.*

Above right: *Anna Pavlova in* The Dragonfly, *a short ballet, 1915.*

talented young man from St. Petersburg. Roman Petrovich Tyrtov was the son of Admiral Petr Ivanovich Tyrtov, director of the Naval Engineering School. Poiret hired the young man as an illustrator and designer. The Tyrtov family, of Tatar origin, had served the Russian fleet for over two centuries; but from early childhood, Roman showed no inclination for ships or cannons, and drew instead. This is what he told the author: "I began drawing at three with colored pencils, and at six I drew my first dress design. It was a sketch for an evening dress for my mother, which she gave to her seamstress. The dress was a big success. When Mother saw that I was serious about drawing, she introduced me to the famous Russian painter Ilya Efimovich Repin. He praised the style of my work and gave me my first drawing lesson."[18]

Roman Tyrtov first visited Paris at the age of seven in 1900 for the World's Fair with his mother and sister. Ever since, memories of Paris gave the child no peace, and he decided to live there no matter what. He studied drawing in St. Petersburg at the studio of the artist

Losevsky. Roman Tyrtov told the author in an interview in 1987: "When I graduated from high school, Father told me to name my gift, and to his great dissatisfaction, I asked for a passport to travel abroad." But whatever Petr Ivanovich may have felt about his son's request, Russian admirals kept their word and he granted permission for the trip. In 1912 the young artist set off on his own for Paris, which later became his home. He never returned to Russia.

Before his departure to Paris, Roman Tyrtov went to the editors of the fashion magazine *Damskii mir* [Ladies' World] and offered his services as Paris correspondent. The artist arrived in magical, tempting Paris at the peak of the Russian influence on the city of muses. The Diaghilev troupe had one triumph after another. Charmed by the Russian ballet, Tyrtov recalled, "I was present at three scandals involving Vaslav Nijinsky. The first, was *Gisèlle* at the Maryinsky Theater in St. Petersburg, and then twice in Paris. First, with *L'Après-midi d'un faun* and then *Le Sacre du printemps*."

Concern for earning his daily bread forced the artist to work in the small fashion house Caroline. He recalled: "I lived very modestly then in a furnished flat. . . . My first year in Paris was very difficult, and the owner of Caroline did not like my drawings at all, and one fine day she said, 'Young man, do what you like in life, but never try to be a costume designer again, you'll never succeed.' And then she tossed my sketches in the waste basket."

Today, even the most scrupulous historians of fashion do not remember the name Caroline, but our hero became world famous. Pride injured, the young artist pulled his drawings out of the wastebasket, put them in an envelope, and sent them to Paul Poiret. The next morning he received a pneumatic letter with an invitation from Poiret himself.

Once at Poiret, Roman Tyrtov took the pseudonym Erté, based on the initials of his name (R.T.). At Poiret's studio, Erté designed coats, dresses, hats, and hairstyles. In the spring of 1913, he designed the play *Minaret*, with the artist Jose Zamora, at the Renaissance

Above: *Anna Pavlova in a summer dress and "tango" shoes with ribbons, July 1920.*

Opposite: *Olga Orlova, Tamara Karsavina, and Alexander Kazimirovich Kononich at the train station in Zagreb, March 1928.*

Theater in Paris. During his work on the costumes for *Minaret*, Erté dealt with the notorious Dutch adventuress Mata Hari, who at the time danced at the Renaissance. It was during his time with Poiret that the artist created his unique style for illustrating fashion.

In May 1913, drawings signed by Erté were first published in the glossy fashion magazine, *Gazette du bon ton*, and his fame grew. His drawing style of languorously elongated silhouettes evinced his closeness to the Diaghilev aesthetic; but, to the end of his days, Erté denied any influence by Bakst on his work, insisting that he found inspiration in Persian miniatures and red-figured Greek vases that he had seen in the Hermitage.

34

In the summer of 1914, having worked for Poiret for eighteen months, Erté left the house and created his own collection with the help of Poiret's first seamstress. This led to a suit against Erté, which Poiret won, leading to a cooling of relations between the two fashion leaders that lasted up to Poiret's death in 1933.

In addition to its influence on fashion, the Ballets Russes gave rise to the adoration of Russian ballerinas. In fashion, the influence of Anna Pavlova and Tamara Karsavina was particularly evident. Pavlova, without question the most famous ballerina of the twentieth century, had no equal as a dancer. Her name was the standard of perfection, which was why so many tried to imitate her manner of dress. Her perfectionist taste was described vividly in a book by her husband Victor Dandre: "In selecting a design of, say, light blue, she found it necessary to repeat it in another color. Naturally, all the trim had to be changed. Then, perhaps, in addition, Pavlova wanted to change the form of a sleeve, the cut of the corsage, until the confused and dispirited tailor shouted: 'But, Madame, what is left of my design?'"[19]

Alice Vronska, a ballerina in Pavlova's troupe, told the author about Pavlova's need to supervise the smallest details of her personal wardrobe and her finickiness in selecting clothing: "Going to fashion houses and stores with Pavlova was torture. She kept trying on and rejecting things, always dissatisfied by something."[20] Her personal wardrobe was impeccable, and her manner of dress created a special trend. Nina Kirsanova, who had danced with Pavlova, told the author: "Pavlova had a special way of wearing things. She particularly liked Manila silk shawls, which she draped in the Spanish manner. They took the place of dresses for her. It became very popular, and many imitated her."[21]

Another soloist in Anna Pavlova's troupe and a former dancer in Sergei Diaghilev's Ballets Russes—Valentina Kachouba, celebrated for her grace and beauty—shared her reminiscences with the author: "In life Pavlova dressed simply: a modest suit, hat—so that no one recognized her on the street. But she had such individuality, something so utterly special about her face, that people always noticed her, even if they didn't know her. I considered her very beautiful. She always dressed with great taste, usually having her elegant clothes made at Pitoeff. And when she was in evening clothes, it was something marvelous. Pavlova looked like a mannequin."[22]

Her popularity and beauty became the stuff of legend. Naturally, the world of fashion could not let this pass, since it had faith in beauty and obeyed the laws of commerce. In the 1910s and '20s there was a brand of cosmetic soap in South America called "Pavlova." Textile manufacturers also used Pavlova's fame: in 1921 the famous Paris fashion magazine *Art, gout, beauté* [Art, Taste, Beauty] announced a new fabric—Pavlova satin, perfect for dishabille. This was a light, semisheer fabric with a satin sheen, its airiness making it suitable only for marvelous undergarments.

The spiritual beauty of Russian ballerinas attracted photographers and artists. In the 1920s Pavlova was asked by several celebrated fashion houses to pose in their designs. In February 1926 the Paris magazine *L'Officiel* published a cover photo of "the weightless traveler, the Terpsichore of packet boats" in a dress from Drecoll in panne velvet trimmed in sable. The famous French fashion illustrator Georges Barbier wrote of her in 1923, "It seems that she has torn away from the earth and like a flower without a stem, flies up, spinning."[24]

The French press of the 1920s also wrote about the style of Tamara Karsavina. The beautiful ballerina was asked to make silent films, and the popularity of her elegant style was greatest in England, where she led a long and interesting life.

2
RUSSIAN FASHION DURING WORLD WAR I AND THE GREAT EXODUS

An old lady in a soldier's greatcoat regards us through a turquoise lorgnette.
—Nadezhda Teffi, *Reminiscences*

World War I moved fashion into a different channel. The military situation and the departure of men to the front fundamentally changed the status of women in Europe. Many had to take the places of their fathers, bothers, and husbands. New kinds of jobs, previously untenable for women—in factories, stores, schools, transport, hospitals, and clinics—led to a sharp transformation in women's clothing.

In the blink of an eye, the fantasies of Bakst, the Callot Soeurs, Paquin, or Poiret became unthinkable and inappropriate. It would have been ridiculous to ride a trolley in a lampshade skirt, stand in a bread line in a Minaret dress, or care for the wounded in a smoky turban with a spray of bird-of-paradise feathers. The new rhythm of life dictated a new style of dress, simpler to wear. War demanded different cuts and styles—skirts and blouses that fastened in front; sailor collars; small, clinging hats such as sailor caps; and dark, unstained colors combined with pure white became fashionable. The lack of fabrics led many fashion houses to reduce production of their wares.

The fashion in shoes, however, defied

Opposite: *Vera Kholodnaya, 1918.*

Above: *An advertisement for a fashionable store in Petrograd in the magazine* Stolitsa i usad'ba, *1915.*

the spirit of wartime, reflecting instead an interest in ballet. The 1915–16 season showed shoes with ribbons laced crisscross over the ankles. Since skirts were shorter, the ribbons were very noticeable. Spanish motifs in women's dresses were popular, such as wide bell-shaped skirts with ruffles that were reminiscent of the silhouette of the costumes by Bakst for Fokine's *Carnival* and *Papillons*. The famous Iza Kremer sang about this fash-

ion: "First a dress from Paquin, then a wave of white skirts, then laces like seafoam, and then her, then her."

Such skirts, wide and shorter, took hold in Russia, too, and were a subject of discussion in the Moscow *Zhurnal dlia khoziaek* [Magazine for Housewives] in 1915: "Along with the skirts and corsages of the first half of the eighteenth century, at least the crinoline, in the infinite expanses of which our great-grandmothers drowned, had its place. But how are we going to travel in our overcrowded trolleys and railroad cars with narrow doors?"[1]

The shortage of fabrics during the war and the high prices of fashionable goods led many Russian women to take up sewing and embroidery. Magazines started printing and selling patterns for their fashions, and embroidery and macramé became very popular. The Petrograd *Zhurnal dlia zhenshchin* [Magazine for Women] wrote on July 1, 1915: "Fashion is weary, fashion is exhausted, wilted in the summer heat. . . . Everything seems too hot, too heavy. The finest linen will not satisfy, it wants to be lightened even more, sprinkled with slits and stitches. Every voile, tulle, and

muslin is broken up with embroidery to let in a microscopic stream of fresh air."[2]

For the duration of the war years, high society in Petrograd, haughtily maintaining its dignity, did not permit liberties in its dress. Despite the war, linen and underwear were still sent to London for laundering and starching. The magazine of beautiful living *Stolitsa i usad'ba* [Capital and Estate] gives us an entire gallery of portraits of refined Petrograd beauties of high society. In the last prewar years the exquisite luxury of Petrograd society had reached its apogee. Pedigree dogs, first-class automobiles, priceless art collections, a slight drawl in pronunciation, refined manners, and flawless wardrobes set the inhabitants of the northern capital apart from Muscovites and provincial ladies. In describing one lady, *Stolitsa i usad'ba* reported: "Slender, graceful, delicately bred like a hothouse flower.

Above: *Princess Mary Shervashidze (Mary Eristova) in a masquerade costume in the style of Bakst. Photograph from the magazine* Stolitsa i usad'ba, *1913.*

Right: *The Russian beauty Marina in a summer dress of a prewar style, St. Petersburg, 1912.*

Above: *Grand Duchesses Olga and Tatyana and the Empress Alexandra Feodorovna at a hospital in Petrograd during World War I.*

Below: *The actress Valentina Mironova in a hat of black panne velvet, c. 1914.*

Right: *Film actress Natalya Kowanko in a dress without a corset, Moscow, c. 1916.*

She has dark bronze hair, innocent eyes the color of a Parma violet, and incredible eyelashes. Tons of chic, liveliness, and charm. She astonishes, captivates, and drives men mad, even though she is not very beautiful. Something between an ancient portrait by Vigée-Lebrun and a fashionable picture from *Vogue* magazine. This is not a woman, but a work of art—*une oeuvre d'art.* . . .

"Perfume is her passion. She cannot live without it. Perfume gives her mood, oblivion, and ecstasy. She intoxicates herself with it as with morphium, and she makes every part of her body be scented with a special aroma.

"Swaying on eight-centimeter-high heels of her hundred-ruble shoes, in the most simple outfit, a chemise style embroidered with old silver (a Poiret design), hair smoothly combed, she looks like a teenager, so innocent, touchingly simple, when she tells her admirers, 'You see, I too am combating luxury, it's really not at all difficult' . . . and, too, she is 'a bit of a barefoot, sings a bit the melodies of Grieg, declaims the poetry of Igor Severyanin and collects ancient

39

Архив автора. Париж

Архив автора. Париж

Архив автора. Париж

kokoshniki [women's headdresses].'" [3]

During the war an upsurge of Russian patriotism was felt in every realm, including fashion. Not a single charity ball or dinner passed without Russian "boyar" costumes, which became popular after the ball at the Winter Palace in 1903. Collecting ancient Russian costumes was considered bon ton among aristocrats, and appearing in them at costume balls was de rigueur. At such parties, everyone wore boyar clothes, old-style peasant dresses, and traditional pearl headdresses.

Singers of Russian folk songs—Nadezhda Plevitskaya, Varya Panina, Nadezhda Vyaltseva, and Yuri Morfessi, Mikhail Vavich, and Igor Seversky—became popular during the years 1914 to 1917. On May 14, 1916, the now-famous "Evening of Russian Fashion" was held in Petrograd at the Palace

Opposite top left: *Ballerina with the Bolshoi Theater and film actress Vera Karalli in a coat stylized to resemble a military uniform, Moscow, 1916. Photograph by M. Sakharov and P. Orlov.*

Opposite top right: *Ekaterina Geltzer, a ballerina with the Bolshoi Theater, in a dress without a corset and a broad-rimmed "Spanish" hat with a veil. The outfit is completed with a fur-trimmed throw and fashionable accessories—a large Italian cameo and silver cigarette holder, Moscow, 1917. Photograph by A. Gorinstein.*

Opposite below: *Tatyana Pavlova, dramatic actress, Moscow, 1916. Photograph by M. Sakharov and P. Orlov.*

Above: *Vera Kholodnaya in a hat with a veil and a chinchilla palatine, Moscow, 1916.*

Right: *Lidia Ryndina, an actress at the Nezlobin Theater in Moscow and a film actress during the war years, in a blouse with a sailor collar, Moscow, 1916.*

41

Архив автора, Париж

Архив автора. Париж

Theater. The beauties of the day modeled clothing created from the sketches of famous Russian artists: the charming Tamara Karsavina wore a red evening dress from Anisfeld; Olga Glebova-Sudeikina showed a red manteau by her husband Sergei Sudeikin; the ballerina Ludmila Barash-Mesaksudi wore a dress of old Russian quilted scarves from a drawing by Prince Alexander Shervashidze. According to those who were there, the other designs were overdone and impractical.

The elegant Tamara Karsavina made a patriotic appeal to Russian artists: "We need but ask our dear artists to draw dresses for us, oh naturally, completely fashionable, the kinds they are wearing now, but composed of motifs from Russian national dress, and order them to be sewn by Russian seamstresses from Russian materials, and we will have Russian fashion. And then? Oh, then we will go

Left: *Klara Milich, an actress at the Operetta Theater, in a batiste blouse ornamented with embroidery, Moscow, 1916.*

Above: *Zoya Barantsevich, an actress in Russian silent films, one of the first in Russia to bob her hair, Moscow, 1916.*

to Paris and show Paris our fashion, and Paris will bow before us and will order dresses from our best seamstresses made of Russian materials, from designs by Russian artists. And then the banks of the Moika and Fontanka, not to mention the Morskaya, will completely resemble the sidewalk of rue de la Paix."[4]

The observer from *Stolitsa i usad'ba*, who wrote under the nom de plume "Russian Parisian," was harshly critical of both the evening of Russian fashion and the attempt to give fashion a national color: "Of course, I know, that the clothes of our domestic fashion plates very often sin by the absence of that nobility which the French call 'distinction,' and also modesty, nevertheless, I am willing to bet that not many would dare to wear some of the dresses shown that evening. Of course, forget about our elegant ones. I looked at the large audience gathered at the Palace Theater that evening and was confirmed once more in my conviction that we have so little taste,

Above left: Nathalie Lissenko, an actress at the Korsh Theater in Moscow and a partner of Ivan Mosjoukine in silent films, in a fashionable bobbed cut, 1916. Photograph by M. Sakharov and P. Orlov.

Above right: Vera Kholodnaya as a femme fatale, Moscow, 1916. In her fashionable hairdo, a carelessly stuck pin, on her shoulders, a chinchilla palatine.

refinement, and sense of measure. Festooning oneself with precious stones, all kinds of bangles, everything that glitters, like Negroid people and the cannibals of 'Niam-Niam'—that is what we love and do well. And on which we spend all our money.

"The neurotic passion for trumpery and tinsel, for external signs of wealth—an indicator of low and coarse culture—suffices to fulfill all aesthetic needs for some. And, anyway, who is there to teach grace, measure, and nobility? Who can set an example of refinement and 'bon ton'? Our artists? Actresses? Or our men from 'society'? But our homegrown Brummells and Oscar Wildes behave and dress like dandies from the black Republic of Liberia. Rather, there can be no talk of male elegance here at all: after all, two thirds of the male population of Russia wear uniforms and walk around in uniform caps. That leaves our representatives of the fair sex. And how many of

them are the trendsetters in fashion, bon ton, and all the rest?"[5]

These sharp remarks regarding the tastes of Russian nouveau riches, alas, have not lost their appropriateness at the turn of the twentieth century. And this article was published in a time and place when style was plentiful—1916 in brilliant Petrograd, a city of grand dukes and personalities, such as Prince Felix Yusupov, and great artists, such as Mstislav Dobuzhinsky, ballerinas Anna Pavlova and Mathilde Kshessinska, poets Zinaida Gippius, Nadezhda Teffi, Anna Akhmatova, and Nikolai Gumilev, whose refined tastes and artistic talent were beyond reproach.

In one sphere Russian fashion in the pre-revolutionary years did not look to Europe—the sphere of winter clothing and furs. Parisian designers, due to the milder winters in Europe, did not pay attention to warm clothes and furs, and Russian seamstresses were ahead in these styles. During the war years of 1914 to 1917 they created many unique designs of fur hats, such as plush berets, Turkish turbans, and Hungarian and Russian toques, as well as all kinds of muffs, stoles, scarves, and bags. The most popular furs were seal, mole, karakul, ermine, chinchilla, and sable, often used in combination. There was a huge number of furriers in Russia, often Jewish, and their mastery was at a level bordering on art. Designs for women's winter coats *à la Russe* were developed during these early war years, as well as dresses were trimmed in fur. The fashion writer for *Zhurnal dlia khoziaek* wrote in 1915: "Many dresses, party

Above: *Vera Karalli in evening dress and a cape of chinchilla, Moscow, 1916. Photograph by M. Sakharov and P. Orlov.*

Opposite: *Elsa Kruger, the Moscow "Queen of Tango," 1916.*

44

Архив автора. Париж

Архив автора. Париж

blouses are trimmed with small bits of fur. Large furs collars and cuffs are put on coats and suits. Furs acceptable for mourning are primarily karakul, skunk, and silver fox, which became fashionable a long time ago and is still holding on."[6]

In the male wardrobe, fur-lined coats with beaver collars and hats were of vital importance in the snowy Russian winters. A famous portrait by the early twentieth-century painter Boris Kustodiev of the popular bass Feodor Chaliapin in a beaver hat and "boyar" fur coat illustrates this fashion perfectly. It should come as no surprise to learn that furs were often the first thing to be packed by the Russian elite, both men and women, when they were forced to flee abroad after the Bolshevik revolu-

Архив автора. Париж

Above left: *Olga Petrova, a Russian actress in Hollywood, 1918. Photograph by A. de Meyer for British* Vogue.

Left: *Zoe Karabanova, an actress at the Kamerny Theater, in silent film, and at Nikita Baliev's La Chauve Souris cabaret, in a feather-trimmed hat, Moscow, 1917.*

Above: *Vera Kholodnaya, Moscow, 1916. Photograph by M. Sakharov and P. Orlov.*

tion. They traveled with their wonders all over the world—from city to city, country to country. In her memoirs, the writer Nadezhda Teffi brilliantly describes the adventures of a sealskin coat: "A sealskin coat is an era in a woman's refugee life. Who didn't have such a coat? It was put on leaving Russia, even in the summer, because it would have been hard to leave it behind, it represented a certain value and was warm—and who could say how long the exile might last? I saw the sealskin coat in Kiev and Odessa, still new, with even, shiny fur. Later in Novorossiisk, worn along the edges, mildewed on the sides and elbows. In Constantinople with a soiled collar and bashfully rolled-up cuffs, and then finally in Paris between 1920 and 1922. In 1920, worn down to the shiny leather, shortened to knee-length, with a collar and cuffs of new fur, blacker and oilier—a foreign imitation. In 1924 the coat vanished. Fragments of souvenirs of the fur would remain on a cloth coat, around the neck, around the sleeve, sometimes on the hem. And that was the

Above left: *Savely Sorin*, Portrait of Nyusya Rotwand, *1918.*

Above right: *Savely Sorin*, Portrait of Princess Dadiani, *1918.*

Below: *Savely Sorin*, Portrait of Princess Mary Eristova, *1918.*

end. In 1925 the horde of dyed cats that attacked us devoured the meek and gentle sealskin."[7]

The February 1917 revolution and the chaos that followed made life in Petrograd anxious. Many who predicted the worst decided to move to Moscow temporarily, where it was comparatively tranquil, or, even better, to the Crimea. The more far-sighted left for the summer places in Finland. The lynchings, robberies, requisitions, and murders coupled with hunger, disease, and lack of firewood forced most of the people who could to move far away. The October Revolution made returning to Petrograd, and then to Moscow, impossible. Everyone believed in the imminent fall of the Bolsheviks and therefore they took only their most expensive and most necessary things. Some made the mistake of placing the family jewels in the bank safes of the capital, certain that one key would be all it would take to get them back. Others hid them in hard-to-reach places: they sewed them into corsets, secreted them in children's

toys, flower pots, in plaster casts on broken arms, in candle wax, and ink pots. One Russian aristocrat, Princess Vera Lobanova-Rostovskaya, née Princess Dolgorukaya, managed to hide so many jewels in her thick hair that there was enough for an auction lasting six days.

People leaving "for a while," took various amounts of luggage—from a small case with a change of underwear and a family album, to an entire arsenal of trunks. The trunks, sturdy and roomy, have often survived to this day in émigré families. In Paris we would sometimes see these huge trunks, often with labels from Russian railroad stations. Some were not opened because their owners were so sure of a speedy return.

We can get an idea of what the elegant Russian beauties were wearing in the years 1910 to 1917 from the wardrobe of the millionairess Tatiana Nikitichna Samsonova, née Nalbandova. She was married to Nikolai Mikhailovich Samsonov, a scientist of the Pavlov

Opposite: *Vera Kholodnaya in a summer dust-cover coat with a sailor collar, Moscow, 1916. Photograph by M. Sakharov and P. Orlov.*

Above left: *Alexandra Balashova, a ballerina with the Bolshoi Theater in an embroidered hat, Moscow, 1913.*

Above right: *Iza Kremer, a star of the Russian musical stage, in an embroidered hat shaped like a helmet, Petrograd, 1916.*

Архив автора, Париж

Архив автора, Париж

Коллекция автора, Париж

Above left: *Lidia Lipkovskaya, a soprano at the Maryinsky Theater, in a manteau with polar fox collar, Petrograd, 1914. Photograph by K. A. Fisher.*

Left: *A coat of silk faille with mole collar, Petrograd, 1917. This coat, which survived evacuation and emigration, was acquired by the author in Paris in the 1990s from an émigré family.*

Above right: *Alexandra Balashova in an ermine muff and palatine, St. Petersburg, 1912. Photograph by K. A. Fisher.*

Right: *Elena Lukom, a ballerina at the Maryinsky Theater, in a karakul fur coat, ermine muff, hat with a sultan feather, and leather boots, Petrograd, 1917. In the war years furs stopped being a luxury and turned into a necessity. Photograph by D. Bystrov.*

school and wealthy heir to the Petro-
vskaya Vodka fortune. She came to
Paris with her husband, who was doing
research before the war. In 1908 she had
the opportunity to dress well and elegantly in both St. Petersburg and Paris.
During the war, Tatiana Nikitichna
packed up her entire wardrobe and
stored it in her Paris apartment. It remained that way for almost eighty years
and was gone through only after the
death of her son in 1994.

The author had a part in this event
and saw for himself how marvelous the
arsenal of a fashion plate of old Russia
could be. The wardrobe consisted of a
dozen silk dresses in bright colors, sewn

Above left and right: *Ekaterina Fokine, a
ballerina at the Mariinsky Theater, wearing
dresses in the Spanish style, Petrograd,
1916. Photograph by D. Bystrov.*

Opposite below: *Matilda Kshessinska,
a ballerina at the Maryinsky Theater,
in a dress in the Spanish style, Petrograd,
1916. Photograph by K. K. Bull.*

Opposite above: *A drawing by
Deruzhinsky, printed in the magazine
Stolitsa i usad'ba, 1916, depicting the
impractical fashion of the "Spanish"
dresses, or "military crinolines,"
as they were also called, that
developed during wartime.*

Overleaf: *Maria Dolina's
patriotic concert in Petrograd, 1916.*

in Parisian and Moscow ateliers between 1908 and 1916. One could sense the Bakst color palette in many of them. They featured incredible color combinations: mouse-gray with emerald green, raspberry and gold, candy pink with black and tobacco. Each dress had a pair of matching satin slippers. A special section of the coffer was devoted to shoes. Dozens of hats—from the enormous wide-brimmed ones fashionable in 1912 to the small, helmetlike ones from 1916—were packed in hat boxes. A sea of feather trim, sprays, and aigrettes, completed these immortal works. Then came the coats, cloaks, and *"sortie-de-bals."* Cut and color put them in the Oriental style: they were made to resemble

the kimonos of panne velvet with silk lining from the famous Jennie fashion house in Paris. After the manteaux, came the suits. Then all sorts of minor accessories: boas, scarves made of silk ruffles, ties, gloves, bags, and veils. The section with fur coats, moth-eaten, was a pitiful sight. The wardrobe was completed by a collection of the finest silk underwear and stockings.

The mistress of this collection did not open it at first because she thought she would be repacking soon; then by 1920 almost everything in it was out of fashion and would have needed complete remodeling, which sealed its fate, preserving it for study by our generation. Of course, this is a unique case,

Архив автора, Париж

Архив автора, Париж

but in earlier times there were probably many such wardrobes in the homes of Russian émigrés.

The classic road for emigrants leaving Russia was to the south—first to Kiev, then Odessa or Yalta. The hardest part was crossing the border with Ukraine, where many were "undressed." For instance, Nikita Baliyev's cabaret troupe, called La Chauve Souris, had most of their things confiscated. Teffi joked, "Well, if they strip even bats there, what hope do the rest of us have of getting through?"[8] Cautious ladies bought up "the last rags" and even curtains before heading south. Kaza-Roza, the famous singer of the Starinny Theater, once told Teffi, "On the corner there's a woman selling a piece of curtain. She just pulled if off the window, it's fresh, still got the nails. It would make a wonderful evening dress."[9] They didn't lose their sense of humor even under those conditions.

After a spree in Kiev, where the leading artistic forces of Russia were gathered, the refugees moved on to Odessa,

Opposite: *Tamara Karsavina, Petrograd, 1916. Photograph by D. Bystrov.*

Above left: *Ludmila Barash, a ballerina at the Maryinsky Theater, in Paris, 1924.*

Left: *A silk dress in the "Byzantine" style from the Russian fashion house Kissel-Zagoriansky, 1914–18.*

Above right: *Olga Glebova-Sudeikina, a ballerina, Petrograd, 1916. Photograph by M. Nappelbaum.*

Архив автора, Париж

from where they could be evacuated to Constantinople. Our ladies, never losing their personal dignity, rushed to the beauty shops. "The Bolsheviks are advancing, we have to flee. You're not going to run like that, without your hair done? Zinaida Petrovna was a trooper: 'I realized the situation was terrible yesterday,' she said. 'So I immediately went for a manicure and permanent wave. Today the beauty parlors are chock full.'"[10] wrote Teffi about Odessa in those days.

After Odessa came Yalta, Novorossiisk, or Batumi. The good clothing was kept for a return to St. Petersburg or for Paris, depending on how people pictured the end of their exile. A wise observer of those migrations, Teffi wrote, "We wore what we didn't care about, saving our dresses for the shore, since we knew that there wouldn't be anyplace to buy new ones. We wore things that would not be needed in the near future: bright shawls,

Архив автора, Париж

ball gowns, satin slippers."[11] And here is a description of men's wear during the exodus: "The young dandies in patent leather shoes and silk socks, holding heavy baskets in hands with yellow gloves, hauled coal."[12]

The bloody war of the Volunteer Army with Bolsheviks was coming to an end. Never receiving the support of the entente with its arms, uniforms, or food, the Whites gave up their positions, bleeding. Loading up on ships, boats, and dinghies, a large part of the populace of enormous Russia, the main consumer of the Russian fashion market, was forced to choose the path of long exile—an exile

Above: *The family of Elizaveta Solonina, Kiev, 1918.*

Below: *The Epple family in Kislovodsk, before leaving Russia, 1918.*

Архив автора, Париж

that led to an unprecedented interest in Europe in all things Russian.

"The ship trembles, billowing black smoke. I watch with eyes open so wide they feel cold. And I won't budge. I violated my vow and looked back. And now, like Lot's wife, I am turned to a pil-

Above: *The Odessa port during the evacuation, 1919.*

Below: *Natalya Kowanko in the Crimea on the eve of her evacuation, 1920.*

lar for centuries, and for centuries I will see my country leaving me, softly, softly."[13] This is the sad, heart-wrenching ending of Nadezhda Teffi's memoirs. Let us end this chapter the same way. And from fashion in Russia, we will move on to Russian fashion abroad.

Архив автора, Париж

59

3
RUSSIAN CONSTANTINOPLE

The Golden Horn—a curved crescent in pale, beckoning clouds,
On the pale earth, amid laurels and roses,
Amid mosques, languishing in cypress groves,
The Golden Horn, ancient tradition holds it, are waters rushing from tears.
—Igor Korvatsky, *The Golden Horn [Zolotoi Rog]*

The exodus of many tens of thousands of refugees crossed the Bosporus with the ancient capital of Byzantium spread wide along both its sides—magical Constantinople. Hundreds and hundreds of ships, boats, and vessels flying the Russian white, blue, and red colors, or the flags of the allied entente arrived in Constantinople. An eyewitness of the events, Yevgeny Rogov, wrote in his memoirs, *Unwilling Wanderer,* "More than 120 Russian vessels of all sizes and functions dropped anchor at Constantinople: military and passenger ships and even barges attached to others. All were overloaded, listing, but with Russian flags. Over 130,000 heroes and their families left their beloved Russia as we later learned."[1]

It was November 1920. Those who had the proper documentation moved from this scrap of floating Russia into Constantinople. Others, without permission to go ashore because of the quarantine, traded the last of their belongings for food and water, which was brought by Greeks in rowboats. Another contemporary of these events, the talented Russian writer and playwright Ilya Surguchev, describes the arrival of Russian ships in the Bosporus: "On an autumnal November day 65 ships came to Constantinople from the Crimea. My God! What happened to that noisy, merry, and old crooked city! Reporters, Armenian monks, filmmakers, pashas, Englishmen, Turkish women in impenetrable veils, dervishes in tall gray *kamilavkas,* representatives of the patriarchate, smart lads

Архив автора. Париж

Opposite: *Namik Ismail,*
A View of Constantinople, *1920.*

Above: *A Russian émigré couple,*
Constantinople, 1921.

Overleaf: *The arrival of Russian ships*
in Constantinople, 1921.

in shorts with 9 x 12 cameras, people with Zeiss binoculars—everyone came up on the shore to look at the 65 Russian ships with raised yellow sanitary flags, overloaded to the bursting point, feebly listing to one side from the weight. The people who had arrived on these ships ate American crackers and unheated British red corned beef. The one thing they had lacked for the last few days was fresh water."[2]

The exchange of fresh drinking water for Russian military uniforms and clothing, and for family jewels, was the first contact between the battered refugees and the local population. Surguchev recalled: "Smiling mysteriously,

the Greeks demanded a lira for a bucket—in those days two million rubles. There were no liras, and soon, after some vacillation, coming down on ropes from the high ships into a Greek rowboat painted with the sign Megala Ellas came leather vests, wedding rings, military jackets with orders still on them, boots, and modestly bundled underwear. The Greek carefully examined the clothing in the light: any moth damage? He knocked his knuckles on the soles of boots, listening with a subtle ear for the right sound. He weighed the rings thoughtfully and melancholically on the palms of his hand, as if on a scale: first on the left, then the right. The people who got water drank it as if it were Holy Communion."[3]

Not all of these innumerable ships managed to land: many were sent to Burgas, Bulgaria; Greece; Egypt; Malta; and Marseilles. Most of the Volunteer Army, under the command of Baron Wrangel, with their wounded were sent to settle on the semidesert Turkish island of Gallipoli, which the Russian refugees called "*Goloe Pole*" (Empty Field). The conditions were inhumane, but thanks to strict military discipline and good army organization, the soldiers and officers managed at least to live in trenches they dug themselves.

Prince Pavel Dmitrievich Dolgoruky gives a truthful account of the life of Russians on Gallipoli in his book, *The Great Collapse*: "There is an entire literature about Gallipoli, and I won't give a detailed description of the deprivation

and terrible conditions suffered by the army in the city and the camp six kilometers away, where they were transferred in the winter. My detailed account was reported to Wrangel and POK [the union of field officers]. We had just begun getting settled. Later conditions, thanks to the exceptional energy of Kutepov, improved. Many families of the officers and soldiers also lived in the city in horrible conditions. At first some even lived in caves and under rowboats. Women and children often lived in rooms of destroyed buildings with three walls and no ceiling, using boards and fabric to plug the breaches. The hospitals were still in the most primitive state, most of the patients lay on the floor, and there were almost no medicines or instruments. Then the Americans supplied us with everything. Patients with various contagious diseases had to be in the same quarters."[4]

Top and bottom: *A panorama of the European part of Constantinople, viewed from the Bosporus, 1910s.*

Above: *Reviewing the troops in Gallipoli, 1922.*

Opposite: *Baron Wrangel visiting an orphanage for Russian children, 1922.*

The camp on Gallipoli was a settlement with military organization, where eventually French tents were erected, military parades were held as if in an active army, food service was organized, and a Russian field amateur theater was even established. Nadezhda Plevitskaya performed Russian songs in open concerts, and handwritten brigade newsletters were published. The majority of soldiers believed that they were not there for long, that bolshevism would soon fail, and that they would all be fighting in the near future to save their homeland. Alas, those hopes were not to pass. Some of the soldiers, who could not take the deprivations and no longer believed in the future of Wrangel's army, quit the camp and moved to Constantinople.

The city was then a picturesque and colorful sight. The Golden Horn, filled with light, the domes of the Byzantine Cathedral of St. Sofia, the minaret of

Constantinople le

the Blue Mosque, the towers of Top-Kapi Palace built during the Crusades, the round majestic dungeon Galata Tower of Emperor Justinian, the vaults of the Big Bazaar, the Rumeli Fortress, the semiruined but once impregnable crenellated walls of Constantinople, the impressive palace of the last sultan Dolma-Bakhche—all this on the European side. And on the other side of the Bosporus—noisy, Asiatic Istanbul, palaces and minarets drowning in fruit orchards, the Prince Islands melting in the morning mists. Add to this the cries of the mullah, the din of homeless cats and dogs, the fishing boats skimming the waters, and the uniforms of soldiers and officers of various entente allies in the streets—that's an approximate picture of Constantinople in the autumn of 1920.

The Russian refugees settled mainly in the European part of the city, on the west bank of the Bosporus in the region

Архив автора. Париж

of Galata near the famous tower by Pera Street, the city's main artery. This was the location of the foreign embassies, including the Russian one, and it was also near Taksim, the shopping square, and the traditionally Russian neighborhood of Karakey. It is here, not far from the port, that a Russian hotel, a Russian monastery, and a Russian church—the only surviving one of three, with an active parish to this day—still stand. The church is famed for its ornamentation by the decorator and artist Vladimir Petrov.

The refugees found housing as best they could, with no reference to titles and ranks. Conditions were very hard. They lived in hotels, monasteries, hospitals, and factories. Some found shelter with the Russian ambassador Neratov, in rooms and even on the stairs of the embassy, a marvelous red mansion with columns on the facade in the style of St. Petersburg palaces. Only a few celebrities with money, such as Alexander Vertinsky, could afford to live in the deluxe Pera Palace Hotel. The terminal of the Orient Express, preserved for the ages by the talented pen of Agatha Christie, was nearby. The Allies, the Zemsky Union of Khripunov, the Turkish Red Crescent, and the American Red Cross helped with canned goods, medicines, and some clothing. Due to the huge influx of refugees, Russian could be heard everywhere.

Opposite: The interior of the Russian church in Constantinople. Photo by Alexandre Vassiliev, 1994.

Above: The wharf in Karakey, Constantinople, 1910s.

Below: A tramway on a bridge in Constantinople, 1910s.

Vertinsky, who later returned to the Soviet Union, left a vivid and sarcastic description of the situation of Russian refugees on the shores of the Bosporus. "Old, yellow-toothed ladies from St. Petersburg, in men's mackintoshes, with turbans on their heads, took out from their purses their last cigarette cases— 'gifts from the tsar' with diamond eagles—and pawned them or sold them to the Odessa jeweler Puritz in the naive hope of better times. They were all very similar—straight as a staircase, with their flat and big feet in men's shoes, with Crimean, two-horned walking sticks in their hands—and they made a 'poor but proud face.'"[5]

The calamitous situation of the refugees caused various international committees to take active measures. The French Ladies' Committee of Constantinople decided to open a free kitchen in January 1921, at the Catholic school of Saint Pulcheria, where up to 700 Russian refugees a day had lunch. The Committee of the Italian Royal Embassy under the chairmanship of Marquis Vittorio Garoni organized the distribution of warm clothing and lunches. The Belgian Committee to Aid Civilian Refugees from Russia brought hundreds of orphans and single women with children to Belgium. The refugees also were helped by the Dutch, Greek, Swedish, and British missions.

Unfortunately, there wasn't enough help to go around. Only steady work, rather than occasional paying jobs, could give the Russian émigrés a roof and bread in those difficult times. British journalist J. D. Quirk wrote in his article "The Constantinople Paradox,"

"The coming of the Russians to Constantinople was the coming of a paradox. Constantinople has seen refugees of all descriptions—refugees from unsuccessful wars, refugees from panic, and a hundred other kinds,—but none more pitiful than those who came crowded on Wrangel's ships. It was a human catastrophe on an enormous scale and none but thought it would add another element of misery to Constantinople.

Nevertheless, though there was always this element of misery present and it was always on object and pity and relief, yet in a very short time it was the Russians who began to display to Constantinople the initiative of the artist, the energy of the artisan, and all the achievements of an unconquerable vitality. After losing everything, they came not to complain but themselves to give. They gave light, colour, comedy, beauty, song, ambition and hope. They showed themselves to have that eternally enviable quality of throwing off the past, throwing off the fear of the future and making gay the present."[6]

On Pera Street Russians opened restaurants, cabarets, pastry shops, and pharmacies. Practicing Russian doctors, lawyers, and handymen appeared, and cockroach races were even organized by a Russian army officer, Petr Boerodaevsky.

Above: *Alexander Vertinsky in the makeup of "sad Pierrot," Moscow, 1918. Photograph by A. Gorinstein.*

Below: *Acrobats in a Russian nightclub in Constantinople, 1928.*

The energetic Anna Zhekulina founded a Russian school. Russian newspapers of every stripe were published: *Novoye vremya, Obshchee delo, Rul'*, and others. In April 1921, Grigory Pakhalov opened Kultura, the first Russian bookstore, and Grigory Gordov, a judge and city leader of Kherson, Ukraine, opened the first Russian newsstand on the corner of Pera and Bruss streets.

Former army officers became very active in Constantinople as drivers. They even organized a special section for Russian drivers in the Turkish automobile club, chaired by Sergei Feodorovich Vinogradov and Vasily Ivanovich Zhirnov. Burnakin's almanac, *Russians in the Bosporus*, published in 1928, stated: "'Russian' driver, 'Russian' mechanic in Constantinople means 'best' driver, 'best' mechanic, and this excellent reputation is honorably supported by our auto repairmen to this day."[7] There were also Russian athletes in Constantinople. Quite famous among them was a Don Cossack born in Novocherkassk, Georgii Petrovich Kirpichev, who had done trick bareback riding from the age of fourteen. Arriving in Constantinople in 1920, he became a professional boxer under the stage name Kirpit, and maintained an unbeaten record.

However, the Russians' greatest influence was, without a doubt, on the city's artistic life. In October 1921, the Union of Russian Artists of Constantinople held the first exhibition of their works at the Mayak Club, under the aegis of antiquities collector Stanley Harrison. There were thirty people in the Union of Artists then, and the chairman was Vasily Iosifovich Ivanov, a student of the watercolorist academician Vasilkovsky. One particularly talented artist was Vladimir Konstantinovich Petrov, a graduate of the Tiflis Art School from the class of Professor Sklifossovsky. A passionate lover of Byzantine art, he created a number of charming genre interiors in the Oriental manner, which were very popular with foreign tourists.

The most respected of the Russian artists in Constantinople was probably the Odessa painter and portraitist Boris Isaevich Egiz, who had studied in Odessa with Kiriak Kostandi, in the St. Petersburg Academy with Pavel Chistyakov, and in Paris with Jean-Benjamin Constant and Jean-Paul Laurens. He was a master of sentimental salon portraits of women and children.

The Russian colony of performers in Constantinople was large and influential. Almost all the Russian performers who were evacuated through the Crimea passed through the Bosporus. Some gave only a few concerts and moved on, others stayed for several years. The Levantine audiences responded best to the lighter genres. The operetta artist

Après le Ciné le monde élégant va souper chez „MAXIM"

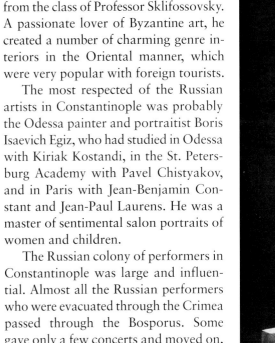

CE QUI NOUS ATTEND:

Au CINE „OPERA"

NATALIE KOVANKO

se présentera prochainement dans le beau film le

„Prince Charmant"

Top: *An advertisement for the Russian restaurant Maxim in Constantinople, 1920.*

Above left: *Valentina Piontkovskaya, an operetta prima donna, 1910s.*

Above right: *Xenia Fiz-Polyakova, a dancer in a Constantinople cabaret, late 1920s.*

Left: *A Turkish advertisement for the film* Prince Charming *starring Natalya Kowanko, Constantinople, 1920s.*

Top: *A drawing from a Turkish newspaper of Caucasian folk dances in a Russian cabaret in Constantinople, 1926.*

Left: *A cartoon from the Turkish newspaper* Aidede, *Constantinople, 1922, depicting a joke about the mores of Russian émigré women who abandoned their children with their Turkish fathers before leaving for other countries. It reads: "Ah, my dear* kharasho, *you're going away and leaving me alone." "Don't cry, I'm not leaving you empty-handed."*

Right: *A cartoon from the Turkish newspaper* Aidede, *Constantinople, 1922. "What would you like?" "Dear* kharasho, *nothing but God's help."*

Below: *A cartoon from the Turkish magazine* Aine, *Constantinople, 1922. "Where does the money go? We wanted to have a glass each, and we've had three bottles." "Even if you have twenty-one glasses each, I still won't be satisfied."*

Vladimir Petrovich Smirnov, famous in old Russia, organized the production of Smirnoff Vodka in Constantinople and with his wife, the operetta prima donna Valentina Piontkovskaya, opened the Parisienne Cabaret Theater. Here, as eye-witness Prince P. P. Isheev wrote in his memoirs *Oskolki proshlogo* [Shards of the Past], "the cream of the expeditionary corps gather in the evenings." But, he relates later, "The distillery's business wasn't very good: the Turks didn't drink vodka, the Greeks preferred their own *duzinka*, and besides which, there was a

tumes, you can understand the stunning success of *La Belle Hélène*."

Grigori Ragozin reported enthusiastically on the Russian operetta *Printania* in Constantinople in 1922: "The operetta troupe of Davetskaya and Ardatov has marvelous audiences. . . . The repertoire: *Silva, Geisha, La Belle Hélène, Good-Hearted Sinner, Bells of Corneville, Eve, Pharaoh's Daughter, Priestess of Fire*, and so on. The greatest successes of the operettas were Valentinov's *Priestess of Fire* and *Pharaoh's Daughter*, turned by the director's will into one of the *Mysteries*

Après le Ciné faites un tour de
fox-trott à la „ROSE NOIRE"

competitor, a Russian colonel. And the Parisienne flourished at first but then withered away for some reason."

In the Constantinople summer gardens Smirnov, Piontkovskaya, and Polonsky, under the direction of Lyubin, produced Offenbach's *La Belle Hélène* with great success. Apparently, this production was a typical example of the "decadent" St. Petersburg tastes of the pre-revolutionary years, heavily influenced by Bakst's Oriental exotica. Prince Isheev writes, "Hélène–Piontkovskaya was carried out by black slaves in a palanquin, and these were not extras covered in soot but enormously tall real Negroes and Nubians. Agamemnon came out on a donkey, and Menelaus–Polonsky was brought out on stage by a hamal, a Turkish stevedore. If you add to this the participation of Yuri Morfessi, the corps de ballet, the chorus, the original production, the stage action being brought out into the audience under striking lighting, and the colorful cos-

Above top: *Namik Ismail*, A European Ball in Constantinople, *c. 1926.*

Above center: *An advertisement for Alexander Vertinsky's Black Rose cabaret, Constantinople, 1920s.*

Above left: *A drawing from a Turkish magazine of dinner in a Russian cabaret in Constantinople, 1924.*

Above right: *An advertisement for a Russian commercial enterprise, 1920s.*

روس كورك مغازه‌سی

م. قوريس

حاضر وسپارش اوزرینه‌انواع كوركلر و كوركلك اعمالات قبول اولنور. كمال اعتنا ایله سپارشات اعمال امدیلر فینلادر رقابت قبول ایتمز.

MAISON RUSSE DE FOURRURES

M. KOURISS

409, Grand'Rue de Péra, 409

Vis à v's de l'hôtel Yanny   Tél. Péra 3667

GRAND CHOIX DE FOURRURES

Prêtes et sur Commande

EXECUTION SOIGNÉE,

PRIX HORS CONCURRENCE.

Gypsy singer Nastya Polyakova, as well as Elena Muravyova, who sang Gypsy love songs, performed there. The dramatic soprano Anna Pavlovna Volina was wildly popular with Turkish and Russian audiences: she was one of the first to sing Russian love songs in Turkish. Language in Constantinople was not such a difficult barrier for the Russian émigrés. The majority of Europeans and Levantines there spoke French, which had been the most popular foreign language in tsarist Russia as well.

One of the most experienced concert singers of that period was Natalya Ivanovna Zhilo, a soprano and graduate of the Moscow Conservatory. She had a wide-ranging chamber repertoire of Russian classics and would appear in a pearl-embroidered headdress and a festive "Grand Duchess" dress. Another concert

of the Harem, and Lehar's *Eve*. They have announced *Rose of Stambul* and *Blue Mazurka*. Of the actors, first place goes to V. I. Piontkovskaya, who has won a permanent place in the hearts of the audience. Also to be noted is Mrs. Selivanova, the marvelous Priestess, Angel, and Widow. Of the men, besides the already acknowledged N. Seversky and A. Polonsky, the young artist G. Klarin enjoys constant success—a wonderful tenor with brilliant highs and an unusually caressing timbre."[9] The productions were so vivid and the repertory so varied (although the Oriental exotica still dominated), that today we are amazed by the Russian actors' energy and persistence during such a difficult time.

A particularly important contribution to the popularization of Russian art and style were the performances of Russian women singers. The famous

Top: *An advertisement for M. Kouriss, a Russian fur salon, Constantinople, 1920s.*

Above, left and right: *Drawings of dresses worn by Russian émigrés in Constantinople, 1923–24.*

Right: *An advertisement for Tourtchikhine, a Russian furrier, Constantinople, 1923.*

Opposite: *An illustration from the Turkish magazine* Hanym, *1921.*

خانم افندیلر !

اكر شیق كینمك وذوق سلیمكزه موافق نویلی مانطولر اكسا اتمك ایسترسه‌كز، موسقوا كوركلر تزیسی تور چیخین

بتون سپارشاتكزی درعهده رایدر. درس بك اوغلی جادة كبیر نومرو: ١٠٥ آیوك پارمق قپو مدخلی نومرو: ٢

Mesdames, Si vous voulez être élégamment vêtues et avoir en ordre vos fourrures faites vos commandes au fourrurier moscovite

TOURTCHIKHINE

Grand'Rue de Péra, 105

Entrée de Buyuk Parmak Kapou, 2

Коллекция автора. Париж

Gypsy repertoires to the Constantinople audiences, all these artists promoted the popularization of Russian taste and style.

A real symbol of "beauty in exile" in Constantinople was the Russian ballet. Before the arrival of Russian émigrés there had been no ballet there at all, but then the famous ballerina of the Warsaw Theater, Olga Alexandrovna Mechkovskaya, had come to the city with her daughter, Anna, and opened a ballet studio. As *Russians on the Bosporus* put it, Mechkovskaya could "justly be considered the inspiration of the Russian ballet in Constantinople." After her, Lidia Krassa-Arzumanova, who was born in St. Petersburg and studied ballet there, opened a studio at which she continued to teach even after the war. One of Arzumanova's students, Elena Gordienko, who now lives

Национальная библиотека. Анкара

performer *à la russe* in Constantinople was Natalya Ivanovna Polyanskaya, who had a lovely luscious soprano voice and had trained in Kharkov with the famous teacher Natalya Davydova. A favorite of the cosmopolitan audience in the Bosporus, receiving great publicity, Natalya Polyanskaya appeared on the stage in a richly decorated headdress in the style of the 1903 Winter Ball in St. Petersburg and sang arias from *The Tsar's Bride, Oprichnik, Eugene Onegin,* and *Queen of Spades.* The soprano Tarakanova sang in one of the cabarets on Pera Street. Among the performers of the Russian repertoire, the basses Alexander Sokolov and Artamonov were most outstanding. In presenting the masterpieces of Russian classical, folk, and

Дом-музей Ататюрка. Анкара

Above, left: *A silk blouse with a side fastening, like a Russian shirt, decorated with Ottoman embroidery and made by Russian émigrés, Constantinople, 1921–24.*

Above: *A cartoon from the Turkish newspaper* Diken, *Constantinople, 1920. "How do accidents happen? Russian women cross the street."*

Left: *An evening dress handcrafted from silk with appliques of machine-made lace from the wardrobe of Mevibe, the wife of the president of the Turkish Republic.*

Opposite: *An evening dress of "Cairo work," tulle trimmed with woven silver threads, from the wardrobe of Princess Maria Iliodorovna Orlova, Constantinople, c. 1922.*

in Istanbul, recalls, "Everyone started at Arzumanova's. But she taught more the atmosphere, the ballet air, so to speak."[10] Nevertheless, Arzumanova is considered both in Ankara and Istanbul one of the creators of the Turkish national ballet.

Famous performers in the Russian ballet troupe were the character dancer Zavarikhin, the ballerina Trappoli, and a former dancer with the Diaghilev troupe, Vladimir Karnetszky, who had soloed for the celebrated impresario in *Polovtsian Dances*, partnered Vera Nemchinova in *Le Pavilion d'Armide,* and danced the Charlatan in *Petrouchka* and the trepak in *Sleeping Beauty* with Slavinsky and Voitsekhovsky. He had graduated from the Warsaw Theater School in Valishevsky's class, danced in the Kiev City Theater, and perfected his work with Bronislava Nijinska. His partner in Constantinople was Marta Kruger, and they danced variations from Diaghilev's repertoire in the Fokine style.

The production of *Scheherazade* by the choreographer Victor Zimin played an important role in promoting Russian art. The costumes were created by the highly talented Paul Tchelichew, who did the design for six productions by Zimin's troupe and was closely tied in Paris to the Diaghilev company and the fashion world. Grigory Ragozin, the Constantinople correspondent for the Russian journal *Teatr i zhizn'* [Theater and Life], published in Berlin, wrote in 1922 about this production at the Les Petits Champs Theatre: "Rimsky-Korsakov's *Scheherazade* was an exceptional success, repeated several times. This production was a true artistic event. The brilliant and colorful ballet won the audience's heart. G. Butnikov's wonderful orchestra, familiar to Russians from the Kislovodsk and Kharkov seasons, sounded marvelous. *Scheherazade* was danced by E. Gluk, who had wide success in the divertissement *Dying Swan*, but in this ballet there was something lacking in her dancing. It needed more exoticism, color, everything that Rimsky-Korsakov's musical palette has in abundance. V. Zimin moved well and danced handsomely, but nothing more. And yet *Scheherazade* requires a 'face.' But

expression was unquestionably the talented young dancer's weak point. Technically he was prepared, but he had not thought through the character's image. The group scenes were brilliantly conceived, but the execution was technically lacking, which is due to the weakness of the corps de ballet. In general, *Scheherazade* was a marvelous spectacle; after the amateur productions, hastily and carelessly thrown together, this was a true triumph of Russian art."[11]

The language barrier was harder for Russian theater actors in Constantinople. They were forced to seek other Russian-language centers and often traveled on guest tours to Riga, Paris, Prague, Belgrade, Berlin, and Sofia. Nevertheless, successful appearances were made by the pretty Julia Gorskaya and the famous actor Alexander Mursky, about whom *Teatr i zhizn'* wrote in 1922, "A. A. Mursky ended his guest tour in Constantinople. His acting revived in the memories of Russian-theater lovers the glorious days of the classical school. His lush incarnations, so full of life force, were performed for the local audiences. From here, A. A. Mursky is starting a tour of Europe."[12]

It was much easier for singers, particularly those with a foreign repertoire. Thus, the refugees founded an Italian opera troupe. The magazine *Teatr i zhizn'* wrote: "Performances of Italian opera are continuing successfully. The cast: the misses Vasenkova, Silivanova, Tabassi, Pankova, Milosh, Vasilkova, Kaizer; messieurs de Neri (an Italian tenor who fled from Odessa), Dubinsky, Kondratyev, Glinoetsky, Grigorovich, Lampi, Vekov. The chorus is Savitsky's, the ballet Zimin's, the artistic director is Uzunov, an artist from the Moscow Art Theater, the director is Dubinsky. Orchestra, M. Skarselli. The repertoire: *Aida*, *Faust*, *Carmen*, *I Pagliacci*, *Cavalleria Rusticana*, *Madame Butterfly*, *Tosca*, *Manon*, *Lucia di Lammermoor*, and others."[13]

Published in 1924 in Constantinople, the almanac *Na proshchan'e* [In Farewell], wrote about the contribution of Russian artists to the city's artistic life: "The Russian ballet, operetta, opera, and Russian concerts were the crown of artistic evenings, extraordinary in content, where so often the residents of Pera met, delighting in the musical and artistic genius of the Russian people."[14] How much more accurate this assessment is than the gloomy pictures of life as an émigré depicted by the "red count" Alexei Tolstoi or by Mikhail Bulgakov.

The Russian influence was also enormous on the restaurants and night life of the city. The famous "Moscow Negro" Fedor Fedorovich Tomas, formerly the owner of Maxim's cabaret in Moscow, opened a similar establishment in the Stella Gardens of Constantinople. The violinist Mikhail Ivanovich Goulesco played at the gambling house run by Sergei Altbrandt of Odessa. Born in Romania, since 1912 Goulesco had performed all over Russia: from Baku and Kislovodsk to Moscow's famous Strelnya restaurant; then, evacuating to Constantinople in 1921, he thrilled crowds at Les Petits Champs and Maxim.

In almost every restaurant, cabaret, and film theater in Constantinople were Russian musicians and even entire Russian orchestras. At the fashionable Pera Palace Hotel, Pavel Alexeivich Zamulenko led a jazz orchestra that included V. I. Porjytzky, A. de Matei, P. Charkovsky, A. Ivanov, and V. Bekker. Maria Vladimirovna Obolenskaya, a graduate of the St. Petersburg Conservatory, accompanied solo performers in cabaret; Pavel Lunich was a classical concert pianist, Konstantin Stepanovich Stengach conducted musical evenings; and the young pianist Konstantin Dmitrievich Nikolsky, who began composing in Constantinople, wrote numerous love songs and ballet numbers.

The Russian orchestra at the Magique film theater on Taksim Square—under the baton of maestro Ivan Ivanovich Polyansky, a graduate of the Rostov Musical School and the Don Philharmonic—was also celebrated.

The author had the fortune to meet in Istanbul with Baroness Valentina Yulianovna Clodt von Jürgensburg, who took an active part in the Russian musical life of Constantinople in the early 1920s. She was a colorful "attraction" of the city's Russian community throughout her life and died there in 1992. Around 1921, during the silent-film era when all movies had musical accompaniment, she began playing in the Magique Theater orchestra.

She recalled: "All the musicians in movie theaters then were Russian. In 1920, in the fall, I was evacuated to Constantinople from Feodosia and it was only then I learned that my husband, Baron Konstantin Clodt von Jürgensburg, had been killed by the Bolsheviks. The baronial line of Clodt von Jürgensburg came from Westphalia, its members moved in the early sixteenth century to Liflandia, and their descendants included vice-governors of Riga. The artistically gifted family of the Baron Clodt von Jürgensburg gave Russia three famous artists, of whom the most famous was Petr Karlovich (1805–67), creator of the four groups of horses with youths controlling them on the Anichkov Bridge in St. Petersburg. I was born in 1902 in the Caucasus, in Grozny. My mother was Russian, my father a Pole. My aunt was first married to Count von Keller and then to the famous Cossack *ataman* [leader] Afrikan Petrovich Bogaevsky (1872–1934). When I was evacuated to Constantinople, I moved to the Tarlabasi neighborhood, to the office of Ataman Bogaevsky. Also living there were his wife, Nadya, their children Boris and Yevgeny, my grandmother, Aunt Nadya's elder brother, General Yevgeny Derret, Baron von Maydell, Colonel Nikolai Filimonov, the ataman's secretary Natsev, and my sister, Alexandra. We lived very cramped and crowded on the second floor in a small apartment. I lived there for twenty-four days in December 1920. In Constantinople I married my second husband, Alexander Alexandrovich Taskin. He was a godson of Emperor Alexander III, and his father was the inspector of the royal lands."[15]

In 1929 Valentina Yulianovna performed on Turkish radio as its first pianist; she worked there for the rest of her life. In the late 1980s she accompanied her partner, Theodore, a Greek, at the Yalim restaurant.

A special place in the nightlife of Russian Constantinople was held by the

aret and restaurant Hermitage, where the chef was a former governor; and the Russian pastry shops Moskva and Petrograd were known for their *kulichi* (Easter cakes) and pirozhki. *Russians on the Bosporus* reads: "The cafe and pastry shop Petrograd plays the same role in the life of Constantinople that the famous Filippov cafe in Moscow and Petrograd used to play. This is a Russian pastry shop where everything is prepared and served Russian-style, in accordance with Russian customs and generosity. Only here, at the Petrograd, can the customer have coffee, chocolate, pastries, pies, *kulich* and cheesecake *paskha*, made just the way it was done in Russia."[17]

Other famous spots included the Gapontsevs's restaurant and the Turquoise and the Luxe. Even today in Istanbul the Regence, an old Russian restaurant, is a place where you can get good borsch and unforgettable duck. As Vertinsky

singer Vertinsky, who had fled Russia with Boris Putyata, moved into the Pera Palace Hotel, and then with the help of the Russian Jewish émigré Glenbaum opened the very popular Black Rose cabaret. The Russian at the coat check was a former senator, and the waitresses were pretty Russian ladies who made up for their inept service with their adept flirting. Nights at the Black Rose, infamous for their cocaine and opium, were described thus by Vertinsky: "There was only one wish—to forget. Forget at whatever cost. First they played baccarat, then dined, then drank *champitre*. Men got together in small groups and drank, remembering old St. Petersburg."[16] Prince Isheev writes about the cabaret as well, and about the singer Elena Nikitina, who performed there with great success. The Black Rose cabaret building, on Istiklar Street, survives to this day and currently houses a billiards club.

The Russian restaurant Ugolok (Little Corner) served an excellent borsch; wealthy foreign clients went to the cab-

Above and right: *Illustrations from the Parisian magazine* L'Art et La Mode, *1920, of "Oriental" dresses.*

Bayanlar :
Son model ve ucuz şapkalarınızı ancak;

"MOD OLGA„

Şapka salonunda bulursunuz

Sultan Hamam Havuzlu Han yanında 22
İSTANBUL
TELEFON : 22305

BAYLAR:

Toptan şapka satışı için

"NAP„

Şapka Fabrikasından

Şapkalarınızı temin ediniz..

Rekabet edilmezsiniz.

so accurately noted: "Caviar, Filippov's pirozhki, Smirnoff vodka, Ukrainian borsch teased the appetite and called to the stomach."[18] The hurly-burly of artistic and night life in Russian Constantinople imbued the émigrés with hopes of an early return to Russia. Insouciance was in the air, helping them forget reality.

Fashion merits a special chapter in the history of Russian life in Constantinople. On Pera Street there were Russian clothing and fur shops, as well as various salons. Initially, they dealt with reselling dresses and furs brought in by elegant but needy ladies. A large fur establishment owned by the Muscovite Turchikhin was located at number 105; the Odessa tailors Kaminsky and Shulman also opened a salon on Pera Street; the Society of Russian Trade at 58 Pera Street handled used furs, Russian jewelry, and silver; the shoe store Vladimir opened in the Oriental Passage; and Grigorian, a Russian-Armenian store and workshop for handbags, opened in the Alhambra Passage.

Russians on the Bosporus notes, "Walking along the Alhambra Passage on Pera, you can't help noticing the shop windows with elegant ladies' purses of beautiful manufacture, with original and exquisite designs and rich encrustation—the work of the 'master from Rus-

sia' Mr. Grigorian, who in the past had an art-binding workshop in Tiflis and a haberdashery workshop in Rostov, and now in emigration has decided to concentrate on haberdashery works, having become immediately distinguished at it. Arriving in Constantinople just seven years ago, Mr. Grigorian open a store and workshop and expanded his work and has a solid clientele. Ladies' handbags made by Mr. Grigorian are often masterpieces of applied art, astonishing in their artistry and filigreed detail."[19]

Of the number of Russian fashion enterprises on Pera we should mention Ferajal fashions, belonging to Natalya Nikolayevna Lazareva and her daughter Irina Feodorovna. An artist from St. Petersburg and a former student of the St. Petersburg Academy of Arts, she was perhaps the first émigré to open a fashion house. A French journalist wrote: "At first alone and then after some time with the help of a young work woman, she created things that quickly gained her fame. Her House of Ferajal soon became one of the very premier ones on Pera."[20] It lasted three years, from 1920 to the end of 1923, when Lazareva left with her daughter in search of a better life in Paris, where she opened a small fashion house called Aneli in 1924. Unfortunately, the author's long search for models from Ferajal, either in Istanbul or Paris, was unsuccessful. It is quite possible that the clothes did not have labels, that is, they were unsigned, which naturally complicates finding them.

Above: an advertisement for the Russian hat salon Mod Olga from the Turkish magazine Moda, *Istanbul, mid-1930s.*

Opposite, left: An advertisement for the Russian lingerie salon Korsak from the Turkish magazine Moda, *Istanbul, mid-1930s.*

Opposite, right: A cover of a Turkish fashion magazine with a photograph of Countess Liza Grabbe in a dress from the house of Chantal, 1920. Photo by George Hoyningen-Huene.

The Russian fashion house Sidan was opened in 1920, run by the Crimean prince Takhtamysh Girey, who inherited it from his sister. The two primary designers at Sidan were Anna Alexandrovna Frolova and Elizaveta Anisimovna Cenol, and the house's specialties were evening gowns, suits, and coats trimmed with fur. Sidan, which flourished throughout the 1930s and '40s, was closed only in the 1960s, when Madame Frolova died. Among the longest-lived Russian fashion houses were Korsak lingerie and corsets and Olga hats, which survived until the end of the 1930s. In the early 1920s the Union of Young Christians organized millinery courses for Russian émigrés and offered scholarships. Graduates opened their own salons or took jobs in existing ones.

The fashion of Russian Constantinople was in striking contrast to the traditional Ottoman styles. Turkish women wore national dress with heavy veils over half the face. Russian women wore whatever they wanted, often demonstrating the latest summer styles from the seamstresses of Kislovodsk and Yalta. Their dresses, shortened according to the fashions of 1919, with low waists and worn without corsets, were without a doubt a European innovation in colorful Constantinople. Sunbathing at Florio Beach became fashionable among Russians, and one émigré, Anna Pegova, invented the beauty treatment of facial peeling there.

KORSAK

En temiz ve en güzel kadın çamaşırları ve kumaş üzerine yağlıboya Resimler. Broderi aplikasyon Perdeler umulmuyacak derecede ucuz yapılır. Bir dafa modellerimizi görünüz.

Korsak

Büyük Parmakkapı No. 4

Beyoğlu

There were many articles and cartoons in Constantinople about Russian women then: Turkish men melting with desire for waitresses in coffee houses, traffic accidents caused by the appearance of a Russian woman on the sidewalk, and so on.

In his memoirs, *Notes of a Russian Pierrot*, Vertinsky wrote: "The situation for women was better than for the men. The Turks had lost their heads over them. Our blue-eyed, light-haired beauties seemed like angels, heavenly houries, women from another planet to them, used to their dusky oriental mistresses. . . . The rather crude Americans, the dry and snobbish British, the temperamental and jealous Italians, and the cheerful and confident Frenchmen—all changed completely under the 'beneficial' influence of Russian women. They 'changed' them amazingly—Russian women like to 'change' men. For foreigners the 'conditions' were rather hard. But you put up with a lot for the woman you love."[21]

Without a doubt, Russian women not only attracted universal attention in Constantinople, they often became the bread winners for their families. It was easier

for them to find work, they were courted, they were adored. Naturally, such success on the part of the Russian women brought confusion into the ranks of the Turkish women; in those days there were still harems. Their husbands vanished in the evenings, spending money on expensive presents for the "kharasho" (a Russian phrase meaning "okay," "very good," or "very well," it is what Russians were called then in Constantinople).

The despairing Turkish women collected signatures for a petition, which they handed over to Colonel Maxweld, commandant of Constantinople, demanding that Russian women be deported. Following is the text, translated from Turkish:

PETITION OF THE LADIES OF ISTANBUL

We, the undersigned ladies living in Istanbul, are worried at the very thought that young men called upon to serve the preservation of their Turkish homeland, which was founded at the cost of huge sacrifices by our self-sacrificing soldiers in Anatolia, will scorn their duty, and we bring to your august attention this urgent problem.

Enemy forces have taken over our country, our homes, have arrested our men and imprisoned them; in response to the Mondross Agreement on a ceasefire they have insinuated into respectable Istanbul neighborhoods the remnants of Russian tsarism who fled the Bolsheviks in order to sow evil and bring discord here. They realize that even with the support of the allies they have acquired in our country, they will not be able to break the faith of our nation, neither spiritually nor materially, by oppressing the mothers of

Above: *A view of the Golden Horn and Galata in Constantinople, 1910s.*

Below: *A view of the Bosporus, 1910s.*

Opposite: *A Russian émigré couple in northern Africa, mid-1920s.*

Islam and that, on the contrary, this repression will lead only to the strengthening of our nation's unity.

These libertines from the North, whom even societies close to them ethnically refuse to accept, have not failed to commit the most odious crimes that could be imagined, and they began this criminal activity the very first day they set foot on our soil. Using the enchanting beauty of their wives and daughters, they are corrupting our husbands and children, inculcating in them concepts of charity and honor that are different from ours. They have robbed the Turkish male, taking away his last property, they have destroyed our families, perverted our sons, and become bad examples for our daughters—in other words, in just one or two years they have managed to bring more harm than all the Russian armies over the centuries.

Among young men between 18 and 30 there are few who could resist the evil temptation of such fatal poisons as morphine, cocaine, ether, and alcohol. In Beyoglu, in the neighborhood between Tunnel and Taksim, you can find 25 Russians bars, cafes, and restaurants that are not controlled by the police or the sanitary services. In those dens of iniquity hundreds of Turkish youths are ruined every day, losing their health, wealth, and good-

80

ness. The same thing is happening to some Turkish women, who are forced to deal with women of dubious behavior who have made their way into every level of society. These Turkish women maintain that the Russian women, who were in rags just recently, now show up in luxurious clothing and wear expensive jewelry. All this has a corrupting influence on future mothers called upon to bring up the next generation of our country.

Therefore, in view of the extreme seriousness of this problem, which is a grave threat to our nation, for the salvation of our Homeland, we the undersigned ask our government to take measure against these sowers of sin and adultery, which is much worse than syphilis and alcohol, and to throw them out of our country."[22]

The petition was signed by twenty-eight odalisques from several harems and the legal wife of Gazi Edhem-pasha. In reading this, bear in mind that along with the evacuated Volunteer Army of Baron Wrangel, a lot of girls from brothels in Petrograd, Moscow, Kiev, Odessa, and Rostov also ended up in Constantinople. They often passed themselves off as officers' wives and aristocrats, thereby casting a shadow on all Russian women.

Many émigrés did not lose hope of one day leaving Constantinople. Crowds of Russian refugees wandered along Pera Street, besieging foreign embassies in the hopes of getting a visa. Czechoslovakia and Yugoslavia accepted the intelligentsia, students, teachers, engineers, and doctors; Bulgaria gave shelter to some of the Gallipoli troops; Argentina invited landless Cossacks to Patagonia; bankers and furriers wanted to go to Germany; many tried to get to America; and France needed only cheap labor. . . .

The situation remained dire for many. Particularly sad news came from Gallipoli, where, suffering from deprivation and need, the surviving portion of the Volunteer Army remained. But it was even harder for those who quit Wrangel's army and moved to Constantinople. Prince Dolgoruky wrote about them: "On Pera in Constantinople in the summer you might meet young men cheerfully walking in clean white shirts, with military bearing, saluting generals, and unmistakably recognize them as men from Gallipoli. And at the same time, the miserable, hungry men in torn greatcoats grimly working the streets, selling violets, matches, and pencils—those were the officers who had quit the army. So many of them died, so many were lost. Other officers worked in restaurants, cafes-*chantants*, and various dens."[23]

At first Wrangel lived in the Russian embassy and then moved onto the *Lukull*, a small military steam yacht anchored not far from the Dolma-Bakhche Palace. Its fate was mysterious and tragic. Here is what Prince Pavel Dmitrievich Dolgoruky recalls: "I think it was in August 1921 that an Italian trader traveling from Bolshevik Batumi, in broad daylight turned sharply from the waterway, which is wide in that part of the Bosporus, and heading straight for the *Lukull*, which was anchored near shore at the permanent berth of the Russian hospital, cut it in half and without stopping headed toward Constantinople. The few people on board were saved, except for the duty midshipman Sapunov. And so the last St. Andrew's flag flying in the Bosporus sank into the water on its mast. Baroness Wrangel lost her last pieces of jewelry."[24]

The Turkish monarchy was living out its last days before the rise of Ataturk. The sultan lived as a prisoner in Ildiz Kiosk. The future of the enormous number of Russian refugees in Allied-occupied Constantinople was in question. By 1924 the Russian émigrés had gradually started moving away from the Bosporus, to wherever they could go. Only those who had found good work and the women who had married Turks remained. Russian Constantinople emptied. Now all that is left is the small Russian cemetery with a tiled chapel with its sign: "Their souls repose in peace."

Архив автора. Париж

4

RUSSIAN BERLIN

Along with Constantinople, another major center of the Russian immigration in the early 1920s was Berlin, where close to 200,000 émigrés from Russia had settled. The phenomenon of Russian Berlin, the cultural and intellectual center of the emigration, is of special interest to researchers and art historians. Its formation was fast, its flowering brilliant, and its decline swift. Russian Berlin lasted much longer than Russian Constantinople, until the mid-1930s. Studying the culture and art, fashion and mores of Russian Berlin, one realizes that there are almost no tangible remains of it. You can no longer wander through the old town in Berlin, it is hard to find contemporaries of the events or to sense the spirit of the past—it does not exist any more, just as it does not exist in many other German cities, victims of the emptying that Germany itself started.

Prague, Belgrade, Constantinople, and Paris give us, even today, at the turn of the century, a sense of communing with the past, even if it is a past that has fallen into oblivion. Russian prewar Berlin, with its once-dynamic life, comes back only in our imagination.

Compared to Paris and other émigré centers, Berlin in 1921–27 seemed like the promised land, a city where Russians, despite the crazy inflation, could live better than in other capitals. But then, most of the émigrés who came to Berlin from Russia were wealthy people. They traveled there by train from Riga, Warsaw, Vienna, Bucharest, and Copenhagen, often with "legal" visas or

Архив автора, Париж

Opposite: *Olga Belaieff-Multon, a Russian actress in silent films in Germany, in evening dress, Berlin, 1926–27.*

Above: *An advertisement for the Kruglikova and Elzner salon in Berlin, 1922.*

simply with the permission of Soviet authorities. The deprivations of being a refugee were not so acute in that golden city, the den of iniquity of the 1920s.

"Germany turned out to be particularly welcoming to Russian émigrés, and that's why many who had settled first in other lands, after long and unsuccessful attempts move here,"[1] wrote an observer for the glossy Russian-language illustrated magazine *Zhar-ptitsa* [Firebird]. Four years after the revolution, during the civil war in Russia, émigré Berlin underwent a true flowering of Russian culture—dozens of first-class publishing houses, newspapers, and magazines of the most varied politics and interests appeared, and numerous restaurants and cabarets, Russian

stores, theater companies, and fashion houses all sprung up—and Berlin audiences were drawn to this dynamic artistic life.

An eyewitness of the events, ballerina Nina Tikanova, wrote in her memoirs, "Street life was vibrant. All of Charlottenburg had turned into a Russian colony, there were Russian restaurants and cabarets everywhere. Beneath our windows newspaper vendors cried, 'Ru-u-ul!' *Rul'* was the name of the daily newspaper published by Gessen and where Milukov wrote."[2]

The intellectual life of Russian Berlin was lively, and there were many periodicals and gifted prose authors, poets, and critics. The Berlin editions were exemplary: Ogonki Publishing House was run by the editor Levinson, and the publisher Zinovi Grjebine, and there were also the publishing houses of Ivan Ladyzhnikov, Otto Kirchner, and A. E. Kogan's *Russkoe iskusstvo* [Russian art], among others.

During these years Berlin became a major center of Russian visual arts as well. Many first-rate artists wanted to be there. In October 1922, the Van Diemen Gallery in Berlin opened a large Russian show sent by the Soviet government, with over a thousand works shown—the profits were supposed to aid the starving in Russia. Very popular were the paintings and publications of Boris Grigoriev. In 1923 the Karl Nikolai Gallery held an exhibit of Konstantin Korovin. The magazine *Zhar-ptitsa* constantly printed color reproductions of the works of Georgy Lukomsky,

Alexander Golovin, Konstantin Somov, Leon Bakst, Alexandre Benois, Sergei Chekhonin, Vasily Shukhaev, Konstantin Yuon, Filipp Malyavin, and others.

This flowering of Russian art in Berlin occurred against the backdrop of economic decline and instability. Nina Tikanova wrote, "In Germany inflation was taking on unheard-of proportions. No sooner were bills printed than they lost all value. With incredible speed thousands turned into tens and hundreds of thousands, millions, billions." It is no surprise that in this tense atmosphere the presence of a lively Russian community, with its popular performers, offered relaxation and recreation to the city's population.

It was in Berlin that the best artistic powers of old Russia were concentrated. The stars of Russian ballet, opera, and drama, as well as outstanding musicians and conductors, were all here. *Zhar-*

Above, top: *A group of Russian émigrés in a pension in Altenau, Germany, 1921.*

Above, bottom: *The Simonovich family, Berlin, 1923.*

Opposite above: *Manya Tsatcheva, an actress in German silent films, Berlin, 1927.*

Opposite, below left: *Elisabeth Pinajeff, a Russian actress in silent films in Germany, c. 1927.*

Opposite, below right: *Mura Muravyova, a variety-show stage dancer, Berlin, 1923.*

ptitsa, no. 3, 1922, wrote: "The flow of Russian immigrants covers more of Europe with every day. Everyone who can flees. But lately there has been a powerful wave of people from the arts—one gets the impression that soon the entire Russian artistic world, despite the promises of gentle M. F. Andreyeva of a vacation [Andreyeva, the wife of Maxim Gorky, was the head of the arts commission in the USSR and promised vacations to Soviet artists], will gather here, abroad."[3]

The incredible influx of artists from Russia prompted many in Berlin to join in on the fad of forming émigré performance troupes. One of the first, which brought much joy to Berliners in the depression years, was Yasha Yuzhny's cabaret The Blue Bird, located on Holzstrasse. Artistic cabarets had been amazingly successful in Russia even before the revolution, when the most fa-

mous were The Crooked Mirror, La Chauve Souris, and The Stray Dog.

The popularity of Baliev's La Chauve Souris extended beyond the borders of Russia. Baliev's cabaret delighted first Parisians, then residents of other European cities, and then transatlantic audiences. The name and emblem of The Blue Bird let the "in" people know that it was related in a way to the Moscow Art Theater—the name was a reference to The Seagull emblem on the curtain of the Moscow Art Theater; Chekhov's play was its signature production. An observer for the Berlin Russian magazine *Teatr i zhizn'* [Theater and Life] did not stint on praise: "The Blue Bird does not have the heartrending talent of Agnivtsev; but it has the humor of Yuzhin, the joyous muse Duvan-Tortosov, the daring extravagance of Tchelichew's colors. It has Bekefi's Russian folk dances. . . . It has Berlin gypsies, trembling to the quivering guitar of high-society lovers of gypsy music. It is only a drop, but it contains the sun of Russian art. And the priests of foreign art behold it in awe."[4]

Seeing the astonishing success of The Blue Bird, another group of Russian actors opened a rival cabaret in February, 1922: Vanka–Vstanka on Kurfurstendamm, in house 32. The troupe was a strong one: the repertoire was in the hands of Nikolai Agnivtsev; Moscow Art Theater artist Andreyev designed the sets; and Richard Boleslawsky, formerly an actor with the Art Theater and later a leading film director in Hollywood, directed the plays. *Teatr i zhizn'* wrote: "In order to characterize this unique undertaking, let us quote the three commandments of Vanka–Vstanka, which speak for themselves: 1) the theater's theme is Russia, 2) the theater's repertoire is gesture, sound, and color, and 3) the theater's motto is 'everything our own and nothing that isn't.' The first program presented 'Wandering Minstrels,' 'Émigré Rus,' 'In Old Moscow,' 'Grandson and Grandfather,' 'Kiev Blind Men,' 'Child's Prayer,' 'After the Evening Sunset,' 'Round Dance of Visas,' 'St. Petersburg,' and other miniatures."

Even in a foreign land the émigré artists turned to Russian themes in their

Above: *Iza Kremer, Berlin, 1925.*

Below: *Elena Polevitskaya in the role of Rita in the play* Black Panther *by Vinchenko, Berlin, early 1920s.*

Opposite: *Olga Chekhova, a famous Russian star of German films, dressed and coiffed* à la garcon, *Berlin, 1925.*

work, and the Berlin audiences repaid them with rapturous love. The columnist who signed himself "Bayan" wrote, "It is enough to read a talented Russian book, listen to marvelous Russian

music, watch Kachalov and Germanova, and be enchanted by Russian ballet to forget about the bitter lot of émigré life. Recently I was happy eating a fluffy meat patty at Vanka–Vstanka. And yesterday happy over a glass of tart Moselle at the Blue Bird. In the middle of Prussia there are two Russian cabarets. I don't think there was a single French one in Koblenitz. But the French brought their starched jabots and pride with them to Germany, while we brought our lax bodies, scattered thoughts, and foaming art. It spews out of us just like debauchery and disorder. Starving and spreeing, making up and arguing, shooting and being shot, we will not forget how to sing, dance, and act. And the jets of our talent sparkle amidst the flat cultural equilibrium that does not understand us and therefore forgives us everything."[5]

Another famous theatrical company that conquered Berliners in those years was the Russian Romantic Theater under the direction of dancer Boris Romanov, which opened on October 15, 1922, at 218 Friedrichstrasse. Bringing together a group of leading dancers from Russia's capital cities, such as ballerinas Elena Smirnova, Elsa Krüger, Claudia Pavlova, and Anatoly Obukhov, the Russian Romantic Theater created marvelous programs of choreographic miniatures under the artistic direction of Paul Tchelichew and Leon Zack.

Such success prompted other performers from Russia to think about forming ballet troupes. In 1924 the Bolshoi ballerina Ekaterina Devillier organized her "pseudo-Diaghilev" troupe with Irina Shishkova and Fred Tim. Touring ballet companies also frequently visited Berlin. The semi-acrobatic numbers of Alice Vronska and Konstantin Alperoff charmed the audiences. They also were delighted by the passionate bacchanalian dances of Tamara Gamsakourdia and Alexandre Demidoff. The Sakharov duet conquered them, too. The great Anna Pavlova appeared on the Berlin stage. The returning star Olga Osipovna Preobrajenskaia was an honored artist of the imperial theaters; the embodiment of feminine grace, she was the "lace maker" of classical ballet. At

Гастролей
30 арт. б. Императ. Петербургск. Балета 30
Елены Александровны
СМИРНОВОИ
Б. Г. РОМАНОВА
А. Н. ОБУХОВА
20 КОНЦЕРТОВЪ 20
НАДЕЖДЫ ВАСИЛЬЕВНЫ
ПЛЕВИЦКОИ
Съ предложеніями обращаться.
Hauptstrasse 114, part. rechts, Dr. SIROTA. Отъ 3-4 дня и письм.

Left: Elena Polevitskaya, a dramatic actress famous in Germany in the 1920s–1940s playing roles from a classic Russian repertoire.

Above and below: Advertisements for Russian theaters in Berlin from the magazine Zhar-ptitsa, 1922.

Opposite: A poster by Jean-Gabriel Daumergue advertising guest appearances by Alice Vronska and Konstantin Alperoff in Berlin, 1923.

Русскій Ресторанъ
„СТРѢЛЬНА"

ВИЛЬМЕРСДОРФЪ
Бранденбургишештр. 37
уголъ Курфюрстендамма

Заказы на столы по
Тел. Уланд 12-10

Съ 1 ч. до 4 ч. обѣды съ вкусной 30 мар. амфи.

Цыганскій хоръ князя Б. А. Голицына
СОЛИСТКА: М. Н. БЕМЕРЪ

Кромѣ
того испол-
нительница русско-
цыганскихъ романсовъ
М. А. ЛИДАРСКАЯ

Сообщеніе: Трамваи A, C, W,
5, 10, 62, 76, 77, 78, 162, 176, автобусъ E

ТЕЛЕФОНЪ: Ноллендорфъ 16-13   ТЕЛЕФОНЪ: Ноллендорфъ 16-13

Театръ „СИНЯЯ ПТИЦА"
ГОЛЬТЦЪ - ШТРАССЕ 9

Программа:

1. Бродячій циркъ
2. Диванныя сплетни
3. Китайская баллада
4. Matelote — исп. Юлія Бекефи
5. Бить въ барабанъ велѣлъ король
6. У цыганъ
7. Частушки

8. Time is money
9. Солдатка. Пѣснь Рахманинова
10. Вечеръ поздно изъ лѣсочка. Лубокъ
11. Парикмахерская любовь
12. Русскій танецъ — исп. Юлія Бекефи

Спектакли ежедневные. — Начало въ 8½ час. веч.

Директоръ: Я. Д. Южный.   Главн. режиссеръ: И. Э. Дуванъ-Торцовъ.

Предв. продажа билетовъ въ «Kaufhaus des Westens», и въ театр. кассахъ

Архив Миплин Соломонпис, Париж

Архив Миплин Соломонпис, Париж

Архив автора, Париж

the Berlin Deutsche Teatr, Vera Karalli, the famous ballerina of the Bolshoi, pleased the audiences, dancing in two pantomimes choreographed for her by the Russian director Ivan Shmidt. In Russia she was considered the epitome of beauty, and, along with Vera Kholodnaya, Karalli had been one of the great stars of Russian silent film before the revolution.

Russian singers and musicians had an enormous impact on the lifestyle and fashion of Berliners in the 1920s. Tenor Dmitrii Smirnov, a former artist of the imperial theaters, appeared at the Marmor Salle; opera singer Filippenko came from Sofia, Bulgaria, to perform; and the famous soprano Oda Slobodskaya gave concerts of Jewish folk music. The Berlin audiences loved the music-hall singer Iza Kremer, who was as popular there as she had been in pre-revolutionary Russia.

Opposite, above left and right: *Two photos of Maria Simonovich, daughter of the personal secretary of Grigory Rasputin, who appeared in cabarets in Berlin and Vienna, 1923–26.*

Opposite below: *Irina Shishkova, a cabaret dancer in Berlin, 1929.*

Above left: *A Russian émigré in a home masquerade, 1920s.*

Above right: *Ekaterina Lopukhina, a Russian actress in German films, dressed as a ballerina, Berlin, 1920s. Photo by Leo Hoffman. Diaghilev's triumph began a fad for classical ballet. In the 1920s actresses posed in tunics and tutus, imagining themselves to be Pavlova.*

Teatr i zhizn' wrote in 1922, "Iza Kremer in remarkable miniatures, full of life, weaves a line of light, airy, colorful instants, moods, silhouettes, and unforgettable visions. A wonderful and practiced *diseuse*, she plunges entirely, as if into a bottomless sea, into the waves that are always foaming around her stage—sometimes laughing, sunny, full of sparkle and droplets, sometimes quiet, sad, and obedient."[6] The creative destiny of this remarkable singer, who never returned to Russia and passed away in Argentina, is now forgotten in her homeland.

Dramatic actors also played a role in disseminating Russian culture and art in Berlin. Perhaps the most important event in émigré life was the guest performances in Berlin of the Moscow Art Theater, headed by Konstantin Sergeyevich Stanislavsky. The power and vividness of the acting and the

91

ГАСТРОЛЬНОЕ ТУРНЭ съ 12аго АПРѢЛЯ
по Германіи, Чехословакіи, прибалтійскимъ государствамъ Эстоніи, Литвѣ и Латвіи
прима-балерины государственнаго Московскаго балета

В. А. КАРАЛЛИ

при участіи солистки Петро-
градскаго Маріинскаго балета | **К. М. ГОРЕВОЙ**
и арт. Мар. балета И. КИРЕЕВА.   Дирекція А. С. ПЛАСКОВА

imagery of the productions created an indelible impression on the Berliners. Leonid Leonidov, impresario on another tour of the Moscow Art troupe, wrote in his memoirs *Footlights and Life,* published in 1955 in Paris, "Everywhere our performances remained true to the legacy of the Art Theater, and in every country where we performed, Russian actors definitely laid the foundations for the prestige and influence that Russian art had outside the borders of Russia after the revolution."[7]

When they arrived in Berlin in 1922, the Art Theater troupe began its season in the Lessing Teatr. *Tsar Feodor Ioannovich* won over the Berlin audience and the remaining performances had full houses. In the spring of 1921 the popular Moscow actors Olga Gzovskaya and Vladimir Gaidarov visited Berlin from Riga. Thanks to their efforts, the Russian Theater was opened in Berlin. It included former artists from the studio of the Moscow Art Theater as well as young émigrés. They premiered with Oscar Wilde's *Salome,* and the theater, in particular its stars, attracted a lot of attention from German and Russian audiences. Olga Gzowskaya, who was

Above left: *Nikolai Beriozoff and Mura Muravyova in a Russian dance, Berlin, 1929.*

Left: *An announcement of European guest performances by Vera Karalli, K. Goreva, and I. Kireyev in the Berlin magazine Teatr i zhizn', 1922.*

Above: *The Ekaterina–Devillier Ballet in Berlin, 1924.*

Opposite: *Russian émigré dancers in the troupe Moskauer Kunst-Schpile, dressed by George Pogedaeff, Vienna, 1924.*

92

ic actor Stepan Kuznetsov appeared in Berlin. A few years later, he recalled, "In April 1921, I got time off and went abroad for a cure. During that time I did twelve performances in Sofia (Bulgaria); six in Berlin; eighteen in Revel [Tallinn, Estonia] and Yurev [Tartu, Estonia]; and in Berlin I made three films and took part in two concerts, dedicated to F[yodor] M. Dostoevsky and A[lexander] Blok."[9] This talented actor and master of stage transformations was an idol of the émigrés for a while.

The career of dramatic actress Elena Alexandrovna Polevitskaya was longer lived. She spent most of the period from 1920 to 1943 in Germany and then moved to Vienna. Her success in Berlin was significant—the images Polevitskaya created of the heroines of Russian classics enchanted the audience, who adored her and wrote poetry about her. One of the first actresses from Russia, Polevitskaya performed Russian classics in German and played the heroines of Tolstoy and Ostrovsky even during the Hitler era.

forced to return to the Soviet Union with the advent of sound films, wrote in her memoirs, "We zestfully took up the challenge, and in order to keep it simple, turned to productions that had worked: *Salome* and *Mistress of the Inn*. These plays were done several times in Berlin."[8] Thanks to the popularity of these productions, and the striking photographs of Gzovskaya and Gaidarov in *Salome*'s unusual costumes, the two stars were soon hired for silent films, where they had successful careers.

In 1921, the famous Russian dramat-

Above: *Olga Gzovskaya during the filming of* Psisha, *directed by Yu. Larin, Berlin, 1927. Photo by Binkler.*

Right: *Vera Voronina, a Russian actress in German films, Berlin, 1924.*

Opposite: *Natalia Kowanko, a star of Russian silent films in Germany and France and a partner of Ivan Mosjoukine in many films made by the Russian émigré Albatross Studios, Berlin, 1926.*

Overleaf, left: *Nina Vanna, A Russian silent-film actress in Germany and England, in Berlin, 1926.*

Overleaf, right: *Xenia Desnitskaya, a Russian ballerina and star in German films, Berlin, 1926.*

Above: *Xenia Desnitskaya being elected beauty queen of the Russian colony in Berlin. Next to her are the runners-up E. Fenkel (left) and V. Dassel (right), Berlin, 1926.*

Below: *Xenia Desnitskaya in the years of her Berlin fame, 1927. Photo by A. Binder.*

Opposite: *Olga Chekhova as a femme fatale, Berlin, 1928.*

Архив автора, Париж

The influence of Russian actors on German cinematography was profound. An interest in exotic Slavic beauty and the secrets of the Russian soul, warmed by the Berlin euphoria for everything unusual, brought a bevy of Russian beauties to German silent films. The most vivid and extended career belongs to Olga Konstantinovna Chekhova, née Knipper. A niece of Knipper-Chekhova, the talented Olga visited the Moscow Art Theater's First Studio, where she met and married the outstanding actor Mikhail Chekhov. In 1921 she divorced her husband and moved to Germany, where she lived the rest of her life. She began her career in German film in 1922. She made silent films, gradually transforming herself from a modest Russian maiden to a femme fatale sex symbol of a turbulent era. Her photogenic quality was appreciated—thousands of photos of Olga Chekhova were printed by the Berlin publishing house Ross in those years.

Chekhova's fame crossed borders: in the late 1920s the Ara fashion house in Paris, founded by Armenian émigrés, began dressing her, attracted by her fame. She mastered German fully and continued making films and acting on stage even during the Hitler era, when most Russian émigrés had left Berlin. In the war years her closeness to Hitler, Goebbels, and particularly Ribbentrop was exploited by the Kremlin, as seen in numerous documents. A "Top Secret" report from Berlin in 1945 praising her

Opposite: *Advertisements in the magazine* Zhar-ptitsa *for Berlin jewelry stores opened by Russian émigrés, 1922.*

Above: *An advertisement for Art Deco jewelry from Marshak and Lenzeler, Paris, 1927.*

to KGB chief Lavrenti Beria read: "For many years she played a dangerous game without being unmasked by the vigilant Gestapo. Only in the very last days, when the Red Army was fighting within the limits of Berlin, was her chauffeur arrested, and she managed to escape from the Gestapo at the last moment."[10]

In the late 1930s the far-sighted Chekhova began a new career, moving into the world of beauty and cosmetics. In 1937 she received a certificate in cosmetology in Paris and then founded a cosmetics firm under her name, manufacturing face creams and the per-

fumes "Chapitre," "Deuxieme Chapitre," "Dushenka," and "Theorema."

In the late 1920s there were not many Russian actresses in silent films in Germany who could, like Chekhova, continue their careers in sound films. But the popularity of Russians in Berlin film was so high that the Viking Film Studio brought to Germany films from Ermolayev's Albatross Studio in Montreuil, outside Paris. This unique, purely Russian studio was known for its high quality, thanks to the sparkle of its stars and the lushness of its productions. Berliners loved Turjansky's 1922 film, *Thousand and One Nights*, with cos-

101

tumes and sets in the Diaghilev style. The stars of this bright, entertaining film were the charming Natalya Kowanko as Princess Fulkhanar and the handsome Nikolai Rimsky as Prince Soliman.

Also quite popular in Berlin was a film made in Russia, Yakov Protazanov's *Father Sergius*, starring Ivan Mosjoukine, Nathalie Lissenko, and Vladimir Gaidarov. Russian themes were of great interest to decadent Berlin, whose studios hired an entire group of pretty and shapely Russian film actresses, including Olga Belaieff, Elisabeth Pinajeff, Lida Salmonowa, Vera Voronina, Xenia Desni, Lya Mara, and Nina Vanna. The most famous in Germany was Xenia Desni (Xenia Alexandrovna Desnitskaya), who was selected beauty queen of the Russian colony in Berlin in 1926 and 1927. The beautiful Nina Vanna (Nina Yevgenyevna Yazykova) worked in 1926 at the German Ufa studio and then continued her career in England, where she became more famous.

An invaluable witness of the "Russification" of Berlin, the dancer and choreographer Nikolai Beriozoff, who died in

Архив Андрея Корлякова, Париж

МѢХОВЫЯ МОДЫ

влад АРОНОВ и КАЗАРНО

ОПТОМ, В РОЗНИЦУ, ЭКСПОРТ
BERLIN W50
SPICHERNSTR 22
AM NÜRNBERGERPLATZ
TEL. UHLAND 2335

Архив автора, Париж

Гершманъ

Архив автора, Париж

Below: *Natalya Kowanko in a fur coat with fur trim in a publicity film still from the Albatross Studios, Paris, 1924.*

Right: *Olga Belaieff in a satin coat trimmed with monkey fur, Berlin, 1925. The interest in African-American jazz prompted designers to use exotic African furs—leopard, zebra, and monkey—as well as the traditional Russian and European ones.*

Opposite left: *Varvara Annenkova, a Russian dramatic actress, Berlin, 1923. Photo by A. Binder.*

Opposite, below left: *An advertisement in the magazine* Zhar-ptitsa *for the Aronov and Kizarno fur shop in Berlin, 1922.*

Opposite, below right: *Pola Negri (Barbara Chalupets), a silent-film star, in a "Russian" fur coat, hat, and white "Cossack" boots. Berlin, 1923. This à la* boyar *style was particularly popular in the winter seasons of 1922–24.*

1996, wrote: "In Europe, especially in Germany, the fashion for all things Russian continued. The program of every variety show or concert had to have Russian singers, balalaika players, or dancers. The opera theaters had operas by Rimsky-Korsakov, Tchaikovsky, Borodin, and Glinka. In drama theaters, the most popular were plays by A[nton] P[avlovich] Chekhov. Book shop windows displayed books by Leo Tolstoy, M[aksim] Gorky, and F[yodor] Dostoevsky, whom everyone was crazy about. It was impossible to get tickets to concerts by Sergei Zharov's Don Cossack Choir. All the major opera theaters of Germany put on *Boris Godunov* with the legendary Chaliapin. Russian restaurants with musical shows attracted loads of customers—The Bear, the Samovar, the Balalaika—as well as night clubs like Scheherazade, Fountain of Bakhchisarai, and Kazbek under Moonlight, where gypsy troupes, Alexander Vertinsky, and Petr Leshchenko performed. All of Germany was humming 'Black Eyes,' and the fashion plates

Мѣховой Салонъ

Большой выборъ готовыхъ изящныхъ

Мѣховыхъ манто

Жакетовъ

Лисицъ

и Шалей

по парижскимъ моделямъ

*

Принимаю заказы
и покупаю мѣховыя вещи

М. Рѣзникъ

TAUENTZIENSTR. 18a, I · TEL. STEINPLATZ 62-3

Обратить вним. на фирму
Никакихъ витринъ

Архив автора. Париж

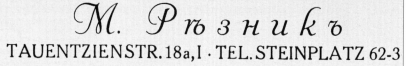

Архив автора. Париж

dressed *à la Russe* or *à la Cossack*. But that was not to last for long: a man with a fanatic's grimace was already on the rise to power—Adolf Hitler."[11]

It is impossible to list every Russian restaurant in Berlin in those days. In Wilmersdorf the Caucasian Alaverdy Restaurant opened with the enchanting Ionesco choir, and the Bear restaurant offered Berliners "borsch with buckwheat kasha at any time of day," hot pirozhki, and meat, cabbage, and fish pies. Dinner at the Bear was accompanied by the gypsy songs of K. L. Istomina. The chorus of I. F. Gill, formerly a soloist of the court orchestra, performed at the Russian–German Restaurant every evening.

The corner of Kurfurstendamm was the location of the Russian restaurant Strelnya, where the gypsy chorus of Prince Boris Golitsyn performed with the soloist Maria Bemer; another performer was Maria Lidarskyaya, who also sang

Left: *An advertisement in the magazine* Zhar-ptitsa *of Reznik's fur salon in Berlin, 1922.*

Below left: *An advertisement in the Paris magazine* Illustrirovannaya Rossiya *[Illustrated Russia] of Magat's fur salon in Leipzig, 1928.*

Below right: *Olga Chekhova in a dress from the Armenian fashion house Ara in Paris, Berlin, 1927.*

Opposite: *A Russian-style fur coat from the fashion house Drecoll, Berlin, 1926.*

Музей моды и костюма. Париж

Архив автора, Париж

from the gypsy repertoire. There were many Russian pastry shops, cafes, and snack bars. One of them advertised itself this way: "Where can you get the very best and real Russian pastries, pies, meat pasties, *coulibiac*, ice cream, Russian vodka, liqueurs, and wines? Only at Roman Dmitrievich Shel'e." The Russian tea, Globus, was for sale, and Gorbachev and Co. produced filtered vodka, Pomerantsev Vodka, Russian Kummel-allasch (Crimean wine), and Kiev Vishnevka (cherry brandy).

There were numerous Russian jewelry stores in Berlin selling the family jewels of the émigrés. Bril and Gershclan, jewelers from Kiev and Odessa, opened their establishment at 14 Unter den Linden. Not far from them was the store of Vesler, Feldman, and Lesnik, who promised to buy diamonds from émigrés at "the highest prices." Orglovsky and Babichenko's store sold pearls and other jewels. Other

Left: *Elisabeth Pinajeff in a summer dress, Berlin, 1926. Photo by A. Binder.*

Below: *An advertisement in the magazine* Zhar-ptitsa *for the Berlin fashion salon Elise, 1922.*

Opposite above: *Olga Belaieff, Berlin, 1929.*

Opposite below: *The Roishman family on a street in Berlin, May 1932.*

stores, such as Artel, sold carvings, embroidery, and other handicrafts, which were the *dernier cri* in fashion. Berlin had several Russian salons for men's and women's clothing. Unfortunately, we could not find the archives of these salons and stores, much less any staff who could tell us about them: many documents and materials were lost during World War II.

The Russian salons in Berlin differed from the Russian fashion houses in Paris. They had all been opened by professional tailors from Russia and were not semicharitable enterprises of Russian aristocrats, as they were in Paris. The Moscow seamstress Maria Medvedeva opened her business in 1922 on Kurfurstendamm, which was thickly settled by Russian émigrés, and made dresses, suits, and hats to order. In Charlottenburg at 46 Kantstrasse, was Anastasia, a Russian hat salon, which advertised its "elegant new spring models" as well as "leather, silk, and straw hats." The Petrograd seamstress Eliza opened a fashion place at 11 Nurnbergerstrasse. The tailor Zhukovsky, known for his elegant lines in men's and women's clothing, also opened a place on Kurfurstendamm. A fur salon selling wholesale and retail was opened by Aronov and Kazarno at 22 Spischernstrasse. Most of the Russian émigrés who were in Berlin in the 1920s were fairly affluent, so the best non-Russian Berlin fashion houses and salons also advertised in

émigré periodicals. The houses of Gustav Kords, Frenfeld, Mikhaelides, Maassen, and many others offered their services in the Russian press.

The first Nazi actions began with pogroms of Jewish stores. One after another, the tailor shops and jewelry stores shut down. The majority of Berlin's Jewish businessmen, including many Russian émigrés, began moving to France, England, and America. Then it was the turn of all the other non-Aryan foreigners and Russians. Berlin, once so brilliant, grew empty for a long time.

The early years of Nazism in Berlin are vividly described in the memoirs of Tamara Lempicka, a Polish artist who studied in her youth in St. Petersburg. She passed through Berlin in 1934, after the burning of the Reichstag: "Hitler was not long in power at this time, but already the streets were filled with Nazi uniforms and the people were afraid. At lunch in the hotel my friend says to me, 'I am so happy to see you, but how did you get a permit to come?' And I say: 'Permit, what permit?' She becomes terribly upset. 'This is terrible,' she says. 'We must go to the police at once.' We leave the hotel. We go to the police. They are rude. They take away my passport. They ask my friend many questions. Finally they take me to the chief authority. He is sitting behind a big desk in a big room. He is wearing the Nazi uniform and the red band on his arm. He had my papers. He looks at them and frowns. 'Madame Lempicka, you are a French citizen?' 'Yes I am.' 'And you live in Paris?' 'Yes I do.' 'And why do you stop in Berlin with no permit?' He looks at me. I am afraid, but I do not show this. I tell him. He looks again at my papers, then he askes, 'Are you the same Mme. Lempicka who paints the covers of Die Dame?' 'Yes, I am.' 'Ah,' he says, coming around the desk to shake my hand. 'I am so pleased to meet you. My wife is most fond of your paintings; in fact, we have collected all your covers from the magazine. I will let you pay the fine, the lightest punishment, and you may go. But you must *never* come back to Germany.'"[12]

5
RUSSIAN HARBIN

The cultural phenomenon of Harbin, a Russian city in the north of Manchuria, China, is unique in the history of Russian emigration. It was the most Russian city outside the borders of Russia, and in terms of the number of fashionable ateliers, shops, and tailors, it surpassed all other émigré centers.

The history of Harbin is only about one hundred years old. It was founded in the spring of 1898 and is closely tied to the start of construction of the Chinese Eastern Railroad (CERR). According to the plan of Yugovich, chief engineer of the construction of the CERR, the track went through the north of Manchuria and connected the Siberian main line with the Ussurian railroad. This created an uninterrupted rail connection between the European part of Russia and Vladivostok—Russia's main Pacific port, in southeast Russia—and Port Arthur in northeast China. Harbin's excellent geographical situation on the shores of the Sungari River, a tributary of the Amur, guaranteed its swift growth as a trade, industrial, and cultural center in the north of China.

Russian builders and settlers appeared in the area after lengthy diplomatic negotiations regarding concessions for building the railroad and obtaining parcels of land for the train stations. Negotiations began in Beijing in 1895 and continued in St. Petersburg and Moscow in 1896. The first steamship with settlers from Russia, *St. Innokentii*, arrived on June 10, 1898, marking the founding

Opposite: *Woman from Shanghai, 1936. Photo by Iwata Nakayama.*

Above: *An advertisement from the magazine* Rubezh [Border] *for Matuzov's fashion salon, Harbin, 1927.*

of Harbin. It quickly grew into three significant settlements: Old Harbin, the New City, and the Wharf, all of which were rapidly built and settled.

The first buildings in Harbin were wooden, but later, in the 1900s, they were built of brick. Even today Harbin's architecture is a mix of eclectic European styles from the late nineteenth and early twentieth centuries. It is a city built on the plans and designs of Russian urban planners, where Art Nouveau finds itself next to neo-Gothic or pseudo-Moorish styles. Architecturally it is reminiscent of many provincial Siberian cities. In 1900 the famous Russian trading house of Churin and Co. opened a store in Old Harbin with a large department of ready-to-wear men's and women's clothing featuring fashions from the European part of Russia.

The railroad began operating on July 1, 1903, which improved the economic and trade ties between Harbin and the West. In 1904 the Ministry of Transport opened shipping on the Sungari River and the number of ships belonging to Russian shipping lines reached as many as eighty. However, the huge flow of Russian settlers met with a hostile reception from the Chinese. Clashes, not infrequent even in peacetime, increased during the Russo-Japanese War. Nevertheless the city grew, its streets were given Russian names, and shop lanes, hotels, hospitals, churches, and schools were built. Education found firm footing: there were the Generozova and the Oksakovskaya high schools for women; a commercial school formed under the aegis of the railroad; Drizul's classics high school for boys; and Tvardovsky's school.

The Russian revolution and civil war turned Harbin into the émigré center in the East. Thousands of refugees rushed

to Manchuria in the hope of escaping war, famine, and disease. This new wave of forced settlers brought the culture of European Russia to Harbin; as a result the city experienced an unprecedented flowering right up until the mid-1940s. "The arrival of a significant number of the intelligentsia with the mass of refugees was a stimulus for the opening of higher and special schools in Harbin. The Harbin Polytechnic Institute, the Law School, the Pedagogical Institute, and others were founded,"[1] wrote V. G. Savchik, historian of the city.

On September 23, 1929, the president of the Republic of China decreed Harbin an international port, stripping the Russian population of the right to extraterritoriality and administrative authority, and the Russian police force was disbanded. The situation changed again on May 31, 1935, when the USSR signed an agreement with China transfering the CERR into joint control, divided equally. Savchik recalls: "Russian white-collar workers and laborers were given the choice of opting for Soviet citizenship, switching to Chinese citizenship, or leaving their work with the Railroad."[2]

Despite the aggravated situation on the railroad with the advent of the new Soviet specialists, life in Harbin was in full swing. In 1923 the city's population was 127,000, most of whom were Russian, which was evident with the consecration of twenty-two Russian Orthodox churches, the first of which, in honor of St. Nicholas Mirlikiisky, was begun in 1899. Then came the wooden St. Nicholas Cathedral in the neo-Russian style with an annexed Iverskaya Chapel, a copy of the one recently restored in Moscow and the one currently standing in the Russian cemetery in Belgrade. The central part of Harbin was once ornamented by Russian Orthodox churches: it also had three

The port of Shanghai, 1920s.

111

Архив автора, Париж

In the beginning the émigrés were helped by charitable organizations, such as the Refugee Committee, the Soviet for Aiding Veterans, and the Yasli orphanage. The émigrés worked to set up public transportation, laying trolley lines and organizing buses. *Rubezh* wrote about émigré life: "Russians in Manchuria preserved customs that people started forgetting even in Russia: Christmas and Easter visits, fortune-telling on Christmas Eve, Red Hill [the first Sunday after Easter and the first time weddings are permitted since the beginning of Lent], wedding train [carriages and wagons carrying the wedding party from the bride's village to the groom's]—these all have roots deep in Russian life. The variety and breadth of Russian life astonished first-time visitors to Harbin, and gave us the right to consider it the most Russian of all the cities abroad. Harbin reminded these people of

Архив автора, Париж

Catholic churches, a Lutheran church, a Russian Old Believer's church, an Armenian Gregorian Church, several mosques, and two synagogues. Other important Harbin landmarks included a museum, which was opened in 1923 by the Society for the Study of Manchuria, and was home to Russian art exhibits.

Numerous Russian newspapers and magazines were published in the city, including *Molva* [Rumor], *Zarya* [Dawn],

Russkoe Slovo [Russian Word], *Novosti zhizni* [News of Life], *Rupor* [Mouthpiece], and *Rubezh* [Border]. The magazine *Rubezh*, founded in 1927 and published weekly from 1929 for eighteen years, was an illustrated journal with a page of fashion news that promoted the popularization of European fashion among the Russian population.

The desire to live "as before in Russia" was typical for Russians in Harbin.

Above left and right: *A corner and a courtyard in Russian Harbin.*
Photos by Alexandre Vassiliev, 1993.

Opposite: *The Church of the Assumption of the Holy Virgin Mother, built in 1908, in the New Cemetery, Harbin.*
Photo by Alexandre Vassiliev, 1993.

a former large Russian city. It astonished those not used to this kind of life—Russian spoken everywhere and signs in Russian on streets and institutions. You could see quite often in the crowded streets real Russian muzhiks in side-opening shirts tied with woven belts with tassels on the end, and country women with bright scarves tied under their chins and wearing dresses with ruffles."[3]

This Siberian color and the desire to preserve tradition created the uniqueness of Harbin. It was home to many old people who remembered the ways of the past. *Rubezh* published an article by Andrei Upshinsky in November 1933, about Avdotya Akimova, a former serf in Moscow, who was born in 1798 and lived to be 135 years old. She had been a serf until the age of sixty-three, had moved to Harbin, where she had lived until 1933, and still remembered Napoleon fleeing Moscow.

The color of Russian life was evident everywhere: prices were given in rubles and kopecks, cloth was measured in arshins (an old Russian unit of length equal to twenty-eight inches), and at the train station there were Russian porters. *Rubezh* described one: "Yes, yes, a real one—in shirt, vest, boots, apron with an oval badge on his chest 'Porter No. 26.'"

The Russians' clothes presented a striking contrast with the Chinese. The Chinese men wore braids and something like skirts, and the women, made up and coiffed severely, swayed on the tiny "hoof" shoes of their bound feet. One settler of our century, Nikolai Baikov, described his Russian nanny's reaction: "A braid like a girl's and walking around in skirts! And you can't tell from the face if it's male or female! The women are dolls, made up and painted, and their feet are like your nanny goat! What does a man need a woman like that for? No joy, no beauty, nothing."[4]

The majority of Harbiners tried to dress in European fashion, following the prescriptions of Paris fashion journals rather than of Shanghai, the largest international center in prewar China. They bought their clothing in fashionable stores or had them made by tailors and seamstresses. A specific trait of Harbin fashion was the city's Russian isolation and homogeneity. While in Constantinople, Berlin, and Paris Russians were only part of the foreign colony, Harbin was filled with them. There was no one to impress with Russian embroidery and furs.

Harbin fashion was for internal consumption. In following it, the émigrés wanted to be dressed well and elegantly, not falling behind Shanghai, and trying to be as close as possible to Paris. A contemporary wrote, "Typical Russians—a sad papa in itchy jacket, mother in a 'flashy' cotton dress with a lace kerchief on her head, and a freckled, snub-nosed daughter with a pancake beret over one

ear, who has stepped out from her native Kineshma straight into Paris."[5]

The directory *All of Harbin* compiled by S. T. Ternavsky in 1926, lists stores of ready-to-wear, where Harbiners bought their clothing. The largest store in the city was Ivan Churin's on the corner of Novotorgovaya Street and Bolshoi Prospect. This store, which is still standing today, called Chu Lin by the Chinese, was an émigré version of Bonheur des Dames and sold everything a large department store is supposed to sell.

As Mary Gurevich-Bloch, now living in Hong Kong, recalled, the designs and patterns were brought to Churin straight from Paris. Nina Afanasyevna Davidenko, one of the three Russians who have lived in Harbin since the 1910s, reported, "Churin's had a workshop with about ten Russian women sewing European styles from *Vogue* patterns. They also had millinery and shoe workshops. The fabrics were cheap, from Harbin. Churin used to have branches in Blagoveshchensk, Khabarovsk, and Vladivostok, as well as Tziamusi. All the customers of ready-to-wear at Churin's were Russian."[6] Although Davidenko's recollections relate to a later period, there is no reason to doubt their authenticity. She worked at Churin's as head bookkeeper from 1939 to 1956.

In her memoirs, *Paths of Exile*, published in the United States in 1978, Zinaida Nikolayevna Zhemchuzhnaya, who had lived for many years in Harbin, described her visit to that department store after her arrival from Moscow: "Churin's seemed so luxurious to me, like the Grand Hotel. I experienced the long-forgotten pleasure of shopping, selecting cloth, trying dresses, shoes, and hats. Soon I was owner of a fur seal cloak, so light and soft after my clumsy fur coat, a new hat, shoes, boots, and several pairs of silk stockings."[7]

Young and pretty Russian émigrés worked at the store, modeling the latest collections. Nikolai Bryansky, who now lives in Australia, writes about one of them, Ludmila Nikolayevna Vasilyeva-Lebedeva, his mother-in-law: "To support her family, Ludmila Nikolayevna took a job as a typist at the CERR, and in the evenings she showed dresses at Churin's Department Store."[8] There she met Nikolai Nikolayevich Vasilyev, a former naval officer and a widower with three children. They soon married. The story of Vasilyeva-Lebedeva, who subsequently became a famous dramatic actress, was typical of the period. She was born in Moscow in 1901 to Kazimir Iosifovich Serafinovich, a doctor born in Vienna, and Tatyana Kachaganova, from the family of the Italian sculptor Cacciagani, who came to Russia in

Opposite: *The Church of the Protection of the Holy Virgin Mother, built in 1930, in the Old Cemetery, Harbin.*
Photo by Alexandre Vassiliev, 1993.

Above: *A view of Shanghai, 1920s.*

the reign of Catherine the Great to ornament St. Petersburg. Ludmila's father died young of tuberculosis and her mother moved to Siberia in 1908. During the revolution, young Ludmila, who had just graduated from the seventh grade of the Romanov Gymnasium in Tomsk, was sent to Omsk, away from the disorder and chaos of the city. There she took a job as a typist first in the Artillery Department and then in the office of Admiral Kolchak. Ludmila Nikolayevna recalled, "His personal orders had to be typed without a single mistake of type. I remained with Supreme Commander Admiral Alexander Vasilyevich Kolchak right up until the evacuation, 14 November 1919. We evacuated, and I had to travel in the admiral's train, continuing my work along the way. At the Yenisei Station near Krasnoyarsk, we were separated by the Czechs, who took Admiral Kolchak, his wife, Anna Vasilyevna, and his retinue in one car under their guard. I was left to the fates."[9]

Ludmila Nikolayevna met her future husband, Innokentii Ivanovich Lebedev, during this time. With great difficulties, she managed to escape with her mother and infant daughter, Natalia, to Manchuria via Verkhneudinsk and Chita. After working as a model at Churin's, Ludmila Nikolayevna took part in amateur theater and by the late 1930s had become a favorite of the public, playing leading roles in the troupes of Vassily Tomsky and Vera Panova. In 1956, with her third husband, Abram Pevzner, she emigrated to Australia, where she continued her stage career until the end of her life.

In addition to Churin's store, Harbin had several other houses of ready-to-wear clothing. Among them was Volga-Baikal at 61 Kitaiskaya Street, which belonged to the brothers Krinkevich, Kirillov, and Kamov and specialized in dresses and lingerie. Konsovsky had a special store of ready-to-wear at 168 Kitaiskaya Street. On the same street, at 152 was the Viennese Association, managed by Karsha, Khutoryansky, and Blyakhman. Nearby were several other stores: Petrov's, which sold "coats, cloaks, and suits"; the Oborot Store, which belonged to Mazursky and Yankilovich; and the Louvre atelier, run by Kazachkov and Bergolson. Felix Pisarsky, an émigré now living in Hong Kong, recalls, "Most of the stores dealing with fashion and custom dresses in Harbin were situated on Kitaiskaya Street. The ladies then dressed in a first-class way. When winter came, Kitaiskaya Street was the site of competition of furs, dresses, and everything festive."[10]

Many stores were also found on Mostovaya Street, including Luxe, Manchurian Association, Clothing, Cheap Bazaar, and Depot of Ready-to-wear. The owner of the Luxe ready-to-wear salon, Galina Andreyevna Vinogradova, lived in China for a while before she moved to Australia with her daugh-

Архив автора, Париж

ter in 1956 and started a dressmaking business. Olga Stefanovna Koreneva, publisher of the magazine *Politekhnik*, supplied details about the store's work: "The Luxe salon had a workshop with seamstresses, some of whom took sewing home. The salon had a millinery workshop, where they sold ladies' hats. The salon made, besides dresses, blouses with cross-stitch embroidery that were very popular. I bought dresses for myself at the Luxe as well as at Churin's store at the Wharf, and in New City I bought dresses and had them made to order."[11]

Vinogradova's daughter Kaleria Mikhailovna Avramenko recalls that the women of Harbin were fashion conscious, but tried to copy Western fashion. They imported French and American magazines, such as *Vogue* and *Harper's Bazaar*. Olga Korneva told me about a light blue dress with silver embroidery that she ordered at Churin's, based on a

Vogue pattern, that still hangs in her closet in Australia.

Two other famous fashion houses— Varshavsky and Antoinette—were owned by Russian Jewish women. The latter had an enviable reputation from the 1920s through the 1950s. It was located on Rynochnaya Street, not far from Kitaiskaya, in house number 58, as part of Louvre, and advertised itself as a Salon of Ladies' Finery that "always has a large selection of ladies' coats, dresses, hats, and every kind of trim. Afford-able prices for everyone." The Salon Antoinette is remembered fondly by Olga Sergeyevna Morozova, who was married to the owner of the highly regarded Cosmopolitan chocolate factory and now lives in Japan. The author also located another client of Antoinette: the famous Harbin opera singer, coloratura soprano Galina Achair-Dobrotvorskaya, who lived in Australia and she reported, "I ordered

my dresses from Antoinette; they were rather expensive, but in the 1940s I was making a good salary and I could afford it."[12]

Stores selling linens for men and women flourished in Harbin. The previously mentioned Volga-Baikal, on the corner of Kitaiskaya and Konnaya streets, offered its shoppers: "Shirts of linen, zephyr, silk, poplin, and others. Collars of every style, ties, braces, studs. Ladies' lingerie—ready-to-wear and custom. Pajamas. Tricot knit lingerie—wool, silk, and fildex." Another flourishing lingerie salon was the Belosol, managed by Iosif Iudovich Belokamen. The atelier was at 17 Koreiskaya Street, and the retail store at 169 Kitaiskaya. Other linen workshops included Rybachenko's atelier at 65 Novotorgovaya Street, the salon belonging to the Eskin brothers, and the Konros Salon, owned by the Tysmenitsky brothers.

Of the corset salons, we must men-

Opposite: *The Mikheyev family, Russian émigrés in Harbin, 1922.*

Above top: *Ludmila Vasilyeva-Lebedeva, Tsingtao, 1920s.*

Above bottom: *Ludmila Vasilyeva-Lebedeva with a friend, Tsingtao, 1920s.*

Above right: *Olga Driabina-Vassilieva, concert master of the Russian opera at the Railroad Assembly, Harbin, 1928.*

Overleaf: *A ball for the Russian colony, Shanghai, 1922.*

tion Elegant, which was owned by Anna Alexeyevna Tostoganova, at 76 Novotorgovaya Street, and Sofia Mikhailovna Braun's salon at 59 Kitaiskaya Street. Small lingerie orders were accepted by the workshops of Ekaterina Petrovna Evstigneyeva, Emilia Kazimirovna Pavlovskaya, and Alexandra Arsenyevna Chervinskaya, as well as by the Ob-Enisei, located at 23 Mostovaya Street.

In the early 1920s various tailoring and sewing schools opened in Harbin; the best known were Woman's Work, run by Krasheninnikova, Kosheleva, Zherbenina, Kurdumova, Rotkegel, and Miller; Yevgenia Ivanovna Emelyanova's Worth at 61 Novotorgovaya Street; Elizaveta Andreyevna Zhilina's Teodor; and Classes by Vladimir Ivanovich Yuzhanov.

The demand for clothing was great—the city's population was growing due of the influx of émigrés, as well as the Soviet workers with the CERR—so not only experienced seamstresses, but many graduates of the tailoring and sewing courses opened ateliers out of their homes. Natalya Timofeyevna Vatunina made hats and dresses to order; Praskovya Vasilyevna Zozulin-

САЛОНЫ ДАМСКАГО ПЛАТЬЯ
ЧУРИНА
в Новом гор. и на Пристани

ПРИНИМАЮТ ЗАКАЗЫ
на всевозможныя дамскія
ПЛАТЬЯ
вечернія, бальныя, дневныя и домашнія,
КОСТЮМЫ, БЛУЗКИ, ЮБКИ и проч.
— и —
ДАМСКІЯ ШЛЯПЫ
парижских моделей.
БЕЗУКОРИЗНЕННОЕ И АККУРАТНОЕ ИСПОЛНЕНІЕ.

Библиотека Харбинского университета

Вниманию дам!
Киевский САЛОН
ДАМСКИХ НАРЯДОВ
М. Я. Матузов
Харбин, уг. Пекарной и Китайской,
№ 47 (2-ой этаж).

Принимает заказы:
**пальто,
манто,
костюмы,**
а также обновку меховых вещей.

Особое внимание уделяется подборке и чистке мехов.

Работа выполняется по образцу столичных городов, под личным наблюдением.

При салоне постоянно имеются последния новости сезона.

Заказы выполняются из своего материала и гг. заказчиков.

Цены внеконкур.

Единственная на Дальнем Востоке усовершенствованная фабрика
БЕЛЬЯ и ПЛАТЬЕВ
„БЕЛОСОЛ"
Фабрика, склад и магазин:
Корейская ул., № 17.

Оптово-розничный магазин
(I отделение) Китайская улица,
дом Окунь.

Всегда Колоссальный выбор белья:
дамского, мужского, детского и постельного.

ПЛАТЬЯ новейших фасонов из лучших загранич. материалов. ОДЕЯЛА.

При магазине салон дамских ШЛЯП.

Прием заказов.

Цены строго фабричные.

ВСЕМ ИЗВЕСТНО,
что в фабричном магазине „УРАЛ"
Харбин-Пристань, Китайская 87, против Мостовой улицы.
Цены на мануфактуру, галантерею и готовое мужское и дамское платье на 40% ниже существующих цен в Харбине.
Продажа исключительно по фабричному прейс-куранту.

От 40% до 50% Вы получите дешевле, чем в других магазинах **мануфактуру, галантерею** и **готовое мужское и дамское платье** в магазине
„НАДЕЖДА"
Г. Харбин, Пристань, Мостовая 38/11, угол Китайской улицы.

Библиотека Харбинского университета

Подвенечные туалеты
исполняются по журналам
Bride's Magazine
непосредственно полученным из Америки.
ЭЛЕГАНТНЫЯ ПЛАТЬЯ БАЛЬНЫЯ и AFTERNOON.
Изящныя
блузки и белье
Салон дамских нарядов
„ЛЮКС"
Китайская № 130.
Тел. 67-20.

Библиотека Харбинского университета

Первоклассный
мужской
портной
И. Т. Кремер
Пекарная ул. № 16.
Тел. 33-58.

Безукоризненное выполнение заказов.

skaya opened a small business called Viennese Chic; Sofia Ilyinichna Orlova's company was called Madame Sophie; Mila Grigoryevna Varaksina owned Record; and Elizaveta Ivanovna Malyavina had her atelier at 28 Yamskaya Street. Noteworthy workshops for ladies' clothing were Moscow Seamstress Avdokhina, who took orders at 59/5 Borodinskaya Street, and Artel of Ladies' Seamstresses at 25 Yamskaya Street. There were shops that sewed for both men and women, including the famous Riga Tailor Workshop owned by Petrovsky at 54 Belgiiskaya Street; the Association of Tailors owned by Ruvin Aaronovich Tsivian at 1 Birzhevaya Street; B. M. Grinshpunt owned by Rudolf Ionovich Obertik at 18 Pskovskaya Street; and Andrei Ivanovich Alexeyev's atelier at 8 Shkolnaya Street. All in all, there were more than seventy ladies' tailors in Harbin who made "dresses for all occasions in life."

Some tailors in Harbin specialized in outerwear for women, such as cloaks

and coats. At 47 Pekarnaya Street, Nikolai Modestovich Averkiev opened a tailor shop and Mikhail Filoppovich Polizhak opened his Salon of Ladies' Dresses. The demand for knitwear, so necessary in the fierce Manchurian winters when temperatures went down to minus 40 degrees centigrade, prompted Vladimir Gavrilovich Bilan to open the Salon of Knitted Goods at 23 Artilleriiskaya Street.

Shoe manufacturing was a thriving business in Harbin. Large stores like Churin's sold fashionable and warm shoes and all kinds of high boots, according to Zinaida Zhemchuzhina. Matvei Stepanovich Borisov owned a shoe store called Goods from Nizhny

Opposite: *Advertisements in the magazine* Rubezh *for fashion ateliers and cloth manufacturers in Harbin in the 1920s–30s.*

Above left: *A window of the Russian art supply store, Shanghai, 1930s.*

Below left: *A window of a Russian Siberian fur store, Shanghai, 1930s.*

Above: *A dress of beige silk with hand embroidery (from the wardrobe of Driabina-Vassilieva), Harbin, c. 1927.*

Novgorod at 109 Novotovarnaya Street and the Armenian Vichat Stepanovich Atoyan opened the Atoyan Brothers shoe store at 111 Kitaiskaya Street.

Harbin had numerous men's tailors. I will list only a few: Rakhmiel Khaimovich Sandler, Ivan Matveyevich Dryazgov, Yan Fritsevich Goldman, and Pavel Andreyevich Voronin.

The harsh climate and the cold, snowy winters made furs, which were relatively inexpensive, quite popular. A resident of Harbin, Zuev, described the Harbin flea market:

"'Greatcoat! Greatcoat!' a Tatar called out in pure Russian. 'I'll sell it for seven rubles. It's not a soldier's greatcoat, it's a general's, with a red calico lining. Seven rubles.'

"'Coat like a fur coat, with a fur collar!' cried an unshaven fellow with red eyes. 'A fur coat, as is, fur coat, I'm giving it away!'

"'Sure, a fur coat,' a wiseguy echoed and then added, 'Selling it cheap, practically giving it away. A fur coat without sleeves, without a back, with a hundred rubles' worth of repairs.'"[13]

Fur stores were located on Kitaiskaya Street as well, and notable among them were Balikoff and Grigorieff at number 174; the wholesalers the Bent brothers; and Boris Isakovich Palei. Felix Pisarsky recalls, "The fashionable fur ateliers were Palei and Bent, which gave exhibits of their works in the winter."

There were also two fur stores on Mostovaya Street: Barnaul Society, at number 5, and Vinokurov and Sons at number 25. The store of Semyon Gurevich, on Mostovaya Street not far from Kitaiskaya, had a good reputation and was particularly well known for its karakul hats and collars. They sold fur coats, jackets, hats, collars, and pelts and had a workshop for retailoring furs. Not far from Churin's on Bolshoi Prospect was the fur store belonging to Khariton Maximovich Velikanov; at 4 Yamskaya, was the fur atelier of Solomon Moiseyevich Tsyngauz; and at 1 Mostovaya, the shop of Khaim Isaevich Trotsky. In the late 1920s dyed furs were popular, and Ivan Efimovich

Terekhov opened the Condor atelier for dyeing furs at 2 Vtoraya Korotkaya Street.

Harbin was up on women's beauty, and its proximity to Shanghai assured it a ready supply of perfume, powder, and lipstick. Dozens of Russians opened manicure salons or hair salons. Apparently, the best known hair salon was Prima at 20/36 Bolshoi Prospect, opposite Churin's. Calling itself a Theatrical Hair Salon, Prima had many clients from Harbin's artistic world. Another famous hair salon was Malyshevsky's Universal at 19 Kitaiskaya Street. There were several smaller establishments and individual hairdressers.

The elegant women of Harbin were known for their beauty. Outstanding among the beauties of the 1920s was the prima ballerina Olga Pavlovna Manzhelei, who came to Harbin in 1928 to appear at the Apollo Theater. A student of Boris Romanov and Lavrenti Novikov, she was a soloist at the Odessa Theater of Opera and Ballet, and then toured China, Japan, and the Philippines with her partner, Boris Serov. They were popular in Harbin until the end of the 1930s.

Harbin also liked the ballet duos Gorskaya–Kazandzhi, Rogovskaya–Shevlugin, Ogneva–Davydov, and many others. The fame of the Harbin Ballet, founded by Elizaveta Vasilyevna Kvyatkovskaya, a choreographer from Moscow, and Nikifor Ivanovich Feoktistov, an artist of the Bolshoi Theater, was well deserved. It brought Harbin several young and talented ballerinas who were known for their beauty, including Serafima Chistokhina, Nina Kozhevnikova, Vera Kondratovich, Nina Nedzvetskaya, and Elena Trutovskaya, who later moved to Paris to perform at the Folies Bergères.

A group of pretty dancers—Bashurova, Altayeva, Rozetti, and Kvasnitskaya—ornamented the stages of variety

Opposite: *Advertisements in the magazine* Rubezh *for fashion ateliers and hair salons in Harbin, 1930s.*

reviews and cabarets, of which there were quite a few. Kozlovsky wrote about Harbin's nightlife: "One of the oldest cabarets was the Pompeii, which was distinguished by its mirrored room and 'living statues.' It was located in the New City; at the Wharf was the famous Fantasia cabaret, at the end of Offitserskaya Street next to the fire station. Those two cabarets were considered the most popular, known for their rich programs starring the best ballet and cabaret performers in the city, exquisite cuisine, and a variety of the best local and imported drinks. There was another cabaret, Aetna, which was in the house of Gibello-Socco in the New City. Aside from these fashionable cabarets, Harbin had lots of third-rate ones, say, for instance, Palermo, Sorrento, and Taverna."[14]

Among the most famous concert performers were the singers Sofia Reggi, Maria Sadovskaya and Elena Novitskaya. Harbin had a special love of operetta. The favorite prima donnas were the beauties Lystsova and Gaidarova. They performed at the Ves' Mir (the Whole World) Theater, and then moved to the Gigantic Theater, which was later renamed Asia.

The Harbin opera was strong, too. Feodor Chaliapin performed there at the end of his career, and the famous soprano from the Maryinsky Theater, Lidia Lipkovskaya, and bass Alexander Mosjoukine, brother of the film star, also sang in Harbin. Thanks to a handsome subsidy from Ivan Mosjoukine, an opera troupe was organized in 1926–28 under the aegis of the railroad. It was directed by Ivan Polikarpovich Varfolomeyev, a tenor from the Diaghilev enterprise, and starred the young Sergei Lemeshev, sopranos Sprishevskaya and Baturina, and mezzo-soprano Zelinskaya. The quality productions with sets and costumes by Zasupkin, Domrachev, and Smirnov guaranteed that the operas were a great success. The émigrés founded their own costume shops for theatrical costumes; one belonged to Yevgeny Andreyevich Chapovetsky and was located at 3 Kommercheskaya Street, and another,

Архив Николая Брянского, Австралия

Left: *Sergei Lemeshev, Harbin, late 1920s. The famous Bolshoi Opera tenor began his career in Harbin under the direction of Varfolomeyev.*

Right: *Olga Manzhelei, a variety hall dancer, Harbin, 1927.*

Below: *Lidia Lipkovskaya, an opera singer from the St. Petersburg Maryinsky Theater, Harbin, early 1920s.*

Opposite top: *Performers in* Coppelia *on the stage of the Railroad Assembly, Harbin, 1930s.*

Opposite bottom: *Vera Kondratovich, poet and ballerina, Harbin, 1940s.*

Библиотека Харбинского университета

which also rented costumes, belonged to Zinovy Mikhailovich Kogan at 13 Turemnaya Street.

Almost all the operas were staged at the Railroad Assembly, whose auditorium seated 1,200 and had excellent acoustics. Olga Stefanovna Koreneva, a Harbin historian living in Australia, wrote about the theater. "The entire building was luxuriously appointed: plasterwork ceilings, beautiful lighting fixtures on the walls, crystal chandeliers, wood paneling, deep red velvet curtains with gold trim; paintings by famous artists in the lobby. The audiences were always well dressed in exquisite taste."[15]

In a later period the opera showcased lyric coloratura soprano Achair-Dobrotvorskaya, dramatic soprano Erdyakova, lyric soprano Khokhryakova, mezzo-soprano Engelgardt, and the bass Sayanin, the baritone Borisevich, and the dramatic tenor Shemansky. Russian drama was performed at the Buff Theater, where Vera Fedorovna Komissarzhevskaya appeared in 1909. In pre-revolutionary times, such stars as Orlenev, Roshchina-Insarova, Ge, and Davydov toured Harbin.

With the massive emigration, many Russian actors from the capital and the provinces ended up in Harbin, as did many actors on tour. In 1923 the brilliant beauty of the Alexandrinsky Theater, Verdinskaya, starred in *Dame aux camélias*, and in 1925 the famous actress from the Maly Theater, Pashen-

Архив автора, Париж

naya, the sister of Roshchina-Insarova, visited Harbin on tour. Orlov, a graduate of the studio of the Moscow Art Theater, produced plays from the Moscow Art Theater's repertoire for nine seasons with young actors from Harbin, including Verlen, Vasilyeva-Lebedeva, Marulina, and Svetlanova-Dvorzhetskaya.

The most productive drama troupe was that of Vasily Ivanovich Tomsky, producing 650 plays between 1938 and 1942. In addition to Russian drama, Harbin also had Ukrainian drama and operetta, the Polish artistic society Gospoda Polska, a Tatar amateur theater, and the Imaldag and Kunst Jewish theater societies.

Along with the opera, operetta, drama, and ballet stars, were the Russian beauties from Harbin society. There were many charity balls—the Polytechnic Ball, the Rose Ball, and others—where beautiful women showed off their finery. Occasionally there were beauty contests to elect a Miss Harbin. Similar contests, a tradition among Russian émigrés, were held in Shanghai, Tsingtao, and Tianjin, where there were significant Russian colonies. In the 1930s the winners of the Miss Harbin contest were Xenia Garetta-Ermolayeva, Baroness von Sieberg, and Olga Pushkareva.

Felix Pisarsky recalled, "Our young women worried about their reputations and tried to avoid working as models. It was considered inappropriate even to

Архив автора. Париж

Архив автора. Париж

work as a saleswoman in a store or a waitress in a café. In Harbin we had a beauty contest for Boyarynya [Boyar Woman]. The most famous Harbin beauties were considered to be Princess Tatyana Uspenskaya, who later moved to Shanghai, Vera Razheva, the daughter of a baker who moved from the USSR, and the student Lidia Shishkanova. Many girls seeking husbands left for Shanghai, where there were more opportunities."

Questions of beauty were discussed quite often. A sampling of topics from the Women's Page of *Rubezh* reads as follows: "Breathing and Beauty," "Skin Care," "Evening Toilette," "Beauty Milk, "Fashionable Line," "Bathing Benefits," "Learn to Wave Your Hair," and "Protect Yourself from Freckles and Wrinkles."

Here is what *Rubezh* recommended to the women of Harbin in 1930: "Very thin women are not in fashion today. Fashion demands rounded forms and feminine curves. Therefore, if you are very bony, try to gain weight. It is just as difficult as losing weight for the heavy, since thinness often has deep internal causes and can be the result of anemia or glandular problems. To gain weight, you must eat well. A bottle of cream, drunk between breakfast and lunch and again between lunch and dinner, will be a great help in putting on needed pounds. Cream of wheat or oatmeal eaten on an empty stomach with fruit is also very good."[16]

Another source of information of fashion and beauty for émigrés was the Russian-language magazine *Sovremennaya zhenshchina* [Modern Woman],

Opposite: *Elena Pavlova,
a Russian ballerina, Harbin, 1922.*

Right: *Alexander Shemansky,
a dramatic tenor with the Harbin opera,
in the role of Cannot in* I Pagliacci, *1930s.*

Below left: *Igor Shvetsov,
a Russian dancer, Harbin, 1930.*

Below right: *An advertisement for
the Shanghai nightclub where
Alexander Vertinsky performed, from the
magazine* Sovremennaya zhenshchina
[Modern Woman], 1937.

ВСѢ
РЕКОРДЫ
ПОПУЛЯРНОСТИ

ПОБИТЫ

DD's Night Club

815, Avenue Joffre   Tel. 71609

ЕЖЕДНЕВНО
А. Н. ВЕРТИНСКІЙ
В СОБСТВЕННОМ
РЕПЕРТУАРѢ

Архив автора. Париж

Архив Николая Брянского, Австралия

Above top: *Performers in the ballet*
Swan Lake *at the Railroad Assembly.*
In the center, in the costume of Odile,
is the ballerina Nina Nedzvetskaya,
Harbin, 1940s.

Above: *Maria Baturina, a soprano of*
the Harbin opera, 1920s.

Right: *The ballet troupe at the Railroad*
Assembly after a performance of the
operetta Maritza, *Harbin, 1940s.*

Архив автора. Париж

Библиотека Академии арендных искусств, Гонконг

Библиотека Академии арендных искусств, Гонконг

129

Мисс Шанхай 1937 года.

Помѣщенное в настоящем номерѣ журнала письмо нашей уважаемой подписчицы, скрывшей свое имя под псевдонимом «Ажур», касается вопроса, который волнует громадную часть прекрасной половины Шанхая, а потому не может не интересовать живѣйшим образом редакцію СОВРЕМЕННОЙ ЖЕНЩИНЫ.

Устроители конкурса на соисканіе званія «Мисс Шанхай 1937 года», содружество богемы ХЛАМ, имѣют от французских властей полномочіе на производство выборов «Мисс Шанхай». Такое довѣріе обязывает, и, раз объявляется о производствѣ выборов, то их слѣдует производить именно в выборном порядкѣ, а не в видѣ какого то аукціона.

Вмѣсто выборов с подачею голосов, будь-то всѣми присутствующими или специальными жюри, устроители на этот раз задались цѣлью собрать с публики деньги, что им с успѣхом и удалось.

В данном случаѣ налицо явное нарушеніе принципа выборности. Титул «Мисс Шанхай» фактически оказался пріобрѣтенным за деньги и не присужденным публикой или жюри. Довѣріе французских властей грубым образом нарушено, а лучшія чувства женщины жестоко оскорблены

Дурной примѣр заразителен. Стремленіе к наживѣ соблазнило подражателей анонсировать новый конкурс красоты. В то время, когда настоящій номер печатался, в русских газетах появились объявленія, приглашающія «красивых РУССКИХ дѣвушек» принять участіе в конкурсѣ Им обѣщалось покрытіе расходов и безплатное предоставленіе купальных костюмов, являющихся установленной формой на конкурсѣ.

Какая профанація!..

Данный вопрос внѣ всякаго сомнѣнія имѣет общественный характер, несмотря на то, что наши ежедневныя газеты не подняли его на своих страницах.

Происшедшаго не исправишь. Желательно лишь, чтобы в будущем выборы «Мисс Шанхай» проводились в здоровой атмосферѣ выборности, а не служили средством обогащенія.

Считая выборы «Мисс Шанхай 1937 года» неправильными, Редакція воздерживается от помѣщенія в журналѣ портрета побѣдительницы конкурса.

published in Shanghai. Its first issue came out in February 1937. It consisted of useful hints for women, fashion reviews, humorous stories, replies to readers' letters, and crosswords. Here is an excerpt from the Mail Box section of the March 1937, issue: "To Olga Polubanova. Question: 1) Is Russian embroidery in style? 2) Where can I get some? 3) What dresses can be embroidered with Russian designs? Answer: 1) Russian embroidery is very much in fashion now, and there is one pattern, not Russian however, in this issue. 2) The E Dvorzhets Salon, 77 Gascogne Apartements, 1202 Avenue Joffre manufactures these works for export. If you mention our magazine, you will get a reduced price for the embroidery. 3) Embroidery is done on canvas or cotton for summer dresses and house dresses."[17]

Between 1947 and 1949, Lydia Vinokurova, a former Harbin model who later became a sculptor, ran a very successful fashion business in Shanghai. She owned three shops featuring her designs: one, on avenue Joffre, was called Femind, and another, on rue Cardinal Mercier, was named Altai. Vinokurova was often referred to as the "Chinese Dior" by the local socialites. Her main Russian competitor in Shanghai was Mrs. Garnet, whose creations were highly regarded.

In Shanghai, Russian émigrés, who

Page 129, top: *Russian girls in a variety review, Shanghai, late 1920s.*

Page 129, bottom: *Russian jazz, Shanghai, late 1920s.*

Opposite: *The cover of* Sovremennaya zhenshchina, *published in Shanghai, 1937.*

Above: *An editorial in* Sovremennaya zhenshchina *about the Russian Miss Shanghai competition, Shanghai, June, 1937.*

Right: *Elections for beauty queen at a ball for Russian youth, Tianjin, December 1940.*

ПАСХАЛЬНЫЙ

РУБЕЖ

№ 18 (639)

Цѣна — 65 ф

lived primarily in the territory of the French concession, had more international influences than they did in Harbin. The acknowledged beauty of the Russian colony in Shanghai was Vera Sennikova, who later moved to Tianjin. They had regular Miss Shanghai contests, which were done in a more European manner.

Life for Russian émigrés in Harbin changed in the early 1930s. On March 1, 1932, the state of Manchukuo was founded, subordinate to the Japanese administration. The Russian émigrés, suffering from unemployment, took jobs in Japanese institutions. In March, 1935, the USSR ceded its rights in the CERR to Japan: numerous Soviet railroad workers and their families returned to the USSR and some moved to Shang-

hai and Tianjin. By a decree of the Japanese administration, the Bureau on Affairs of Russian Immigrants was formed to help the Russian population in finding new jobs.

Hard times were ahead for the residents of Harbin. In August 1945, after Japan lost World War II, Harbin was occupied by Soviet troops. Many émigrés were arrested and taken to the northern regions of Siberia. The civil war in China worsened the position for the remaining émigrés. In 1954 many Russians from Harbin were sent into forced labor in the remote areas of the USSR. The rest, knowing what awaited them in the north, headed abroad, gradually leaving via Hong Kong for Australia, Canada, Brazil, Chile, or Europe. By the mid-1960s, Russian Harbin was empty.

Opposite: *The cover of the Harbin magazine* Rubezh, *no. 18, 1940.*

Above and left: *Advertisements for hair salons and cosmetics from the telephone directory* Ves' Kharbin [All Harbin], *1927. The magazines of Harbin and Shanghai often published advice on skin and hair care. The cult of feminine beauty reigned among the émigrés.*

6
RUSSIAN ÉMIGRÉ HANDICRAFTS

World War I and the 1919 Versailles Peace Treaty, which redrew the map of Europe, introduced the "exotic" Slavic countries of eastern Europe to the West. The First World War became the demarcation line that separated twentieth-century fashion from nineteenth-century fashion. The new occupations women engaged in during the war—work in factories, plants, and hospitals—helped to transform rigid societal stereotypes and, accordingly, fashion.

An entirely different rhythm of life mandated the creation of a new dress silhouette: the new straighter, shorter, uncorseted styles were more comfortable to wear while working, riding city transportation, and standing in queues. The shortage of elegant fabrics and the creation of artificial viscose silk also influenced the fashions of the 1920s. Clasps on dresses were moved from the back to the chest; hair was cut short. The new rhythm and conditions of life were fertile soil for new trends in fashion, such as the previously unknown Eastern European "folk-peasant" style in clothing.

The enormous demand by Western Europeans for Slavic handcrafted articles prompted many émigrés to take up fashion handicrafts at home, or in the hotels where they were often living at the beginning of their emigration. Russians made a wide range of articles by hand, such as furnishings used in interior decoration—lampshades, pillows, napkins and drapes—as well as dolls and toys,

ПОРТНОЙ

Б. З. Рукин

24, rue du Faubourg Montmartre, 24.
Téléphone: Provence 37-59

(раньше: Киев, Николаевская 3)

доводит до сведения русской колонии и особенно киевлян, которым фирма моя была известна, как одна из лучших,

что мною открыт

ПРИЕМ ЗАКАЗОВ МУЖСКОГО ПЛАТЬЯ

Opposite: Katyusha Ionina, a Russian model, in a headdress made by the house of Caris, Paris, 1923.

Above: An advertisement for a Russian tailor, Boris Rukin, Paris, 1928.

and items for the fashion industry—hats, embroidered handbags, umbrellas, and costume jewelry, and painted silk batik shawls and scarves, which were especially popular in the 1920s.

At first these crafts were marketed through exhibits organized by Western charitable organizations; then individuals active within the émigré circles became more involved in selling the crafts. One of the first such exhibitions was organized in Constantinople in 1921 by the American Red Cross under Admiral Bristol's chairmanship and featured crafts made by Russian children. Judging from an extant archival photograph, there were embroidered napkins, pillows, boxes, and other crafts, as well as paintings. The energetic Grand Duchess Maria Pavlovna organized a charitable

sale of Russian handicrafts in Paris in early 1921. The Paris magazine *Fémina* wrote about it: "A group of Russian refugees from the highest social strata opened an exhibit of works by participants under the direction of the Grand Duchess Maria Pavlovna. At the exhibit, you will find toys, embroidery, drawings, sculptures, and lingerie which are both exquisitely tasteful and very original. This exhibit of national art, at once charming and useful, is a great success."[1]

Judging from the photograph accompanying the article, the exhibit also displayed wooden shelves carved in the neo-Russian style, popularized by artists from the Abramtsevo estate, and handmade Russian dolls used as teapot cozies or simply for interior decoration. This exhibit launched a new émigré craft as well: rag dolls in Russian peasant clothing, a stylized version of traditional Russian costume. The largest doll workshop in Paris in the 1920s was Mrs. Lazareva's establishment, which produced not only Russian dolls, but all kinds of dolls dressed in national, or simply fashionable, costumes. The most avant-garde in style were those produced by the painter and sculptor Maria Vassilieff; they are now considered rare antiques.

The handicraft arts required skills. The Russian Art School was opened in the sixteenth arrondissement by Nikolai Vasilyevich Globa, with such eminent professionals as Mstislav Dobuzhinsky and Ivan Bilibin teaching classes.

Russian-style embroidery, drawing, painting, and sewing were taught, and the school's graduates filled the ranks of émigré artists circles.

With the increase in the number of people producing crafts and a wider variety of articles being produced, a sales network developed for the handicrafts. The artisans joined together into cooperatives and the cooperatives delivered production to shops. Certain shops specialized in handmade items. Many émigrés placed their wares at famous Paris fashion houses, others used the services of *placiers*—merchandise distribution agents. Avgusta Damanskaya writes about the popularity of Russian-style crafts in the early 1920s in the novel *Miranda*, tracing the path of one of the émigré characters: "In Constantinople he was the chairman of something, in Sofia a teacher, in Prague a temporary

deputy to a half-Russian official in the Ministry of Land Ownership, in Berlin the co-owner of a Russian crafts shop— they were fashionable—and finally, in Paris, a shareholder of the bar 'Kinechma' with fresh *rasstegai* [open-face meat or fish pies] served round the clock."[2]

Top left: *A "Nansen" passport issued in Paris in 1937.*

Top: *A square in front of the Cathedral of Alexander Nevsky in Paris nicknamed "Chatterbox Place," 1926.*

Above: *Count Baranov, formerly a colonel in the Tsarist army, working as the doorman at the Russian restaurant Casanova, Paris, 1938.*

Left: *A family of émigrés in front of a Russian shop in a Paris suburb. On the right is N.M. Polezhaeva, c. 1925.*

Opposite top: *An advertisement for a French store that sold clothing to Russian émigrés, Paris, 1926.*

Opposite, above left: *Russian General Erdeli, a taxi driver in Paris.*

Opposite, above right: *A drawing by Pem in the magazine* Illustrirovannaya Rossiya *[Russia Illustrated] of a Russian taxi driver on the grand boulevards of Paris, 1928.*

Opposite below: *The interior of the Russian restaurant Boyarsky, Paris, 1926.*

The society columnist Pierre de Trevier wrote enthusiastically and in great detail in *L'Art et la mode* about the popularity of Russian crafts in Paris in 1924: "Russian restaurants aren't the only thing Paris has. We have something else besides the taxi drivers and dance teachers who assure you that they were adjutants to the Tsar. . . . We now have all these attractive, multicolored Russian fabrics and decorative objects, created with rare artistry by craftsmen and women who, by strange coincidence, have situated themselves along the entire rue du Faubourg St. Honoré from the Place Beauvau to the rue Royale. In these unique shops with their enchanting window displays you can admire attractive fabrics, indescribable shawls and patterned fabrics with ornamental designs blending the naive and sophisticated, with color combinations that sing to you, that play with you, which scatter and then re-collect once again

Above: *A boarding house for Russian aristocrats in Brookline, Massachussets. Second from the left is the owner, Charles Whitmore, to his right is his Russian wife and her father, Mikhail Peltsig. Everyone is doing embroidery, mid-1920s.*

Left: *Nadezhda Plevitskaya, a famous émigré folk singer and a GPU (precursor to the KGB) secret agent, in a handmade dress, mid-1920's.*

Right: *An advertisement by the Berlin underwear company "Olga" from the magazine Zhar-Ptitsa [Firebird], 1922.*

„OLGA"
SEIDEN=WÄSCHE=VERTRIEB G·M·B·H·
BERLIN W 35, LÜTZOWSTR. 46
TEL. NOLLENDORF 40 54
*
Художественное изготовленіе дамскаго шелковаго и другого тонкаго бѣлья Гарнитуры, Капоты, Блузы, Пиджамы и пр. (Вышиваніе и рисованіе).

Срочное выполненіе заказовъ
Продажа оптомъ и въ розницу

138

into a captivating, inspiring, spiritual harmony. There are tunics trimmed with lace of unsurpassed artistry. Unforgettable scarves, remarkable embroidery, belts that marry leather, braids and ribbons, following the dictates of a taste at once barbaric and magnificent. You'll find Russian furs there, selected by these natural-born artists, and decorative items done in the Moscow-style right next to the sign 'Russian sale.'

"There are beads made of wood, ivory, carnelian, nephrite, and semiprecious stones cut into bead shapes,

Above left: *An exhibit of Russian handicrafts, Geneva, 1927.*

Above right: *An exhibit of handicrafts entitled "Russkii Ochag" (The Russian Hearth), Prague, 1927.*

Below: *An exhibit of Russian handicrafts, Paris, 1922.*

squares, rings, which seem to be strung chaotically, totally haphazardly, without any forethought, but which create an impression of such tonal unity and decorative brilliance that one is captivated, enchanted. I fervently believe that our fashions will fall under the direct influence of these naive but experienced artists.

"Bakst's creations and Stravinsky's efforts did not pass through without leaving a trace, but the Russian influence undoubtedly has manifested in an even more dynamic and striking form

Национальная библиотека. Сантьяго

Ранюк Сан-Тельмо. Буэнос-Айрес

due to the large-scale participation of Russian craftspeople who settled in Paris. Do not doubt that the tunics of Parisian women will soon be illumined with a Slavic spirit or a Russian mood. The Cossack coat, which made an appearance last season, will fade in comparison to these stylized creations, obscure recollections of Holy Russia's endless suffering."[3]

A dress made by the Rosa Ratner cooperative, which was located in the center of the Russian craft trade, at no. 58 rue du Faubourg St. Honoré, was donated in 1997 to the Musée de mode et du Costume in Paris. This embroidered black dress has the label "Aux Bibelots Russes" with the note "Robe Russes" ("Russian dress").

Inna Sergeevna Mishchenko (née Senkevich), who was born in Odessa in 1900 and came to Paris in 1924 from Belgrade, reminisced about Russian workers' co-

Архив автора. Париж

operatives: "In Paris several Russian aristocrats opened so-called *oeuvroirs*, that is, cooperatives that assigned work to be completed at home. The situation for Russians then was very dramatic. We were all young, poor, and had no work experience. As émigrés, Russian women were the first to begin working. They were first to get work—sewing—while living in horrible third-class hotels."[4]

The daughter of an Odessa government official, Inna Sergeevna fled from Odessa with her mother in 1920 on the English warship *Leonardo* to Thessaloniki, Greece, then moved to Yugoslavia under the protection of the Society to Aid Victims of Soviet Rule. Living in Zemun, near Belgrade, Inna Sergeevna met Aleksei Danilovich Mishchenko, her future husband, a journalist who later had a successful career in France.

After Mishchenko moved to Paris to work as a correspondent for the Belgrade newspapers, he had no steady income, and Inna Sergeevna was obliged to earn money with her handiwork. She recalled: "Our situation was better than that of others: we lived in the sixteenth arrondissement, which was considered a very good neighborhood. My husband was thirty-three then, a university graduate who spoke English and French well. Many of my Russian émigré acquaintances began to sew at home. They were often given lingerie to satin-stitch and adorn with lace. At that time, the émigré women embroidered at night in the hotels, earning pennies, while their husbands became taxi drivers."

The aristocratic craft co-ops of that time specialized in work done by hand, most often embroidery. They would re-

Opposite above: *Lazareva in her doll workshop, Paris, 1926.*

Opposite, below left: *A doll in a Russian costume created in a crafts workshop, Paris, 1920s.*

Opposite, below right: *Alexandra Balachova and Mikhail Mordkin as Russian dolls in La Chauve Souris cabaret, Moscow, November 1916.*

Left: *A drawing of a Russian doll from the French magazine* L'art et la mode, *Paris, 1925.*

Above: *Lazareva's daughter with dolls from their craft workshop, Paris, 1926.*

ceive orders, sometimes from the big Paris fashion houses, for trim and embroidered finish work, which was usually very intricate and labor intensive. According to Inna Sergeyevna Mishchenko's memoirs, at that time they were paid 75 francs for an embroidered dress, while the owner of the co-op sold it for 275 francs.

Taking advantage of the incredible popularity of Russian embroidery, in 1924 Mrs. Meyers, the enterprising wife of the Secretary of the American Mission in Paris, decided to open an atelier featuring embroidered dresses. This atelier was located on the rue Visconti, one of the narrowest streets in the St. Germain neighborhood and, according to the eyewitness Inna Mishchenko, "had no name." She recalls: "Women from the highest Russian society worked there, Princess Kutuzova in particular. They made dresses in one style: straight silk dresses with no waistline, like a shirt without sleeves in blue or black.

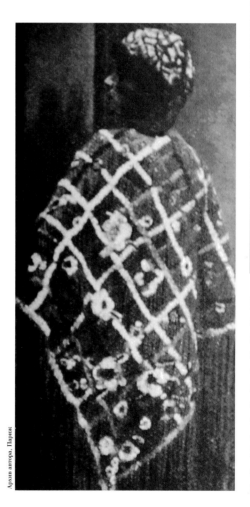

HENRI MANUEL

Архив автора. Париж

Архив автора. Париж

Russian-style embroidery was done on the collar and the shoulders, and sometimes they did the embroidery in bouquets. The clients, mainly American women, enjoyed shopping at our place, since Mrs. Meyers sold the dresses more cheaply than other houses. I worked in this atelier for three years until a young woman, whom I knew as a young girl back in Russia, suggested that I become a model, since this profession was so much in demand."

Among the Russian émigrés, there were a great many seamstresses who worked at home, sewing on commission. Not all of them had professional experience and training, not all possessed sufficient taste and the sense of proportion so essential in the art of sewing. Aristocrats who had never worked before, as well as actresses, teachers, and physicians, became seamstresses. Teffi gives an amusing description of one of these woebegone seamstresses in

suits: midwifery courses, then work at a hospital. Well, yes, I got quite a taste of medicine. No use for my doctoring here. Who needs it? You look around, the professors, even they've joined Gypsy choruses. But I'll always be able to support myself with my needle. I turned in a dress yesterday—a scrumptious little number. A button right smack on the appendix, piping across the left kidney, and gathered all around the peritoneum. Very sweet. Take a look—your little blouse here, as they say, is a total fantasy. The neckline isn't very low, just

Paris in her collection of stories titled *Gorodok* [Small Town] :

"I've brought your little blouse, yes I have. I wanted to suggest a little frill on the stomach, but I'm thinking that you wouldn't take a liking to it. Did I ever think that I'd wind up a seamstress? I lived my life in completely different pur-

Opposite left: Marevna, a Russian artist, in a shawl she created, Paris, 1927.

Opposite right: Vera Serguine (Marie Roche), a French actress, in a handmade dress, Paris, 1924.

Above left: A handcrafted purse embroidered with wool and beads, Paris, c. 1925.

Above right: A detail of a hand-embroidered summer dress, Paris, early 1920s.

Below: An advertisement for hand-embroidered blouses in the French magazine L'art et la mode, *Paris, 1923.*

touches the tips of the lungs. Buy yourself a little hat, just big enough to cover the gray matter of your brain. It's very fashionable. . . . What, the belt's too wide? Look here, I've sewn on two buttons, you can fasten it on either side, the liver side if you like, or the spleen side—it's fashionable either way."[5]

LA BRODERIE DANS LES BLOUSES

143

Vladimir Mayakovsky's great loves, arrived in Paris from Penza, in the southern Soviet Union, in 1925, and also opened a hat business in her Paris apartment. In the late 1920s, Yakovleva, who became the Viscountess du Plessix, took a millinery course with a professional Armenian hat designer and learned the trade that supported her in New York during the postwar years. Her daughter, Francine du Plessix Gray, describes Yakovleva's atelier: "On the table lay mountains of felt, tulle, rolls of ribbons large and small, feathers, and roses made from fabric scraps. An enormous round steam press, which compelled all this to take on the necessary shapes of berets and hats, completed the picture. Mother never made any sketches, using her own reflection in a mirror as her only creative instrument hour after hour—eight hours a day, three hundred days a year; the mirror became the symbol of her life."[6] After moving to New York during the war, Yakovleva worked for twenty-eight years in the hat salon at

In addition to the seamstresses, a great many Russian milliners set up shop in Paris, serving mainly other émigré women. One of them was the former Muscovite Natalya Yevgenyevna Trzhetsyak, née Firenkrantz. She made hats for a long time—from 1920 to 1940—and sometimes did embroidery to order. She sold to the author a dress she embroidered with beads for Kitmir, the Russian fashion house in Paris.

Inna Mishchenko, with whom we are already acquainted, also made hats. After working as a model at the O'Rossen House on Place Vendôme, she opened a hat business at home, producing copies of other well-known milliners' designs. Natalya Yakovleva, another former model at the O'Rossen House, was Mishchenko's assistant. Mishchenko's atelier also sold patterns for hat designs to émigrés in other countries, dividing the patterns into halves and sending them through the mail in two separate envelopes in order to keep them from being copied.

Tatyana Yakovleva, the niece of a well-known artist and one of the poet

Saks Fifth Avenue, where her clients included Marlene Dietrich, Claudette Colbert, and Edith Piaf.

Yakovleva married Alexander Liberman, who later became the art director at Condé Nast Publications, and she became one of the arbiters of elegance and taste in New York: Christian Dior, Valentina Sanina, and Yves Saint Laurent all took her opinion into account.

In Paris during the 1920s, even beauties such as Lady Abdy (née Iya Grigorevna de Gay), who later became famous in Parisian high society, at one time had to resort to doing crafts work in order support herself and her family. A few months before she died, Lady Abdy told the author: "My best friend Misia Sert thought that I had a talent for dressmaking because I would dream up designs for dresses, various parts of garments, and handbags. Around 1929 I made handbags that I had designed myself. Many of them were sold everywhere at that time. Later I gave the production of these bags and drawings of purses to a small lingerie house, 'Annek,' which my mother, Anna Ivanovna Novikova, a former actress at the Aleksandriinsky Theater, had established with her friend Madame Kamenskii.

"One fine day I saw models at Chanel with our 'Annek' handbags and I said to her [Chanel]: 'Why these are the bags that I designed for my mother's house!' But Chanel wasn't at all ashamed and replied: 'Now you work for me, so it's all the same.' But I knew that this was not the case. My mother's Annek House was a small business and we couldn't sue her. Chanel was well aware that no lawsuits would be brought against her, and several of my craft designs from Annek were copied and sold at Chanel."[7]

Painting on silk was a handicraft that was very widely practiced by the émigrés. It captured everyone's hearts in the 1920s and the large ornamental designs and vivid combinations of colors from Bakst's palette were clearly a tribute to the Ballets Russes. Aniline dyes, which appeared in the 1850s, produced bright and rich colors, making possible the creation of unusual designs on silk. The Lutovinov atelier was among the silk painting workshops in the 1920s–30s that was well known for its painted scarves, shawls, and kerchiefs. It was established by Pavel Nikolayevich Lutovinov, a former naval officer and his wife Valentina Alexandrovna (who died in New York in 1984). This atelier was located at no. 10 avenue Stefan Mallarmé

Opposite, above left: *An unknown woman at the Longchamps races near Paris in a hand-painted dress, Paris, early 1920s.*

Opposite, above right: *Princess Elena Trubetskaya in a handmade dress with patterns from Russian embroidered towels as the trim, Paris, 1923.*

Opposite below: *An autumn coat embroidered in the Slavic cross-stitch style, Paris, 1922–23.*

Above left: *A detail of a dress with wool embroidery, Paris, 1922–23.*

Above right: *Hand-painted dresses with Slavic ornamentation, Paris, 1922*

Right: *Galia Mushkina, owner of Galia, House of Handmade Fashion, in an embroidered design from her atelier, Paris, 1929. Photo by D'Ora.*

145

Архив автора. Париж

in the seventeenth arrondissement and produced magnificent painted batik items. Russian artisans worked in it, and at one point it employed about ten people. One of the head scarves created in 1933–34 by the Lutovinovs is in the collection of Irina Holman de Koby in England.

George Wakhevitch, the famed French film and theater designer who was born in Odessa in 1907, recalls working in the Russian silk painting atelier: "Since I needed to support myself while attending school, I painted flowers on fabrics for the mothers of my classmates who were more prosperous than I was. Evenings I created designs for the art objects made in the workshops run by Russian émigré ladies."[8]

One of the leading talented applied artists who achieved great fame with her modest work in Paris was Maria Bronislavovna Vorobyova-Stebelskaya, who became a celebrity under the pseudonym Marevna. A child of Parisian bohemia and Russian Montparnasse, she created a collection of shawls with

Архив автора. Париж

Opposite: *Inna Sergeevna Mishchenko, an employee of a millinery workshop and a crafts cooperative, and a model for the O'Rossen House, Paris, 1932.*

Above left: *N. Ye. Trzhetsyak, who later became a milliner in Paris, Moscow, 1914.*

Above right: *A Russian émigré in a handmade hat, Warsaw, early 1920s.*

Left: *Advertisements for Russian tailors in Paris from the magazine* Illustrirovannaya Rossiya [Illustrated Russia], *1920s.*

147

creations something spring-like, spontaneous, free and candid, which delights and, at the same time, there is something profound, something of the young, free people who still have many centuries of trials and incredible experiences in store for them."[9]

Marevna, who was born in Cheboksary, USSR in 1892, wrote a book, *Mémoirs d'une nomade*, in which she also talks about her handicraft work of the 1920s. She exhibited her works in the Soviet pavilion in 1925 at the Exhibit of Contemporary Decorative and Industrial Art in Paris at the invitation of its organizers, who knew her back in Russia. Her creations were an enormous success. She recalls: "My tapestries, handbags, belts, trim for dresses and coats, and my shawls, all were loved by the French and Russian visitors alike. If I were a Russian citizen today, I'd be awarded a medal. This possibility was seriously discussed, but they crossed me off the list of recipients so as not to arouse any jealousy among the 'real'

large floral designs trimmed with fringe. The fashion journalist Edme described Marevna's work in the Parisian magazine *L'Art vivant* in 1927: "Marevna's Russian shawls all share wildness, primitiveness and modernity. She wove small, brightly colored squares with a needle on a net background of wool strips and scattered it with flowers. . . . The wool strips recall primitive natural life before the advent of machines, when the spinner and weaver were the masters of the canvas. Returning to one's roots gives one's creations freshness and youthfulness, and there is in Marevna's

Above: *A summer jacket made by Russian tailors, from the poet Irina Odoevtseva's wardrobe, Paris, 1935.*

Right and opposite: *Drawings from the French magazine* L'art et la mode *depicting designs from the fashion house Annek, 1929.*

Opposite right: *A detail of a silk batik shawl from the Lutovinov workshop that was a wedding gift from the Lutovinovs to Irina Holman de Koby, Paris, 1932.*

Russians. But still, everything I had on display sold out very quickly!"[10]

The artist and jeweler Vladimir Makovsky was a master craftsman of the highest caliber. He created the technique of making miniature mosaics from semiprecious stones and mother-of-pearl, which resembled a Florentine technique, and created sets of plaques for brooches, rings, earrings, and boxes. His works, reminiscent of Bilibin's illustrations for Russian fairy tales, were very popular in the 1920s in famous Parisian jewelry houses such as Cartier. Today Makovsky's mosaics are valued very highly at auction.

To be sure, not everyone achieved such a high level of perfection. The house of the Guchkov sisters made simple but elegant ornaments for the Russian firm Caris; and in the early 1920s the writer Elsa Triolet, who was Louis Aragon's "Soviet" wife and Lili Brik's sister, made cotton "beads for swimming," which were coated with "a pearl solution" of fish scales. These irregularly

Библиотека Ла Камбр, Брюссель

Коллекция Ирина Холодная де Кобб, Биэборо, Англия

shaped white, pink, and gray beads apparently had a very characteristic odor. Elsa recounts the saga of their sale in her story *"Busy"* [Beads] in the Soviet magazine *Krasnaya nov'* [Red Virgin Soil], in which she describes her encounter with an American magazine publisher:

" 'Where did you get that necklace?'
'I made it.'
'Is it for sale?'
'No.'
'Would you like to sell it?'
'Very much.'
'Come to my office tomorrow. You'll sell a lot of them.' "

As a result of this sudden acquaintance Elsa Triolet sold several consignments of her beads to the major fashion houses of Paris—Jean Patou, Madeleine Vionnet, Elsa Schiaparelli. Only at Chanel (about which Triolet wrote maliciously, "Chanel has gone out of fashion") did Prince Kutuzov refuse to see her. How did Elsa Triolet deal with this unexpected windfall? She wrote with pride: "Louis and I used the money from the sale of this design to go to the Soviet Union."[12]

7
THE KITMIR HOUSE OF EMBROIDERY

The House of Kitmir, which operated in Paris from 1921 to 1928 and had an exclusive contract with Chanel, brought together many Russian embroidery workers who worked at home. The constant demand for their work turned would-be artisans into haute couture professionals. The founder and artistic director of the house was the Grand Duchess Maria Pavlovna Romanova (1890–1958), a cousin of Emperor Nicholas II, a granddaughter of Emperor Alexander II, and the daughter of Emperor Alexander III's younger brother— Grand Duke Paul Alexandrovich, who was executed by the Bolsheviks. Her mother was Grand Duchess Alexandra Georgievna, the daughter of George I, the King of Greece, and the Grand Duchess Olga Konstantinovna Romanova.

Alexandra Georgievna died at the age of twenty-one at the Ilyinsky estate near Moscow, six days after giving birth to her second child, Grand Duke Dmitrii Pavlovich, Maria Pavlovna's brother. In 1902 Paul Alexandrovich entered into a morganatic marriage with Olga Valerianovna Pistolkors in Livorno, thereby losing the right to raise his children. Maria and Dmitrii were left virtually orphans and were raised by their uncle Grand Duke Sergei Alexandrovich, the governor-general of Moscow, and his wife, Elizaveta Feodorovna (Empress Alexandra Feodorovna's sister), who was pious and artistically gifted but— according to Maria Pavlovna's description—rather cold and unfeeling.

Opposite: *The Grand Duchess Maria Pavlovna, proprietress of the Kitmir fashion house, with embroidered articles. Photo by Meurisse.*

Above: *An advertisement for Kitmir from* Jardin des modes *magazine, 1925.*

At home Maria and Dmitrii learned English—their governesses were English and French—and Maria Pavlovna spoke Russian badly until the age of six. At the age of seven she traveled in her own personal railway car accompanied by a servant and her loyal governess, Mademoiselle Hélène, to visit Germany and France. To be sure, Maria Pavlovna and

Dmitrii Pavlovich were brought up exclusively, as befitted their rank. During their walks they were accompanied by servants and footmen, and on Sundays they were allowed to play only with children from aristocratic families. Despite these refinements during her childhood, Maria Pavlovna was able to find the inner strength to live by her own labor as an adult.

Maria Pavlovna's personal life was not a simple, smooth one. In 1906, the crown prince of Sweden, Duke Wilhelm of Södermanland, visited St. Petersburg and was introduced to the sixteen-year-old Maria Pavlovna. Grand Duchess Elizaveta Feodorovna, her guardian, told her niece that it was her destiny, and Maria Pavlovna agreed to the crown prince's proposal, which soon followed. The wedding was postponed until her eighteenth birthday, and bride and groom were married in St. Petersburg on April 20, 1908. The marriage was positive politically and diplomatically for both Russia and Sweden, but unhappy due to the absence of feelings on the part of the newlyweds for each other. On the occasion of his cousin's wedding, the tsar pardoned the bride's father, Grand Duke Paul Alexandrovich, permitting him finally to return to Russia with his new family.

After a honeymoon in Germany, Italy, and France, the newlyweds went to Sweden, where an official ceremonial reception awaited them with the state flags of Russia and Sweden waving all

Архив Жака Феррана. Париж

over Stockholm. In Sweden, Maria Pavlovna went hunting, attended horse races, and even played field hockey on Crown Princess Margaret's team. While living in the Oak Hills palace in Stockholm, she decided to study the applied arts. Maria Pavlovna (or the Duchess of Södermanland, which was her title in Sweden) had little interest in her husband, and vice versa, but the marriage endured and, in May 1909, their son Prince Lennart was born.

During the winter of 1911–12 Maria Pavlovna departed with her husband on a long journey to attend the king of Siam's coronation. The Swedish journalist Staffan Skott, in his recent book, *The Romanovs,* relates how the King and Duke of Montpensier, "a hunter of wild beasts," began to court her. Relations between the couple cooled even more. When they returned to Stockholm, doctors found that Maria Pavlovna had a serious kidney ailment, and it was decided that the duchess of Södermanland be sent to Capri for treatment in the fall and winter of 1913–14.

Returning to Moscow briefly for the celebration of the 300-year anniversary of the Romanov dynasty, Maria Pavlovna

Above: *Grand Duke Dmitrii Pavlovich, St. Petersburg, c. 1908.*

Right: *Maria Pavlovna in a court dress, St. Petersburg, c. 1908. Photo by Bergamasco.*

Архив Жака Феррана. Париж

then set off for Capri, but got only as far as Berlin, where her brother Grand Duke Dmitrii Pavlovich was waiting for her. Taking leave from her husband at the first opportunity, Maria Pavlovna changed her travel plans and left for Paris with her brother. Commenting on this, Princess Zinaida Yusupov wrote to her son from Coreïz, in the Crimea, on November 27, 1913: "Maria Pavlovna of Sweden is also a sad example of a disorderly life without any principles or a foundation."[2]

It was obvious to close relatives in both Russia and Sweden that divorce was unavoidable and finally, on March 13, 1914, their marriage was officially dissolved, an action then confirmed by an edict issued by Nicholas II on July 15, 1914. Unfortunately, Maria Pavlovna's son remained at the Swedish court, and she was unable to see him until she fled Russia.

In Paris Maria Pavlovna studied at a painting school, then traveled in Italy and Greece. A true Russian patriot, she returned to Russia when World War I began and set out for the front as a nurse. For two and a half years, the grand duchess worked as a nurse in Pskov, treating and bandaging wounded soldiers and officers, and even performing simple surgery herself. This difficult labor served Maria Pavlovna well—without this crucial experience her success with the fashion house of Kitmir might not have been possible.

Maria Pavlovna was stunned by the news of Grigory Rasputin's murder in the Yusupov palace in Petrograd in December 1916, in which her brother Dmitrii Pavlovich was directly involved; her cousin Nicholas's abdication from the throne followed soon thereafter. Maria Pavlovna left Pskov for Petrograd. There she made the acquaintance of Prince Sergei Mikhailovich Putyatin, the son of the palace commandant at Tsarskoe Selo, the tsar's country residence. The meeting grew into a happy affair and, in love for the first time, Maria Pavlovna married Putyatin in the Pavlovsk Palace on September 9, 1917, two months before the tragic events that forced millions of Russians to abandon their country. As Maria Pavlovna wrote

Above: *The Bolsheviks selling off the Romanov jewels. Photo from the magazine* Illustrirovannaya Rossiya *[Russia Illustrated], 1927.*

Below: *Maria Pavlovna, Duchess of Södermanland, Stockholm, 1910.*

in her memoirs, *A Grand Duchess in Exile*, in 1932: "Old Russia ceased to exist and will never be restored."[3]

Maria Pavlovna was expecting a second child at the time. Through stormy Moscow and a calmer Kiev, Putyatin, his parents, and Maria Pavlovna made their way to the south of Russia. Maria Pavlovna left everything behind: her father, Grand Duke Paul Alexandrovich, was arrested and killed soon after by the Bolsheviks; the entire Romanov family lost their country, which they had ruled for three centuries.

After reaching Kishinev, Moldavia, Maria Pavlovna and Prince Putyatin received an invitation from the Romanian royal court to stay a while with Queen Marie of Romania, whom Maria Pavlovna had not seen since her first wedding in 1908. Maria Pavlovna wrote: "Of the royal families remaining on the throne who were in more or less close kinship with us, they were the only ones who met us with real sympathy and compassion."[4]

Romania, with all its comforts and amenities, surprised her after so many years of military adversity. Russian officers strolled the streets of Bucharest in full regalia. It was at the court of the Romanian queen that Maria Pavlovna made friends with Crown Princess Elizabeth, who later married King George of Greece. The princess had a passion for embroidery, collected Romanian folk em-

Left: *Gabrielle Chanel,
Paris, c. 1911.*

Right: *Grand Duchess
Maria Pavlovna, 1924.*

Below: *Russian émigré
women, Biarritz, France, 1924.*

Архив автора, Париж

Архив автора, Париж

Библиотека декоративных искусств, Париж

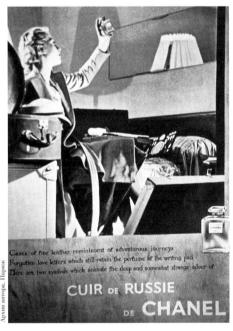

Cases of fine leather reminiscent of adventurous journeys
Forgotten love letters which still retain the perfume of the writing pad
Here are two symbols which animate the deep and somewhat strange odour of

CUIR DE RUSSIE
DE CHANEL

Une jolie robe de WORTH, très nouvelle, en crêpe Javanais marron. Elle est ornée d'un motif égyptien, brodé de différents tons.

Brown Javanais crape. Egyptian ornament, embroidered in several shades.

Ce très beau manteau est un modèle de CHANEL. Il est entièrement brodé; col et bande de zibelinette.

Mantle, entirely embroidered; zibelinette — a kind of sable fur — collar and band.

De JENNY, ce manteau très enveloppant, en velours Frisson noir; col, larges parements et bande de renard gris.

Black Frisson velvet, with collar, large cuffs and band made of grey fox fur.

TROIS JOLIS MODÈLES DE WORTH, CHANEL ET JENNY
Remarqués dimanche dernier à Longchamp

Above top: *An embroidered black satin coat with a squirrel collar by Chanel, 1921.*

Above: *An advertisement for the Chanel perfume "Russian Leather," c. 1950.*

Above right: *A drawing from the magazine* L'Art et la mode, *depicting winter coats in the "Russian style" from the fashion houses of Worth, Chanel (center), and Jenny, Paris, 1922.*

Overleaf: *A sketch for the cover of* La Mode à Paris, *showing "Russian style" embroidered winter coats, 1922.*

broideries and embroidery with Ottoman motifs, and then copied them on her hoop. Like her mother Queen Marie, she worshiped Romanian folk handicraft. After the breakup of the Austro-Hungarian Empire, the Romanian royal house did everything "to put Romania on the map of the world." The princess's other passions were fashion and perfumes, and it was unquestionably in Bucharest that an interest in such things was stimulated in Maria Pavlovna. Embroidery, fashion, and perfume became the grand duchess's longtime traveling companions.

In the meantime, Grand Duke Dmitrii Pavlovich, exiled by Emperor Nicholas II to the Persian border, wound up in Tehran, where he spent about two years. Thanks to the sympathetic attitude of Sir Charles Marling, the British envoy to Persia, Dmitrii Pavlovich not only found compassion there, but was able to locate his beloved sister, who was also wandering around the world.

Having settled in the Cotroceni palace with Prince Putyatin, Maria Pavlovna finally attended to her poor wardrobe. As she writes in her memoirs: "I had

Библиотека декоративных искусств, Париж

Музей искусств, Цинциннати, США

with me only one or two worn dresses, altered from my pre-war outfits, which were four years old, and also unbleached linen underwear. I didn't even have a pair of silk stockings, just the remnants of former luxury in the form of a few handkerchiefs with holes where the monograms had been cut out. While I still lived at the hotel, I sent for a seamstress who brought me several Parisian designs; among them was a brown dress of heavy silk. This dress, I was told, was a design from the house of Chanel. At that time Chanel was the rising star on the Paris fashion horizon. These designs cost much more than I could pay at that time, and I didn't buy anything.

Above left: *A drawing from* Vogue *magazine depicting the Grand Duchess Maria Pavlovna (left, in profile) at a ball in the Ritz Hotel, Paris, August 1928.*

Above right: *A beaded evening dress in panne velvet from the house of Jean Patou, Paris, 1921–23.*

Opposite left: *A detail of a beaded chiffon evening dress, Paris, 1923–24.*

Opposite right: *A beaded evening dress with a fur wrap, Paris, c. 1925.*

I didn't even know how these clothes were supposed to be worn, because I had lost all touch with the world of fashion. But I remembered that name— Chanel. A young woman with the same name owned a small lingerie shop on rue Cambon before the war. And I thought: was this the same woman?"[5] In the near future both Maria Pavlovna and Dmitrii Pavlovich would link their destinies with Chanel's.

Fortunately, Maria Pavlovna received as a gift from the Romanian queen several dresses that did not fit the queen, but which were immediately altered to fit the grand duchess. Prince Putyatin received several suits from the

158

wardrobe of the king. On ceremonial days, Maria Pavlovna, like all the women of the royal house of Romania, wore Romanian national costumes.

In the meantime, successively more tragic news came from Russia. Maria Pavlovna learned in the British Mission in Bucharest that her aunt, Grand Duchess Elizaveta Feodorovna, and Prince Volodya Paley, her stepbrother, and several other close relatives were savagely murdered in Alapayevsk. She was in despair, and wrote: "None of us Russians believed that our exile would last, we thought that the fall of the Bolsheviks would be a matter of a few months, no more, and that, of course, we would all then return to Russia."

Maria Pavlovna's desire to meet with her brother in Europe at that difficult time was so great that she decided to leave with Putyatin for Paris, then London. Taking leave of the cordial Romanian court, she left her young son in Romania. Maria Pavlovna settled in Passy, and visited her deceased father's palace in Boulogne-sur-Seine, where he had lived in exile from the Russian court for twelve years with his second wife and three children. When he returned to Russia, his sumptuous furniture and rich art collection had been taken to the newly built Paley palace in Tsarskoe Selo.

The Alexander Nevsky Cathedral in

Национальный музей моды и текстиля. Париж

Архив автора. Париж

159

288

Paris was the place where Russian émigrés met and socialized. Christmas and Easter holidays were especially splendid, and on Sundays crowds of Russian émigrés filled the church courtyard and garden. Maria Pavlovna was in deep mourning for her father: she wore a trimmed black crepe dress and a black hat with a crepe veil—this is the way her contemporaries remember her.

In Paris Maria Pavlovna was forced to face everyday problems for the first time in her life. In spite of the fact that she was nearly twenty-eight years old, she did not understand the value of money very well. She recalled: "I had never before carried cash with me, nor had I ever written a check. I knew the approximate price of jewels and dresses, but did not have the vaguest idea how much bread, meat and milk cost."[6]

Maria Pavlovna greeted her brother Dmitrii Pavlovich with great joy when he arrived in London. Having sold his St. Petersburg palace during the revolution, he had some means and lived modestly but comfortably in the Hotel Ritz. However, his move from Tehran to London had entailed enormous suffering. He had set sail for Great Britain on an English military boat via Mesopotamia and Bombay and along the way had contracted typhoid fever; fortunately, he was nursed back to health by his Russian boatman. Dmitrii Pavlovich got to Marseilles by way of Port Said and Cairo, then to Paris, and then getting to London was easy.

In order to conserve their resources, Maria Pavlovna and Putyatin rented a small apartment on Berkeley Street in London and would visit Dmitrii at the Ritz. The British court exhibited extraordinary coldness in those years toward their Romanov relatives. However, in London Maria Pavlovna managed to find the address of her father's widow,

LES JOLIES
BRODERIES DE
KITMIR
7, Rue Montaigne

Ensemble en Kasha blanc, belles broderies russes, en laine rouge et verte jupe unie et plissée.

White Kasha ensemble, russian embroideries of red and green wool. Plain and pleated skirt.

Библиотека декоративных искусств. Париж

Princess Paley, who was then in Finland with her daughters.

Fortunately, the crown prince of Sweden and his wife brought Maria Pavlovna's jewels—some of which she had left there for safekeeping even before World War I, and others that she had prudently concealed in inkwells, candles, and paperweights and had sent to Sweden from Russia—when they came to London to visit. Maria Pavlovna was advised to sell her entire jewelry collection at Christie's auction house, but the power of the sentimental memories associated with them was too great—many were family jewels of the Romanov House, and besides, Maria Pavlovna still naively believed in the possibility of returning to Russia. Meanwhile, the European jewelry market was saturated with Russian jewelry. Jewelry store displays were bursting with tiaras, diadems, necklaces, bracelets, earrings, and rings. These were difficult times, and demand was low and the supply enormous. The rarest of pieces went for very low prices—the same situation was occurring in Constantinople and Harbin.

Summoning up her courage, Maria Pavlovna went to a jeweler on Bond Street to sell the family's matching ruby set and recalled: "'You are deeply mistaken if you think that this jewelry is very valuable,' they usually told us

Opposite above: *An advertisement for Kitmir from* L'Officiel *magazine, Paris, February 1925.*

Opposite below: *A drawing from the magazine* L'Art et la mode *of an embroidered ensemble from Kitmir, Paris, 1926.*

Above: *An advertisement for Kitmir from* Vogue *magazine, drawing by Dorland, Paris, July 1926.*

Below: *Grand Duchess Maria Pavlovna with Kitmir designs, 1927. The painting on the wall is by Stelletsky.*

Тургеневская библиотека. Париж

everywhere. Our jewels were always either too large or too small, or faceted instead of cabochon or vice versa, and never in an appropriate set. If they knocked the price of the Romanov jewels down so low, what did other families have to face?" The grand duchess was forced to sell all her adornments over the course of the next few years.

Another blow befell Maria Pavlovna in London: in a letter from her mother-in-law Princess Putyatina in Bucharest, she learned about the sudden death of her one-year-old infant child. To be closer to his sister in this difficult time, Dmitrii Pavlovich rented a small house in the London suburb of Kensington, where the Romanovs and Putyatins had settled together. Unfortunately, relations between Dmitrii Pavlovich and Prince Putyatin soon soured.

Given the situation, Maria Pavlovna decided to become involved in something in order to earn a living. She had loved to sew, knit, and embroider as a child in St. Petersburg. As a little girl she loved to embroider after lunch, sitting in the grand duke's palace library. How useful her childhood passions turned out to be in her London exile! Knitted sweaters and dresses had just become fashionable in London and Paris at that time, in 1919. Knitting, a craft that had been practiced since the Renaissance,

was lifted to the level of virtue in the Victorian era; during the difficult years of World War I, when many women first experienced a shortage of clothing, especially of warm children's clothes, knitting and crocheting became a necessity of life. Women took to knitting in order to pass the time while riding the underground or waiting in queues for milk or bread. At the end of the war in 1918, there was still a shortage of good fabrics and thus knitted articles became not only practical, but fashionable.

Maria Pavlovna bought some needles, yarn, and a guide to home knitting. After a botched sweater, with characteristic persistence she started working on a new sweater, but that became one she wore at home because of an error in counting the loops. She recalls: "I found out about a shop where I took my first successful sweater, wrapped in paper and tucked under my arm. The shop owner had no idea who I was, and was very surprised when she learned about the purpose of my visit. I opened the package, held up my work for her careful examination, my heart sinking. She bought the sweater from me for 21 shillings and asked me to bring others."[8]

Maria Pavlovna began knitting sweaters and dresses for the London shop. Every four or five days she would finish up a new sweater; dresses took up to ten days. She knit constantly, from rising early in the morning, at the table at lunchtime, when she read, and on the underground. But no matter how hard she tried, for this work it was impossible to earn more than six pounds sterling a week, which was a drop in the sea of the family budget. Something more substantial had to be devised.

In her closet, Maria Pavlovna had only a few shabby dresses that she had had altered in Bucharest. Life in London and changes in fashion required a new wardrobe, and she made the decision to sew her own. She bought a cutting and sewing magazine and fabric, and made a pattern, then boldly cut her first dress directly on the parquet floor of her home with enormous dressmaker's scissors. Maria Pavlovna had no sewing machine, nor did she know how to use one, so she basted and sewed her first dress by hand, occasionally asking her husband for his opinion. She sewed herself a copy of a dress from the Callot Soeurs fashion house, with a skirt that used a kilometer of tulle. Encouraged by her first success, Maria Pavlovna began sewing dresses for herself and her Russian friends, and designed a fanciful dinner jacket for her husband and a robe for her brother Dmitrii in a fabric with a pattern of a flock of birds scattered across a black field.

In the early winter of 1919, a group of Russian émigrés in London appealed to Maria Pavlovna with a request that she become the head of a sewing atelier that made military and medical supplies for the Volunteer Army fighting on the Don River in southern Russia. After finding a suitable building, she, together with other Russian émigré women, began sewing for the soldiers. Meanwhile, more groups of Russian refugees kept arriving in London. The dowager Empress Maria Feodorovna arrived in London from the Crimea on board an English military boat with her daughter Grand Duchess Xenia Alexandrovna and her grandchildren. The English Queen Mother Alexandra met her beloved sister, now a tired woman with a lifeless gaze wearing a black traveling suit, a small hat embroidered with sequins, and a short boa, pinned with a brooch at the throat. Europe did not yet know about the tragic death of the tsar and his family, and many people, especially Maria Feodorovna, religiously believed in their miraculous salvation.

In the spring of 1920, Maria Pavlovna went to Paris to meet with the widow of her father, Princess Paley. Marisha, as she was called at home, had changed radically: her suffering due to the execution of her beloved husband and her losses in Russia had completely undermined her health and she had grown thin and aged. The warm-hearted Maria Pavlovna met with her every day and eased her grief. Paris was gradually

Opposite: Grand Duchess Maria Pavlovna, Paris, 1924.

filling up with Russian refugees, and Maria Pavlovna decided to sell her house in London and settle down in Paris. Her brother Dmitrii followed her to Paris, where their enchanting stepsisters—Princesses Natalya and Irina—had already settled. Maria Pavlovna rented a small apartment on rue Courcelles and furnished it with the bare essentials of her new life: a table for cutting and a sewing machine.

From 1921 on, Maria Pavlovna devoted a great deal of time to philanthropy for the Russian Red Cross, organizing parties and special sales of handicrafts to raise money for Russian refugees. At one of these evenings in the International Circle club, she was noticed by a journalist from *Vogue* magazine in a remarkable dress she had made—a long chemise of raspberry crepe, scattered all over with silver brocade leaves, a belt at hip level and a necklace of large pearls from the collection of the murdered Grand Duchess Elizaveta Feodorovna.[9]

Maria Pavlovna missed her son, who had been left in Sweden, and with help from the Swedish King Gustav, Maria and Dmitrii Pavlovich went off to Denmark, where she finally saw Prince Lennart, who had grown up and matured, and the Dowager Empress Maria Feodorovna, her aunt. After returning to Paris, Dmitrii Pavlovich went to work at a major champagne firm because his financial resources had run out. In early 1920, destiny brought the grand duke together with the talented fashion designer Gabrielle Chanel. They became completely inseparable, and the affair determined to a large extent Chanel's favorable attitude toward the Russian émigré community. Thus two worlds—that of imperial Russia and that of peasant France—met in Biarritz. Chanel despised titles and once said: "I always feel pity for born, blueblood princes: their trade, when they have one, is the saddest in the world, and when they don't have one—it is doubly sad."[10]

In fact, Dmitrii Pavlovich rather liked older women, and, back in Russia, he had had quite a romance with the splendid countess Natalia Brasova, the wife of Grand Duke Mikhail Alexandrovich, the tsar's brother.

In the fall of 1921, Maria Pavlovna met Chanel for the first time. Chanel already had a solid reputation and clientele in those years. She was a born businesswoman, but not a born seamstress. However, she was the one who created the image of the new woman in the 1920s. In the new economic situation of the day, Chanel, in defiance of her rival Paul Poiret, democratized fashion and transformed the wardrobe of Parisian women with her designs, which were simple in cut and often copied for the mass market.

Maria Pavlovna decided to try her luck with Chanel and, knowing her rather intimately through her brother, set off for a meeting at her studio, located on the third floor of the House of Chanel on rue Cambon. At the time Chanel was interested in embroidery and even imported colored knit sweaters from the Faeroe Islands in the hopes of transferring their ornamentation to her silk blouses. Just at the point that Maria Pavlovna appeared at the studio, Chanel was bargaining with her permanent embroiderer, Madame Bataille. Chanel, certain of the stability of her reputation, assumed that everyone should consider it an honor to embroider for her house, even for a low price. Madame Bataille was asking 600 francs for an embroidered blouse and, not obtaining it, was withdrawing.

Maria Pavlovna recalled: "I suddenly addressed Chanel and offered to embroider the same blouse for 150 francs less."[11] Chanel gladly agreed, afraid only that Maria Pavlovna was unfamiliar with the methods of machine embroidery. Maria Pavlovna immediately

Robe de taffetas et tulle « vert émeraude » toute semée de fleurs modernes, en laine passée et tricotée de tons vifs.
Emerald green coloured taffeta gown, with modern wool flowers in bright shades.

LES JOLIES BRODERIES
DE
KITMIR
7, Rue Montaigne

Châle de crêpe de Chine « rubis » tout brodé
de laine, en camaïeu, sur un grand volant
de lièvre gris.

Ruby coloured crêpe de Chine shawl embroidered with wool in camaïeu shades, over large grey
hare flounce.

Robe de mousseline de soie blanche brodée
de perles et de strass. Crevés de deux mousselines noire et blanche, plissées soleil.

White chiffon gown, embroidered with beads and
rhinestones, «crevés» made of two black and white
plaited chiffon.

LES JOLIES BRODERIES DE
KITMIR
7, Rue Montaigne

devoted so much of her energy and strength.

The beginning was the most difficult: for all her effort and passion for handicraft, Maria Pavlovna did not, of course, know how to use an embroidery machine. When she bought her first embroidery machine, she asked the proprietor of the shop to teach her how to use it. Trying to hide her too-famous name, Maria Pavlovna enrolled under an assumed name in a course for machine embroidery at a factory, where her first awkward attempts elicited only the ridicule and contempt of the workers. Finally, the work began to go well, and the idea of founding a fashion house of embroidery dawned on her.

The story of how the house got its name is as follows: among Maria Pavlovna's close friends in Paris was a former Russian ambassador to Washington, Bakhmetiev, a monarchist and great lover of animals. The name of one of his three sweet Pekinese dogs was Kitmir—in honor of the legendary dog of Persian mythology. This was the name that Maria Pavlovna chose for her house.

The grand duchess and her mother-in-law Princess Putyatina found a place in the back courtyard of a wealthy private residence on fashionable rue Francois 1, not far from the Champs Elysees. She invited two Russian girls to work for her and sent them to take the same embroidery courses that she herself had just completed. They bought two more embroidery machines, and the Kitmir atelier was ready to take orders. As Maria Pavlovna recalled: "Suddenly the machine became the emblem of my new life."

In early January 1921, Chanel began

Opposite and above: *Drawings from the magazine* L'Art et la mode *depicting "Beautiful Embroidery from Kitmir," Paris, March 1926.*

Right: *An advertisement for Kitmir from* Vogue *magazine, Paris, 1924.*

promised Chanel that she would buy an embroidery machine and thus began her first professional experiment in Paris.

Nearly three months later, Maria Pavlovna, happy and proud of her work, appeared at Chanel's carrying her first machine-embroidered silk blouse, for which, as agreed, she was asking 450 francs. This work was the first order of the future Kitmir—the fashion house of embroidery—to which Maria Pavlovna

165

Тургеневская библиотека, Париж

working on her spring collection, which she ordinarily showed on February 5. There was very little time left. She instructed Maria Pavlovna to design the embroidery patterns and choose the fabric and threads. Chanel spent hours explaining her ideas to Maria Pavlovna, discussing the sketches of the embroideries and the fabric samples. All of this was completely new for Maria Pavlovna. She had to go to all the suppliers' shops, bargain with them, and solve the many organizational and commercial problems with which she had been unfamiliar until then.

The fabrics were cut at the house of Chanel, brought over to the Kitmir atelier where the embroidery patterns were transferred onto them from tracing paper, and then the Russian artisans got to work. The first set of orders from Chanel consisted of a series of blouses, tunics, and coats. For this series, Maria Pavlovna made several of the same tunics of light

gray silk herself, embroidered in the same shade thread with a sprinkling of red motifs. This Kitmir house design, which was created for Chanel, became especially popular. With pride, Maria Pavlovna happened to see her tunic once on a lady who was having lunch at the Ritz.

Chanel and Maria Pavlovna met daily at the time. Chanel dressed very simply, even in everyday style. She loved to work in a warm studio near the fireplace, dressed in a sporty suit, a dark sweater and dark skirt—the embodiment

Above: *Grand Duchess Maria Pavlovna, Paris, 1926.*

Opposite above: *An illustration from* Jardin des modes *showing beaded dresses from Kitmir, Paris, 1925.*

Opposite below and right: *Beaded crepe de Chine dresses from Kitmir, Paris, c. 1927.*

of her fashion revolution that changed women's clothing for the twentieth century. According to Maria Pavlovna's recollections, that season Chanel always wore the same clothing, and changed only when she went out to meet people, dressed in a coat of priceless fur.

Chanel worked often in Maria Pavlovna's presence: cutting away, trimming, and pinning. Her word was law for her employees, her will unshakeable, her thinking quick and precise. She made decisions in the blink of an eye, surveying the entire collection at once. Chanel was capable of executing, or saving, any one of her dresses; her concerns were to ensure the harmony of everything she created, its clarity of line, its comfort, and the prestige of her label. When the crucial day finally arrived—the day when designs were to be shown to foreign clients at the house of Chanel on rue Cambon—Maria Pavlovna could hardly hold back her tears

when she saw the embroidered work of her brainchild, Kitmir, on the models (some of whom were also Russian). The procession lasted nearly three hours and, when it ended, it was the embroidered articles that clients competed with one another to order from the Chanel saleswomen. Their originality and the freshness seemed completely novel. Maria Pavlovna was ecstatic—it was Kitmir's first triumph.

The success of the Kitmir embroideries surpassed all expectations. Maria Pavlovna literally drowned in orders immediately. At that time there were only three or four embroiderers working at Kitmir, including herself. They worked for weeks without days off, sleeping at their embroidery machines, thinking only about the deadlines for completing their orders. Maria Pavlovna's right hand was, undoubtedly, the loyal Princess Putyatina, who helped her daughter-in-law with everything. Before a fabric with a pattern already transferred onto it was embroidered, it was basted onto rigid, chemically treated mousseline that burned away when it was pressed with a blistering hot iron. Its ashes floated around the room, mak-

Библиотека декоративных искусств. Париж

ing it difficult to breathe, but Maria Pavlovna, her hands scorched from working with the iron, kept on embroidering and embroidering Chanel's orders.

The summer of 1921 was in full swing. Nearby, ladies in garments embroidered by Maria Pavlovna were strolling under the tree canopy in the Bois de Boulogne while the grand duchess herself was climbing the back stairs to her small atelier. Work began early in the morning and the fatigued Maria Pavlovna would often fall asleep after lunch right on the floor of the Kitmir workshop, lying down on her fur coat instead of a mattress.

Kitmir's main problems were always organizational. Soft-hearted Maria Pavlovna kept hiring more and more Russian émigré workers, giving them preference not for practical reasons but from a desire to help her needy compatriots. Many advised her to hire professional embroideresses, but she firmly followed her patriotic convictions. The expanding business required more and more substantial outlays and, in order to cover them, Maria Pavlovna was again forced to sell her jewels. This time a valuable Romanov family matched set of large emeralds was sold, the price of which, in spite of the considerable sum received, was obviously incommensurate with its real price. Financial "advi-

sors" rushed to Prince Putyatin like vultures to carrion when they found out about the major proceeds from the sale of Maria Pavlovna's emeralds. Inexperienced in commercial affairs, the grand duchess agreed to entrust all her money to a Dutch industrial society, which not only did not accrue any interest on the capital she invested in it, but swallowed up the entire sum when it went bankrupt. Kitmir did not get a single franc. In the meantime, Prince Putyatin, who had once worked in a private bank, mastered the subtleties of the profession—thereby surprising even Chanel's meticulous accountant—and began working as Kitmir's accountant.

Kitmir received twice as many orders during its second year of operation and its troubles increased. Despite additional staff, the quantity of orders noticeably surpassed the possibility of fulfillment. The Chanel saleswomen rang Kitmir's phone off the hook, demanding more and more embroidered goods, the fashion for which had reached its apogee.

It should be noted that Chanel wasn't the only house showing embroidered things. Jeanne Lanvin, who showed garments with Romanian and Slavic embroidery, was serious competition. After World War I many houses were experiencing a shortage of elegant fabrics and needed beautiful trim, so Kitmir's pro-

Коллекция автора. Париж

duction sold like hotcakes. The firm Babani, located on boulevard Hausmann, did a great deal to support this needlework fashion. Its exclusive specialty was embroidered articles with folk art motifs from the outlying areas of the former Ottoman Empire and the Slavic provinces of the former Austro-Hungarian Empire.

In spite of the competition, demand exceeded supply that season, and Kitmir was so besieged with work that it could not keep up with the plethora of orders. Some of Chanel's clients complained and rejected their orders, there-

Opposite above: *An advertisement from* Vogue *magazine, October 1925, announcing Kitmir's participation in the 1925 Exhibit of Contemporary Decorative and Industrial Arts in Paris.*

Opposite below and this page above left and below: *Beaded silk evening dresses from Kitmir, Paris, 1927.*

Above: *An advertisement for Kitmir from* Vogue *magazine, May 1925.*

by arousing a storm of indignation on the part of Chanel's saleswomen. Maria Pavlovna was afraid even to come to rue Cambon and would sometimes hide in the closet in Chanel's studio just so she wouldn't have to listen to the severe reprimands of angry saleswomen who were losing good clients. In addition, Kitmir did not have the right to copy Chanel's orders. However, it could copy orders in volume if they came from abroad and, thanks to this, Kitmir got some American clients. One of them, Mr. Kurzman, ordered a set of embroidered blouses on condition that he receive them in a completely ready-for-purchase form. All of this was so new that Maria Pavlovna stayed up nights with her English maid, completing the sewing on these blouses herself.

Money soon came from Kurzman in America, along with newspaper clippings of an interview in which he proudly announced that he was the first in the United States to import articles from Kitmir. The advertisement was accompanied by an image of the Russian imperial crown and the initials of the grand duchess, as well as her full title. This type of commercial advertisement was alien to Maria Pavlovna. She earned money with her labor, not her background, and had never mentioned her title before in

Robe en lamé blanc et argent, brodée de perles de corail et de paillettes d'or.

White and silver lamé gown, embroidered with coral and gold spangles

LES BRODERIES DE KITMIR 7, Rue Montaigne

BRODERIES ET IMPRESSIONS 7 RUE MONTAIGNE PARIS KITMIR

representing Kitmir. More American clients followed, including the New York fashion designer Francis Klein, who remained loyal to Kitmir's embroidery right up to the day it closed down.

Maria Pavlovna recalled: "I loved the feel of silk, the play of its half-tones, contrasting transitions. In it I saw the fabrics which spoke to me about my past. I once found a piece of yellow cord which reminded me of the thread used in Moscow monasteries. In the past I had learned from the nuns the old method of embroidering saints' faces with silk floss of one shade, on which the play of the light and shadow was

achieved merely by the change in the direction of the stitch. I found the same non-tarnishing silver and gold threads which were used to embroider in relief the cotton-stuffed nimbuses and crowns around the saints' faces. Are these kinds of things still used?"[12]

Chanel taught the somewhat old-fashioned Maria Pavlovna Parisian practicality. She once told her: "You're harming yourself by dressing like a refugee. Don't think that you can elicit sympathy in this way. On the contrary, in the end, people will avoid you. If you want to do business, first and foremost you have to look appropriate, remember this!"[13] Maria Pavlovna, taking the wise advice, began to take care of herself, to dress better, wear a little makeup, and even hired a Swedish masseuse in order to lose a few pounds. Chanel also advised her to cut short the long hair that she wore in a bun all the time, taking a pair of scissors and cutting Maria Pavlovna's hair herself in the rue Cambon studio. Her influence on Maria Pavlovna did not stop there. The tenacious and smart Frenchwoman wanted to help her Russian friend. The grand duchess lacked toughness. Chanel demanded that she completely root out any spirit of "charity," which should not be mixed with commerce.

On Chanel's insistence, Kitmir updated their selection of embroideries each season. Initially it consisted of Maria Pavlovna's designs in a pseudohistorical style. She studied antique ornament and collected a basic library, essential for making sketches, and used ornamental motifs from Oriental carpets, Persian ceramics, Bulgarian and Russian embroideries, and decoration from Coptic fabrics, Chinese porcelain, and the jewels of Indian maharajahs. The most popular embroidery method at Kitmir was the *cornély* stitch (twisted silk thread) and, from the 1922 season on, Maria Pavlovna began embroidering not only in silk and gold, but also with seeds, beads, and sequins.

One of the employees of the house of Kitmir, Kira Alexandrovna Sereda (née Baroness von Medem), recalls: "Having arrived in Paris from Constantinople in 1922, my mother and I were hungry and looking for work. We came to Kitmir to Grand Duchess Maria Pavlovna and got an order to embroider evening bags with beads and sequins. Colored purses were very fashionable at that time. The Duchess asked us: 'Do you know how to embroider the *cornély* or Chinese stitch?' We said that we did, and got more orders for embroidered belts, and my mother, Baroness Nina Vladimirovna von Medem, née Shlitter, got an order to embroider shawls with an elaborate design, like an entire picture. There were many Russian women working there and all were gifted. The

Duchess gave us work to take home and paid decently. And we were so poor then, that we were happy to do any work!"[14]

Rostislav Mstislavovich Dobuzhinsky, the son of the remarkable Russian painter Mstislav Dobuzhinsky, gave the author the following account of his wife's work for Kitmir. The young Rostislav had arrived in France by boat with his lovely wife, actress Lydia Kopnyaeva, on June 24, 1925. He recollects: "When my wife came here, of course, for her as an actress, the French theater

Opposite below and this page above:
Advertisements for Kitmir from
Jardin des modes *magazine, 1926.*

Opposite above: A drawing from
the magazine L'Art et la mode,
"Embroidery from Kitmir,"
Paris, January 1926.

was out of the question. She had much experience making theater costumes, and she got work as a cutter and draper at Kitmir. She worked there under the name of Dobuzhinskaya with Vera Sudeikina, Stravinsky's future wife. Kitmir, which belonged to Grand Duchess Maria Pavlovna, was a very interesting atelier. Only Russian ladies worked there. They were jacks of all trades. Their specialty was beaded articles, embroidery, different kinds of inlay work which they did for many big houses like Lanvin, Chanel. . . . They sewed an especially large number of "beaded" dresses. Kitmir's manager was Baltic Baron Gerst, a fat, broad-shouldered giant."[15]

In addition to purses, belts, and shawls, Kitmir produced embroidered mules, slippers with motifs from Persian miniatures, which, despite their high price, were very much in demand. The revival of embroidering in chenille should be added to the list of Maria Pavlovna's contributions. This yarn, popular as far back as the end of the eighteenth century, was widely used in needlework in the Victorian era and then half forgotten. Maria Pavlovna undertook the production of hats crocheted in chenille, Chanel started selling them, and many thousands of such hats were worn around the world.

In August 1923, Maria Pavlovna rented an entire private residence at no. 7 rue Montaigne to expand production. The office and showroom were on the first floor; the workshops were on the other two. Professional French embroiderers were added to the staff after several Russian needleworkers left Kitmir, using its production secrets to open ateliers under their own names. More than fifty embroiderers worked for Kitmir in 1923, with additional cutters and technical people. The name Kitmir was proudly written in gold letters at the entrance to the courtyard. Maria Pavlovna settled into the spacious office with a mahogany desk, a fireplace with a mirror, two chairs, and a small table on a blue carpet. She bought most of this furniture from the previous tenants of the house; it seemed luxurious compared to the refugee furniture of the old atelier.

Several French fashion houses contacted Kitmir with extremely enticing offers. Among the possible clients was the house of Jean Patou, one of Chanel's main competitors, who became especially famous in the 1920s for his jersey and knit sportswear. Patou's popularity, right up to his death in 1936, was enormous. Many Russians worked in his house not only as models but as stylists as well; in particular, the young artist Dmitrii Dmitrievich Bouchéne, who created several designs for Patou.

Afraid to offend her patron Gabrielle Chanel, Maria Pavlovna decided to seek her advice and share her plans for expansion with her. Chanel seemed glad about her plans, but immediately created a list of big houses with which Kitmir was forbidden to work—all of those in competition with her. Not only was Patou on the list, but also other potential clients. This list became the stumbling block between Chanel and Kitmir. An enraged Chanel, accusing Maria Pavlovna of ingratitude, forbade her to come to her studio fearing that the grand duchess would pass on production secrets to competitors. However, she did not limit herself to working exclusively with Kitmir; she took her orders to other houses of embroidery, of which there were a great many by that time.

The loss of the exclusive connection with Chanel was very costly to Kitmir. Having acquired new clients, Maria Pavlovna was obliged to create up to 200 new embroidered designs to suit all tastes by the coming season; due to this, Kitmir lost its unity of style and originality.

Maria Pavlovna had to spend long hours in the salons waiting to meet with Paris's dictators of fashion, listening to their comments and criticism, and continually changing the patterns, shades, and manner of embroidery in order to satisfy the taste of each fashion house. There was such an avalanche of orders that they were dispatched to other ateliers in the provinces. By that time, hundreds of embroiderers across all of France worked for Maria Pavlovna.

Maria Pavlovna rarely left Paris for vacations because she could not live for long away from her beloved creation, Kitmir. The vacation place she and Putyatin chose was Biarritz or Saint-Jean-de-Luz. There, on the Atlantic shore, in the company of Princess Paley and her stepsisters Irina and Natalya, she forgot about difficult everyday life in Paris. Biarritz was the fashionable vacation spot for European titled aristocracy and American millionaires in the early 1920s, and a sizeable colony of Russian émigrés settled near it. The proximity of the Spanish royal family further increased the attractiveness of this expensive resort. Grand Duke Dmitrii Pavlovich's

Туркменская библиотека. Париж

Above: *Grand Duke Dmitrii Pavlovich at his wedding with the American Audrey Emery in Biarritz, November 21, 1926.*

Opposite: *Grand Duchess Maria Pavlovna in the house of Kitmir, Paris, 1927.*

affair with Gabrielle Chanel had developed in Biarritz, and after they parted ways, it was there that Dmitrii Pavlovich met the young, attractive American millionairess Audrey Emery, who later converted to the Russian Orthodox faith. A few years later, in 1926, she married the grand duke and received the title of Princess Ilyinskaya, after the name of the estate owned by Maria's and Dmitrii's father near Moscow.

The family jewels ran out, Kitmir ate up most of the profits, and Maria Pavlovna wound up heavily in debt. A financial disaster was imminent. Maria Pavlovna's family life was also crumbling: her marriage with Putyatin had developed a crack. The grand duchess devoted all her energies to work while Putyatin preferred to spend his time in the company of Russian officers, fast-living squanderers of money and time. His lifestyle did not correspond to Maria Pavlovna's notions of duty, and the family atmosphere became strained. When her patience came to an end, Maria Pavlovna left Putyatin in the company of his friends in Paris and departed for Scotland, then the Netherlands, alone. Handing over the business to the care of her mother-in-law, she was finally able to withdraw from everyday concerns and be alone. Putyatin wrote her long letters every day.

After four months of voluntary exile, Maria Pavlovna returned to Paris only because the business required it. She decided to send her husband to Vienna without seeing him; the family had financial interests there connected with a failed bank. In Paris, Maria Pavlovna took the management of Kitmir into her hands again and continued to meet daily with her husband's parents, who lived in the same house in which the Kitmir atelier was located. Warm relations with her in-laws made Maria Pavlovna reconsider many times her pending decision to break with Putyatin; but a return to the past was no longer possible. In 1923 Maria Pavlovna made up her mind to get a divorce.

Serious changes were on the horizon for Kitmir's work. While from the end of World War I through the early 1920s,

Тургеневская библиотека, Париж

Russian folklore in all its manifestations was extraordinarily in vogue, now a new trend was replacing it. The archeological excavations in Egypt and the discovery of Tutankhamen's grave by the Englishman Howard Carter in 1922 gave rise to Egyptomania in the full sense of the word. The gaze of the fashionably dressed of the world turned to Egypt, its burning hot landscape, mysterious graves, and eternal pyramids. The legislators of fashion were attracted to the geometric forms of Egyptian art, the precision of its lines, the balance of its composition, and contrast of its color combinations. In 1923–24 everything Egyptian sharply crowded out everything Russian, which could not but be reflected in what Kitmir produced. Embroidery, however, did not go out of style but merely changed its forms, and Kitmir successfully created numerous geometric patterns on Egyptian themes. Kitmir's style stayed in tune with the

times and Maria Pavlovna began appearing in the public eye more. Fashion magazines of the time wrote about her often, and in 1924 Paris *Vogue* published a large-format photo portrait of her in profile by Havrah.

After her divorce, Maria Pavlovna became close friends with one of Chanel's main competitors, the famous fashion designer Jean Patou, a lover of the fair sex and an inveterate bachelor. Patou was ten years older than the grand duchess, had a large fortune at the time, and surrounded himself with extravagant luxury. Maria Pavlovna began appearing with him at society receptions and even spending time at his private residences in Biarritz, Deauville, and on the Riviera. *Vogue* published a drawing portrait of Maria Pavlovna in a red crepe Chanel dress at a soiree at the Hotel Ritz arranged by Count Cyril de Beaumont, a society lion of Paris, who was well known in the period between

the wars. The splendor of Parisian society captivated Maria Pavlovna, and she was its natural and esteemed decoration. The relationship between the grand duchess and Patou, the Parisian prince of fashion, went so far that rumors about a possible marriage spread in 1925. The Parisian press even wrote about it; the well-known fashion reporter Elsa Maxwell talks about it in her memoirs.[16] This was the first time Patou's name was ever mentioned in connection with an affair of honorable intentions. We can only speculate why the marriage did not take place. It seems likely that the obstacle was Jean Patou's character, his habit of living as a bachelor; he never did get married. At that time Russian women were in vogue. Picasso, Dali, Léger, Rolland, Maillol, and many other European celebrities succumbed to the charms of Russian beauties.

Kitmir was past its golden years of prosperity. Its finest hour had been in

173

1925, during the Exhibit of Contemporary Decorative and Industrial Arts (l'Art Deco) in Paris. This major international exhibit summed up the work of artists during the post–World War I period. Many countries opened their own pavilions at it, granting complete representation of applied arts of that time. Parisian fashion houses took their places in the main pavilion. An exception was the house of Paul Poiret, the great dictator of prewar fashion. Seeing his business as superior everywhere and in everything, he constructed on the banks of the Seine three barges with the romantic names "Amour," "Délices," and "Orgues," where one could visit the exhibit hall and restaurant and delight in "an orgy of fragrances" at the presentation of the famous perfume from his subsidiary house, Rosine. Initially, the house of Kitmir had not planned to take

part in the exhibit, but as soon as Maria Pavlovna found out that there would be a pavilion from Soviet Russia representing Russian art, the blood of the Romanovs boiled up in the grand duchess. She recalls: "I found out that the Soviet Russians were going to have a separate pavilion at the exhibit, and made the decision that we, too, must show our work to the general public. It would be especially fair that everyone know what we refugees, most of whom had never worked before and who comprised the majority of my atelier, were capable of in our exile."[17] Maria Pavlovna succeeded with great difficulty in renting a space in the main exhibit for an extensive showcase of samples of embroidered articles from Kitmir.

The exhibit lasted several months. The USSR pavilion exhibited samples of Soviet textiles: cotton prints with the

hammer and sickle, wool challis scarves from Pavlov-Posad, as well as several dresses by Davydova, Lamanova, Pribylskaya, Mukhina, and Makarova. The real professional of Russian fashion among them was Nadezhda Petrovna Lamanova. Born in 1861 in the province of Nizhny Novgorod, Lamanova opened her prominent fashion house in 1885. She began to supply the court with her designs and it is possible that she even dressed ten-year-old Maria Pavlovna. Lamanova's dresses (she worked primarily in the technique of pricking out a pattern) were distinguished by the cleanness of their lines and forms. For many years Lamanova was associated with the Moscow Art Theater, for which she began making costumes in 1901.

Remaining in Russia after the revolution, Lamanova survived many troubles and lost a great deal, most significantly her fashion house with its convenient linden-tree cutting tables. She was eventually arrested and sent to Butyrskaya prison. Thanks to Maxim Gorky's help, she was finally freed and continued working on her own, making dresses out of towels and coats out of blankets due to the shortage of fabrics. She wrote articles for fashion journals and maintained continuous authority in the field of fashion. Familiar with the success of the "Russian style" in fashionable 1920s Paris from rumors and magazine articles, Lamanova decided to create a series of handcrafted Russian designs for the international exhibit of 1925.

As Tatiana Strizhenova, a Soviet specialist on the history of fashion, writes: "Simple homespun fabrics—canvas, linen, cotton linen weave—became the basis for chemise-style dresses. They were trimmed with embroidered inserts of either genuine folk embroidery, which the artists had found, or embroidery which they did according to Vera Mukhina's sketches. She also prepared and showed her own original embroidery as separate art works."[18]

All the designs were shown with the appropriate accessories: shoes, belts, hats and beads made of soft bread paste. Lamanova's design, which completely corresponded to the demands of the day, won the Grand Prix. The artist was awarded, it was written, "for clothing based on folk art." This fact, while a very happy one in and of itself, was presented in the USSR as the triumph of "Soviet fashion," as true Russian folklore conquering Europe. Excessive indulgence in this style later affected fashion in the USSR in a sad way. Naively believing in the permanence of Parisian taste and fashion standards, fashion designers there, encouraged by Lamanova's success, became engaged almost exclusively in decoration and embroidery, copying the "Russian style" that had been elaborately developed by the émigrés in the 1920s. However, for obvious reasons, in the USSR the success of the other Russian participant in the exhibit was passed over in silence.

When the exhibit ended, Maria Pavlovna was invited to take down her

Opposite: *An advertisement for Kitmir from* L'Art, goût, beauté, *1927.*

Below: *A sequined evening dress by Kitmir with an asymmetrical design, Paris, 1928.*

Коллекция актеры. Париж

showcase in the main pavilion, where her embroidered designs were displayed. Some time later, Kitmir received a letter from the executive committee with a request that the manager of the atelier, Baron Gerst, stop by the board of directors. Maria Pavlovna expected another routine annoyance. How great was her surprise when she found out that Kitmir had been awarded a gold medal and an honorary degree as an exhibit participant, both of which were addressed to Mr. Kitmir: the board had not even suspected who the real owner of Kitmir was.

Success at the Paris Art Deco Exhibit, especially receiving the gold medal, boosted Kitmir's reputation tremendously. From 1925 through 1927, fashion magazines of France—*Jardin des modes, Vogue, L'Art, goût, beauté,* and *L'Art et la mode*—continually published striking drawings advertising the house of Kitmir. It is no wonder that Kitmir responded to the fashion of beadwork on embroidery so easily: beadwork and knitting were widespread in Russia in the nineteenth century. Many Russian ladies who embroidered for Kitmir were familiar with the technique of beading from childhood. In 1925 Kitmir specialized in producing beaded fringe. Short, straight party dresses of silk crepe georgette or crushed velvet were trimmed with beaded fringe that was especially mobile when the wearer was dancing the Charleston. The preferred color scheme was the black-gray-white spectrum with a sprinkling of other colors.

Maria Pavlovna devoted a great deal of time to philanthropic and religious activities. Through her efforts, land was bought around an abandoned Protestant chapel on the outskirts of Paris, which was rebuilt into a Russian seventeenth-century-style church. Maria Pavlovna commissioned the painter Dmitrii Semyonovich Stelletsky, well known at the time, to work on the iconostasis and murals; it took him nearly two years to complete them. To this day the Sergievsky monastery church on the rue Crimée is one of the most significant monuments of émigré creativity.

After her divorce from Putyatin,

175

Maria Pavlovna moved to Boulogne, the southwest suburb of Paris where Russians loved to take up residence. There were several Russian Orthodox churches, Russian restaurants, and shops there in the 1920s. Life in Boulogne was cheaper, and Maria Pavlovna rented a small three-story summer house on the street where her father Grand Duke Paul Alexandrovich's palace had been; it had been sold by Princess Paley and made into a Catholic school. The proximity of Boulogne to Paris was convenient for Maria Pavlovna for her communication with Kitmir's office, which was located not far from the Champs Elysées. The grand duchess furnished her new dwelling with antique furniture acquired at the flea markets. The dining room was Louis Philippe, with a set of mahogany furniture somewhat reminiscent of the

Russian furniture of Tsar Nicholas's time and the salmon-color boudoir was furnished in Empire-style Karelian birch Russian furniture. Maria Pavlovna spent a great deal of time in the garden, resting in her pajamas under the canopy of large trees. The household was managed by the old Russian valet Karp, who served for many years abroad in the families of the Romanov grand dukes. Maria Pavlovna, following good old country estate traditions, surrounded herself with animals. Living with her in Boulogne were a Scots terrier, three Persian cats, rabbits, white doves, nightingales, and a pheasant.

In the meantime, Kitmir began to experience increasing financial difficulties. It often placed advertisements in the leading fashion magazines in order to attract new clients. In 1926 articles

Opposite above: *An advertisement for Kitmir from* Vogue *magazine, Paris, March 1926.*

Opposite below: *An advertisement for Kitmir from* Jardin des modes *magazine, 1925.*

Below: *A beaded silk evening dress by an unidentified fashion house, Paris, 1926–27.*

Right: *A detail of a beaded silk evening dress by a handicraft atelier, Yugoslavia, 1926–27.*

made from printed fabric, such as shawls, scarves, and fabric borders with large floral patterns were added to the atelier's repertoire. Unfortunately, Maria Pavlovna was unfamiliar with the laws of commerce. She paid too much for embroidery patterns, she allowed herself to be shortchanged, and she sold the finished goods at too much of a reduced price. Her atelier did not have professional managers, which she avoided because she felt so helpless in business matters. Trying to save the failing business, Maria Pavlovna accepted financial assistance from a well-to-do Russian émigré. In order to pay back the debt to her partner, she was forced to sell the last of the remaining Romanov family jewels, including a famous necklace with large pearls that had belonged to her mother.

In about 1928, embroidery began to go out of fashion. People grew less interested in it, showing a preference for smooth printed fabrics. Art Deco was living out its last days on the eve of the 1929 Wall Street crash. Maria Pavlovna attempted to revive her dying business up until the day the ruined Kitmir was swallowed up by the experienced old French embroidery firm Fritel and Hurel, who still owns the most extensive collection of Kitmir embroidery samples. Maria Pavlovna obtained the right to use the

177

Kitmir name on articles produced by the firm. Many of the Russian embroiderers who had worked for the grand duchess began working for the new owners.

Having suffered a defeat, but not wishing to surrender, Maria Pavlovna departed for London in the spring of 1928 in search of a new business. A new passion was sweeping over the Parisian fashion houses at that time—perfumes. Both large and small fashion houses followed the infectious example of Paul Poiret, who as early as the 1910s had established a subsidiary perfume company, and began to create their own fragrances. Many of these fragrances, such as Chanel No. 5 and Jean Patou's Joy are still with us today.

Russian émigrés also enthusiastically took up creating new perfumes. Many well-known fragrances were created with the participation of Russian specialists. For example, Ernest Beau, chief perfumer of Moscow's Rallé cosmetics, was one of the creators of Chanel No. 5, which was inspired by an image from Pushkin's short story "The Queen of Spades." The fragrance was infused with "the fresh scent of Finnish lakes" and the "bouquets of Yalta." The idea of creating her own perfume inspired Maria Pavlovna. The Paris market was saturated, so she decided to try her luck in London. She spent hours searching for the right combination of scents. She called her first perfume "Prince Igor" and she launched it in a small trial series in bottles bearing her name. Clearly lacking in commercial sense and business abilities, Maria Pavlovna did not generate the necessary advertising for it and did not distribute it properly. Failures plagued and pursued her, but she did not lose hope: Europe seemed to be a lost battlefield, so she set her sights on America, which was the promised land to many. One of Maria Pavlovna's American friends invited her to stay with her for a while, and new unexplored opportunities opened up.

Preparations to leave for the United States were cut short by the death of Maria Fedorovna, the widow of Alexander III, on October 13, 1928. She had lived her last years in her native Denmark and was for many the last symbol of the imperial dynasty. Maria Pavlovna returned to Paris via Berlin in December 1928 and set sail for America from Le Havre. Grand Duchess Maria Pavlovna Romanova's arrival was greeted by the press with great enthusiasm and curiosity. She was photographed and interviewed a great deal. In America she finally realized the seriousness of the state of her health, which she had constantly neglected in Paris. For many years she had suffered from pain in her ankle and even limped a little: the necessary surgery was performed in New York in January 1929.

In the United States Maria Pavlovna hoped to find a market for her "Prince Igor" perfume and to publish the memoirs of her life in Russia, which she had been working on for many years. She took the advice of her friends and sent her manuscript to a publisher. How great was her surprise when on April 18, 1929, on the eve of her birthday, she received a proposal from the editor to publish the first volume of her memoirs. The book was translated from Russian into English and French and was published in two volumes: the first was entitled *The Education of a Grand Duchess,* and the second was *A Grand Duchess in Exile.* They subsequently became bestsellers in the United States and Europe, which improved Maria Pavlovna's financial situation.

It seemed that a period of success had begun. In May Maria Pavlovna was invited by the New York department store Bergdorf Goodman's to serve as a consultant, purchasing fashionable clothing from France; for example, from the Russian fashion house YTEB. She returned to France with a light heart and got busy selling her house in Boulogne. Bidding farewell to Princess Paley, Maria Pavlovna departed for the Gare de Lyons, where she was seen off by her stepsister Princess Natalya Paley and the latter's husband, the owner of the fashion house Lucien Lelong. In August 1929, she sailed from Marseilles to the United States a second time, bringing along her favorite seven-string guitar, a typewriter, and $300 (all that the grand duchess had, besides, naturally, her large debts).

Maria Pavlovna worked at Bergdorf Goodman's, prepared her memoirs for publication, and gave lectures at universities. Hearst Publishers invited her to write fashion articles and reviews, and in 1935 Maria Pavlovna was sent by them to Germany as a photojournalist. This new profession completely engrossed her and she mastered the technique down to its subtleties.

While living in New York, Maria Pavlovna began a new hobby: collecting Russian books. A fortunate incident helped her acquire several volumes from her deceased father's library. In 1937, by order of the King of Sweden, who sympathized with the grand duchess, she received a Swedish diplomatic passport to replace her old Nansen passport, which gave her broad freedom of movement. She was frequently published at the time: for instance, on December 8, 1937, *Vogue* ran her enchanting description of Russian Christmas. At Bergdorf Goodman she began to create hat collections.

In 1937 there followed a series of divorces in the family. Her brother Dmitrii Pavlovich divorced his American spouse. Their stepsister, Princess Nathalie Paley, a society beauty and Hollywood actress at the time, divorced Lucien Lelong and moved to New York to become even closer to Maria Pavlovna.

In 1941 the United States entered World War II as an ally of the Soviet Union. America's friendly attitude toward the Communist nation was unendurable for Maria Pavlovna. She could not live in a country that supported the government that had executed her father and most of her relatives. Taking leave of her New York friends—Princess Paley, the well-known German photographer Horst, Valentina Sanina, founder of the fashion house Valentina, and her husband George Shlee—she moved again, this time to Argentina.

Maria Pavlovna rented a small house with a garden in the Barrio Norte, the best section in Buenos Aires, and devoted her spare time to painting, even managing to sell several of her paintings. Argentine newspapers published her ar-

ticles about interior design, fashion, and art. The Russian fashion house belonging to Natalya Nevolova opened around this time—this is where Evita Perón, the beautiful wife of the Argentine president, got her clothes.

A large number of Russian émigrés took up residence in Argentina. Landless Cossacks from Gallipoli were invited. There was a marvelous Russian church, decorated in majolica, that had been consecrated at the turn of the century. Maria Pavlovna felt peaceful, and became especially close friends with the family of Prince Mestchersky, who had moved there from Paris. In 1947, Maria Pavlovna's son Prince Lennart came to visit from Germany for several months and for the first time genuinely got to know his Russian mother. Two years later Maria Pavlovna visited Europe

where, at the home of her son on a little island called Mainau, in Germany, she met her first husband, Prince Wilhelm of Sweden, for the first time in many years. In spite of the unexpectedness of the meeting and the awkwardness of the situation, they parted good friends.

In November 1952, Maria Pavlovna became the Honorary Patron of the Organization of Young Russian Scouts in Argentina. Throughout the 1950s, the last years of her life, Maria Pavlovna often visited Europe, where she would live with her son or with friends. She would unexpectedly appear in Mainau with her camera, easel, and paints. Grand Duchess Maria Pavlovna died from pneumonia on December 13, 1958, in Konstantz, Germany. She is buried in a side altar of the Palace Church in Mainau next to her brother Grand

Duke Dmitrii Pavlovich, who died in Davos in 1942.

Foreseeing her coming death, the grand duchess bequeathed the family icon, which was at Prince Mestchersky's home in Buenos Aires, to her son, Prince Lennart. However, Miguel Kireeff, the chief editor of the Russian-Argentine newspaper *Nuestro Pais* told us: "The icon remained at the Mestcherskys when she moved to Europe. Unfortunately, the icon never did reach her son and is in the possession of Father Vladimir Shlenev, who inherited all the Mestcherskys' personal articles."[19]

Most of Maria Pavlovna's memorabilia, such as her court dress, her portraits, and her photographs, are in Prince Lennart's possession at the family castle at Mainau. In 1999 a memorial exhibition of her life was held there.

Above left: *The building in which Kitmir was once located, avenue Francisco, Paris. Photo by Alexandre Vassiliev, 1997.*

Above right: *A building in which Kitmir was once located, avenue Montaigne, no. 7, Paris. Photo by Alexandre Vassiliev, 1997.*

8

THE EMERGENCE OF RUSSIAN FASHION AND FASHION HOUSES IN PARIS

As we have discussed, the influence of Russian folk art became more and more palpable in the collections of the major Paris and London houses beginning in 1920 and continuing throughout the decade. The popularity of embroidery, including Russian, Hungarian, and Romanian designs, can in part be explained by the wartime shortage of rich fabrics. Also feeding the trend was the sudden availability of skilled, inexpensive labor due to the influx of émigré women who needed work and knew how to sew and embroider.

Famous Paris fashion houses of the early 1920s, such as Chanel, Lucille, Martial et Armand, Paul Poiret, Agnès, Germaine, Drecoll, Augusta Bernard, and others, each created *à la russe* designs during the seasons of 1920 to 1923. The fashionable new shapes of these years followed the traditional lines of Russian national costumes. The names of the designs themselves showed their derivation: Martial et Armand designed a "Babushka" (an old woman); the house of Alice Bernard the suit "Muzhik" (Russian peasant man) in 1922; and the London house of Vladimir created a blouse called "Cossack" in 1921.

Paris *Vogue* wrote on December 15, 1920: "The calamities in Russia have drawn attention to the originality of peasant costumes. We are all aware of the wave of interest in Russian costumes in the world of elegant fashion."[1] Fur trim, hats in the shape of *kichki* (an old-

Opposite: *Mary Garden, a Scottish opera singer, as Aphrodite in a production in New York, 1921. Her costume is clearly inspired by traditional Russian costume. Photograph from* Vogue, *Paris, January 1921.*

Above: *An advertisement for the Parisian fashion house of Myrbor, where the Russian painter Natalya Goncharova worked in the 1920s.*

style Russian women's round headdress with gold embroidery), embroidered sleeves, the *kosovorotka* (a man's shirt that buttons to the left side), and high boots were just a few of the elements of "Russian fashion" shown in the collections of the big houses during these years. But possibly the most popular feature of Russian national costume was the northern Russian *kokoshnik* (woman's crownlike, festive headdress).

The history of the *kokoshnik* is full of mystery, and no one knows the exact date of its origin. It is known that in the early eighteenth century, Peter I, in one of his attempts at Westernizing Russia, issued a decree forbidding boyars' wives to wear these headdresses; *kokoshniki* survived among the peasants as a feature of festive and wedding apparel. By the end of the eighteenth century, Catherine the Great permitted the wearing of it, but solely as a feature of carnival costumes.

Then, the war with Napoleon stirred up an unprecedented wave of Russian patriotism and revived an interest in everything national: clothing as well as literature, music, and art. From 1812 to 1814, Russian red and blue *sarafany* (peasant dresses) with Empire waistlines and filigree buttons down the front became fashionable in Europe. Portraits from that time depict Englishwomen, Frenchwomen, and the Russian Empress Elizaveta Alexeyevna, Alexander I's wife, wearing them. The pro-Russian movement in fashion brought back *kokoshniki* to fashionable society. In 1834 Nicholas I issued a decree introducing a new court dress comprising a narrow open bodice with long boyar-style sleeves, a long skirt with a train, and the *kokoshnik*. By the end of the nineteenth century, these dresses were often sewn in various colors with velvet and, for the empress and grand duchesses, brocade with insets of white satin. The pattern of the rich gold embroidery was predetermined by decree in accordance with a lady's position in the court. The proto-

181

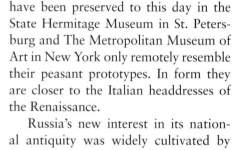

col for wearing these dresses was followed in Russia right up to Nicholas II's abdication in February 1917.

General Alexander Mosolov, the head of the ministry of the court, cites in his memoirs, *Pri dvore poslednego imperatora* [In the Court of the Last Emperor] some remarkable examples of the Russian court's taste: "'Russian' dress is described in great detail in the 'Court Calendar.' This white satin dress must leave both shoulders bare; the train must be of red velvet with embroidery in gold (the ladies in waiting of the grand duchesses had trains of other colors, according to a special table). A *kokoshnik* of red velvet must prominently adorn the head.

"The dresses and, implicitly, the *kokoshnik*, can be decorated with precious stones in accordance with the level of wealth of the particular individual. In this regard, I will cite an instance that once struck me—Olga Zinovieva, the wife of the leader of the nobility in one of the districts of the Petrograd province, wore nine or ten emeralds, each the size of a robin's egg, as buttons. In my day the diamonds worn by Countess Shuvalova, Countess Vorontsova-Dashkova, Countess Sheremetyeva, Princess Kochubei, Princess Yusupova, etc., were particularly remarkable."[2]

To be sure, the court *kokoshniki* that

have been preserved to this day in the State Hermitage Museum in St. Petersburg and The Metropolitan Museum of Art in New York only remotely resemble their peasant prototypes. In form they are closer to the Italian headdresses of the Renaissance.

Russia's new interest in its national antiquity was widely cultivated by Slavophile historical novelists, opera composers, architects, and artists. The historical canvases of such artists as Vassily Vasnetsov, Ilya Repin, Mikhail Nesterov, A. P. Ryabushkin, and Konstantin Makovsky acquainted the public with the boyar—pre-Petrine—costume, albeit in stylized form. The works by the artists of the Abramtsevo and Talashkino crafts workshops helped to create an unprecedented interest in Russian folk art and costume, inspiring numerous crafts exhibits and the creation of folk art museums, and prominent figures such as Princess Tenisheva, Shabelskaya, and Stanislavsky became great collectors of Russian antiques.

The imperial Bolshoi and Maryinsky theaters especially did a great deal to popularize traditional Russian costume. Frequent productions of Russian operas with historical and folkloric themes, such as *Sadko, Prince Igor, A Life for the Tsar, Rusalka, Snow Maiden,* and Mussorgsky's *Boris Godunov,* as well

Opposite, top left: *George Dow*, Portrait of Charlotte Augusta, Princess of Wales, *in a Russian costume, 1817.*

Opposite, top center: *Franz Krueger*, Portrait of the Empress Alexandra Feodorovna, *in a traditional Russian costume, 1830.*

Opposite, top right: *Vladimir Makovsky*, Portrait of the Dowager Empress Maria Feodorovna, *in traditional Russian costume, 1912.*

Opposite below: *A portrait of an unknown woman wearing a kokoshnik, Pskov, late 1870s. Photograph by Dmitriev.*

Above: *Ekaterina Geltzer in the costume of the Tsar Maiden based on a sketch by Korovin for the ballet* Konyok Gorbunok [The Little Humpbacked Horse] *by Pugni, Moscow, c. 1912.*

Right: *Grand Duke Andrei Vladimirovich in a masquerade costume as a stol'nik [table server at the imperial court], St. Petersburg, February 1903.*

Overleaf: *Russian émigrés in masquerade costumes at a patriotic soirée. Far left: Elena Shreter, Belgrade, 1934.*

184

as the ballet *The Little Humpbacked Horse* in stage sets designed by the talented artists Korovin, Solomko, and Ponomaryov, were some of the examples of this pan-Slavic focus. At the turn of the century, the Moscow Maly Theater, with its productions of plays by Alexei Tolstoy and A. N. Ostrovsky, and the Moscow Art Theater, with its historically accurate, museum-quality productions by Stanislavsky and Nemirovich-Danchenko, such as *Tsar Fedor* and *The Snow Maiden*, were unparalleled in the way they paid meticulous attention to national culture of the past down to every last detail on the costume. National traditions were also preserved by concerts at which singers such as Vyaltseva, Plevitskaya, Panina, and Dolina-Gorlenko sang traditional Russian songs.

Recognition of this "Russian style" peaked at the 1903 costume ball at the Winter Palace, where guests wore magnificent boyar costumes based on seventeenth-century royal court attire. The noble ladies were resplendent in their *kokoshniki*, often exaggerated in an operatic style. Since many of the participants in this event became refugees, this style was later to serve as the model for fashions produced by Russian émigrés in the West. "Sokolsky," the little fortress near St. Petersburg that was built to re-

Библиотека декоративных искусств. Париж

Opposite: *Sophia Madero Crenwell in a diadem in the shape of a Russian* kokoshnik, *1920.*

Above: *A headdress shaped like a Russian* kokoshnik *that took first prize at a fashion ball in Paris in April 1925.*

Below left: *Elena Makowska, a Polish silent-film star, in an evening dress with a tiara shaped like a Russian* kokoshnik, *Berlin, early 1920s. Photograph by A. Binder.*

Below right: *The English Princess Mary on the day of her marriage to Henry Laceless, the Duke of Heirwood, in a bridal ensemble with a tiara shaped like a Russian* kokoshnik, *London, 1922.*

others were stored in the treasure-house of the Russian church in Nice, and still others traveled around to museums in various American cities until the 1930s. The collection is now divided among the Brooklyn Museum of Art in New York, the Museum of Fine Arts in Boston, and the Art Museum in Cleveland.

Due to the influence of these exhibitions, bridal headdresses in the form of a crown/*kokoshnik* became popular in Western fashion of the 1920s: it is impossible to list all the famous brides of the world who got married in the 1920s in variations of Russian headdress. It is, perhaps, sufficient to mention that Queen Mary, Elizabeth II's grandmother, was married in a headdress reminiscent of a Russian *kokoshnik*.

The freely interpreted *kokoshnik* become a feature of everyday wear. Jeanne Lanvin created a collection of hats in the shape of Russian headdresses, and in the early 1920s, the house of August Bonaz in Paris produced plastic *kokoshniki*. This staggering success in the West compelled many Russian émigré fashion ateliers to start producing them. The house of Caris in Paris, which made designs exclusively in the Russian national style, created a collection of *kichki*, *kokoshniki* and *povoiniks* (a head scarf worn by married Russian peasant

Архив автора. Париж

semble a medieval village for the entertainment of the nobility, was the last memorial to this fashionable revival of Russian history.

It is no wonder that these articles of exaggerated Russian style, which are now scattered around the museums of the world, were among the items the aristocracy took with them when they set off into forced exile. A great deal of genuine antique Russian clothing, as well as reconstructed articles, had gained renown outside of Russia in the early part of the century. For example, part of M. L. Shabelskaya's unique collection of Russian national costume, embroidery, and headdresses, which she collected in Russia from 1880–90, was exhibited in Chicago in 1893, Brussels in 1894, and Paris in 1900. Some of the items in this valuable collection remained in Russia,

Национальная библиотека. Саппоро

Музей МХАТ, Москва

Национальная библиотека, Сантьяго

women). Variations on motifs from the Russian headdress and the Russian bo-yar costume also appeared in the early 1920s in the designs of such famous émigré fashion houses as Yteb and Irfe.

All through the long years of emi-gration the *kokoshnik* remained a cer-tain symbol of old Russia. It was a feature of Russian stage costumes and it could be seen in small Russian cabarets from Constantinople to Harbin and at performances by famous émigré theater troupes—from the Bluebird in Berlin to La Chauve Souris in Paris and New York and Maria Kuznetsova's Private Russian Opera in Paris. There was no star who did not perform in a *kokoshnik*: Anna Pavlova, Olga Baklanova, Alexan-dra Balashova, and Tamara Karsavina all wore one. Many of the creators of these fantastic headdresses used the orig-inal drawings of the artist Sergei Solomko

Above left: *Olga Baklanova, a Moscow Art Theater actress who became a Hollywood star, in a Russian costume, Hollywood, 1929.*

Above right: *Hope Hampton, an American film actress in an evening dress beaded in a double-eagle motif, 1924.*

(he also died in exile in Paris in 1928) as a foundation. Others, using only photographs, copied the costumes of the lavish ball of 1903 held in the Winter Palace. The author has in his collection several such examples: the rarest of them is the ballerina Nina Kirsanova's *kokoshnik*; it is Art Deco in style, made of lightweight pearl beads of various shapes with insets of green lead-glass gems and stones. Nina Kirsanova, a soloist in Anna Pavlova's dance troupe, performed in this *kokoshnik* at concerts featuring Russian dances.

In the early 1920s, before Soviet Russia was recognized by world governments, the attitude toward Russian émigrés was one of warmth tinged with sympathy. Various private and government foundations were organized in Europe and America to support refugees. They organized charity shows, concerts, and sales to raise money. A *Russkaya izba* (Russian Hut) was organized in 1920 in King's Hall in London, consisting of Russian choral singing, folk dances, and balalaika players. The London public responded to the concert with enthusiasm. British *Vogue* wrote about it in January 1920: "The concert was over before we had a chance to come to our senses. As we left, we took away a feeling of strong sympathy for Russia in our hearts. Was this not an appeal of her people? Could we allow its partition as a nation?"[3]

Similar activities to help Russian refugees were organized in the Paris Grand Opera with the participation of Alexandra Balashova, Vera Karalli, and Maria Kuznetsova, stars of the imperial Russian stage. Exhibits of Russian craft arts—held by the émigrés themselves in Constantinople, Paris, London, and Prague—were another form of aid.

Witnessing the triumph of the Russian style, many émigrés began thinking about establishing their own small private enterprises of "Russian fashion." Ateliers and workshops were opened in Berlin and in Paris. By 1921 France had accepted nearly 150,000 Russian refugees. After chaotic Constantinople, sleepy Sofia, and provincial Belgrade,

Above left: *Lidia Lipkovskaya, a famous soprano, in a costume from the opera* Tsarskaya nevesta *[The Tsar's Bride], St. Petersburg, c. 1914.*

Above center: *Ekaterina Kudryavtseva, a cabaret dancer, in a* kokoshnik *she made, Paris, c. 1927.*

Above right: *Mary Pickford in a Russian* kokoshnik, *Hollywood, late 1920s.*

Below left and right: *Drawings from the French magazine* L'Art et la mode *showing* kokoshnik-*style hats from the Parisian atelier Nandine, 1923–24.*

Национальная библиотека, Сантьяго

glamourous postwar Paris seemed like the real capital of the world to Russians. But life in this splendid city was not easy for them. Vladimir Zeeler, the editor of the guide *Russkie vo Franttsii* [Russians in France] wrote: "Every Russian needs work today. Long gone are the days when some people had something left over from the resources that they had taken out with them, when everything that one had brought in the hopes of a speedy return, was spent. The black days for the emigrés soon came, in which, while searching for work, they were forced to confront many obstacles and limitations which did not alleviate but made the objective of finding work much more difficult."[4]

Ruined and bewildered, deprived of shelter, and living only for the hope of a happy end to the civil war, Russian émigrés literally sat on their suitcases in anticipation of a miracle. Citizens of a country that no longer existed, Russian refugees finally obtained legal rights on July 5, 1922, with the establishment of

the Nansen passport, a refugee document that was recognized by thirty-eight governments as proof of identity.

For the majority of Russians, hopes for a return to their homeland remained an unfulfilled dream. Family valuables spirited out in hiding places in their baggage, the folds of their clothing, in dolls, or even in their hairdos, were sold for a pittance to European jewelers. The proceeds from their sale instantly evaporated, and the aid from the many charitable societies was insufficient to live on: only work could rescue the refugees in those difficult years. France had lost a consider-

able part of its male population during World War I, and working hands were needed everywhere. But the emphasis was on labor, and many highly educated refugees were forced, for lack of better earnings, to get jobs at plants all over the country, from Alsace to the Pyrenees. In spite of their ranks and titles, a great many of the newly arrived Russian nobility worked at the Renault and Citroen automobile plants on the outskirts of Paris. Another important source of émigré earnings were Russian taxis, whose number grew steadily, reaching 6,000 by the early 1930s. Also, a myriad of Russian

clubs, restaurants, snack bars, cabarets, and ateliers were opened in Paris. Such a mass appearance of Russians evoked surprise—Russian exotica astonished the imagination with its novelty.

The continuing glory of Sergei Diaghilev's Ballets Russes, the triumph of Anna Pavlova and Feodor Chaliapin, the success of Maria Kuznetsova's Private Russian Opera on the Champs Elysées, the work of the Russian film studio Albatross, which put Ivan Mosjoukine and Natalya Kowanko on the world screens, the Prague Art Theater troupe with Maria Germanova, and Nikita

Above left: *A drawing from a French fashion magazine of a design called "Tsaritsa," early 1920s.*

Above center: *A silk dress embroidered in coral designed by the house of Lanvin, Paris, 1922–23.*

Above right: *A drawing from a French fashion magazine of a dress embroidered in the Russian style designed by the house of Lefranc, early 1920s.*

Below left and right: *Details of embroidered dresses designed by the house of Lanvin, Paris, 1922–23.*

191

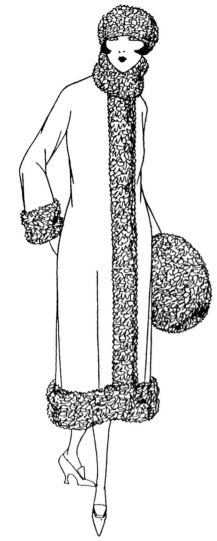

Библиотека Ла Камбр, Брюссель.

Baliev's theater-cabaret La Chauve Souris all helped to raise the morale of Russian émigrés.

The long history of the collaboration between Russians and the Parisian world of fashion begins at this time. Marina Gorboff writes in her book *La Russie Fantôme* [The Ghost of Russia], which came out in Paris in 1995, that by 1931 nearly 42 percent of the women of the Russian emigration were involved in the fashion industry.[5] Russian women worked sewing, knitting, making hats and lingerie, and painting on silk. They also worked as models, artists, and saleswomen in the Russian houses of fashion. They were the first famous models: these titled, or simply elegant, ladies of the first wave of Russian emigrants pioneered the road to this profession, raising its prestige, as far back as the early 1920s.

One of the first Russians who began advertising Russian fashions in France was Mrs. Polyakova, the chairwoman of the organization of Russian invalids in France. The Paris magazine *Fémina* wrote about her on May 1, 1921: "She is modeling two embroidered blouses, the color and shape of which are inspired by Russian art. The blouses were sewn for a charitable purpose. In this

Национальная библиотека, Сантьяго.

Архив автора, Париж.

192

Музей моды и костюма, Париж

Opposite, top left: *A drawing by the illustrator Marian in the French magazine* L'Art et la mode *of a winter coat in the Russian style, Paris, 1920.*

Opposite below: *A worker manufacturing fashionable "Russian boots" at John Rowson's factory in Leicester, England, early 1920s.*

Opposite, top right: *A winter outfit: jacket, straight skirt and "Russian boots," Paris, 1922.*

Above: *A ladies' winter coat in gold brocade with a fur collar and trim, Paris, early 1920s.*

Right: *Count Sheremetyev in a boyar costume at the 1903 ball in St. Petersburg that revived the interest in pre-Petrine Russian national dress. Photograph by Boissonas et Eggler.*

Архив автора, Париж

193

Chapeau en taupé souple garni de crosses noire et blanche, porté par la Princesse Troubetzkoy

CHAPKA

362, Rue Saint-Honoré

PARIS   Tél. Gut. 1

Библиотека декоративных искусств. Париж

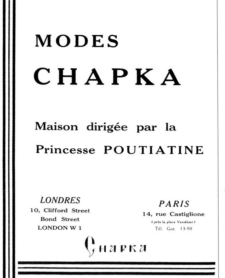

MODES

CHAPKA

Maison dirigée par la

Princesse POUTIATINE

LONDRES   PARIS
10, Clifford Street   14, rue Castiglione
Bond Street   (près la place Vendôme)
LONDON W 1   Tél. Gut. 13-90

Chapka

Архив автора. Париж

La Princesse Troubetzkoy porte ce nouveau béret souple en velours bleu marine garni d'un petit gros-grain du même ton.

CHAPKA

362, Rue Saint-Honoré

PARIS   Tél. Gut. 13-90

Библиотека декоративных искусств. Париж

way the highest level of Slavic society is devoting itself to aiding unfortunate refugees."[6]

Princess Olga Urusova (Ouroussow in the French spelling) also opened a fashion atelier in Paris, at no. 108 boulevard Haussmann, in the early 1920s. The Urusov family has Tatar-Mongol roots; their ancestors were Tatar-Mongol princes who settled in Russia, and they are direct descendants of the Murza of Urus. During the reign of Alexander I, the Urusov princes were recognized as princes of the Russian Empire by an imperial decree. It is not without interest that they were related to the Tyrtov family.

Princess Urusova announced in a 1924 advertisement that her atelier made dresses, coats, sportswear, hats, and designed Russian embroidery. There is

Архив графини Натальи Сумароковой-Эльстон. Лондон

Top left and right: *Princess Trubetskaya advertising items from the fashion house of Chapka (which means "hat" in Russian). Photo from* Vogue *magazine, Paris, October 1926.*

Above center and bottom: *Advertisements for the house of Chapka and its other branches in Paris and London, 1920s.*

Center: *Ye. D. Zinovieva, an employee at the London branch of the house of Chapka.*

an outfit from the house of Princess Ouroussow—a silk dress and coat with embroidered trim—in the collection of the Musée de la mode et du Costume at the Palace Gallierà in Paris.[7] This lilac silk outfit with insets of fabric ornamented with Eastern patterns is beautifully cut and the dress has a zipper in the back, which was a novelty in the 1920s. There

Архив автора. Париж

10, Clifford St.
Bond St.
LONDON W.1

CHAPKA

MODES

362, Rue Sʲ-Honoré
PARIS (Iʳ)
Gutenberg 13-90

ЦѢНЫ ШЛЯПЪ ОТЪ 200 ФРАНКОВЪ

are not many signed garments from Russian fashion houses in museum collections throughout the world: the Ouroussow fashion house label, which is intact on this dress, is very rare and therefore quite valuable. Judging from this one ensemble, the house of Ouroussow had a folkloric profile.

The fashion house of Caris was also established in Paris in the early 1920s. Judging from the photographs of its designs preserved in a private archive in England, Caris made Russian-style dresses, *kichki, kokoshniki*, beads, and small bags. Katyusha Ionina, Caris's leading model, showed them in a striking manner. An embroidered red silk dress from this house, as well as a par-

Above left and right: *Drawings by Cora Marson from the French magazine* L'Art et la mode *of headdresses in the Russian style, Paris, 1921–22.*

Above center: *An evening headdress of orange panne velvet with embroidered and pearl trim, Paris, early 1920s.*

Below left and right: *Drawings from the French magazine* L'Art et la mode *of headdresses in the Russian style, Paris, 1921–22.*

Below center: *Countess Anna von Bennigsen in a Russian-style hat she made, New York, 1922.*

rure, a matched set of jewelry consisting of handmade beads and earrings, are preserved in her daughter Irina Sergeyevna de Koby's collection. According to de Koby's recollections, Caris employed exclusively Russian émigrés to make their "folk style" designs.

Princess Maria Ivanovna Putyatina [Poutiatine in the French spelling], née Princess Endogurova, established a millinery business called Chapka ("hat" in Russian), which occupies a special place in the history of the fashion houses and ateliers founded by Russian aristocrats. The Putyatin princes belong to one of Russia's oldest families and trace their lineage back to 862. Ivan Semenovich Drutsky-Putyata gave the family the

ROBES
MANTEAUX
CHAPEAUX SPORT
BRODERIES RUSSES

PRINCESSE O. OUROUSSOW

108, BOULEVARD HAUSSMANN
PARIS

362

Left and right: *Silk walking suits from the house of Princess Olga Ouroussow (the French spelling), Paris, c. 1923.*

Above: *An advertisement in* Vogue *magazine for the fashion house of Princess Olga Ouroussow, Paris, 1924.*

Below: *A clothing label from the house of Princess Olga Ouroussow.*

Putyatin name, linking it forever with another Russian princely family—the Drutskys. The founder of the Chapka business was the spouse of Major General Prince Mikhail Sergeyevich Putyatin and the mother-in-law of Grand Duchess Maria Pavlovna, who owned the Kitmir House of Embroidery. Chapka prospered in the 1920s, producing embroidered cloche-style hats. Only skilled Russian women worked there. Princess Trubetskaya was the top model; her title attracted clientele. With time, the Chapka house opened its own shop in London, where Elizaveta Dmitrievna Zinovieva, née Princess Galitzine, worked as a saleswoman.

On January 15, 1922, Countess Orlova-Davydova opened the Russian house called Mode at 114-bis boulevard Malesherbes in Paris. At first, it specialized in hand-knit articles. The countess's sister, Maria Zografo, and cousin

Countess Orlova-Denisova assisted her. Together they decided to specialize in hand-block-printed wool and silk fabrics. Countess Orlova-Denisova was the chief expert in dyeing; using stencils, she produced remarkable, incomparable fabrics in imitation of antique brocade. A French magazine wrote about them in 1925: "The originality of their patterns, inspired by ancient Russian, Coptic, Egyptian, Persian and Chinese ornament, as well as the stability and brightness of the dyes they used, made it possible for them to be brilliantly successful with French and foreign clients."[8]

Enthused with this success, Countess Orlova-Davydova moved her Mode business to a more prominent building at no. 23 rue du Faubourg St.-Honoré. She had 125 skilled women working for her, mainly Russian and Armenian refugees. Nearly all of them were home-based workers: they took home fabrics,

dyes, and stencils, and brought back finished products. A dozen needleworkers knitted garments in jersey, which Chanel had made fashionable. Countess Orlova-Davydova opened another atelier in the northern suburb of Clichy in February 1924, specializing in reproducing antique Russian brocade with embroidery with Prince Yuri Lvovich Dodukov-Izedinov, a man of great taste, a talented graphic artist, and an expert in antique styles, as the head of the department. These expensive embroidered fabrics were used for interior decoration, upholstery, and dresses. Many major Parisian houses of fashion ordered fabrics from the countess for their collections. As a French commentator wrote: "The first piece of embroidered fabric from the Clichy atelier was presented as a gift to the Russian church on rue Daru, and ceremonial vestments for major religious holidays were sewn from

Below: *Countess Anna Ilyinichna Vorontsova-Dashkova, owner of the Ymedy fashion house, Paris, 1925.*

Right: *Princess Wiazemskaya, who, together with the American millionairess Vera Vanderbilt, opened an institute of beauty and an atelier on rue Rude in Paris, shown here in a dress from her atelier, Paris, 1922.*

Архив автора. Париж

it."[9] The house's business in the early 1920s was good: the total annual earnings of the employees in 1922 was 100,340 francs, tripling in 1923 to 320,000 francs. The business folded at the end of the 1920s due to the economic recession and because decorative and embroidered fabrics fell out of fashion.

The fashion house Anely was opened by Natalya Nikolayevna Lazareva, née Markova, with her daughter by her first husband, Irina Fedorova, in Paris in 1924. Intelligent, energetic, and gifted, Lazareva had received an education in the arts in St. Petersburg and was a tal-

ented portraitist. She opened her first house of fashion, Ferajal, in Constantinople, then moved to Paris with her three children. Natalya's other daughter and her son, Yuri, children from her second marriage to Nikolai Nikolayevich Lazarev, were still too young to be involved in the work of the fashion enterprise, but she was helped by one of the Tolstoy countesses. A Parisian commentator wrote in 1925: "Like all other houses of fashion established by high-society ladies from Russia, the house of Anely is very young. Owing to the boldness and taste of its creator, Mrs.

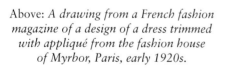

Above: *A drawing from a French fashion magazine of a design of a dress trimmed with appliqué from the fashion house of Myrbor, Paris, early 1920s.*

Above right: *A detail of an appliqué on a tunic dress from the house of Myrbor, based on a sketch by Natalya Goncharova, Paris, c. 1925.*

Right: *A dress with an appliqué from the house of Myrbor, based on a sketch by Natalya Goncharova, Paris, 1924.*

Far right: *A sketch by Natalya Goncharova of an evening wrap for the house of Myrbor, Paris, 1925.*

Библиотека декоративных искусств. Париж

MYRBOR

Lazareva, it deserves a place of honor in the world of Parisian fashion."[10]

Lazareva's most loyal assistant was her daughter Irina Feodorova, who subsequently became the personal secretary of the well-known French actress Françoise Rose, and then the secretary of Prince Rimsky-Korsakov while he was director of the house of Nina Ricci. The house of Anely did not survive the depression following 1929. In the 1930s, Lazareva opened a boarding house on boulevard Raspail, and in the late 1930s she left for the United States to be with her younger daughter and two grandchildren; she died there in the mid-50s.

The Russian fashion house Ymedy opened in Paris on August 1, 1924, at no. 5 rue de Colisée. Its founder and owner was Countess Anna Ilyinichna Vorontsova-Dashkova, née Princess Chavchavadze. A French commentator wrote about this enterprise in detail in 1925: "It is difficult to exaggerate the courage with which ladies of Russian high society, exiled from their Homeland by revolution, threw themselves

Cape en crêpe de Chine blanc, brodé noir et or et en crêpe de Chine noir, brodé blanc et or.

White crêpe de Chine cape embroidered black and gold, and black crêpe de Chine embroidered white and gold.

MYRBOR

Библиотека Ла Канбр. Брюссель

Robe en satin noir, avec applications de satin de couleurs rebrodé d'or.

Black satin gown, with applications of satin in colours, embroidered with gold.

MYRBOR

Above left: *A drawing from* Vogue *magazine of a dress trimmed with appliqué from the house of Myrbor, Paris, February 1925.*

Above: *Drawings from the magazine* L'Art et la mode *of dresses trimmed with appliqué and embroidery from the house of Myrbor designs, Paris, June 1925.*

into work. Running the business Imedi has turned out to be extremely difficult, and the countess was completely unprepared for it. After all, the former position of her husband, the son of Count Vorontsov-Dashkov, Minister of Alexander III's Court, then governor-general of the Caucasus during Nicholas II's reign, guaranteed her a carefree, happy life.

"The recently opened Imedi fashion house expanded so rapidly that it was soon necessary to move from the rue de Colisée location, which had become cramped; and in July 1925, the House moved to enormous, luxuriously decorated salons at no. 84 avenue d'Iéna.

"With the assistance of ladies—Princess Tumanova, Princess Eristova and Mrs. Gamerkelli—who, like the owner of the house, wound up in exile, Countess Vorontsova-Dashkova attended to everything, down to the small details, managing at the same time to create her designs and personally supervise the execution of work. These efforts were rewarded: elegant clients from the high-

Архив автора, Париж

Above left and right: *Advertisements from* Vogue *magazine, and from the program of the Russian Private Opera on the Champs Elysées, for the house of Anna Sergueeff, Paris, early 1920s.*

Above center: *Nikita Baliev and his wife, Zoe Karabanova, on a transatlantic ocean liner, c. 1927.*

Below left and right: *Drawings by Paul Slavone, from the magazine* L'Art et la mode, *of designs from the house of Anna Sergueeff, Paris, early 1920s.*

Opposite: *Faina Zelinskaya, an actress at the cabaret La Chauve Souris, in a dress from the house of Anna Sergueeff, Paris, 1929.*

est strata of French, English, American, and Dutch society, who, from the very start, appreciated the talent and taste of Ymedy's founder, demonstrated a preference for her House."[11]

While studying the history of this entirely forgotten fashion enterprise, we contacted the relatives of Anna Ilyinichna and her spouse, Alexander Illarionovich Vorontsov-Dashkov. Prince Gleb Iraklievich Eristov de Ksani told the author in 1991 that, according to his aunt Princess Mary Eristova, Princess Anna Chavchavadze worked for Chanel as a high-society model. "This meant that she was exceptionally elegant and went out a lot to various receptions in Paris, and Chanel dressed her and paid her a salary to do it."

Another Georgian house of fashion in Paris in the 1920s, which belonged to the Princess Nina Shervashidze, née Princess Mkheidze, was located in a five-room apartment at 32 rue Washington. According to the recollections of one of her contemporaries, the Princess

Архив автора. Париж

Архив автора. Париж

Архив автора. Париж

Библиотека «Ла Камбр», Брюссель

Costume de drap violet, jaquette cintrée à la taille, garnie de tresse noire. Gilet de soie rouge brodé or et violet.

Violet cloth costume, jacket trimmed with black braid. Red silk waistcoat embroidered in gold and violet.

(1025)

Costume de velours Van Dyck noir, brodé de soies de couleur. Blouse moujick en drap de soie blanc ceinturé de noir.

Black Van Dyck velvet costume embroidered with silk in colour. Russian blouse of white silk cloth, black belt.

(1026)

Costume de drap vert. Jaquette ajustée à la taille par des brandebourgs, très ample du bas, garnie d'astrakan gris. Plastron brodé de soies de couleur.

Green cloth costume, jacket with gimp, trimmed with grey astrakan. Breast-piece embroidered with silk in colour.

(1027)

A LA MANIÈRE RUSSE

Opposite, top left: *Ivan Petrovich (Svyatislav Petrovič), a Serbian silent-film actor in a* cherkesska *(a Caucasian tunic), Berlin, c. 1926. Photo by A. Binder.*

Opposite, top center: *Lia Mara, a Latvian silent-film actress, in a* cherkesska, *Berlin, c. 1927.*

Opposite, top right: *Ivan Mosjoukine, a silent-film star, in a* cherkesska, *Paris, 1927.*

Opposite below: *Drawings from the magazine* L'Art et la mode *of dresses and coats in the "Russian manner," Paris, 1926.*

Below: *Vivian Gibson, an American silent-film star, in a stylized Caucasian costume, Hollywood, 1926.*

Right: *Alexander and Ekaterina Kudryavtsev dancing the* lezghinka *in a cabaret, Paris, c. 1932.*

herself sewed dresses to order for wealthy American women and had an assistant.

The houses of fashion of Georgian descent that appeared in Paris introduced Caucasian motifs into the fashions of the 1922–23 season. For example, in 1922, *L'Art, goût, beauté* [Art, Taste, Beauty] advertised the very fashionable crêpe "Tiflis," rapturously describing it: "The crêpe 'Tiflis' was a great success this season. Very soft, but at the same time with a beautiful finish, it drapes agreeably in elegant daytime dresses and in ravishing evening wear. It hugs the figure marvelously, gives dresses rare style and uniqueness. It is splendid unadorned or with decoration, is suitable for embroidery, but excellent on its own, without trim. Its color range offers a most rich palette of nuances."[12]

Caucasienne, a house of *"sortie de bal"* evening coats and wraps with fur "boyar" and "Caucasian" trim opened in Paris. The vogue for everything Caucasian flourished especially luxuriantly in Parisian night life. Expert horsemen, *shashlik* (pork shish kebab), and the *lezghinka* dance were in vogue. The evening cabaret Caucasus Cellar was popular and drew famous performers such as Alexander Vertinsky. The Caucasian Prince Vladimir Arbelov opened a small fashion atelier called Anart in 1923, in which Baron Tiepolt's family worked: Baron Nikolai Apollonovich Tiepolt sketched the designs, his wife

Elizaveta Sergeyevna sewed, and their pretty daughter Katyusha modeled the dresses for clients.

Possibly the best-known of all the "Caucasian" houses was the atelier of Pierre Pitoeff, who hailed from a famous theater family. His designs were distinguished by originality of design and trim. We were able to locate the Diaghilev ballerina Valentina Ivanovna Kachouba, one of this house's clients. She was ninety-eight years old when we met with her, but she remembered the most interesting details about the house of Pitoeff's work: "Pitoeff was a good house. I ordered many dresses from him, sometimes based on Erté's sketches. I still even have a photograph of a checkered redingote coat pinched at the waist. . . . Pitoeff loved to dress me. He always told me: 'You could have been a model.' But I full well knew that I couldn't, since I was too short, and models were often very tall. Pitoeff loved to make dresses especially for me. I always bought his dresses. Otherwise I would go grab a dress here or there and buy it, but he created designs for me. The design that Erté drew for Pitoeff, for instance, I wore only twice because it created such a furor that I didn't risk going out in it. The dress was remarkably beautiful: black gauze with gold stripes, long drooping sleeves, soft, draped folds. One day I set off for the Théâtre des

Champs Elysées to the Diaghilev Ballet, and right then and there a crowd gathered around me to look, so that I couldn't bring myself to go out during the next entr'acte anymore. The second time I went out in this dress I was with a handsome Spaniard in Biarritz to a big party in a stylish cabaret. We came out to dance a tango, and in the end were left dancing alone, because everyone got up on their chairs to watch us; from that time on I didn't want to wear that dress.

Left: *An advertisement for a Caucasian restaurant in Berlin featuring five o'clock tea, an evening cabaret, and a "cozy" bar, 1922.*

Above center: *A cartoon from the magazine* Illustrirovannaya Rossiya *[Russia Illustrated] about the Caucasian restaurants in Montmartre. "It's strange, the French say that Montmartre is full of foreigners. But we don't see any."*

Top: *A Cossack chorus, Paris, 1925.*

Opposite: *A Georgian princess in a dress from a Caucasian fashion house, Paris, 1920s.*

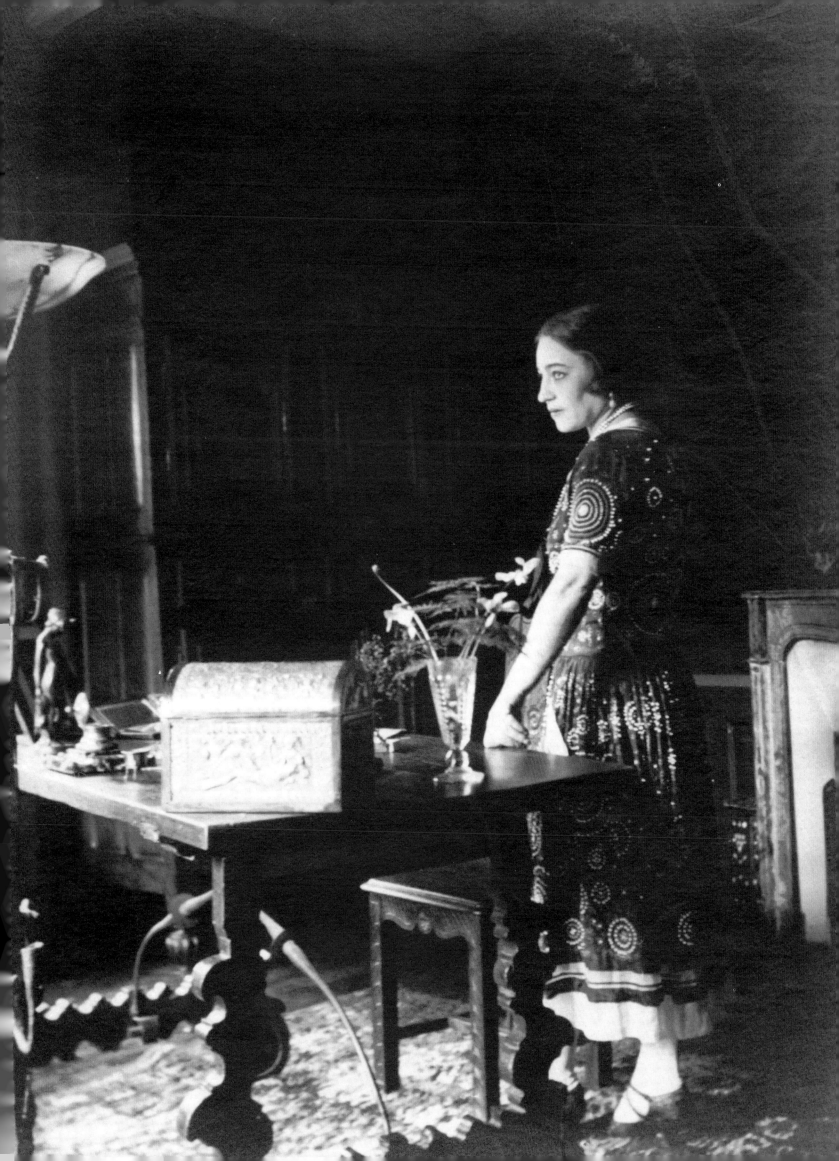

Библиотека «Ла Калибр», Брюссель

Above: *A drawing by Cora Marsen from the magazine* L'Art et la mode *of a "Caucasian" astrakhan hat, Paris, 1922.*

Below: *A drawing from the magazine* Paris-élégant *of a winter coat with fur trim, a design from the fashion house Caucasienne, 1925.*

Right: *A Georgian princess in the salon of a Caucasian fashion house, Paris, 1920s.*

Библиотека декоративных искусств, Париж

Архив автора, Париж

206

Архив Валентины Кашубы, Мадрид

I wore a turban when I went out in Pito-eff's dress. Generally I would often wear a turban since my hair was long and came down to my waist. All of Paris knew me then, and I was called 'la belle Kachouba.' Many famous Russian performers dressed at Pitoeff's; Tamara Karsavina and Anna Pavlova were among his clients."[13]

Eyle, another Caucasian house of fashion, opened in 1921 in Paris, and was located in no. 6 rue Boissy-d'Anglas. It belonged to the wealthy Armenian Tamara Agadzhanovna Mailova, née Dildarova, the wife of Ilya Lazarevich Mailov, a merchant of the First Guild. This house specialized in artistic knitting, and produced coats embroidered

Above: *Valentina Ivanovna Kachouba in a spring coat designed by the house of Pierre Pitoeff, Paris, 1922.*

Right: *A drawing from the magazine* Paris-élégant *of silk evening dresses with bead embroidery designed by the house of Pierre Pitoeff, Paris, 1922.*

in silk, and embroidered purses. Eyle's workshops were funded by money obtained from the sale of jewelry smuggled out of Russia. According to the owner's son, about seventy Russians, mainly aristocratic women, worked there. The fabrics at Eyle came from the house of Lessure and the articles were sold in Paris, Nice, and Cannes. The clients were mainly American women, who adored Caucasian exotica. Tamara Agadzhanovna drew the designs, and the artist Aslanov assisted her. Many of Eli's needleworkers, as was the case in other Parisian houses founded by Russian émigrés, took embroidery work

home, and did not spend whole days in their workshops. The house of Eyle folded with the death of the owner in 1926.

The appearance of such a large number of émigré Caucasian houses of fashion created fierce competition. The fashion house of Anna Sergueeff (the French spelling of Anna Sergeyeva), stands alone among the houses appearing around this time; it opened in 1922 at no. 54 rue Galilée, not far from the Champs Elysées. Little is known about the history of the house, although the former main conservator of the Musée de la Mode et du Costume, Guillaume Garnier, ranked it as one of the leading

Библиотека декоративных искусств, Париж

Архив автора. Париж

Библиотека декоративных искусств. Париж

enterprises of the Russian emigration. We were able to locate the only known design from this house in Billy Boy's magnificent collection in Lausanne. Judging from it, the level of dressmaking skill there was extraordinary. The extant evening dress of silk and lace is sewn according to all the rules of haute couture of the 1920s, and is notable for the execution of its inner and outer hand seams, choice of trim, and quality of fabric. The fate of this dress is interesting: it was acquired by its present owner in Moscow in the 1980s, where, apparently, it arrived in the baggage of émigrés repatriated from France.

With time, around 1938, the house of Anna Sergueeff expanded and moved to more spacious quarters, also near the Champs Elysées, at no. 45 rue Pierre Charron. We were able to locate one of Anna Sergueeff's clients, the actress Faina Zelinskaya from Baliev's cabaret La Chauve Souris. Elegant and attractive, Zelinskaya dressed well and became famous in Paris and New York in Baliev's popular skit "Katinka." She recalled: "I ordered dresses from Felix Yousoupoff and from Sergueeff. When I left Paris, Baliev told me, 'Ryzhik [Red] (since I was a redhead then), please take several of Sergueeff's designs with you

Архив автора. Париж

Библиотека декоративных искусств. Париж

Left: *Silk pajamas designed by the house of Mary Nowitzky, Paris, 1926.*

Above: *A drawing from* Vogue *magazine of a dress pajama designed by the house of Mary Nowitzky, Paris, September 1926.*

to New York.' And since we would travel there with wardrobe trunks, there was plenty of room. I went over to see her for lunch. Anna Sergeyeva was married to a prince. She had a marvelous salon, and she dressed me at a discount. I brought her dresses over to America without paying any duty. She even had a special mannequin with my measurements so that I could always get a dress without having a fitting."14

We should also add to the number of small houses founded by Russian émigrés the tailor Jacob Matline and the atelier Guenièvre, named after Queen Guinevere, the wife of the legendary King Arthur and the beloved of the knight Lancelot. This house, located near the Place Madeleine in Paris, was established by the Countess Alexandra Ostenburg, known in the fashion world by the name of Sasha Verola ("Sasha" is the diminutive of her first name and Verola is her last name by marriage), who was the daughter of Princess Oldenburg from

Above: Drawings from the magazine L'Art et la mode *of beachwear designed by the house of Mary Nowitzky, Paris, 1922.*

Below: An advertisement from Vogue *magazine for the house of Mary Nowitzky, Paris, 1926.*

PYJAMAS
VÊTEMENTS
DE SPORT ET
D'INTÉRIEUR

**MARY
NOWITZKY**

MONTRE SA COLLECTION D'HIVER
A PARTIR DU 27 JUILLET
82, RUE DES PETITS CHAMPS, PARIS
(PLACE VENDOME) TEL. GUTENBERG 58-52

402

St. Petersburg. Her daughter, the half-French Mary Madeleine Verola, who later married Count Alexander Mordvinov and became Countess Maria Mordvinova, worked as a model for the house; Irina Sergeyevna Pokrovskaya was one of the seamstresses.

The well-known professional Moscow seamstress Nikitina, the aunt of the Diaghilev ballerina Alise Nikitina, ran a small tailor's business in the 1920s on rue de Colisée not far from the Champs Elysées. Her clients were predominantly Americans who flooded Paris at the end of World War I.

We should mention the fashion house of Myrbor, which was among the important salons of fashion in Paris and which adopted a Russian name, a Russian sign, and the work of distinguished Russian artists—even though it was not owned by Russians. It was founded by Marie Cuttoli, the wife of a French senator, and it created designs for clothing and for interior design, such as rugs

211

based on the sketches of Picasso, Léger, Miró, and other artists.

Natalya Goncharova, one of the most prominent artists of the Russian emigration, was invited to work in the fashion department of Myrbor, where she created clothing designs for several seasons from 1922 to 1926. The author discovered several Myrbor designs preserved in the costume department of the Victoria and Albert Museum in London, which were apparently made following Goncharova's drawings since they are very similar to sketches she made for the house, which remain intact in a private collection in Paris. Among the things found in the collection are dresses, wraps, a blouse, and a coat, all of which are rare in their originality of conception and technique. They are abstract in ornamentation with pronounced Slavic colors; done in appliqué and produced in a manner reminiscent of the costumes of the Diaghilev venture. The entire collection is from the wardrobe of Emily Grigsby, a rich American who was a lioness of London society and who often dressed at the house of Myrbor.

The fashion house of Mary Nowitzky (the French spelling of her name) was also popular. Opening around 1924, it had a

405

sensational success with elegant silk pajamas, firmly establishing them in women's fashion of the 1920s. The garments from Nowitzky's house, where Vladimir Poretskii was director, were perfectly sewn and often decorated with hand-painted silk. The house also made jersey sweaters whose originality of trim and color combinations set them apart from those of other houses. The word "pajama" is derived from the Hindi word *pājāma* (meaning "leg garment"), and the house of Nowitzky used the Indian exoticism to its advantage. Nowitzky's success was extraordinary; the leading fashion magazines of the time—*Vogue, L'Officiel, Revue de la femme, L'Art et la mode*—devoted much space to her sweater designs, pajamas, and bathing suits. In early 1928, *Harper's Bazaar* wrote about the house of Nowitzky show: "In this collection, entirely devoted to sportswear, leisure wear and bathing apparel, we will note the amusing and original jackets with unevenly cut hems. These jackets drop down to the hipline, to the knees or are gored . . . and would never seem ordinary to the eye, well-defined or distinct.

"Another reason for interest in this collection is related to the unusual cut

Top: *Z.S. Rashevskaya, the morganatic wife of Grand Duke Boris Vladimirovich on the beach at Cannes. Photograph from the magazine* Fémina, *Paris, September 1931.*

Center: *Drawings from the magazine* L'Art et la mode *of bathing suits from the house of Mary Nowitzky, Paris, July 1930.*

Right: *A close relative of Rashevskaya on the beach in Cannes. Photograph from the magazine* Fémina, *Paris, September 1931.*

of the bathing pantaloons, whose width is created with pinched gathers that fan out from the waist.

"Most of the sportswear outfits and light dresses are made of printed Moroccan and Flamenco crepe, Ikatny silk and printed Ducharne silk with a pattern reminiscent of wool weaving, of patterned taffeta, and Kasha, a silk fabric from the house of Rodier of printed jersey, a natural or dyed silk and linen blend called shantung or georgette.

"The combinations of colors are notable for their brightness and fancifulness. They include white polka dots on a black or green field, yellow stripes on a grey background or pink ones on blue. One of her black pullovers was shown with a peach-colored skirt and three-quarter length coat of crepe georgette. Pajamas and negligees stand out, in particular, for their bold yet harmonious color combinations."[15]

Maria Novitskaya married Prince Victor Kochubei and in the 1930s emi-

Beachwear from the house of Mary Nowitzky, from Vogue *magazine, Paris, July 1927. Photo by George Hoyningen-Huene.*

grated to the United States; she began designing shoes and continued her business with enviable success. Novitskaya's competition among the Russian houses were the Melikov House of Pajamas and Lingerie and the small house of Maria Iodko, whose specialty was sportswear. In the field of fashion accessories, the leaders were the Isakoff house and the Volokhoff house, both of whom specialized in fashionable bags, purses, and gloves.

In the 1920s, Russian émigré houses of fashion began appearing in London. One small atelier called Nadya and Rina was opened by Princess Ekaterina Ivanovna Lobanova-Rostovskaya, née Shatyenstein, who at the age of twenty-one had married Prince Konstantin Anatolyevich Lobanov-Rostovsky, the son of Prince Anatoly Grigoryevich Lobanov-Rostovsky, a tsarist diplomat, and Chariklea

Rizo-Rangabe, a Greek woman from an old Byzantine princely family.

After emigrating from Russia with her small son Andrei, Princess Ekaterina Ivanovna first wound up in Malta, and only later made her way to London, where she opened her small fashion house with her friend Nadya Becker. The house specialized in embroidered summer dresses, and there are photographs showing Ekaterina Ivanova dressed in one while vacationing on Capri. The house of Nadya and Rina was closed when the princess died on January 25, 1927; however, Nadya Becker continued to sew and in 1946 created the wedding dress for Milbrough Walker, the English bride of Prince Andrei's son.

These ateliers, needlework workshops, and small fashion houses that sprang up everywhere Russians exiles settled, especially in Paris, became the backdrop against which emerged larger, more solid fashion enterprises such as Paul Caret, Yteb, and Irfe.

9

THE PAUL CARET HOUSE OF FASHION

The fashion house of Paul Caret operated from 1919 to 1929 with boutiques in London, Paris, Cannes, and Beaulieu. Lady Olga Nikolayevna Egerton, née Princess Lobanova-Rostovskaya, founded it and created the designs. Born in Russia in 1863 in the Lobanov-Rostovsky ancestral estate in the village of Lobanov, Yefremovsky district of the province of Tula, she was from an extensive and ancient noble family. The Lobanov-Rostovsky princes were descended from Rurik, the Scandinavian prince who settled in Russia in the middle of the ninth century. Prince Igor, Saint Vladimir of Kiev, and Vladimir Monomakh are among the Lobanov-Rostovskys' ancestors. One of their ancestors, Prince Yuri Vladimirovich Dolgoruky, became ruler of the principality of Rostov in the twelfth century; subsequently, Rostovsky princes ruled over Rostov from the thirteenth through the fifteenth centuries. Alexander Ivanovich was the last Rostovsky prince; he left Rostov in 1495. It was his son, Prince Ivan Alexandrovich, nicknamed Loban, who founded the Lobanov-Rostovsky line around the year 1500. From that time on, beginning with his son Prince Ivan Ivanovich Lobanov-Rostovsky, who fought against the Tatars, the entire line of descendants used this hyphenated name.

In 1860, at the age of thirty-four, Prince Nikolai Lobanov-Rostovsky married the noblewoman Anna Ivanovna Shablykina (Shenshina by her first marriage), and the couple had nine children, two of whom died as infants. Olga was

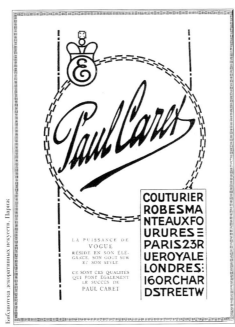

Opposite: *Maria Kieva, a variety-show actress, wearing a design by Paul Caret, Paris, 1925.*

Above: *An advertisement from* Vogue *magazine for the house of Paul Caret, Paris, 1923.*

the second eldest child and the first daughter. Her parents owned three estates: Lobanovo in the province of Tver where Olga was born; and the country estates of Khvorostovo, in the Toropovetsky district, and Lobanovskoye in the Dmitrovsky district of the Orlov province. On December 4, 1884, Princess Olga Nikolayevna married the nobleman Mikhail Mikhailovich Katkov, a Russian diplomat and secretary in the Russian Embassy in Lisbon. Eight years later, in 1892, she became a widow, and

in 1895 she married again, to Sir Harry Edwin Egerton, an English aristocrat she met in Europe. He was twenty-two years older than Olga Nikolayevna and had a sizeable fortune; he adored his wife and took her off to England.

Sir Egerton had been a member of the privy council of Great Britain and an ambassador in Rome. Upon returning to England, he retired from his affairs and lived with Olga Nikolayevna at Tatton, the family estate in Cheshire county. He died in 1916 during World War I, and Olga became a widow for the second time. Olga Nikolayevna Egerton, a lady of fifty-three at the time, with a large amount of inherited capital, decided to become involved in fashion. Her motives were altruistic: aware of the difficult situation of Russian women émigrés in London, she decided to help them and founded the House of Caret, renamed Paul Caret a year later. The name was based on the Egerton family motto "fair and square," which, translated into French, reads "*juste et carré.*" Lady Egerton changed the spelling of the latter word to "Caret," and then, inspired by the great fashion designer Paul Poiret, added the word "Paul" as the first name.

A French journalist wrote about the house's first seasons: "After a difficult beginning, the house has been so successful that, instead of closing it down when the Red Cross began helping Russian refugees in London, Lady Egerton continued her work. Due to her remarkable organizational abilities and the devotion of her co-workers, the

215

Библиотека „Ла Камбр. Брюссель.

CRÉATIONS DE

Paul Caret

23, Rue Royale, PARIS
16, Orchard Street, Portman Square, LONDRES

house overcame all its difficulties and achieved brilliant success. The firm enjoyed a well-earned reputation in England, and its founder decided that her place was in the center of the fashion marketplace. So in October 1921, she moved her fashion house to 222 rue de Rivoli in Paris. The London office became a branch office, and another one was opened in Cannes."[1]

Advertising for Paul Caret occupied more and more space on the pages of *Vogue* magazine from 1921 on. The collections were varied, fusing Paris chic, Russian expansiveness, and English taste, which attracted an extensive clientele to the house. Lady Egerton invited only Russians to work for her, trying to help them endure the difficult burden of living as refugees. Nikolai Mikhailovich Katkov, Olga Nikolayevna's son by her first husband, ran the business. His wife, Xyusha Katkova, became one of the house's leading models and, subsequently, one of the most

famous Russian models of the 1920s in Paris.

Paul Caret's style was unique and inimitable. Every client was given individual attention. Purity of line was maintained. Well-proportioned dresses with straight silhouettes, with an accented waistline on the hips, which was fashionable at the time, were often adorned with decorative embroidery or appliqués. Lady Egerton, who created the collection, used monochromatic silks, preferring black combined with gold trim or trim in a matching tone, such as embroidery in red beading on red muslin. Pearl or jade necklaces completed these smart and elegant dresses. Paul Caret's signature items were the so-called elegant evening "sortie-de-bal" wraps, which completed the low-cut decolleté ball gowns. They were trimmed with high velvet collars in the manner of boyar *kozyri* and were sewn of fabrics that matched the evening attire. Many fur wraps and articles trimmed with fur were also made.

216

PAUL CARET

PAUL CARET

PAUL CARET

Библиотека Ла Камбр, Брюссель.

Библиотека декоративных искусств, Париж.

Opposite and above: *Drawings from the French magazine* L'art et la mode *of Paul Caret's designs for older and full-figured women, 1922.*

Above right: *Lady Olga Nikolayevna Egerton, founder of the house of Paul Caret, Paris, mid-1920s.*

Below right: *An advertisement from* Vogue *magazine for the house of Paul Caret, Paris, 1923.*

The popularity of the Paul Caret label was so great that many celebrities of the day ordered their clothing exclusively from Lady Egerton's house. A photograph of the actress Jeanne Palerme in a Paul Caret dress appeared in the pages of the Paris *Vogue* magazine in 1923, and the Russian actress Maria Kieva, who was a success in Casino de Paris in New York, became the fashion house's "face." Advertisements announced that Maria Kieva dressed exclusively at the house of Paul Caret.

Always in step with the fashions of her time, and often ahead of them, in 1924 Lady Egerton began to show a

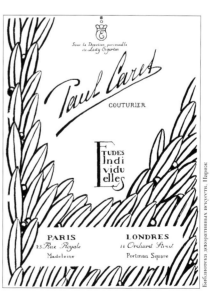

Библиотека декоративных искусств, Париж.

preference for the empire line combined with a long skirt, which lengthened the female silhouette considerably; these proportions did not become popular until the season of 1931–32. Delighted by this uncommon novelty, *Vogue* magazine wrote in 1924: "We find the empire line in several collections, but nowhere is it so clearly delineated as in Paul Caret. This design with a raised waistline in a brocade of old gold is almost a historical reconstruction: the skirt is slightly draped under the bust and gathered at the sides. The slit in the back reveals a tighter underskirt decorated with a floral border which is repeated on the ends of the matching scarf."[2]

Paul Caret revived trains for evening dresses, which were an evident novelty in the fashions of the 1920s. We see them in Lady Edgerton's designs as early as 1922, whereas it was not until 1937 that they became fashionable in Paris. The best fashion illustrators worked for Lady Edgerton, including Etienne Drian, one of the founders of Art Deco.

Reporting on the collections of the Paris fashion houses in 1924, *Vogue* wrote: "The collection from the House of Paul Caret leaves an impression of great simplicity in combination with subdued harmonious colors. Designs "for the street" are simple in tone and line. Evening coats of luxurious, embroidered fabrics and evening attire and dresses are draped with graceful, soft folds. Ravishing fabrics are used for the evening wear. Many of the dresses are lengthened by trains either at the back or on the sides.

Above: *An illustration by Etienne Drian from* Vogue *magazine advertising the house of Paul Caret, Paris, 1923.*

Opposite: *Maria Kieva, the "face" of Paul Caret in* Vogue *magazine, Paris, June, 1926.*

218

Below: *An advertisement from* Vogue *magazine for the house of Paul Caret, Paris, 1924.*

Right: *A Russian model in a design from the house of Paul Caret, Paris, November 1926. Photo by George Hoyningen-Huene for* Vogue *magazine.*

Библиотека декоративных искусств. Париж

Библиотека декоративных искусств. Париж

FABIOLA, FRAC et FUGITIVE, trois robes de la collection Paul CARET,
qui soulignent de la plus spirituelle façon trois types féminins très divers.

PAUL CARET
222. RUE DE RIVOLI
P A R I S

Above left: *Drawings from* Vogue *magazine of dress designs from the house of Paul Caret, Paris, May 1928.*

Above right: *Drawings by the illustrator Dorland for* Vogue *magazine of dress designs from the house of Paul Caret, Paris, October 1926.*

"The predominant colors are green, brown and black, in any case, for day-time wear. For evening, printed velvets, patterned brocades are enlivened by an even richer palette of colors. Among the fabrics we find, as with other houses this season, varieties of ottomans and velvets, crepes, satins and lightweight wools. For evening, a great many brocades and velvets, printed or in solid colors."[3]

With time, Lady Egerton's collections became increasingly diverse. When she turned sixty, she began including outfits for older women in her collections—an unbelievable success. The French *Vogue*, which repeatedly ranked Paul Caret among the most prestigious fashion houses of Paris, wrote in 1926: "Simple, well-cut and austerely finished dresses are part of this collection. Another group of designs, decoratively trimmed for the most part, especially suits older women. This category includes certain embroidered dresses. . . . Simpler dresses emphasize the waistline. In most cases, the skirts are flared at the bottom, either gored or with straight pleats. In addition to embroidery, metal ornaments, lace, bows, edging, jabots and braids are used as decorative motifs.

"Dresses embroidered with beads and sequins in colors ranging from light blue, pink, green to white, will be especially enchanting for evening. The wraps over them are mostly in brocade trimmed with fur."[4]

When Renée Marguerite's novel *La garçonne* was popular, Paul Caret was the first among the Russian fashion houses to incorporate motifs from men's clothes, taking advantage of the androgynous silhouette that was fashionable in the 1920s. In 1926 Lady Edgerton created a dress-suit in black satin that she called "Tailcoat," to be worn with bobbed hair slicked back in male fashion like Francesca Gahl's haircuts in the film *Peter*. From that season on, Paul Caret favored a "Charleston" line in its evening wear, with a shortened hemline and dropped waist.

Lady Egerton showed her collections twice a year: the summer line in February and the winter line in July. She also presented regular showings of her designs in her luxuriously appointed salons on rue de Rivoli. Her success in Paris greatly increased the house's reputation everywhere: her designs sold well at the London branch of Paul Caret at no. 16 Orchard Street; in Cannes, she opened a boutique in the Carleton Hotel, which was known for its high prices and choice clientele; and even opened a third boutique in the resort town of Beaulieu.

In 1928, French *Vogue* was still writing about Paul Caret's well-deserved reputation: "This collection is particularly distinguished by the excellence with which all the evening dresses are created. They are sewn of black,

« JAVANAIS ». ENSEMBLE EN SHANTUNG « CHEN-SI » DOUBLÉ DE CRÊPE IMPRIMÉ « JONQUE ».

PAUL CARET

TISSUS PREVOST DE LYON

Left: *A detail from the cover of the magazine* L'art et la mode *of a drawing of a dress from the house of Paul Caret, with its fabric from the Lyons factory Prevost, March 1929.*

Above: *Gali Bajenova models a dress from the house of Paul Caret, Paris, 1929. Photo by George Hoyningen-Huene for* Vogue *magazine.*

Opposite above: *Gali Bajenova, the former model who became head of the fashion house of Paul Caret, renaming it Elmis.*

Opposite below: *The building in which the atelier Paul Caret was located, Paris. Photo by Alexandre Vassiliev, 1997.*

beige or unbleached lace (made by the house of de Marescot and de Prévost), as well as from printed marquisette, lamé brocade, muslin, satin or very rich-colored silk satin from the house of Bianchini. These dresses retain a long and straight line to the hips, on which a stiff flounce cut on the bias is placed, which sometimes extends down to the floor in the form of a long side train. Among the designs for the young, you will find pressed frills and little short gathered flounces placed horizontally in front and rounded in the back.

"A group of evening dresses in printed crepe from the house of Rodier is presented with coats in black, navy, brown or beige which are lined in the same crepe fabric as the dresses.

"Several coat-dresses are done in blue-grey or dark grey flannel. Several sportswear jackets and suits are made of printed flamenka alpaca or silk corduroy from the house of Bianchini. The preferred colors for sportswear are yel-

low, green, and grey and a range of natural hues."[5]

During the season of 1928, Lady Egerton's age—she had just turned sixty-five—began to take its toll. She grew fatigued and her son Nikolai Mikhailovich took charge of the house's

business. For a time, the famous model of the 1920s Gali Bajenova had modeled Paul Caret designs; she was a former saleswoman at Chanel and director of Paul Poiret's Rosine perfume shop in Deauville. Seeing the creative and administrative abilities of this beautiful woman, Lady Egerton proposed that Gali Bajenova become the new mistress of the fashion house, and Gali agreed. In 1929 the house of Paul Caret nominally ceased its existence in name and was renamed Elmis (an abbreviation of Bazhenova's Kabardinian name, Elmiskhan Hagondokova).

The house of Elmis stayed at the same address as Paul Caret—222 rue de Rivoli. The entire staff—fifty seamstresses and three main cutters—worked for the new house. Unfortunately, the house of Elmis did not survive the economic depression and was sold in 1931 to George Ochmiansky, who ran the business until 1936. Lady Egerton departed for England, then for America, where she died on January 3, 1947.

10
THE TAO HOUSE OF FASHION

The Russian fashion house TAO was established in Paris in 1921 and lasted until 1928. The house was founded by Princess Maria Sergeyevna Trubetskaya, Maria Mitrofanovna Annenkova, and Princess Lyubov Petrovna Obolenskaya, who created its name from the first letters of their family names.

These three aristocratic women, who at one time had been radiant figures in Moscow high society, originally opened their fashion establishment on rue St. Honore, and, after expanding in 1923, moved it to no. 32 avenue de l'Opera, opposite the famous fashion house Paquin. With the help of the founders' daughters and the former model Countess Belevskaya, we were able to reconstruct the history of TAO.

Princess Maria Sergeyevna Trubetskaya was born in Tula on August 25, 1886, to the family of Senator Prince Sergei Alexeyevich Lopukhin and Aleksandra Pavlovna Baranova. Like many young Russian girls from good families, she learned to sew and embroider at an early age. She married Prince Vladimir Petrovich Obolensky, the brother of Princess Lyubov Petrovna Obolenskaya (née Princess Trubetskaya). These women spent their youth on the Trubetskoi estate near Moscow, and Princess Maria Sergeyevna also lived in the Trubetskoi house on Prechistenka Street in Moscow.

Princess Lyubov Petrovna Obolenskaya was born in 1888 in Moscow to the family of Peter Nikolaevich Trubetskoi, a member of the nobility and the

Opposite: *Princess Lyubov Petrovna Obolenskaya, Princess Maria Sergeyevna Trubetskaya, and Maria Mitrofanovna Annenkova in the fashion house of TAO, Paris, 1926.*

Above: *An advertisement for the house of TAO, Paris, 1929.*

owner of the picturesque estate Uzkoye along the Kaluzhskaya Road near Moscow, as well as the Kazatskoye estate and a distillery on the Don River. He was married to Princess Alexandra Vladimirovna Obolenskaya, a member of one of the oldest Russian princely families. Princess Lyubov Petrovna Trubetskaya married Prince Alexei Alexandrovich Obolensky, an officer of the

Horse Guards and a distant relative on her mother's side. Lyubov Petrovna and Alexei Alexandrovich had five children: a son and four daughters. At the beginning of World War I, in order to be closer to her husband, Lyubov Petrovna became a nurse in a military hospital.

During the revolution the Trubetskoi and Obolensky families moved to the Crimea, and then sailed to Constantinople on the ship *Hannover* along with other Russian refugees.

During the first winter in Constantinople, and then later in Paris, the Obolenskys lived on the money from the sale of the diamonds they had managed to smuggle out hidden in a doll's head. The third co-owner of the house of TAO, Maria Mitrofanovna Annenkova, a Moscow amateur painter and a friend of the Trubetskoi and Obolensky families, also emigrated with them to Constantinople.

As soon as the three ladies arrived in Paris, after a forced departure from Turkey, they began plans for setting up a fashion atelier. Lyubov Petrovna took sewing and cutting courses to better acquaint herself with the business. The knowledge she gained there helped her immensely in her future work in the fashion world. Her husband, Prince Alexei Alexandrovich, sang and played the violin well, and she accompanied him beautifully on the piano, since she had studied music with Professor Leschetinzky as a child. The prince's musical abilities stood him in good stead in his émigré years: he often performed at

musical soirees, and Nellie Melba, a famous Australian prima donna with a
marvelous soprano voice, heard him at
one of these performances. She advised
the prince to take voice lessons from
Henri Roussel in Monte Carlo and
promised to make him a member of her
touring opera company. Prince Obolensky's musical career subsequently influenced the course of TAO's affairs.

At TAO Maria Annenkova, who was
artistically gifted and had a splendid
sense of color, worked exclusively as
the creator of designs. Maria Alexeyevna Yanushevskaya, née Countess
Belevskaya, a model for TAO, recalls:
"TAO's colors were very beautiful—
nothing loud. There wasn't much too
much imagination in the designs, but
there was a great deal of good taste. The
designs were often trimmed in fur. There
were simple dresses for thin women, and
entirely different ones for the fat Russian
merchants' wives who had fled Russia."

Annenkova drew the sketches for the
designs, working closely with the main
cutter, Madame Restori, who came from
Madeleine Vionnet's atelier. Annenkova

Above: *A portrait of Princess
Obolenskaya by Savely Sorin, 1918.*

Below: *The salon at the house of TAO
on avenue de l'Opéra, Paris, c. 1926.*

Opposite: *Countess Maria Belevskaya
in a pale pink silk evening dress
designed by the house of TAO, Paris,
February 1926. Photo by Arthur O'Neill
for* Vogue *magazine.*

went out with her clients often and,
since she was a friend of Countess Belevskaya's mother, she invited the young
and charming Maria Belevskaya, Sver-
beeva by her first husband, to work as
TAO's permanent model.

Maria Belevskaya recalls: "TAO began as a business among friends. For example, at 4 o'clock, everyone sat down
to have tea. My husband Sverbeev would
always come to meet me. He feared my
work as a model then and didn't allow
me to wear makeup. Initially, business
was bad at TAO, it was difficult to sell
dresses. We had no inexpensive dresses.
The atelier was quite small, no more
than ten people. TAO had another model besides me, a nice Russian brunette
who soon left France."

The choice of Belevskaya as the leading model was impeccable. A tall blonde
with fine features and marvelous porcelain white skin—a face reminiscent of a
cameo—she embodied the classical type
of a Russian noble girl. It's no wonder,
since she was the descendant of one of
the most distinguished families of old
Russia. She was the great-granddaughter

and direct descendant of the poet Zhukovsky, and her godmother, Grand Duchess Elizaveta Feodorovna, was the sister of Alexandra Feodorovna, the last Russian empress. At first Belevskaya did not know how to walk like a model, but Princess Meshcherskaya, who later became a well-known model herself, taught her this skill.

Maria Annenkova conducted the fittings, Princess Lyubov Petrovna kept the books, tracking accounts and bills, and Princess Maria Sergeyevna Trubetskaya supervised the sewing.

Countess Musina-Pushkina worked at TAO as a saleswoman for several months and Maria Belevskaya's sister also worked at TAO attending to the clients as business steadily improved. TAO's clientele was, for the most part, international. French and English women ordered a good deal, delighted at the opportunity to be dressed by "real Russian princesses." There were many clients from Poland, the wives of members of Pilsudski's government, who were still wealthy then and owned vast estates. TAO even received orders from

Архив Марии Янушевской-Белевской, Париж

227

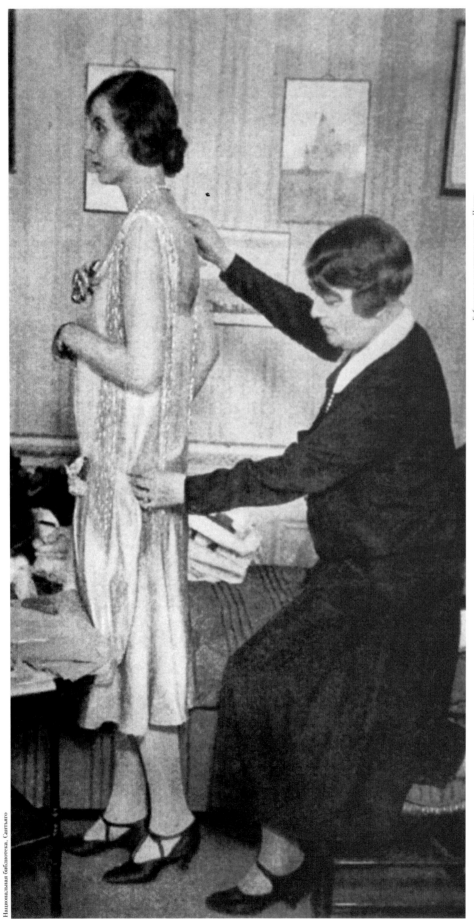

Above: *Maria Annenkova, Paris, 1926.*

Left: *Maria Annenkova measuring a dress worn by Maria Belevskaya in the house of TAO, Paris.*

the highest rung of Polish society—Princess Radziwill.

It was TAO's impeccable taste that distinguished its elegant garments from those produced by other ateliers. Maria Annenkova introduced "Russian style" in TAO's first collections, beginning in the season of 1923 when folkloric motifs were becoming popular. At that time dresses with a straight silhouette and dropped waist (which softened women's shapes) were fashionable; retaining this stylish cut, Maria Annenkova adorned the dresses with Russian embroidery in warm tones. The embroidery was done according to traditional patterns, which assured the success of the garments. At Annenkova's suggestion, TAO created suede cloaks trimmed in fur—a guide to fashion houses published in Paris in 1925 mentions that TAO produced dresses that were trimmed with suede and painted by hand.

According to Belevskaya, all the articles produced by TAO bore the fashion house's name; but unfortunately, after many years of searching in the mu-

Above: *Princess Obolenskaya in the salon at the house of TAO, Paris, c. 1926.*

Below: *Dresses and coats designed by the house of TAO in the salon on avenue de l'Opéra, Paris, c. 1926.*

seums and collections of Europe and America, the author was unable to find a single dress with such a label. In addition, there are very few advertising materials to be found about the house. Outside of TAO's frequent advertisements in the programs for Maria Kuznetsova's Private Russian Opera in Paris, we discovered only one significant piece about the house: it was published in the August 26, 1926 issue of the Argentine magazine *El Hogar*.

The photographs published in this magazine convey the domestic atmosphere of the house with its stylish and comfortable nineteenth-century mahogany furniture, wood paneling, cozy floral curtains, photographs and paintings on the walls, and a small shop window with perfumes and costume jewelry. On display are the fashionable necklaces and elegant bottles of perfume that were sold at TAO. As for the three owners of the house, they look innately dignified in their simple and comfortable dark silk dresses.

Fashion magazines often covered

Библиотека Ла Камбр. Брюссель

TAO, in particular the Paris magazine *Eve*. The February 1926 issue of French *Vogue* ran an oval photograph by the famous Arthur O'Neill of Maria Belevskaya modeling a pale pink silk evening dress with pleated insets and a gored skirt finished with a wide silver lamé belt and decorated at the hemline and neckline in phosphorescent paints, which created a stunning impression at parties.

TAO's salon and atelier were located on the third floor in large and spacious apartments dating from Napoleon III's time. As the house's fame grew, wealthy American clients also began dropping in. It was the 1920s, the depression had not yet begun, and people didn't stop to think about money but lived for the moment, spending merrily and without restraint. Most Russian émigrés, of course, lived differently, working hard and counting their daily earnings. However, as Prince Dmitrii Pavlovich Dolgoruky wrote, "Very different in this respect were certain aristocratic ladies, who did not fear opening fashion workshops in Paris and were able to attract English and American clients."[2]

Princess Obolenskaya's sister, Countess Sofya Petrovna Lamsdorf (née Princess Trubetskaya), created women's lingerie of exceptional quality for TAO. Around 1927 Princess Obolenskaya set off for New York with a collection of TAO dresses and lingerie—it all sold out. Shortly before, Prince Obolensky, who had been studying singing in Monte Carlo, moved the children to his place in Monaco. Princess Obolenskaya was so involved with TAO's business affairs

Above: *Drawings from the magazine* L'art et la mode *of TAO designs worn by France Ellis in the play* Rolls Royce *at the Maturin Theater, Paris, April 1929.*

Opposite, top left: *Princess Obolenskaya, New York, 1928.*

Opposite, top right and below: *The building at no. 32 avenue de l'Opèra, Paris, in which the house of TAO was located. Photo by Alexandre Vassiliev, 1997.*

Архив князя Сергея Трубецкого. США

Архив автора. Париж

that she rarely visited. After a year of study with Professor Henri Roussel, the prince's voice was completely ready for the opera. The soprano Nellie Melba kept her word and took Obolensky on tour, first to Australia, then to the United States, where Professor Walter Damrosch heard him and became interested in his method. He invited the prince to give voice lessons at the Juilliard School of Music in New York. A decision was made: Obolensky liked the United States very much and, since there was very lit-

tle chance of returning to Russia, he sent for his entire family to come to New York from Paris. Thus, TAO was closed down in 1928.

Soon after moving to New York, Princess Obolenskaya opened a store on Park Avenue specializing in first-class lingerie and small items for the boudoir—her sister, Countess Lamesdorf, continued to sew for the New York store. The business was so prosperous that the princess ran it for forty years. She was able not only to support her family, but to help other people and took part in charitable receptions in the 1930s. Obolenskaya loved musical concerts, often holding them in her home until she was very old. She died at the age of ninety-two in August 1980, and is buried at the family plot in the Mount Olive cemetery in Queens, New York.

Princess Trubetskaya and Annenkova remained in Paris. Trubetskaya sewed dresses her entire life and continued to have loyal clients. Countess St. Hippolyte, the daughter of Princess Trubetskaya recalls, "Mother sewed all my dresses and she embroidered. She was very good at handiwork. She sewed for her children and her grandchildren." Trubetskaya was truly in her element satin stitching, in particular embroider-

ing icons. She satin stitched *khorugvy* (saints' images on banners used in Orthodox church processions) for the St. Sergei Church on rue de Crimée, which had been established with the assistance of Grand Duchess Maria Pavlovna. In addition, she worked as the leading saleswoman from 1928–35 at the fashion house of Augusta Bernard on rue St.-Honoré. Princess Maria Sergeyevna Trubetskaya died in the Russian Home for the Aged in Chellè, near Paris, on June 27, 1976, at the age of ninety.

Архив автора. Париж

11
YTEB HOUSE OF FASHION

Yteb was a Russian fashion house that operated in Paris from 1922 to 1933. The founder of the house and its head designer was Betty Buzzard, née Baroness Hoyningen-Huene, who, prior to her exile, was a lady-in-waiting to Empress Alexandra Feodorovna. "Yteb" is the proprietor's name spelled backwards.

Baroness Elizaveta Bertoldovna Hoyningen-Huene was descended on her father's side from an ancient Baltic baronial family that emigrated from Prussia to Kurland, Latvia, at the time of the Crusades. The Hoyningen-Huene family received a barony in 1620; however, the title was not recognized in Russia until the reign of Alexander II, when the tsar issued a special decree giving the family Russian citizenship. Between the years 1864 and 1866, the Hoyningen-Huenes were elevated to the rank of barons of the Russian Empire. The family seat was the Navvast country estate in Estonia, comprising a long low house with many service structures and a well-organized farm.

Betty's father, Baron Bertold Niko-laevich Hoyningen-Huene, was an officer in the Russian Army, a serious and stern man who occupied the high position of principal equerry to Emperor Nicolas II. Horses were the baron's passion. Even at his far-away estate at Navvast, he maintained first-class stables and a collection of carriages imported from Russia, England, France, and America. The baron saw little of his children: his duties placed him in charge of more

Opposite: *A beachwear design by the house of Yteb, Paris, June 1928. Photo by George Hoyningen-Huene for* Vogue *magazine.*

Above: *The house of Yteb logo. Drawing by George Hoyningen-Huene, 1923.*

than 1,000 subordinates, and an enormous amount of his time was occupied by the imperial family's constant trips, horse races, and the tsar's stables.

Betty's mother, the American beauty Anne van Ness Lothrop, met the baron in St. Petersburg, where she had moved in 1885 from Grosse Pointe, Michigan. She was the daughter of George Lothrop, the minister plenipotentiary of the United States to the court of Alexander III. Thus Betty, her sister Helena (Hala), and her younger brother George (Georgy)

belonged to the highest social circles in both the old world of Russia and the new world of the United States.

Baron Hoyningen-Huene's family led a genteel and easy life in St. Petersburg. Their apartments were on Palace Square, and Betty and Hala spent much time dancing cotillions, mazurkas, and polonaises at society balls. Betty's mother was celebrated for her elegance—a correspondent for the *Sankt-Peterburzhskie vedomosti* [St. Petersburg News] wrote of her in the 1880s: "At the third ball, or rather *soirée-dansante* given yesterday, the 30th December, at the hospitable house of the American minister, all the *haut-ton* of St. Petersburg was assembled. . . . Elegance reigned everywhere and the hospitality of the host could be seen at every step. . . . In the salon the guests were met by Miss Lothrop, the elder daughter of the minister. The young hostess was dressed in a charming toilette of sea-water color, which showed itself through the light tulle trimming."[1]

A detailed description of the life of the American envoy's family in St. Petersburg has come down to us through the letters of the minister's wife, Elmira van Ness Lothrop, which were published in Philadelphia in 1910. Anne had apparently become acquainted with the young, handsome Baron Hoyningen-Huene at the horse races. Elmira describes a colorful scene, with a parade of horses and various contests: "They have every year a Carousel, in which twelve or fourteen ladies and gentlemen ride. The *manège* was beautifully decorated

with helmets, cuirasses, flags. . . . Ought I to be so bold as to admit that Anne, in the words of many among the officers and the spectators around us, jumped best of all the women?"[2]

As children, Betty, Helena, and George often took vacations abroad. They traveled in Italy and France and visited some of the celebrated spas of the early twentieth century, such as Bad-Karetznach in Germany and St. Moritz in Switzerland. They were imbued with a love of beauty from early childhood, and studied Russian art and sculpture of classical antiquity at the State Russian Museum (then known as the Alexander III Museum) and the State Hermitage Museum.

Both sisters graduated from the Institute for Noblewomen and became maids-in-waiting to Empress Alexandra Feodorovna. George attended high school during this time and spent summers with his sisters at the family estate Navvast in Estonia, where there was a spacious, well-built country house with its own bakery, mill, threshing floor, sauna, and a village for the domestic servants and local peasants. The country estate had two parks, one in the English style and the other in the French style, along with tennis courts, a croquet court, and, naturally, stables with excellent horses.

When World War I began, Betty and Helena, taken with the patriotic fervor that gripped all of St. Petersburg, went

to work as nurses in a military hospital. There, Baroness Betty Hoyningen-Huene—pretty, splendidly educated, fluent in several languages, and possessed of impeccable taste—met S. N. Buzzard, a colonel in the British Army during the war. He was a professional soldier, a chevalier of the order of the Legion of Honor. The young Baroness fell in love, married him, and took the name Betty Buzzard.

To escape the war, Betty's mother, Baroness Anne Hoyningen-Huene took fourteen-year-old George to Yalta, where the family owned a house. George studied in Yalta until the revolution began. The Dowager Empress Maria Feodorovna also settled in the Crimea after leaving Kiev, and Baroness Anne Hoyningen-Huene paid her a number of visits. The entire Hoyningen-Huene family was soon arrested on suspicion of espi-

onage, but friends intervened, and they were released. Feeling uneasy even in the Crimea, Anne decided to return with her son to Petrograd, where, with the intercession of the American ambassador to the Kerensky government, she received permission to leave Russia.

Anne and George reached London after traveling by land across Finland, Sweden, and Norway, avoiding the Baltic and North Seas, which were full of minefields and military action. Baron Bartold Hoyningen-Huene managed to leave Russia shortly thereafter. All the family's property was expropriated during the Bolshevik Revolution, and the baron, disguised as a peasant, got to the

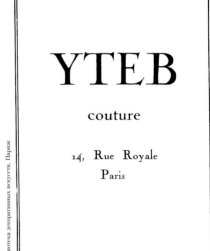

YTEB

couture

14, Rue Royale
Paris

Above left: *Betty Buzzard, or, as she was known in Paris, "Madame Yteb," c. 1925.*

Above right: *An advertisement for the house of Yteb, 1923–24.*

Left: *A drawing from* Jardin des modes *of a dress and coat ensemble designed by the house of Yteb, Paris, 1925.*

Opposite, top left: *An advertisement for the house of Yteb, 1923–24.*

Opposite, bottom left: *A drawing from the magazine* Paris-élégant *of a silk summer dress designed by the house of Yteb, July 1925.*

Opposite, right: *A drawing by Francis from* Vogue *magazine of checked summer outfits designed by the house of Yteb, Paris, April 1925.*

234

235

border with a single suitcase. Betty and her husband had left the country even earlier.

The family received support from their American relatives in England: part of the family savings had been prudently held in American banks. George, then eighteen years old, was sent to a boys' school in the county of Surrey. Deeply affected by the civil war going on in Russia and believing in the possibility of order being restored there, he enlisted in the British Expeditionary Corps as a Russian translator. With the British, George wound up in southern Russia—in Batum, Ekaterinodar, Taganrog, and Tsaritsyn. In 1920 the young baron contracted typhoid fever at Novorossiisk and almost died of the dreadful disease, which was killing so many people in those years. He was evacuated to London and from there to France, where his entire family gathered in Cannes, on the Côte d'Azur.

By this point only work could save the exiles. Betty and Helena did needlework from home. About this time, 1918, the talented young fashion designer Robert Piguet, the son of a Swiss banker, moved to Paris; he opened his fashion house on avenue Montaigne two years later, and Helena went to work there as a seamstress. Seeing the success of Piguet, who, incidentally, became one of the classic figures in Parisian couture, Betty, with the aid and support of her husband, decided to open a Russian fashion house. She named it after herself, but in an encrypted form. Betty began her enterprise very modestly, in a small bare flat on the Left Bank. Her first assistants were Russian refugees who, like herself, needed some kind of work.

Above: *A drawing by George Hoyningen-Huene for* Vogue *magazine of an evening dress designed by the house of Yteb, Paris, October 1926.*

Right: *An advertisement for the house of Yteb in* Vogue *magazine, Paris, 1925.*

Opposite: *A drawing by George Hoyningen-Huene in* Vogue *magazine advertising the house of Yteb, Paris, June 1925.*

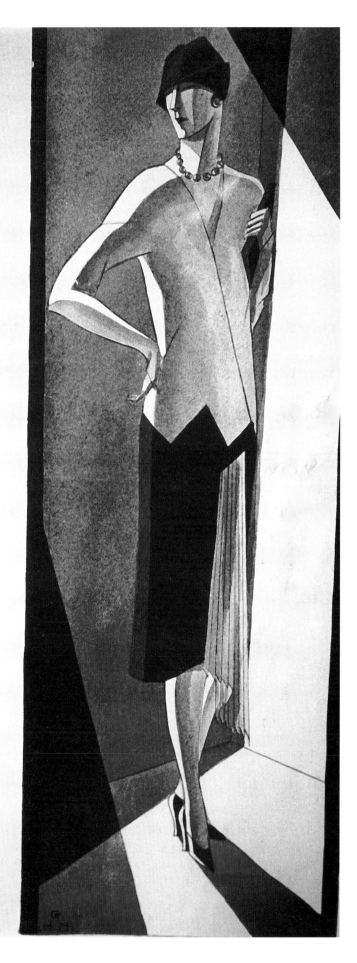

Opposite: *A drawing by R. Just for* Vogue *magazine of an evening dress designed by the house of Yteb, Paris, December 1925.*

Above: *A drawing by George Hoyningen-Huene in* Vogue *magazine advertising the house of Yteb, Paris, October 1925.*

Right: *A drawing by George Hoyningen-Huene in* Vogue *magazine of a cocktail dress designed by the house of Yteb, Paris, August 1925.*

A contemporary wrote of the house of Yteb's first steps: "Extremely capable, with outstanding artistic vision, the proprietress of the house selflessly took up sewing. Besides, she was always up to date on all the whims and demands of fashion."[3]

Betty wanted to understand all the details and learn the secrets of mastering the fashion business. She did not shun even the most mundane jobs, and when her modest business began producing tangible results, she had already acquired considerable experience in needlework. Once she amassed the necessary funds and a small circle of clients, she decided to move her business to what in those days was the center of fashionable Paris; in 1922 she opened her establishment at no. 14 rue Royale (now home to the headquarters of L'Oréal cosmetics). Success ensued with lightning speed.

George Hoyningen-Huene, who had been working as a translator and a movie extra, assumed an active role in the affairs of the business. Artistically gifted, he had loved to draw since childhood, and Betty proposed to him that he illustrate Yteb's advertisements and help design their garments. George worked for Yteb for several years, starting in 1923, creating many vivid, memorable illustrations for fashion magazines. He studied drawing at La Grande Chaumiere and Colarossi studios, and, on his sister's advice, studied at the cubist artist André Lhote's studio, which was famous in the 1920s. Two other Russian artists studied with Lhote during this period: Tamara Lempicka, who became a fashionable society portraitist of the Art Deco era, and Paul Tchelichew, the future luminary of the Paris art world. Under the influence of his studies with Lhote, George designed a cubist logo for the house of Yteb.

In 1923 Betty Buzzard adopted the name Madame Yteb so as to avoid possible misunderstandings with clients, dressmakers, and suppliers. The Art Deco style required simplicity: abbreviating names was fashionable.

A French commercial review wrote

Opposite: *Nina von Hoyer, a model for the house of Yteb, Paris, c. 1926.*

Above: *Maria Efremova, a Russian dramatic actress in a gold lamé dress from the house of Yteb, Paris, 1923. Photo by Vladimir Rehbinder.*

of Yteb: "From the outset, its designs have been brilliantly successful, and the circle of its illustrious clientele has grown with each passing year. Mention must also be made of Madame Yteb's kindness in attracting many of her fellow Russians who, like she, have been forced to earn a living by working."[4]

Yteb was a truly Russian house: almost the entire staff, from the seamstresses and salespeople to the models, was Russian. The first Yteb designs to gain popularity were in the "Russian style." One design from the 1923 season attracted attention at the Chantilly races: a dress in the Byzantine Russian style with shoulder straps and embroidery down the center. This kind of pseudo-historical design was an attempt to re-create the costumes of the Russian ball held at the Winter Palace in February 1903. The design was most reminiscent of the gown worn to the ball by Grand Duchess Xenia Alexandrovna, Princess Irina Yousoupoff's mother. After successfully attracting attention with its ancient Russian exoticism, Yteb became one of the great promoters of Russian style in fashion.

To popularize its collections, Yteb followed the example of other houses and invited famous actresses to pose in its dresses. Madame Yteb brought in Maria Efremova, a former Moscow Art Theater actress, who was performing in Paris at Paul Poiret's Oasis Theater. She was popular in France for her performances in Nikita Baliev's La Chauve Souris cabaret at the Fémina Theater in Paris. In Russia she had performed in *The Bluebird*, *The Living Corpse*, *The Brothers Karamazov*, and *Nikolai Stavrogin* at the Moscow Art Theater, and substituted for Olga Knipper-Chekov in Ivan Turgenev's *Where It's Thin Is Where It Tears*, working onstage with the celebrated Olga Gzovskaya. In Paris, Maria Efremova not only appeared in Baliev's cabaret but also established her own cabaret theater, the *Balaganchik*, with the actress Camille Desmoulins. The scenes in which they "re-created Russia" were a great success with Parisians. As an advertisement for Yteb, Maria Efremova posed in a gold lace dress embroidered with cut-glass imitation gems for the Russian photographer Vladimir Rehbinder, who was well known in 1920s Paris. A gold turban in a splendid brocade gave the picture an exotic flavor.

Yteb's successes in 1923 were so incontestable that Madame Yteb opened a branch in Cannes, at no. 1 rue Grand-Hotel. The fashion magazine advertisements in those days generally occupied half a page, indicating the specialty of the house: dresses, coats, knitwear, or furs. In 1924, sport clothes appeared in the Yteb collection: in the October issue of Paris *Vogue* we find two photographs of Georgian Princess Chalikova (Chalikashvili) wearing a golf dress by Yteb. The dress was brown with a pleated skirt made of the soft woolen fabric known as "*kasha.*" Another design, a woolen winter dress with a fur stand-up collar and lapels, was a veritable fantasy on a Russian peasant caftan called an *armyak.* It was shown with a cloche hat in panne velvet by the Felix Deca house.

The designs in the 1924 winter collection had simplified lines, often with fur trim along the hem or on the cuffs of outer garments. Many Parisian houses during the first half of the 1920s used a combination of fabric and fur, a fashion trend that unquestionably originated in Russia.

Beginning in 1925, the Yteb style changed radically. Fanciful and exotic elements were discarded, and the house presented designs with a straight silhouette that were austere, while retaining a charm and elegance. Like Chanel, the Yteb house increasingly addressed women's everyday wear: a necessity in the wardrobe of working women in the new era. The strong influence of Baron George Hoyningen-Huene's graphic style is evident in the geometric simplicity of the trim. The illustrations and drawings he made for Yteb in 1925 were unusually expressive. Today there is no doubt that Hoyningen-Huene's drawings and photographs made an enormous contribution—equal to Erté's—to the aesthetic of the new style.

Europe was passionately in love with American jazz during the post–World War I period. Its energetic rhythms impelled one to dance, and the availability of gramophones and radios poured oil on the flames of this raging passion. The new dances—ragtime, the foxtrot, and the Charleston—were enthusiastically accepted by women, and the new lifestyle dictated changes in apparel. Skirts were shortened even for evening dresses. There were more women than men after the war, which made for bitter competition among the ladies, many of whom tried to please by baring their boyish bodies ever more revealingly.

Naturally, Yteb echoed the general rage for short dresses by making stylish embroidered garments with dropped waistlines, sometimes trimmed with pearl beads. For accessories, Yteb showed sheer embroidered silk scarves and luxurious *sorties-de-bal* with fur collars *à la boyar.* In order to attract an international clientele, Yteb began to use world celebrities in its advertising. A 1925 Yteb advertisement in *Vogue* featured a drawing by Baron Hoyningen-Huene of the famous British dramatic actress Dorothy Dickson, star of the Royal Theater in London. The success of his drawings for Yteb brought him many new commissions. Fashion magazines competed for him fiercely, and he sold a series of illustrations to other prestigious publications such as *Harper's Bazaar, Women's Wear,* and *Jardin des Modes.*

Most of Yteb's employees had emigrated from Russia to Paris in the early 1920s, and fortunately, we have detailed information about many of them. For example, Baroness Nina Vladimirovna von Medem sewed evening gowns at Yteb for two years. Her husband had once been a chamber page to Empress Maria Feodorovna at Tsarskoe Selo and had fought as a volunteer in the Russo-Japanese War. Baroness von Medem arrived in Paris from Constantinople in 1922 with her daughters Kira and

Lyolya, who later became professional models. The two sisters, each called Princess Paley, also worked at Yteb for a short time.

Yteb's leading model was Sofia Nosovich, an energetic, striking woman with an amazing figure. In Russia she had fought in the White Army against the Bolsheviks, was arrested and imprisoned, and, miraculously, escaped. Nosovich retained her interest in politics as an émigré. She suffered greatly over the disappearance of a member of her family, General Kutepov, who was kidnaped on the orders of the GPU by two Soviet-recruited agents—the White General Skoblin and the well-known singer Plevitskaya. Sofia Nosovich joined the French Resistance during World War II and was decorated for heroism. She was a first-class model, but never spoke a word of English, which was required when working with British and American clients, of whom Yteb had many.

We were able to find one of the first Yteb models, Baroness Elena Sergeyevna von Tiesenhausen, who joined the house around 1925. Her life and work in the Paris fashion industry were typical of many refugees of her generation. Elena Sergeyevna was born in St. Petersburg in 1905, into the family of Baron Sergei Sergeyevich von Tiesenhausen, a director of several tobacco enterprises and also a prominent elected member of the *zemstvo,* a regional council in Russia. He was the proprietor of the vast Torma estate and lived with his family in St. Petersburg at no. 80 Fontanka Embankment, in the home of the Bogdanovs. Elena Sergeyevna's mother, Olga Alexandrovna (née Bogdanov) came from a family of tobacco manufacturers, who made the popular Bogdanovskie cigarettes. The family had six children, all of whom attended the Obolenskaya Gymnasium in St. Petersburg.

Elena Sergeyevna's older sisters, Valentina and Olga, graduated from the Institute for Noblewomen, while Elena studied for two years at Stayunina's well-known school in St. Petersburg. The baron's family was forced to flee to the

Opposite: A drawing by George Hoyningen-Huene for Harper's Bazaar, *1925.*

D'après un dessin par le Baron Huene

VAPOREUSE

Robe pour danser
en mousseline
de soie " pêche "
brodée de perles
sur satin chair
portée par
Miss Dorothy
D I C K S O N

**OF HIS MAJESTY'S THEATRE
LONDON**

YTEB

14, Rue Royale
PARIS

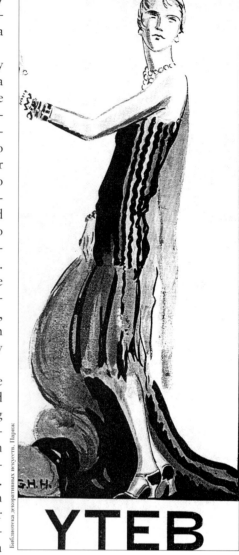

YTEB

and their servants. We lived splendidly in Yalta, without a care. A lady-in-waiting looked after me. We stayed in Yalta until the Bolsheviks came."[5]

Baron von Tiesenhausen's family was evacuated by steamship from Yalta to the Bulgarian port of Varna, where refugees from Russia were accommodated in the auditorium of the municipal theater: the Tiesenhausens had to sleep in one of the dress-circle boxes for a month. They were then evacuated to Serbia along with other refugees. Fortunately, Marquis Artur Palavichini and his wife, née Countess d'Harcourt, who lived in a sumptuous castle there, invited the baron's family to stay with them. After spending several months in the marquis's hospitable castle, the Tiesenhausens rented a house of their own, and Elena entered the Russian high school run by General Erdeli in the city of Selsky Rudnik.

The cultural life of Russian Belgrade was in full flower as the city overflowed with Russian émigrés. The Serbian king welcomed them cordially and even established grants to support Russian writers. Elena Sergeyevna lived in Serbia for five years, from 1918 to 1923. After moving to Paris, she settled with her family in a southern suburb, not far from Versailles. One day Elena Sergeyevna saw a newspaper advertisement by a

Crimea when the revolution broke out. Baroness von Tiesenhausen recalled: "We were fleeing from the Bolsheviks then, and lost our entire fortune. We couldn't take anything with us: Mama didn't even take her diamonds from the safe, thinking we would soon return. When life in St. Petersburg became dangerous, we took the direct train to Yalta: its coaches were still beautiful, with upholstered seats. I was an eight-year-old girl then, and perceived everything with great delight. We owned a house in Yalta, a luxurious dacha. There were few refugees in Yalta when we moved there, but more families began to arrive, one after another. While the Revolution raged in St. Petersburg, the opposite—carousing—was taking place in Yalta. We gave receptions for seventy people

Above, left and right: Drawings by George Hoyningen-Huene in Vogue *magazine advertising the house of Yteb, Paris, 1925–26.*

fashion house seeking shapely young women, which led to her employment with Baroness Hoyningen-Huene at Yteb. Elena Sergeyevna recalls: "They already had several Russian models there: Roslavleva and Nosovich. My temperament and Nosovich's were not compatible, and I didn't want to be in the same fitting room with her. Yteb's designs were marvelous. They were a success, and the business was doing well. The collections began with summer dresses or simple frocks, followed by sportswear; then came cocktail and party dresses, and the showings ended with the evening gowns. The winter collections also included coats and furs. Yteb's designs had clean lines and an original cut; they didn't have pretentious embroidery and were simple

Архив Ольги Вейнанд, Англия

Above: *Baroness Elena Sergeyevna von Tiesenhausen in an at-home dress designed by the house of Yteb, 1925.*

Right: *Princess Lieven in a dress by the House of Yteb, Paris, April 1926. Photo from Vogue magazine.*

Библиотека декоративных искусств, Париж

245

Библиотека декоративных искусств. Париж

Библиотека Ла Камбр, Брюссель.

Библиотека Ла Камбр, Брюссель.

Left: *A model in an evening dress by the house of Yteb, Paris, November 1926. Photo by George Hoyningen-Huene for* Vogue *magazine.*

Above and right: *Drawings from the magazines* L'art et la mode *and* Paris-élégant *of designs from the house of Yteb, 1926.*

246

Библиотека декоративных искусств. Париж

Библиотека декоративных искусств. Париж

Left: *A drawing by Henri Mercier in* Vogue *magazine advertising the house of Yteb, Paris, May 1926.*

Above: *A model in an evening dress from the house of Yteb, Paris, April 1926. Photo by George Hoyningen-Huene for* Vogue *magazine.*

*Tailleur très élégant en
lainage fantaisie rouille,
blouse en crêpe de Chine
assorti, boutons en métal
ouvragé.*

*Ce costume est en trois
pièces Kasha gris-perle,
deux panneaux du même
tissu retombent sur les
côtés, les boutons sont
assortis au ton de l'en-
semble.*

YTEB

14, Rue Royale --- Paris

YTEB

14, Rue Royale   Carlton Hotel
PARIS   CANNES

to wear. All the designs had dropped waists.

"Yteb had about twelve permanent models. The firm occupied two floors in my time. Its proprietress, Russian Baroness Hoyningen-Huene, drew the designs herself, but always had a cutter there, too. She paid us decently for our work but never allowed us to wear the dresses off the job. I worked at Yteb for four or five years and left about 1929."[6]

During the latter half of the 1920s, photographs of Yteb's designs were regularly published in the major magazines: *Jardin des Modes*, *Vogue*, and *L'art et la mode*. Yteb had an enormous advantage in that George Hoyningen-Huene had become a successful fashion photographer. It came about because one day George and his mother, Baroness Anne Hoyningen-Huene, were having lunch at the Hotel Ritz with Edna Woolman Chase, the editor-in-chief of American *Vogue*. Impressed by the baroness's nostalgic tales of imperial splendor in St. Petersburg, Mrs. Chase invited George to take a job as a photographer at *Vogue*. He worked there for many years learning the craft, and it was at *Vogue* that he became a professional photographer. By the 1930s he was an undisputed leader in fashion photography.

George often photographed Yteb designs for the magazine and did a great deal to strengthen the reputation of the family business. For example, he drew one of the house's society models,

Opposite, far left: *An advertisement for the house of Yteb in* Vogue *magazine, Paris, 1926.*

Opposite, above right: *A drawing from the magazine* Paris-elegant *of an autumn walking suit designed by the house of Yteb, 1925.*

Opposite below: *An advertisement for the house of Yteb in* Vogue *magazine, 1926.*

Right: *A drawing by George Hoyningen-Huene in* Vogue *magazine of an embroidered outfit by the house of Yteb, August 1926.*

Библиотека декоративных искусств, Париж

Библиотека «Ла Камбр», Брюссель.

Архив Грея Макхартри. Лондон

Princess Lieven, in a green crepe dress of original cut that especially demonstrated the dressmaker's high level of craft. Another design from the summer season, a beige crepe georgette dress, was presented in an ensemble with a three-quarter length summer coat of the same fabric.

Mousselines and georgettes were Madame Yteb's favorite fabrics for evening-wear collections. During the 1926 season, these dresses were often trimmed at the hemline with orchid designs made of curled ostrich feathers. Yteb's creations were distinguished by a sense of proportion and very expert cutting, to which special attention was paid. The house's main objective was simplicity of line: the 1927 collection featured jersey golf outfits that were simple in silhouette and could compete with those shown by Chanel. The white silk evening dress was exquisitely austere. It was cut on the bias, and the uneven hem resembled a design from Madeleine Vionnet. Yteb presented very interesting evening wear designs in 1927,

Above left: *A drawing from the magazine* Paris-élégant *of an evening dress designed by the house of Yteb, 1927.*

Above: *Nina von Hoyer in a dress by the house of Yteb, Paris, 1926–27.*

Opposite, top left: *A drawing from* Vogue *magazine of an evening dress by the house of Yteb, Paris, 1927.*

Opposite, right: *Nina von Hoyer in a dress by the house of Yteb, 1926–27.*

250

Библиотека „Ла Камбр", Брюссель.

such as the open sleeveless dress, a photograph of which was published in
Paris-élégant. In crepe de chine the col-
or of the Nile, the dress was distinguished by striking trim on the skirt:
horizontal silver-bead embroidery was
followed by two layers of brocade insets
ending in a fringe of ostrich feathers
dyed the same shade as the dress.

Vogue magazine gave Yteb a great
deal of space in 1927, going into rap-
ture over its collections: "Yteb creates
original clothes without resorting to
garishness or eccentricity. They show an
intrinsic inventiveness and good taste.
An elongated straight silhouette is used
for the day wear, while the evening
clothes are simple but skillfully cut.

"A group of outfits in soft wool and
peau-de-soie includes long coats, and
jackets shortened to hip length, forming
ensembles with the dresses. Wide leather
sashes or belts stitched into the dresses
hug the hips.

"The sport dresses are often sleeveless, while the sleeves of the daytime
dresses are fuller from the elbow down,

Архив Грега Мандергине, Лондон.

251

and skirts have dropped waistlines. Fullness is achieved with folds, overlaid aprons, straight flounces, draping, or other means such as shortened capes, jabots, scarves, lapels, and stiff horizontal and vertical pleats. The fabrics are presented in various combinations: *peau-de-soie*, *kasha*, crepe de chine, georgette, jersey, and leather.

"The evening wear includes dresses of silk mousselines and georgettes in pastel shades with gracefully airy drapings, panne velvet capes, soft belts, straight flounces and insets. Embroidery, imitation gems, appliqué flowers, buckles and smoky velvet inserts merely underscore the austerity of these dresses. The more complicated evening dresses of satin or brocade lamé are embellished with sequins or heavy fringe. The

evening wraps match the dresses and are made of brocade lamé, brocade, or silk mousseline. There is one silk mousseline wrap lined with velvet.

"The favored colors are black, white with black, beige, taupe, blue, sapphire and lavender, yellow and blue-green, violet, apricot, salmon, lilac, and coral."[7]

Madame Yteb had shown an interest in small checks and stripes as early as 1925, and in 1928 Yteb came out with new designs in a geometric style. One of Yteb's most popular designs of the 1928 season was the "Success" dress of black satin crepe with white polka dots, which had long sleeves, a dropped waist, and a black gored skirt. There was a dramatic contrast between the two black-and-white Yteb designs shown in *Vogue* that year. One was a dress of black panne

252

NICOLE GROULT

Ce trois-pièces fait de velours anglais et de toile de
soie conviendra à la simple
promenade en campagne
comme au sport. Le sweater
en sose beige unie et la jupe
de même ton se portent avec
une veste en velours beige.
La ceinture de tissu marque
une taille presque normale

NICOLE GROULT

Le costume composé du jum-
per rayé et de la veste en jersey uni est l'un des plus po-
pulaires qui soient. Le sweater en trois tons de bleu est
porté ici avec une jupe en
crêpe de Chine bleu clair et
la veste en tricot de laine bleu
moyen est bordée de clair. Sa
coupe simple le rend pratique

YTEB

Ce trois-pièces " Pour le Golf "
est, comme son nom l'indique,
réservé au plein air. Il démontre
une fois de plus la place pré-
pondérante que tient le jersey
dans les costumes de sports. Le
sweater en jersey vert s'accom-
pagne d'une jupe et d'une veste
de jersey rayé vert et blanc. Des
plis de côté donnent l'ampleur

YTEB

Le jersey est un facteur important de la mode de plein air. Il
apparaît le plus souvent com-
biné avec un autre tissu. " Loi-
sir " se compose d'un sweater en
jersey bois de rose bordé de pope
line assortie ; la jupe de même
ton, en popeline, est finement
plissée devant. La veste est en
tricot bois de rose marron et beige

velvet set off with a large turned-down collar of snow-white ermine. The other was a masterpiece of Art Deco graphic art in alternating black and white satin. *Vogue* wrote of Yteb in 1928: "This collection consists of a large number of practical designs. . . . for young people, which are almost completely in keeping with the names of the designs. . . . The evening wear has a great deal of draping and voluminous detail. Raised ribs and selvages, as well as very small patterns on the latest print fabrics, create a textured effect that works well here.

"Most of the daytime dresses are made of very contrasting textures such as glossy satin and and dull marocain. A combination of solid-color and printed silks is often used.

"The evening dresses are mainly of

Opposite, above left and right: *Nina von Hoyer in daytime and walking outfits from the house of Yteb, Paris, 1928.*

Opposite, below: *A drawing from* Vogue *magazine of designs by the house of Yteb, 1928.*

Above: *A page from* Vogue *magazine of designs created by the house of Yteb with Nicole Groult, Paul Poiret's sister, September 1927.*

Right: *A drawing from* Vogue *magazine of designs by the house of Yteb, 1928.*

mousseline, crepe de chine with small printed patterns scattered on a background, georgette, taffeta, satin, and mousseline trimmed with lace.

"Natural leather colors and shades of yellow are used for the silks and tweeds. We recommend a combination of grey and bright red for dress fabrics. Green and a whole spectrum of reds are everywhere, just as the new combination of grey and green has become a obligatory for evening dresses."[8]

In 1929 Yteb decided to produce its own perfumes, following the sweeping trend at the large fashion houses. Grand Duchess Maria Pavlovna, the founder of the Kitmir house, had introduced her fragrance "Prince Igor" the previous year, and Felix Yousoupoff (the French spelling of "Yusupov") created signature scents for his fashion house of Irfé in 1926. Yteb apparently entered the Paris market with a perfume in its originally designed bottles under the intriguing name "Yteb No. 14" in order

Библиотека декоративных искусств, Париж

Библиотека декоративных искусств, Париж

Left: *A model wearing a silk print dress designed by the house of Yteb. Photo by George Hoyningen-Huene for* Vogue *magazine, Paris, May 1928.*

Above: *A drawing by Francis for* Vogue *magazine of sportswear ensembles from the house of Yteb, Paris, 1928.*

to spite Chanel. Its advertisement, printed in the shape of a triangle, showed
fourteen bottles arranged in a pyramid.
The perfume quickly became a success.
Bottles from the Yteb No. 14 campaign
are now collector's rarities.

A new Russian model, Nina von
Hoyer, came to Yteb at this time. She
was descended on her father's side from
Baltic nobility; on her mother's side she
was a stepsister of Natalia Petrovna
Bologovskaya, née Ivanova, a professional Parisian dressmaker. Arriving in
Paris after the revolution, Nina von
Hoyer and her friend Olga Schwanbeck
earned a living by painting silk scarves,
which were very fashionable in the mid-
1920s. Many Russian refugees painted
on silk using the batik technique, producing shawls, scarves, dresses, umbrellas, and lampshades. When the fashion
for painted silk passed, Nina decided to
try her luck in a Russian fashion house
and started by going to Prince Felix
Youssoupoff at Irfé. Since all their positions were filled, the prince advised her
to apply at Yteb.

Models at that time were chosen to
fit a particular garment size exactly, and
Yteb just happened to have a vacancy.
Nina fit into two evening dresses sewn
for her predecessor and she immediately
got the job. She wrote in her memoirs:
" 'You will do,' " said Mdme. Yteb, 'but,
for God's sake, ask Sophie Nosovitch
to teach you how to walk and show
clothes. Because that you do all wrong.
I like my models to walk in the way that
a lady walks into a drawing room. Without any fuss, and no undulating or
unnecessary movement which so many
French models have. It cheapens the
whole outfit when it is shown like that.'

" 'But, Mdme. Buzzard,' I said, rather
astonished, 'surely I do not undulate or
twist my hips when walking.'

A drawing from Vogue *magazine
of party dresses from the house of Yteb,
Paris, October 1928.*

255

" 'You do quite the opposite my child. You walk like a soldier on parade, which is all wrong, although, personally I prefer it to the other extreme. Don't worry, Sophie will teach you. She has trained the other two very well and they walked like *poules* from Montmartre with their little fingers stuck out in a most gentile manner. It was too awful for words. You will see them now—they begin to walk like ladies.' "9

Nina was happy to find permanent employment with compatriots again. She was paid little at first—800 francs a month—but she was supposed to get a bonus equivalent to 2 percent of the price of every dress that sold when she showed it. Every month Yteb gave its models two pair of new silk stockings, which were constantly tearing since the

girls did not wear them just for work. For showings, the models each got a pair of gold-colored satin slippers that went well with all the dresses. Nina writes further on: "Sophie Nosovitch was our crack mannequin. She had a lovely straight figure and an attractive face rather older for her age; she was only thirty. All the other models were much younger but not nearly so smart. Sophie could put any old rag on herself and it immediately acquired a certain cachet.

"Sophie had had a much more difficult life. She was the sole supporter of her parents and grandmother. Her only brother joined the Foreign Legion. Poor Sophie had had an unhappy marriage which had soon broken up. I loved Sophie and admired her as a model."

Aside from Nina von Hoyer, the Russian girls working at Yteb included twenty-three-year-old Tatyana Guchkova, the twenty-five-year-old Georgian Princess Rimma Eristova (a relative of the leading Chanel model, Mary Eristova), and Erna, who soon married Count Tolstoi and left her job. By law, every Russian business had to employ a specific percentage of French citizens. There was only one Frenchwoman, Jeanni, who modeled at the time. The poor girl understood not a word of Russian and was totally isolated among the Russians.

Working at Yteb turned out to be very lucky for Nina. She writes that, in teaching her to show clothes, Sofia Nosovich formulated the professional credo of a good model in a major house very accurately: "She must not forget

Opposite: *A model in a silk dress with a large print pattern designed by the house of Yteb. Photo by Marant for* Vogue *magazine, Paris, 1929.*

Right: *Lelya von Medem in a silk dress with a large print pattern designed by the house of Yteb. Photo by George Hoyningen-Huene for* Vogue *magazine, Paris, April 1929.*

for what purpose she was walking. It was not for men to want to hop into bed with her. It was meant to show women the dress she was wearing and she had to show it properly, and not sway about like a woman of the streets."

The models began the day by putting on their makeup until ten and beginning work at half-past ten. The fashion of the day made its demands on women's beauty: Nina was forced to pluck her thick eyebrows as it was obligatory for stylish women in the 1930s to have thin eyebrows.

Fashion is an indicator of changes in society and a mirror of history. The economic downturn began in 1929 in France, and it had a powerful effect on fashion: the frivolous license of the 1920s was forever left behind. In 1929, Jean Patou was the first to "restore" the waist to its natural place, lengthening skirts in the process. Keeping in step with the times, Yteb presented a new, elongated, and more feminine silhouette that season.

In March 1929, *Vogue* reported: "Princess de Karaman-Shimay, sitting in Madame Yteb's pale-green salon, simply can't choose between a wool georgette dress and an outfit of matte and glossy beige satin."[10]

The fashion house of Yteb could be proud of its clientele, among whom were wealthy and titled ladies from many countries: Madam Yvonne de la Chapelle, Ladies Hosford and Inverclyde, Mrs. Shepperton, and several American millionaires. Recalling the Americans, Nina wrote: "Nothing satisfied them; they always wanted to impress one with their riches and how much better were the shops and clothes in the U.S.A. In fact, everything was better. I was always wanting to say, why, in heaven's name do you come to Paris to have your dresses made if you can do so much better in the U.S.A.? Tatiana said that they shopped here entirely from snobbishness, so that they could show their friends and neighbours garments made in Paris."

There was a great deal of truth in this; but such clients also helped to keep the establishment going as it continued to create ever newer designs for them. A

UNE NOTE ÉCLATAN-
TE ET FRAÎCHE DANS
L'ATMOSPHÈRE DE
PARIS

YTEB

14, RUE ROYALE. PARIS

Библиотека декоративных искусств, Париж

Библиотека «Ла Камбр», Брюссель

model's work was very fatiguing then, and still is. They must stand for hours, like wooden dummies, in fitting rooms while they are being fitted for a dress. Starting in 1930, the job became even more complicated when Madeleine Vionnet helped to introduce draping to fashion. The lines of antiquity replaced geometric dress silhouettes. Some houses, like Alix, which belonged to Madame Grès, specialized exclusively in draping: ancient Greek sculptures were used to create patterns. Designers as dissimilar in their creative approaches as Elsa Schiaparelli and Jean Lanvin made wide use of draping in their dresses in the 1930s.

Nina wrote about this fashion: "I had to play the part of a plastic or wooden doll, with nothing on except a girdle and bras, though of course we wore our stockings and gold satin shoes with very high heels on. Not only was it hard to stand for so long on such high heels but pins were often stuck into our bodies by mistake when Betty Buzzard was too engrossed in draping a bit of silk over our shoulder."

George Hoyningen-Huene, by this time a well-known photographer, was often present at these tiring fittings. At the beginning the models were shy about standing in front of this handsome young man in only their underwear, but they soon became accustomed to it. Nina explained: "He contemplated us as clothes hangers in the same way

as Mdme. Yteb did. We were wooden dolls to him and nothing more."

Nina's manuscript has enabled us to learn a great deal about both Yteb and the house's proprietress. "Betty Buzzard (whom everyone at Yteb called Mdme. Yteb) was a charming society woman and a very good hostess and everyone liked her, outside Yteb. But something seemed to happen to her when she was in her establishment. She became cold and quite unapproachable. For some unknown reason she didn't like Sophie. They had come from the same de luxe boarding school in Petrograd, and, though Betty Buzzard was a few years older than Sophie, they were at that school for quite a few years together, although in different classes." Sofia Nosovich believed that she and Madame Yteb had different "auras," but all the same they continued to work together, placing the greatest value on each other's professionalism.

In talking about the tedious fittings at Yteb, Nina recalled the following episode: "I was very taken aback one afternoon when Betty kept me standing for hours while she tried to create an evening dress of salmon coloured crepe marocain. It did not look good on me and I said so. Betty looked at me with astonishment, as if a wooden doll had suddenly come to life and started talking.

"'Shut up,' she said, 'You are not supposed to open your mouth while at work.'

Опposite, left: *An advertisement for Yteb No. 14 perfume in* Vogue *magazine, Paris, July 1929. The number in the name of the perfume is the house of Yteb's address on rue Royale, Paris.*

Opposite, right: *A drawing from* Vogue *magazine of an elongated evening dress with asymmetrical draping designed by the house of Yteb, 1928.*

Above: *A drawing from the French magazine* L'art et la mode *of an elongated evening dress, with a train, designed by the house of Yteb, Paris, 1929.*

Right: *An advertisement in* Vogue *magazine for the house of Yteb, Paris, February 1929.*

"I never did after that, only gave a little shriek once in a while when a pin was driven into me." Nevertheless, Nina was one of the few models who was allowed to take dresses home. Nina later learned that her uncle had known Colonel Buzzard and his wife back in St. Petersburg, and this might have accounted for their relatively indulgent attitude toward her.

One day, Colonel Buzzard invited Nina to lunch, and it became clear in the course of conversation that business was going poorly at Yteb. The large staff was a hindrance to the house: at the time, in the years 1930 to 1931, Yteb had a special pattern librarian, a dress packer, and a person in charge of the department where worn garments were cleaned. The colonel wanted those jobs to be done by one woman. In addition, on the top floor of Yteb was a staff dining room, which the colonel proposed to close. But hardly anyone at Yteb took him seriously. The Russian models made fun of him because he stammered slightly. Temperamentally, he was incapable of managing a fashion house. A born soldier and a favorite in his regiment, at Yteb he strolled among the young models like an Oriental sultan. He and Betty Buzzard lived in a private house on rue Nicolo in Paris furnished in English Chippendale; the colonel organized large parties there and spent little time at Yteb.

The change in clothing style in the early 1930s had a tragic effect on most Russian fashion houses, which emphasized decoration. Every kind of Slavic embroidery, sequins, beading, appliqué, and silk painting went out of fashion, leaving many Russian women without jobs. However, Yteb not only remained

Библиотека декоративных искусств, Париж

Библиотека Ла Камбр, Брюссель

Above: *Kira Sereda in an evening dress designed by the house of Yteb, Paris, April 1931. Photo by George Hoyningen-Huene for* Vogue *magazine.*

Right: *A drawing from the French magazine* L'art et la mode *of a dress designed by the house of Yteb, 1930.*

Opposite: *Baron George Hoyningen-Huene, Paris, 1933. Photo by Cecil Beaton.*

unaffected but even benefitted from these changes. Its designs proved to be in keeping with the times. The secret of its success lay primarily in the smart and sensible cut of its clothes. Madame Yteb never forgot that silhouette determined fashion, and she achieved excellent results with the aid of her French cutter Madame Marie.

Yteb's 1931 collection looked extremely elegant. The fitted-waist dresses with wide skirts and oblique insets in the bodice were highly appreciated by *Vogue*: "The straight silhouette is expanded toward the bottom by overlaid flounces. The sleeve is fuller below the elbow. The dresses, coats, and outfits with detachable fur collars are very austere. For evening, there is a fitted-waist 'princess' silhouette. With large bows on the back. Long coats with wide sleeves. Arm-holes are low and wide. The fabrics: baburra, wool in diagonal stripes, marocain, satin, and panne velvet. The colors: green, sand, chestnut, black, and forget-me-not. The furs: beaver, colt hide, and karakul. The belts are black silk and thin."[11] In July 1931, *Vogue* published a drawing depicting Yteb's faithful client Princess de Caraman-Chimay in a golf outfit.

Baron George Hoyningen-Huene continued to take photographs for Yteb, and one of the models the house used at this time was the elegant Russian girl, Kira Sereda, the daughter of Baroness von Medem. Her measurements exactly matched the requirements of the new fashion. In one photo by Hoyningen-Huene for *Vogue*, she posed in a long white satin evening dress with a petal-shaped skirt cut on the bias.

About this time Nina von Hoyer re-

with the clients: always courteous, correct, and attentive. Nina explained: "My life went on quite smoothly working at Yteb, but the more I worked as a vendeuse, the more I was sure that I would never be good at it. A vendeuse is born, not made. Natacha, my sister, would have been a far better one; she had a much more persuasive manner and was so interested in clothes herself that her enthusiasm infected her customers."

All Yteb's patterns were kept under strict security—only once was Nina able to borrow an old pattern for just one night (on her word of honor) from which she sewed her first dress, which delighted her entire family. Nina decided to leave Yteb—something she often regretted—when she received an advantageous offer from a new millinery store belonging to the Greek merchant Stamoglo. They paid 1,200 francs a month, 400 more than she was getting, and that played the decisive role.

When Nina communicated her intention to Colonel Buzzard after dinner, she was very surprised at his reaction, which was pleased rather than distressed. He

quested to be transferred from modeling to sales, where the work seemed much more interesting and promising. She became an assistant in-house saleswoman under the patronage of Tatania Guchkova, who was already working as the primary saleswoman. The job proved to be very difficult for her. Nina wrote: "Think of how many clients you will come into contact with who will behave atrociously and unfairly. You must learn to lump it and pretend to like it. The customer is always right." Yteb required that salespeople behave like true ladies

said: "We are going to either shut Maison Yteb altogether, or drastically reduce the size of the white elephant. Etiquette decrees that the last to come are the first to go and, you, unfortunately, are in that category. We will probably keep two mannequins. One will be Sophie and the other Rima. Tatiana will have to stay as she has to keep her old mother and ailing sister. The trouble with you Russians is that you have great ideas but no commercial sense at all. I have very little but I spark in comparison with Betty."

This page: *Drawings from* Vogue *and* Jardin des modes *magazines of designs for dresses and suits from the house of Yteb, 1932.*

Opposite: *The building in which the house of Yteb was located, no. 14 rue Royale, Paris. Photo by Alexandre Vassiliev, 1997.*

262

Yteb still managed to survive the 1932 season, but the grave economic situation was also affecting many of its clients. Among the most faithful were the very wealthy Belgian Princess de Caraman-Chimay, owner of the ancient Chimay Castle. Yteb continued to make clothes of then-fashionable jersey, often combining it with leather. The fascination with sportswear for golf, yachting, and travel was typical of many other houses, and Hermès, Chanel, Maggy Rouff, Worth, and Martial and Armand specialized in them. These outfits didn't save Yteb: business continued to get worse. Nina, who was working at the Stamoglo millinery store, wrote of the situation: "I was very chagrined that Yteb's business was going downhill very quickly. Rimma, Sofia, and Tatiana were the only girls still there. The dresses were far cheaper and less luxurious. When we met, Colonel Buzzard invited me to lunch, and I gladly accepted. During the meal, he said that they had de-

cided to stay in business as long as possible, but that the house could now no longer be called first class, as it had been before.

"He said: 'We're now trying to make something like a confection, in the spirit of American ideas. We've stuck to several sizes of the same simple design. Naturally that means we now have to make slight alterations on the clothes

when they sell. This is fine with our clients, since they are all having difficulties now and are just glad they can spend less money and still say to their friends in America that their dresses are from the house of Yteb.'"

Before Yteb actually closed, Prince Felix Yousoupoff, owner of the Irfé fashion house, tried to save both failing businesses by making a desperate attempt to merge the two; it ended in the bankruptcy of both. By 1933, Yteb had essentially gone out of business. Nina married the Englishman Mr. MacCartney and moved with him to England. Baron George Hoyningen-Huene continued to work successfully for *Vogue*, but left it in 1935 because of its "Russian-Prussian" character. Betty Buzzard and her sister Helena became salespeople in various fashion houses. After World War II, Betty worked in the Russian Catherine Parel house, which belonged to Ekaterina Nikolayevna Bobrikova-Bonnet.

12

THE FASHION HOUSE OF IRFÉ

The Russian fashion house Irfé was established in Paris in 1924 and lasted until 1931. Its founders and designers were Princess Irina Romanova and Prince Felix Youssoupoff (the French spelling of "Yusupov"), who created the name "Irfé" from the first two letters of their first names.

The princely family of Youssoupoff was a distinguished, old noble family in Russia, descended from Abubekir-ben-Raioc, a descendant of the prophet Ali and nephew of Mohammed, who held the title of Emir el Omar. His successor, Termess, migrated from Arabia to the Caspian shore. His heir, Edigei Mangit, who took part in the campaigns of Tamerlane, moved to the Black Sea coast and established a Crimean khanate there. The descendant of the last Musa Mirza was the ruler of the Nogai Horde and an ally of Tsar Ivan III in the late fifteenth century. It was one of his sons, Khan Yusuf, who began the line of the Youssoupoff princes. Yusuf's great-grandson Abdul Mirza converted to Christianity, took the name of Dmitrii, and was given a princely title by Tsar Feodor.

One of the most educated and wealthy people at the court, Prince Nikolai Borisovich Youssoupoff became especially renowned during the reign of Catherine the Great. The owner of numerous estates, including the famous Arkhangelskoye, he was a refined connoisseur of art, a collector of jewelry, and a passionate lover of young women. Felix Youssoupoff, the hero of our nar-

Opposite: *Princess Irina Youssoupoff in an evening dress from the house of Irfé, Paris, 1924.*

Above: *An advertisement for the house of Irfé from* Vogue *magazine, Paris, 1925.*

rative, inherited from him all these properties and passions except the last one.

Prince Felix Felixovich Youssoupoff, Count Sumarokov-Elston was born in the Youssoupoff palace on the Moika Canal in St. Petersburg on March 24, 1887. He realized very early in life that he was the owner of an immense fortune and was closely linked to the noble families of the Russian and European aristocracies. His mother, Princess Zinaida Nikolayevna Youssoupoff, was a woman of rare beauty and exquisite manners. When Felix was born, she had been expecting a girl and had prepared a layette in pink for the newborn. Felix was enchanted by his mother's beauty and ardently worshiped her, delighting in her impeccable clothes and her legendary and fabulously expensive diamonds and pearls. In his memoirs, published in Paris, Felix Youssoupoff devotes much space to describing the luxurious dresses, sables, silks, and vel-

vets that he saw in his youth. Another passion of his childhood that he retained in his adult years was his love of Eastern exotica; he often idiosyncratically played "the sultan."

The prince recalls: "Next to my father's office was a Moorish hall that led out into the garden. Lavishly decorated with mosaics, it was the exact copy of the palace in the Alhambra: marble columns surrounding a central fountain, couches upholstered in Persian fabrics lined the walls. I liked this room for its Oriental style, full of languor: I liked to give myself up to daydream there. Sitting on a couch with my mother's jewels, I imagined myself a satrap surrounded by slaves."[1]

Another experience of the prince that was to influence the house of Irfé's exotic Eastern decor was the interior of the Youssoupoff estate in the Crimea; it was called Koccoz, which means "blue eye" in Tatar. It was a large and elegant palace, reminiscent of Bakhchisary. There were Turkish-style furniture, Turkish carpets, stained glass, and even a copy of the "fountain of love, the fountain of sorrow," immortalized by Pushkin, completing the dreamy, voluptuous decor. High-concept Eastern dinners were arranged, and a wardrobe full of clothing in the Ottoman style was kept on hand for guests. All this excited young Felix's passion for disguises, performances, and festivities.

Neither fights with his parents nor embarrassing situations in the city could stop Felix from pursuing his inclina-

tions—he liked to dress up. Friends of the Youssoupoff family once by chance saw him dressed in a women's evening dress of silk tulle with silver sequins and a luxuriant headband of pale blue ostrich feathers, singing obscene couplets on the stage of the fashionable St. Petersburg coffeehouse "Aquarium." Felix recalls one such escapade in his memoirs: "That cold, icy night, a young woman in a ballroom gown, covered with diamonds, was racing at full speed in an open sleigh down the streets of St. Petersburg. Who would have recognized that this crazy woman was the son of one of the most venerable families in the city!"[2]

Felix not only liked to wear disguis-

Above left: *Francois Flameng, Portrait of Princess Zinaida Nikolayevna Youssoupoff, 1894.*

Above center: *Valentin Serov, Portrait of Prince Felix Youssoupoff, 1903.*

Above right: *Prince Felix and Princess Irina Youssoupoff at their wedding, St. Petersburg, February 1914.*

Below: G. *Vigstrem, Portrait of Princess Zinaida Nikolayevna Youssoupoff, c. 1900.*

Opposite: *Princess Irina Youssoupoff, Paris, 1923.*

es himself, but often dressed up his favorite bulldog, Gugus, in amusing outfits, too. Once he even disguised himself as a wetnurse and Gugus as an infant whom he carried in his arms so he could smuggle him into England from Europe, undetected, in violation of the quarantine rule for cats and dogs. Felix's trip to England in 1909–1910 and his "studies" at Oxford University were an unending series of pleasures and entertainments. The eccentric prince found steady amusement through his friendship with Anna Pavlova, Diaghilev's triumphs in London, costume balls, and dinner parties. He was invited everywhere and his outrageous behavior become the sensation of the day. Felix recalls: "A little while later I

Архив Ксении Сфирис. Афины

received an invitation to a grand costume ball at Albert Hall. Since I still had some time to spare, I ordered a Russian costume of gold brocade with red flowers in the style of sixteenth-century St. Petersburg. The costume was magnificent: embroidered with gems and trimmed in sable, with a matching hat—it became a sensation. I met all of London at the soiree, and the next day my photograph figured prominently in all the newspapers."[3] As early as 1910, Felix Youssoupoff was one of the harbingers of the "Russian style," which was later to become so popular in Western Europe.

Above: *An advertisement for the house of Irfé from* Vogue *magazine, 1926.*

Opposite: *Princess Irina Youssoupoff in a design from the house of Irfé, New York, 1924. Photograph by Edward Steichen.*

Felix rented a large apartment near Hyde Park and skillfully decorated it. He liked black rugs, silk lampshades, soft furniture—in short, refined comfort. Prince Youssoupoff was probably the first of the Russian aristocrats to acquire what was at that time entirely new and unusual furniture from the Martin atelier, a subsidiary of the Parisian fashion house of Paul Poiret. Eccentric taste and extravagance always characterized Felix.

After returning to Russia in 1912, Felix finally began thinking about the future. He was twenty-five years old, and the combination of a refined appearance with fabulous wealth and exquisite manners made him one of the most desirable eligible bachelors in pre-revolutionary Russia, an enviable partner for many titled aristocrats. However, each time his notorious name was pronounced, excited whispers ensued. His overly close friendships with Grand Duke Dmitrii Pavlovich, the athlete Vasilii Soldatenkov, Eric Hamilton, Serbian Prince Pavel Karageorgievich and King Manuel of Portugal threw a shadow on Felix's reputation.

When young Youssoupoff's choice for a bride fell on the Princess Irina Alexandrovna Romanova, it provoked a sea of talk and gossip. Prince Felix had met Princess Irina, the granddaughter of Emperor Alexander III, at the Youssoupoff estate Koccoz in the Crimea. A girl of innocence and incomparable beauty, Princess Irina was born on July 3, 1895, in Peterhof, the eldest daughter of Grand Duke Alexander Mikhailovich, the founder of the Russian Air Force and a childhood friend of Emperor Nicholas II. At the age of twenty-three, Alexander Mikhailovich fell in love with Nicholas II's fourteen-year-old sister, Princess Xenia Alexandrovna. Despite the fact that the bride and groom were closely related (Xenia's suitor was her father's cousin), their union was not only happy, but exceptionally fruitful. In addition to the beautiful daughter Irina, there were six sons in the family, all of whom were saved from the revolution and continued the Romanov line in emigration.

Felix recalls his first encounter with

Туреневская библиотека. Париж

Irina Romanova: "From that day, I was sure that this was my fate. Since then, the adolescent had turned into a young woman of dazzling beauty. Shyness made her silent, but intensified her charm and surrounded her with mystery. Seized by a new feeling, I realized the poverty of my past adventures. I, too, had finally found that complete harmony which is the basis of every true love."[4]

Felix and Irina's wedding took place in the Anichkov Palace in St. Petersburg on February 22, 1914. The newlyweds moved into the left wing of the Youssoupoff palace on the Moika Canal, but soon after set off on a honeymoon voy-

age around Europe and the Near East. Upon the young couple's return to Russia, Irina gave birth on March 21, 1915 to a daughter, also named Irina, the only child from the marriage.

Felix's future destiny was tragically and inextricably linked with the name of Grigory Rasputin, whose influence on the tsar and his family during World War I was, to the prince, unendurable. After thoroughly studying the habits and temperament of the "spiritual advisor," Prince Youssoupoff made up his mind to take a step that forever inscribed his name in world history. On Youssoupoff's initiative, Grand Duke Dmitrii

Pavlovich, Purishkevich, Sukhotny, and Doctor Lazovert worked out a plan to murder Rasputin in the basement of the Youssoupoff house. The events of that night, December 28, 1916, have been described in detail by both the conspirators themselves and historians.

Felix Youssoupoff's participation in Rasputin's murder soon became a generally accepted fact. The prince and Irina were put under house arrest and sent to the Youssoupoff estate Rakitnoye while awaiting the investigation. Grand Duke Dmitrii Pavlovich was exiled to Persia, which saved his life during the revolution.

Туреневская библиотека. Париж

270

Opposite, above and below: *Photographs from the magazine* Illustrirovannaya Rossiya *[Russia Illustrated] of the living room of the Youssoupoff house in Boulogne decorated with murals by Yakovlev, Paris, 1927.*

Left and right: *The founders of the house of Irfé, Princess Irina and Prince Felix Youssoupoff, Paris, 1927.*

In 1917 the Youssoupoffs moved to their estate Ai-Todor in the Crimea. Living out the last peaceful days in Russia, Felix made two trips back to St. Petersburg from the Crimea: the first one to retrieve two Rembrandt portraits, and the second to hide the family diamonds under the staircase of the house. The jewelry was discovered by workers doing repairs on the house in the mid-1920s and was confiscated by the Bolsheviks.

On April 13, 1919, when the evacuation of the Volunteer Army and the civilian population from the Crimea began under the onslaught of the Red Army, the couple accompanied the dowager Empress Maria Feodorovna and Irina's brothers and mother, the Grand Duchess Xenia Alexandrovna, on the English dreadnought *Marlborough*—they were leaving Russia forever.

At first, the Youssoupoffs lived comfortably in exile: they had a large villa in Italy, and Paris seemed to them a temporary romantic refuge. Trying to settle into a new life, the Youssoupoffs bought a small house in Boulogne, a southeastern suburb of Paris, where they later founded their fashion house, Irfé. Erté, who lived near them on rue Gutenberg and knew them intimately,

recalls: "I first met the Youssoupoffs around 1921 at Ganna Walska's house in Paris. What a handsome couple they were! The Prince had been regarded as one of the best-looking men in Russia. Even in old age his finely structured face, though wrinkled, was still striking. He had a wry sense of humour. In reminiscing about his life in Russia, he once said to me, 'I married my wife out of snobbery. My wife married me for money'—a not-so-subtle reminder of the fact that the Youssoupoffs had once been the richest family in Russia, much richer than his wife's family, the Romanoffs."[5]

This candid admission may well explain their somewhat surprising marriage. We should not forget, however, that the Youssoupoffs did live a long and difficult life together, filled with love and mutual understanding.

Erté writes: "When the Youssoupoffs finally left Russia in April 1919 on the British dreadnought *Marlborough*, they were able to bring out many valuables—paintings, furniture, decor, and art. The proceeds from their sale supported them for many years, making it possible for them to live in, if not imperial, then relative, luxury. In addition to an estate in Corsica, they had a house

with a large garden near the Parc de Prince in Boulogne-sur-Seine not far from my apartment. The prince had a wing added to the house, in which he created a charming theater. The walls were decorated with murals by the famous Russian painter Yakovlev. This house was destroyed several years ago in order to free the space for a large apartment house. My heart broke when I saw the empty lot, strewn with the shards of these remarkable murals."[6]

Photographs of the interior Youssoupoff and Yakovlev created were published in one of the unique books of the 1920s about fashion houses. The Youssoupoff house comprised stylish furniture, silk lampshades, a large fireplace, and murals on the walls with figures in perspective in the spirit of the Italian quattrocento. The prince came up with a creative touch: a small, intimate theater with a decorative curtain for fashion shows and at-home concerts—a distant relative of the luxurious theater at the Youssoupoff house in St. Petersburg. Princess Tatyana Metternich, who attended this theater in her childhood, writes: "The Youssoupoffs always had theaters in their palaces. For them it was a normal thing. They constructed and decorated their theater in Boulogne with

Библиотека декоративных искусств, Париж

their artist friend Alexander Yakovlev. There were gracefully arranged odalisques all along the walls, painted in cream, beige and pale green shades in Art Nouveau style. The theater itself was carpeted and shaped like an oval salon, with a curtain and a small staircase in the middle separating it from the stage."[7]

Prince Youssoupoff writes in his memoirs that the idea to open his own fashion house arose when he and his wife returned from a trip to the United States in 1924. Irfé was started modestly: together with a group of Russian friends, the Youssoupoffs rented a building on rue Obligado. This is where the first designs were cut and sewn. Prince Youssoupoff recalled that a Russian émigré woman, an eccentric creator of designs that were beautiful but difficult to wear, worked as his cutter.

Not knowing how to proceed in this new business, the Yousoupoffs launched

their first collection without the necessary advertising. Happily, a new occasion to prove themselves presented itself rather quickly. A few months later, in the winter of 1924, there was a fashion show by the big Parisian houses at the Hotel Ritz on the Place Vendôme, which ended with a ball. The Irfé atelier was furiously working late into the night: the last designs were still being sewn as the Irfé models arrived at the Ritz well after midnight with the ravishing Irina in the lead. It created an indelible impression even on the jaded Parisian public, who had seen it all. A French reporter wrote: "Originality, refined taste, meticulous work and an artistic sense of color immediately placed this modest atelier in the ranks of the big houses of fashion."[8]

Encouraged by these first signs of recognition, Felix and Irina Youssoupoff organized showings at their home in the theater wing. In those years, when Ras-

putin's murder was still fresh in people's minds, the opportunity to dress elegantly at the fashion house of "the very same" Prince Youssoupoff appealed to the imagination of snobbish European and American clients.

Irfé's success exceeded all expectations, and the Youssoupoffs rented a new building, more advantageously located—in the center of Paris near the grand boulevards, Place de la Concorde, and rue de la Paix, where most of the large fashion houses were found—which bolstered Irfé's reputation. The building in which the Youssoupoffs continued their business, on rue Duphot, still stands today. They occupied the first floor of an old-style house, and the prince had the entire interior renovated. The wood paneling was painted a light gray, the walls covered in gray velvet. The reception room, as was the custom in all decent houses in Russia, was furnished in mahogany furniture, its walls

Opposite: *An advertisement for the house of Irfé in* Vogue *magazine, 1926.*

Below: *A drawing from the magazine* Paris-élégant *of a design from the house of Irfé, 1927.*

Right: *Princess Mia Obolenskaya in a design from the house of Irfé, Paris, c. 1930.*

273

covered in gray floral cretonne. There were yellow silk drapes on the windows and, to create a feeling of coziness, antique engravings and showcases for family knick-knacks were brought in. The elegant decor was completed with several touches in Irina Youssoupoff's style, such as unusually shaped crystal bottles and Irfé embroidered shawls draped casually on the backs of armchairs, as if the mistress had left them there by chance.

From 1925 on, virtually the entire staff of Irfé consisted of Russian émigrés. In addition to the Youssoupoffs, Irina's twenty-five-year-old brother, Prince Nikita Alexandrovich Romanov, and his wife, Princess Maria Illarionovna Romanovskaya, née Countess Vorontzova-Dachkova, worked there. Mikhail and Nonna Kalashnikov took an active part in the organization of the business.

Yelena Trubetskaya and the Obolensky princesses, Salomiya and Nina, worked as models. None of the employees of the house, as Prince Youssoupoff himself admitted, had any idea of how to organize and run a modern enterprise. For instance, Youssoupoff's favorite servant forgot to deliver hundreds of invitations to Irfé's first show on rue Duphot, so no one got to see the mysterious lighting, delightful bouquets, and hundreds of gilt Napoleon III–style chairs especially rented for the occasion.

Fortunately, Felix entrusted the management of the house's social contacts to the Chilean Marquis Jorge de Cuevas, an elegant habitué of formal Parisian receptions. Thanks to the marquis, Irfé got so many orders that Felix had to rent the second floor of the building. Since the work was organized *à la Russe*, that is, poorly, Felix invited an experienced and knowledgeable French

director, Madame Barton, to enforce discipline.

Irfé's clientele was international, and many of the women ordering dresses insisted on seeing "the Prince himself," as they referred to him in French. Some of them sought Russian exotica, in vogue in those days, others were captivated by the fashions. In his memoirs, Felix singles out the American millionairess Mrs. Whobee. He describes her first appearance colorfully: "'Damned powerful!' our new client cried. 'So you're the Prince? You don't look like a murderer. I'm glad that you were able to save your hide from those dirty Bolsheviks.'

"She raised a shotglass full of vodka in her ringed and braceleted hand and grinned, looking at me with her remarkable eyes under heavy, thickly lined eyelids, drank it bottoms-up to my health. 'Make me a *kokoshnik* and fif-

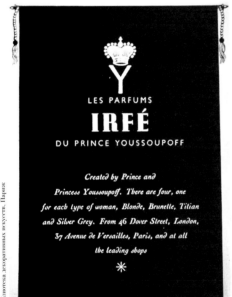

Opposite: *Drawings from* Vogue *and* Paris-élégant *of daytime and evening dresses designed by the house of Irfé, Paris, 1925–27.*

Above: *Advertisements from British* Vogue *for perfume and bath essence from the house of Irfé, October 1936.*

teen dresses. And another ten for this imbecile,' she added, nodding toward her sponger, the small Austrian baroness."[9]

Either the *kokoshnik* that Nonna Kalashnikova sewed for Mrs. Whobee was really to the latter's liking, or the vogue for things Russian truly had no limits, for the client never parted with this brocade headdress embroidered with pearls. Thanks to customers like her, Irfé's fame spread and increased. Beginning in 1925, Parisian fashion magazines published modest advertisements for the house, and then drawings

of its best designs. Painting on silk defined Irfé's style in that period. During the 1925–26 seasons the Youssoupoff house created several successful elegant designs in silk batik. *Vogue* featured the originally cut dress "Bat" and "Water Lilies," shaped like a Russian peasant shirt. The textile pattern and the silhouette of the latter design were obviously old-fashioned. If in the early 1900s it had been difficult to get by without using water lilies and their pliable stems, in the Art Deco period such botanical investigations were obviously

275

beside the point. Nevertheless, the fluidity of the lengthened silhouette in defiance of the popular short styles of the day, and the elegance of the ensembles, attested to Princess Irina Youssoupoff's exceptional taste.

In 1920s Paris, Irina was renowned for her beauty. Tall, slender, "a purebred Romanov," she was photographed wearing Irfé dresses by many famous photographers, although she was never a model in the real sense of the word. Princess Tatiana Metternich, who now lives in Germany and knew Irina as a child, recalls in her memoirs: "Ephemeral, draped in silk dresses trimmed with fringe, with an ageless face like her husband's, she reminded one of a cameo. But sometimes, losing her usual restraint, she dispelled her charm with a dry remark uttered in a low and squeaky, purely Romanov voice."[10]

The Youssoupoff venture became very popular, and soon three branches

were opened. The first one, in Le Touquet, a resort town in Normandy, was managed by Antonina Nesterovskaya, the wife of Grand Duke Gavriil Konstantinovich, a cousin of Irina's. She had her own fashion business in Paris—the house of Bery. The second branch of Irfé was in London at no. 42 Berkeley Street, run by an Englishwoman, Mrs. Ansel. The house stands to this day. The Berlin branch was located on the Pariserplatz in the private residence of the Radziwills. The charming but unpredictable Princess Thurn-und-Taxis ran things there.

Because of Irfé's success, Prince Youssoupoff began to receive various enticing offers in other fields. Together with the Belgian Baron Edmond de Zuylen, Felix opened a shop of Youssoupoff porcelain on rue Richepanse called Monolix, which was designed by the Russian émigré architect Nikolai Iszelenov. Prince Youssoupoff also took part in designing three Parisian restau-

276

rants: Mrs. Tokareva's La Maisonnette on the rue Mont-Thabor; the Lido on the same street, with murals of Venetian carnivals by Schoukhaieff; and Mon Repos, run by Makarov on avenue Victor Hugo and decorated in the Russian peasant style. Youssoupoff-mania was so widespread in those years that one London restaurant offered "Fatted fowl à la Youssoupoff" on their menu.

For the 1926 season, the house of Irfé's new offerings were evening dresses embroidered in tiny round and bugle beads, which had become fashionable due to the success of the Kitmir House of Embroidery, and more sporty designs. Paris *Vogue* describes Irfé's 1926 winter collection in detail: "You have before you a collection which is at the same time a selection, because it does not include any bad designs. It is virtually the best line of designs ever created by this fashion house. The aura of amateurishness inherent in its first creations has disappeared completely. The level of technical execution has obviously risen. Prince Youssoupoff, the founder of Irfé, brings to his clothes his refined taste and striking personality, which expresses itself exceptionally well in the choice of lines and range of colors.

Opposite: *Drawings from the magazine* Paris-élégant *of designs for daytime summer dresses from the houses of Irfé, Les Soeurs Willy, and Christiane, November 1927.*

Right: *Princess Irina Youssoupoff in the salon of her residence in Boulogne, outside of Paris, February 1926. Photo by E. Scaioni for* Vogue.

Библиотека декоративных искусств. Париж

"The sportswear deserves special attention, although there isn't much of it. One of the best is a red pullover of wool jersey-kasha with a wide leather sash-belt of the same shade, and a Scottish wool skirt in a beige-red-brown mix with a matching scarf.

"The dresses, both for daytime wear and for evening, are elegant and noble in their calm lines. Inset decoration breaks up the surfaces of the fabrics, as do flounces, narrow and slightly gathered insertions, embroidery, softly moving and light draping. The hemlines on evening dresses are, as a rule, uneven. Evening coats, usually cut straight, captivate with their choice of fabrics—velvet, brocade, and fur—and by their elegant lines.

"The following fabrics are used: wool, velvet, satin, satin crepe, black Chantilly, gold lace, muslin, solid-color lamé for dresses and printed lamé for coats."[11]

Irfé was the first of the Russian houses to come out with their own perfume. Following Chanel's example, Felix and Irina Youssoupoff presented their perfume, Irfé, in 1926. It came in

different scents: for blondes, brunettes, and redheads. According to Xenia Sfiris, who is the prince's granddaughter and his favorite, both Felix and Irina took part in developing the perfume. All three versions of the fragrance had a sharp, spicy Eastern quality. Princess Margarita of Greece designed the advertising, which depicted a rectangular bottle with a faceted black glass cap.

Around this time Irfé began to sell colored fabric belts made by the Russian artist Marevna, who had just had a daughter fathered by Mexican artist Diego Rivera, and was in great need of a steady income. A needleworker, she went to the Russian Red Cross where she sewed shirts and longjohns for the demobilized White Army. Marevna designed a hand-printed sash with a pattern of antique Russian bridles with pompoms. Marevna made the rounds of all the Russian houses of fashion looking for work before she finally came upon Irfé. She writes in her memoirs: "Several weeks later, Countess Youssoupoff offered me work exclusively in her salons. Marika could be

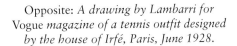

Opposite: *A drawing by Lambarri for* Vogue *magazine of a tennis outfit designed by the house of Irfé, Paris, June 1928.*

This page: *Drawings from the magazines* Paris-élégant *and* L'art et la mode *of designs from the house of Irfé, 1928.*

with me. We would live in a servant's room with an attic, and I could cook on an alcohol burner. She offered me 350 francs a month. Alas, this wasn't enough to live on and feed a child."[12]

The costs of production and the lack of interest in financial affairs on the part of the Youssoupoffs, who had once been so wealthy, brought the house to a financial crisis. Irfé was temporarily saved from ruin only by the infusion of a large sum from the accounts of Mrs. Vanderbilt and Mrs. Whoobee. Whoobee's help cost the Youssoupoffs their private residence in Boulogne, which they sold to her to cover their debts, and they moved to temporary quarters in the pavilion, which had served as the private theater.

Nonetheless, Irfé continued to create the obligatory number of simple, well-cut, elegant dresses for the new 1927–28

collections, and interest in the house did not fade in the least. The magazines *Paris-élégant, L'art et la mode,* and *Vogue* included Irfé's designs on their pages among the designs of the best houses. *Vogue* wrote about their 1928 collection: "A line of suits and coats, in tweeds and men's fabrics, sets the tone for this collection. Jackets and coats are slightly tapered at the natural level of the waist, and instead of the usual fur collars—small, stiff standing collars or classic folding European suit collars.

"There are quite a few dresses cut entirely from silk madras or patterned crepe de chine among the sportswear designs, sewn so that their lengthened bodices remind one of a sweater worn loose over a pleated skirt.

"Walking suits are popular at Irfé; the heavy morocain crepes and printed

Opposite above: *Prince Felix Youssoupoff
with his bulldog in his house
in Paris, c. 1929.*

Opposite below: *Princes Fedor
Alexandrovich and Nikita Alexandrovich
Romanov, Irina Youssoupoff's brothers,
during the years they worked for the
Red Cross, London, 1919.*

Above: *Prince Felix Youssoupoff in a
salon at the house of Irfé, Paris, 1920s.*

Above right: *Princess Irina Youssoupoff in
a dress from the house of Irfé, Paris, 1920.*

alpaca are exceptionally well suited for them. Evening dresses are done in various silks: taffeta, satin, crepe de chine, gauze and chiffon, in most cases with a printed design.

"Semi-transparent fabrics, such as tulle, muslin, lace, Roman crepe, crepe georgette, gold muslin, are preferable for evening. Skirts, lengthened either at the side or with trains in the back, are combined with slightly fitted bodices."

In creating a narrower, elongated feminine silhouette at the end of the 1920s, the house of Irfé predicted the lines of the next decade, that is, the post-crisis fashion of the 1930s.

But the Youssoupoffs were in a terrible mental state during this time, depressed by the death of Princess Irina's grandmother, the Dowager Empress Maria Feodorovna, the auction of the family's personal belongings organized by the Bolsheviks in Berlin, and the death of the Grand Duke Nikolai Nikolayevich in January 1929. To complete the family troubles, the financial crisis on Wall Street erupted in 1929, and they lost their well-to-do American clientele and a large part of the capital they had invested in American banks.

The house of Irfé tried to survive in difficult new conditions, and although

281

Архив автора, Париж

the personnel of the house changed a bit, it nonetheless remained staffed almost entirely by Russians. Princess Lieven was one of the seamstresses, assisted occasionally by the young Natalya Petrovna Bologovskaya. Irfé's main model was the Spanish model Carmen; of the Russian models, in addition to the aforementioned two Obolensky princesses and Princess Trubetskaya, we'll mention Kira Sereda, Baroness Anastasia von Nolken, General Nikolai Aleksandrovich Lokhvitsky's daughter Nelli Lokhvitskaya, Valya Speranskaya, Leka Kazachka, and Tamara Brodskaya, the Countess de Boucoiran by marriage.

The Baroness Anastasia Vladimirovna von Nolken, formerly a well-known Parisian model, who knew the Youssoupoff family well, recalls working at Irfé: "Felix Youssoupoff was a very eccentric man. He once noticed me at a naval ball in Paris and, as he had been

Above: Prince and Princess Youssoupoff in London, 1930s.

Opposite: The building in which the house of Irfé was located at no. 19 rue Duphot, Paris. Photo by Alexandre Vassiliev, 1994.

an acquaintance of my father's back in St. Petersburg, he invited me to work for him. My name, Anastasia, seemed too long to him, so he changed it to Asia, which is the name I used when I modeled designs at Irfé. His house was reminiscent of an Eastern palace: all the fitting rooms were lined in gray velvet, as if they were in Turkey. Felix himself received clients in a turban and Eastern robe, looking like a khan with his favorite bulldog. His spouse, on the contrary, was very modest and didn't like us, the models, to curtsey when we met. Apparently because of his eccentricity, Felix was not averse to trying on one dress or another to show everyone how it should be worn."[13]

It is difficult today to judge how much the clothes from Irfé cost. We were able to find only two people who were clients of the house during the 1920s—Valentina Kachouba, the Russian ballerina from the Diaghilev company, and Lady Abdy, an English aristocrat of Russian descent. Valentina Kachouba told us: "Prince Youssoupoff invited me to perform in his theater and offered several of his garments for sale. I took great pleasure in wearing one of them, a red evening dress."[14] The ninety-four-year-old Alexandra Dionisievna Danilova, a star of the Diaghilev seasons in the 1920s who lived in New York, recalled things in a somewhat different light: "Felix Youssoupoff suggested that we, the performers, should dress at his fashion house, but it was too expensive for us, and so instead we ordered copies of designs from the big houses which the Russian seamstress Vera Frank brought to us in a suitcase."[15]

Lady Adby adds another brushstroke to Felix Youssoupoff's portrait: "I bought a small and simple light-brown daytime dress from him. He didn't have anything especially beautiful. He was a very kind man, and whenever money would come his way, he gave it away to all the Russians who were in need."[16]

Prince Youssoupoff's memoirs, *Konets Rasputina* [The End of Rasputin], were published in 1927. The book turned part of the Russian colony in Paris militantly against him. The weekly *Dni* [Days] published by Alexander Kerensky printed an exposé on January 10, 1928, telling of a major scandal relating to the prince's private and financial affairs, Youssoupoff's impending deportation to Basel, and the closing of the Irfé business. Although this information was fabricated by the "enemy camp," the fashion house's business had become less than brilliant. Felix himself was preoccupied with receptions, exhibitions, and social life, and without serious daily management such enterprises are doomed to failure. Furthermore, some of the Irfé staff had defected to Elmis,

the fashion house run by Gali Bajenova.

Unfortunately, we have been able to locate only two dresses from the house of Irfé: one, a black silk dress, is at The Metropolitan Museum of Art's Costume Institute in New York, and the other is in the collection of a well-known American collector who wishes to remain anonymous. At that time, because of the large customs duties on European goods imported into the United States, many American clients cut out the Parisian fashion house labels from their clothes, passing them off to customs inspectors as American goods. This practice, incidentally, continued for many years, which partially explains the lack of large numbers of signed dresses from Russian fashion houses in American costume museums.

Suffering losses at Irfé, Prince Youssoupoff made a desperate attempt to unite Irfé with the Russian fashion house Yteb. After the most difficult and ruinous year of 1930, the financial affairs of Irfé were so bad that Parisian banks refused credit to the once fabulously wealthy Youssoupoff. He wrote in his memoirs: "We were forced to ask our clients to pay

for their orders upon receipt, which we were not accustomed to doing in the past."[17] Under the oppressive financial circumstances of 1931, the decision to liquidate the Irfé business and its branches was made. Sales of Irfé perfume were the only trade that continued for a time. The Prince himself recalls: "After this total defeat, I came to the conclusion that I wasn't cut out for commerce!"[18]

The completely ruined Youssoupoffs moved to a small two-room apartment on the first floor of a house on rue des Tourrelles. Felix and Irina's daughter, Irina, married Count Nicholas Sheremetyev in Rome in June 1938. The only child from this marriage, Xenia Nikolaevna Sfiris, née Countess Sheremetyeva, now lives in Athens and Paris. Her daughter, Felix and Irina Youssoupoff's great-granddaughter, Tatyana Ilinichna Sfiris, was born in Athens in 1968.

Prince Felix Felixovich Youssoupoff, Count Sumarokov-Elston, died in Paris on September 27, 1967, at the age of eighty. Princess Irina Alexandrovna Youssoupoff died in Paris on February 26, 1970, at the age of seventy-four.

13

THE BERY HOUSE OF FASHION

The Russian fashion house Bery was established in Paris in 1924 and lasted until 1936. The founder of the business and creator of the designs was Princess Antonina Rafailovna Romanovskaya-Strelninskaya (née Antonina Rafailovna Nesterovskaya), the wife of Prince Gavriil Konstantinovich Romanov.

Prince Gavriil Konstantinovich Romanov was the grandson of the brother of Emperor Alexander II, Grand Duke Konstantin Nikolayevich. Gavriil's grandmother, Alexandra, Princess Saxen-Altenburg, was an extraordinary beauty who had been immortalized by the brush of the talented artist Winterhalter.

The father of Gavriil Konstantinovich was the literarily gifted Grand Duke Konstantin Konstantinovich Romanov, who had served in the tsar's navy, as befitted grand dukes, and then shifted to the army due to weak health. He became famous for his poetry, using the *nom de plume* K. R. In St. Petersburg he owned the famous Marble Palace, located not far from Mars Field. Grand Duke Konstantin Konstantinovich was commander of the Preobrazhensky Regiment, founder of the Higher Women's Course in St. Petersburg, and a fervent proponent of universal establishment of village schools. He served as president of the Academy of Sciences and founded a department of belles-lettres. He corresponded with famous artists, such as Tchaikovsky.

Prince Gavriil, born on July 3, 1887, and his brother Prince Ioann, born a year earlier, were the first to suffer from the reforms of Emperor Alexander III,

Архив автора. Париж

Opposite: *Princess Antonina Romanovskaya-Strelninskaya (Nesterovskaya), owner of the house of Bery, Paris, c. 1927.*

Above: *The Marble Palace in St. Petersburg, photographed in the 1910s.*

who decreed that in the name of economizing the state budget, only the children and grandchildren of the reigning sovereign would bear the title of grand duke. Thus, Gavriil Konstantinovich could be called merely a prince of royal blood rather than a grand duke, which painfully hurt his pride. Grand dukes received 280,000 gold rubles annually from the imperial treasury, which guaranteed a comfortable life, while Prince Gavriil Konstantinovich was given a one-time sum of one million gold rubles, and he could count on nothing else.

As a child, Prince Gavriil had been brought up strictly: he and his siblings were taught to speak pure Russian without an admixture of foreign phrases, and they had to memorize prayers. Following in his father's footsteps, Gavriil Konstantinovich chose a military career, traditional for the Romanovs. At nineteen he was promoted to officer's rank and awarded several orders. He was close to the emperor and spent time with the latter's family, playing games, and often meeting with Grand Duchess Maria Pavlovna and her brother, Dmitrii Pavlovich.

On August 19, 1911, at a ball given by Matilda Felixovna Kchessinska, a ballerina at the Maryinsky Theater, Prince Gavriil met and fell in love with a pretty artist of the Imperial Ballet, Antonina Rafailovna Nesterovskaya, who had just turned twenty-one. She was born March 13, 1890, in St. Petersburg, to an impoverished noble family. Like her sister, Lidia, Antonina entered the school of the Imperial Ballet, and in 1906 was accepted into the troupe of the Maryinsky Theater as a member of the corps de ballet with a salary of 600 rubles. Nesterovskaya performed with the Maryinsky Theater for seven seasons, leaving the troupe in 1913. Tatyana Leskova, a soloist of the Ballet of Colonel de Basil, called Nesterovskaya "a ballerina by the water," a ballet term from the nineteenth century used to describe dancers who were placed in the

back row of the corps de ballet, right by the backdrops depicting lakes and rivers. Alice Frantzevna Vronska, who danced with her on the stage of the Maryinsky, characterized Nesterovskaya as a ballerina "of which there were many."

Nevertheless, perhaps thanks to the protection of Kchessinska or Prince Gavriil, Nesterovskaya danced small solo parts in some large ballets and in smaller productions. She soloed in the now-forgotten ballet *Pharaoh's Daughter* and in F. Gartman's ballet *The Red Flower*; considered more of a character dancer, she often danced mazurkas and Spanish dances. In the 1907–1908 season she toured Russia, appearing in Kiev, Kharkov, Baku, and other cities. For three seasons, from 1909 to 1911, she danced in the corps de ballet of Diaghilev's troupe, touring Paris, Brussels, Monte Carlo, Berlin, and Budapest.

Nesterovskaya was very short and well-built, with a round face and slightly upturned nose. It is not hard to imagine how she looked next to the enormous, more than six-foot-tall Prince Gavriil. Always dressed "in fashion and becomingly," Nesterovskaya was the archetypal saucy little ballerina of the early twentieth

century; but, although young and lovely, she was not the social equal of Gavriil Konstantinovich and could not dream about marriage—her lowly origins were an insurmountable barrier.

At the memorable party where they met, Nesterovskaya was taking part in a skit that parodied the stars of the Imperial Ballet. It was organized for her birthday by Mathilda Kchessinska, then the mistress of young Nicholas II. Even in her old age, Kchessinska recalled that the party had been "most grand and successful." At the entrance to her dacha in Strelna were posters heralding the unprecedented joint appearances of the imperial prima ballerinas: Kchessinska, Anna Pavlova, Olga Preobrazhenska, and Ekaterina Geltzer. For the occasion, the balcony of the dacha was fitted with a real stage with electric lighting, a curtain, and live plants.

Baron von Gotch imitated Kchessinska with success. He got into the role so much that, like Mathilda, he lay on a couch and ate only black caviar sandwiches. Misha Alexandrov portrayed Pavlova in *Giselle* and "flew around the stage like her" wearing a tunic. The virtuoso Preobrazhenska was imitated by von Gotch again. The Moscow prima donna, Geltzer, was parodied by our heroine Antonina Nesterovskaya, who was called "Nina" by the troupe. Kches-

sinska wrote in her memoirs, "Nina Nesterovskaya portrayed Ekaterina Geltzer in variations from *Don Quixote*. She sipped cognac all day and overdid it a bit—'for courage,' as she assured everyone."[1] After the performance a table was set in the garden with a sea of champagne, and the entire garden was lit with lanterns; the closeness of the nearby reservoir reminded the guests of Felicien, the restaurant on the water that was so popular in those years. The party continued until morning, and

Gavriil Konstantinovich was completely charmed by Antonina Nesterovskaya, who became his life companion for the next forty years.

Vladimir Krymov, the editor of *Stolitsa i usad'ba* [Capital and Estate], the first Russian magazine about the good life, knew the secrets of high society in Petrograd and was a friend of Kchessinska's and Nesterovskaya's. In his trilogy, *For the Millions*, he depicted both ballerinas under fictional names, capturing them and the atmosphere of their lives subtly and vividly; in particular, he described the party at Mathilda's house, calling her Felixa Adolfovna in the novel *How Well They Lived in St. Petersburg*. He describes the heroine whose prototype was Nesterovskaya as follows: "Always dressed a bit pretentiously, always in Paris gowns, and only now during the war, a few things from Brisac. She won't wear anything else. She makes a pouty little face, minces and says all kinds of silly things, repeating the same thing several times if it sticks in her head for some reason.

"She practically does not dance in the ballet, but when a pretty figure is called for, they give her mime roles. She is proud of that, her name is in the posters among the personae dramatis, and she considers herself a ballerina."[2]

In 1912 Prince Gavriil Konstanti-

Opposite, far left: *Antonina Nesterovskaya, a ballerina for the Maryinsky Theater, St. Petersburg, 1908–1912.*

Opposite, near left: *Nesterovskaya in a costume for the ballet* The Red Flower, *St. Petersburg, c. 1907.*

Above: *Antonina Nesterovskaya with her sister, Lidia Nesterovskaya, also a ballerina with the Maryinsky Theater, St. Petersburg, 1913. Photo by K. A. Fisher.*

Left and right: *Antonina Nesterovskaya, St. Petersburg, 1908–1912.*

Opposite: *Mathilda Kchessinska in a Russian costume during her last appearance at Covent Garden with the company of Ballet de Basile, London, 1936.*

Right: *Tamara Lempicka,* Portrait of Prince Gavriil Konstantinovich Romanov, *c. 1927.*

Частное собрание

289

novich and Nesterovskaya traveled on the special St. Petersburg–Monte Carlo train with Kchessinska and Grand Duke Andrei Vladimirovich to the French riviera, a famous vacation spot for the titled aristocracy at the turn of the century, to play roulette in Monte Carlo. The riviera idyll did not last long because they soon had to return to St. Petersburg, where the prince was at university. When World War I broke out, Prince Gavriil said good-bye to his mistress and headed to the active army, fighting in advance operations.

Evacuated to Petrograd in the fall of 1914, he joined the Military Academy, graduating at the age of twenty-nine with the rank of colonel. His affair with Nesterovskaya continued openly and was discussed publicly. The two lived together for a long time and in 1916 Empress Alexandra Feodorovna, seeing the sincerity of their feelings, decided to help them get married, even though it was considered a misalliance. Ballerinas were considered appropriate partners as mistresses but not as high-society wives.

However, Gavriil Konstantinovich participated in the conspiracy to kill Rasputin, which ruined his relationship with the empress, and his marriage to Nesterovskaya fell through. In February 1917, when the revolution broke out, Gavriil Konstantinovich was a student at the Military Academy in Petrograd,

Opposite: *Princess Xenia Georgievna Romanova in an embroidered dress, Paris, May 1928. Photo by Edward Steichen for* Vogue.

Above: *Princess Antonina Romanovskaya-Strelninskaya (Nesterovskaya), Paris, 1925.*

Below: *Zinaida Rashevskaya, Princess Romanovskaya, advertising cultured pearls by Tecla. Photo from the magazine* Fémina, *November 1925.*

but Nesterovskaya managed to save him from attack by an armed mob: she telephoned to warn him of the disorder and sent a car and driver for him.

Prince Gavriil Konstantinovich and Antonina Nesterovskaya managed to get married a few months later, on April 9, 1917, and Antonina Rafailovna Nesterovskaya became Princess Romanovskaya-Strelninskaya. The title of Princess Romanovskaya went automatically to

all ladies of unequal origins who married Romanovs, and the second part of the name usually indicated a family estate belonging to the Romanovs. In the case of Nesterovskaya, the second name was apparently a reference to Kchessinska's dacha in Strelna, a romantic reminder of how the newlyweds met.

After the Bolshevik revolt, Prince Gavriil Konstantinovich was arrested and, like other Romanovs, sent to prison. He found himself in the Fortress of Peter and Paul, together with Grand Duke Dmitrii Konstantinovich, his uncle Grand Duke Pavel Alexandrovich, and Grand Dukes Nikolai and Georgii Mikhailovich.

Nesterovskaya used every means fair and foul to get her beloved husband out of the Bolsheviks' hands, including using her "folk" ancestry. In his memoirs, Prince Felix Youssoupoff, who was in St. Petersburg during these tragic events, wrote: "Thanks to the energy and cleverness of his wife, who obtained his release, Prince Gavriil avoided the fate of his relatives. The rest of the prisoners in the Fortress of Peter and Paul were soon executed. Grand dukes Georgii and Dmitrii died in prayer, Grand Duke Paul, gravely ill by then, was killed on his stretcher, and Grand Duke Nikolai died joking with his executioners and holding his favorite kitten."[3]

Nesterovskaya and Gavriil Konstantinovich hurriedly left Russia and made their roundabout way to France. Their material situation was very difficult. Antonina first considered opening a ballet studio, which many ballerinas from the Imperial Ballet did when they found themselves living abroad as émigrés—Nesterovskaya's sister, Lidia, had such a studio in Berlin, and then in Holland. But fate had other plans. Inspired by the work of Russian aristocratic women in the world of fashion, Nesterovskaya decided to open her own house.

The times were quite suitable: everything Russian was in style, and republican France was rather stunned by the lofty Russian titles. *Vogue*, in a 1924 article called "A Russian Aristocrat Finds Salvation in Work" wrote: "We are no longer surprised to encounter Russian society ladies among the sales staff in fashion houses or the directors of fashionable ateliers and houses of embroidery, or the authors of fashion illustrations. They have shown great talent, ability to work, and demonstrated such courage, steadfastness, and determination to forget their past, that now they are the objects of universal adoration."[4]

The house of Bery, opened by Antonina Nesterovskaya and Gavriil Konstantinovich, was at 38-bis rue Vitale. Although magazines began writing about it as early as 1925, praising the particular elegance of its designs, it was still just a small family enterprise. The first clients were naturally attracted by the person and title of Gavriil Konstantinovich, great-grandson of Emperor Nicholas I, but soon the house came to be recognized on its own merit. A Parisian publication wrote of Bery: "You will find luxurious toilettes there, distinguished by the stamp of the most refined Paris taste at the lowest prices."[5]

Unfortunately, the house of Bery did not label its work, which makes it hard to find them in the collections around the world. However, we did manage to find a seamstress from the house—Vera Vladimirovna Pyatakova, who came to Paris in 1929 by ship from Constantinople. She told us: "In those days there were many Russian seamstresses in Paris.

Архив Жака Ферриана, Париж

Above: *Princess Antonina Romanovskaya-Strelninskaya (Nesterovskaya), Paris, 1919.*

Opposite, top and bottom: *Two views of the building in which the house of Bery was located. Photo by Alexandre Vassiliev, 1997.*

As soon as the Russian arrived here, the husbands became taxi drivers, and the wives started sewing. The seamstress Semenova lived in our hotel, and I secretly took sewing lessons from her."[6]

Fate brought Vera Vladimirovna to Bery, which had moved to no. 2 rue de Dardenelles in 1929, taking up the first floor in a large apartment. Clients were received in the large salon, filled with antique furniture. The walls were covered with photographs from the life of Prince Gavriil, the Romanov family, and Antonina Nesterovskaya. This entertained and impressed the clients, including the many American millionaires who had stormed postwar Paris in search of the extravagant life and the opportunity to meet real Russian princes, who were not yet very much in evidence in the United States.

There were six seamstresses and one main cutter, Vera Alexeyevna Shorina, at Bery. Her statuesque demeanor caused some clients to take her for the princess. Vera Vladimirovna recalled: "The collections created by Antonina Rafailovna consisted of day wear and chic evening gowns, suits, and cloaks. We did not do furs at the atelier, and if necessary sent them out to a furrier. The Bery did not have models." In order to improve and simplify the quality of production, the princess bought designs stolen from the big fashion houses and produced copies. Thanks to the high quality of the sewing, Bery's garments were still quite expensive.

Antonina Nesterovskaya had indisputable taste, but, as often was the case in Russian houses, the organizational aspect was not the best. The servants often cheated the mistress, and orders were often delayed. The clients waited impatiently in the salon, and then Prince Gavriil Konstantinovich would come visit with them. Vera Vladimirovna recalled, "The prince entertained the clients: he took a long time showing them albums of family photographs, commenting on each one, to drag out the time and let us finish the order." At first Vera Vladimirovna was paid 139 francs a week at Bery, and in the 1930s one could live on that in Paris.

Prince Gavriil Konstantinovich and his wife did not lose their interest in society once they were abroad. They were constant attendees at the many Russian balls, frequently enjoyed evenings out in Russian nightclubs, and continued their close friendship with Kchessinska, who lived near Passy. The couple spent some time at the dacha of Monsieur Binnemet, the director of Houbigant, the cosmetics firm, which was not far from the chateau Marly-le-Roi. Another friend and relative whom Prince Gavriil Konstantinovich often saw was Grand Duchess Xenia Alexandrovna, who lived in London.

Following the example of Prince Gavriil, Grand Duchess Maria Pavlovna, and Irina Youssoupoff, other Romanovs went into the fashion business. Zinaida Sergeyevna Rashevskaya, the wife of Grand Duke Boris Vladimirovich, became a photo model for Tekla, the Paris firm of cultured pearls. Duchess Marina of Kent, née Princess Romanov, and Grand Duchess Kira Kirillovna, sister of Grand Duke Vladimir Kirillovich, both worked as models for fashion magazines.

On October 13, 1938, the head of the House of Romanov, Grand Duke Kirill Vladimirovich, died in Neuilly near Paris. His son, Grand Duke Vladimir Kirillovich, who took over the title, was concerned with preserving the significance of the Romanov titles, since by

then there were only five living Romanov grand dukes. He bestowed the title of grand duke upon Gavriil Konstantinovich on May 15, 1939, marking an important moment in Gavriil's émigré life. This action, however, has been contested by some other Romanovs.

Bery's business slowly declined and the house had to be closed about 1936. After Bery shut down, Grand Duke Gavriil Konstantinovich and Princess Romanovskaya-Strelninskaya lived very

modestly in a Paris suburb, where the grand duke wrote his memoirs, *In the Marble Palace*. To earn money, he organized bridge parties and the princess occasionally gave dance lessons. The antique dealer Natalya Alexandrovna Offenstadt, who knew her in those years, recalls, "The entire hallway in their apartment was hung with family photographs. Gavriil Konstantinovich once said, 'I've begun to like living here, too.' They lived happily and often had tea parties. At an elderly age, Antonina Rafailovna was more like a simple Russian woman than a princess. But once she began talking, you could hear the closeness to the grand ducal circles with their refined turns of phrase. She was a real society lady. Apparently life among the Romanovs had made her that way. But as soon as she shut her mouth, she looked like a Russian peasant woman with a braid around the crown of her head. She always brought my children chocolates, and we called her the 'chocolate princess.'"[7]

Princess Antonina Rafailovna Romanovskaya-Strelninskaya died March 7, 1950, in Paris. Her husband not only survived her, but in 1951 remarried forty-eight-year-old Princess Irina Kurakina, who also became Princess Romanovskaya. Grand Duke Gavriil Konstantinovich died on February 28, 1955, in Paris.

14

ARDANSE HOUSE OF FASHION

The Russian fashion house Ardanse was established in Paris in 1924 and was in business until 1946. The founder of the business and the creator of the designs was Baroness Cassandra Nikolayevna Accourti von Konigsfels. She was born in St. Petersburg with the maiden name Cassandra Coralie.

Never one to shun work, Baroness Accourti was a nurse in St. Petersburg during World War I, and once in Paris followed the example of other aristocratic women and went into fashion. Her sister, Baroness Ekaterina Nikolayevna von Driesen, also worked at Ardanse. Thea Bobrikova, the main model at Lanvin, and then a model at Ardanse, recalled that at first the Baroness Accourti was not made welcome by her fellow countrywomen. "She was looked down upon by the aristocrats of the first wave of emigration because of her very minor title."[1] (Cassandra Nikolayevna's family came from Austro-Hungary and was added to the book of Russian barons by decree of Emperor Alexander III only in 1891.)

Despite the rocky start, the house of Ardanse turned out to be more solid than the rest. The unusual taste of its owner and the lack of grandiose ambitions helped the house survive in a period when many of its competitors were closing down. Cassandra Nikolayevna opened her business on the Right Bank, in a prestigious neighborhood of Paris. A luxurious mansion, at no. 37 rue Bienfaisance, built by the architect Troncoix in 1877, the house was decorated exquisitely in a single color scheme. "Here everything is

Opposite: *A portrait by V. Shtemberg of Baroness Cassandra Nikolayevna Accourti, 1910s.*

Above: *A view of Petrograd in 1914.*

violet," wrote a charmed visitor to the house in 1925, "and not that boring violet shade, but warm and modest, bringing to mind the color and fragrance of violets de Parme. The armchairs, carpets, showrooms, fitting rooms, even the writing paper, boxes and wrapping paper are all the same violet color, and this color unity creates an indescribable charm. The saleswomen and pretty models who inhabit these magical sets are dressed in violet without exception, harmonizing with the interior. I don't suppose you could find a more soothing tone to show off the wealth of color demonstrated in the designs."[2]

The pale violet was not the only "corporate color" of Ardanse. In 1928 it was replaced by aquamarine, which was then seen in every detail of the decor. Baroness Accourti personally met every invited client and presented glorious roses, tied with a ribbon of pale blue with an amaz-

ing aquamarine tint. The color selection, naturally, was not random. Pale violet and aquamarine were the favorite colors of Empress Alexandra Feodorovna. Baroness Accourti's color talent was noted in the press and the reviews of Ardanse collections included analyses of its evolution. The "aristocratic charm" of Ardanse, which all the fashion magazines described, overcame the initial mistrust of the high aristocracy. Ardanse began dressing the noble ladies of the Russian émigré colony.

The feminine and elegant dresses of Ardanse were created by Baroness Accourti herself. She preferred delicate pastels, washed-out color combinations based on the traditional tastes of the Winter Palace. Judging from a portrait done in the 1910s, she had once been a follower of Art Nouveau and liked clothing in those colors. In this portrait Cassandra Nikolayevna is depicted in a dress of light soft fabric in pale colors, contrary to the fashion of the day, which dictated bright contrasting colors in clothing. Her preference for calm, gentle femininity was retained in her own designs. She used the corporate color—Ardanse blue—in many of her day and evening ensembles of the late 1920s, which were "full of charm and brilliance" according to the critics. Noting the beauty of her designs, they were pleased to see that her fashions were suitable for everyday wear as well.

Shows of the Ardanse collection took place in salons elegantly decorated with flowers, on a small stage with fiery

Архив автора, Париж

orange velvet curtains. One such collection was called "A Day in the life of a Parisian Woman," featuring a woman wearing Ardanse perfume and clothing set off by hats, furs, and jewels from Agnès, Ostertag, and Heim, "serving as excellent frames for the designs."[3]

Every collection from Ardanse was an event in the world of fashion, as can be seen from the regularly published reports in the years 1928–1932 in the authoritative and popular Paris magazine *L'Art et la mode* [Art and Fashion]. There were so many magical, enchanting outfits with exotic or romantic names! For instance, "Amourette" from the 1928 collection, made of soft draped black silk jersey with a pleated skirt—a contrast to the dress with the flying collar of snowy organdy. "Fabienne" astonished the imagination of fashion plates with lovely billowing sleeves that revealed the shoulders. It was replaced by a dress of tulle the color of pink champagne ("Petit Sax"), which charmed with its saucy youthfulness. At the waist was a wide belt of taffeta in the same shade, tied in a

bow. But the pearl of the collection was "The Last Goddess," an evening dress made of snowy jersey, embroidered with sparkling strass, it seemed to flow over the model's body, creating an incomparably feminine line.

In the 1928 collection was another design that caught the eye of journalists—"Sister Teresa," a dress of black crepe satin with a snow-white collar "flying up at the slightest breeze and enchanting with its sorrowful charm." The silhouette of "Sister Teresa" was clearly built on the memories of the nursing uniform worn by the baroness in Petrograd during World War I, probably not without a hint of coquettishness. The personal experiences of the creator of Ardanse were reflected in many of the house's designs. Following in the footsteps of Jeanne Lanvin, Ardanse had a specialty clothing line for girls and young women. "It is impossible to resist the dresses for young ladies from Ardanse. There is nothing more adorable than 'My First Dance' of foaming champagne tulle, so appropriate for

our seventeen-year-olds, to be shown with the design 'My First Doll,' a miracle in miniature of taffeta the color of blue porcelain, modeled by a delightful eight-year-old. Both designs were joyfully received."[4] Ardanse had many orders for these dresses as their wealthy clientele was always looking for sweet presents to give to their daughters.

The house of Ardanse survived the economic collapse of 1929, and, even during the most difficult post-crisis seasons from 1930 to 1933, continued to show designs ornamented with precious stones and lace, reacting only slightly to the new economic reality. The reason for the long life of Ardanse was that it never oriented itself to the American market, as had Irfé, Yteb, Bery, and Ymedy. Ardanse was more oriented to the traditional Paris haute-couture market, and its clients were frequently ladies of wealth and family, of the same age as Baroness Accourti.

An interesting description of an Ardanse collection is dated February 1930: "This young house, which is be-

AU BAL DE LA PRINCESSE D'AREMBERG

ing spoken about more and more frequently . . . today showed a complete collection of original beach pajamas, distinguished by excellent taste. Ardanse also has very beautiful evening gowns, which resonate with the aristocratic being of its creator. Herself a woman of society, she works primarily for society ladies who are capable of appreciating the subtleties of her taste.

Opposite: *Baroness Accourti as a nurse in a Petrograd hospital, c. 1916.*

Above: *A page from the magazine* L'Art et la mode *(1929, no. 30) of evening dress designs from the young house of Ardanse, and a design from the famous house of Lanvin, as seen by an illustrator at a ball given by Princess d'Arenberg.*

"Among the spring outfits for women, who are used to being distinguished by their elegance, is the 'Trilby' dress with Scottish skirt. The 'Chiberthe' in light blue with dark blue sheen, which we have come to love and which is now called 'Ardanse,' consists of a bolero with a flirtatious lacy trim reminiscent of Madeira embroidery. Since the elegant clients of this select house are not

297

yet feeling a financial pinch, Ardanse practically tosses over its evening designs charming cloaks, pelerines, or wavy boleros of muslin, covering the arms and décolleté. We hail these new models of elegance, which allow one to head off straight from tea to dinner or the theater, removing if one wants only the airy, intangible veil through which the whiteness of skin glows tenderly. Ardanse has come up with many innovations, and its sense of total harmony is such that the chosen ones say that they make appointments with the refined mistress of the artistic studio so that she can study their figure and create an absolutely individual look for them."[5]

Let us note that it was rare for there to be such a detailed review in the pages of the respected magazine *L'Art et la mode* of a collection of a fashion house established by Russian émigrés. From the descriptions it is clear that Baroness Accourti created first and foremost for herself, that is, she trusted her feminine intuition and knowledge of society. The designs for the February 1930 collection were more practical than before, which is a vivid demonstration of her sense of the times and of the attention she paid to the shifts in the fashion market. In that sense the work of Baroness Accourti deserves the highest praise. Without yielding to the theatricality and decorativeness typical of Russian creators of fashion, she used only the most noble fabrics and had a clear preference for transparent materials with a lacy effect—lace, tulle, muslin, and organdy. From season to season she created varied and unified collections that sold well in Paris for many years.

However, the work of Russians in fashion was often resented by French couturiers. To quote the famous fashion designer of the 1920s, Jean Patou: "Take the Russians, for instance. . . . Their artists had a strong influence on our theater costumes, especially in color and embroidery, but I can't remember if I've ever heard of a great Russian fashion designer."

Ardanse was an exemplary organization. Work was not unsupervised, as in

Opposite: *Drawings from the French magazine* L'Art et la mode *of silk evening dresses designed by the house of Ardanse, 1929.*

Above: *A Russian model in an evening dress of black velvet and white chiffon designed by Ardanse, Paris, April 1929. Photo by George Hoyningen-Huene for* Vogue.

some other Russian houses, but was handled professionally and methodically. Collections were prepared and shown regularly and were widely reviewed in the press. Madame de Mirecour, the reviewer from *L'Art et la mode*, wrote about the collection shown in Au-

gust 1930: "In that luxurious mansion, drowning in extraordinary flowers, it was hard for us to find a free place on the day of the opening, when beautiful, tall and slender girls presented a well-thought-out collection.

"I particularly liked 'Rendezvous,' a cloak of fumikasha of Mediterranean blue trimmed in gray karakul, and 'For Tomorrow,' a housedress in a pale green mother-of-pearl, with long sleeves of silk lace that are just right for coquettes.

"'Sèvres Biscuit' is made of almost intangible lace through which the whiteness of skin shows through, and seems to be a design of rare perfection.

"Another dress with the promising name 'I Always Smile' seems to be named appropriately. Made of light blue taffeta, it will ornament our eighteen-year-old daughters. Without a doubt, everyone will smile at the sight of the outfit."[6]

Although Russian style, imbued with decorative elements, went out of style in the mid-1920s, Ardanse carried nostalgic Russian elements in its collections. Of course, the Baroness Accourti did not introduce Russian folk art in her designs, but her high society style with the sparkle of the St. Petersburg pre-revolutionary splendor retained a delighted memory of Russia. Madame de Méricour wrote: "The ornament of the Ardanse collection is 'Neva Ice,' which consists of a waisted jacket and a slightly A-line skirt out of Russian ermine the color of a white lily. What fashionable woman doesn't dream about this inaccessible ensemble? Let us note that most of the formal afternoon and evening dresses were presented with accessories from Weil jewelers, with whom Baroness Accourti collaborates fruitfully."[7]

A definite advantage of Accourti's house was the presence of permanent models from among the Russian émigré community, slender tall women, brilliant not with noble titles but with stature and beauty. At various times the models at Ardanse included young women from Russian families: Kitty Upornikova, Ksyusha Katkova, Thea Bobrikova, and Nina Tverdaya. In the late 1930s for a very brief time Barbara

Библиотека декоративных искусств, Париж

ARDANSE

ARD

Rapponet—the future star of Schiaparelli during the war years—worked at Ardanse. In 1930 Ardanse hired a finalist of the Miss Russia contest organized by *Illustrirovannaya Rossiya* (Illustrated Russia). Nina Vasilyevna Egorova, married name Tverdaya, was one of the two runners-up, and her photograph was published in the Paris magazine, which was distributed in all the countries of the Russian diaspora, so that the contest finalists were known from Harbin, China, to New York. They received fan letters and were adored.

Nina Egorova was invited by Boris Evelinov, an organizer of fashion shows, to enter the "Elegance" competition for models that took place on the Côte d'Azur. Baroness Accourti saw her there and took her into her fashion house, where she modeled for several seasons. Nina recalled: "The designs of Ardanse were quite varied. There were many silk dresses with lace in pastel tones. I often showed evening gowns, since I was tall."[8] Another model, Thea Bobrikova, also recalled the house's special predilection for lace trim.

L'Art et la mode wrote on February 20, 1931: "In the overflowing lovely mansion, where the celebrated fashion designer set up her Penates, at the impressive staircase decorated with garlands of flowers, gathered famous Parisian women in obedient anticipation of a marvelous festival of beauty. This anticipation was the result—and everyone knows this now—of the creations of Baroness Accourti being completely devoid of banality. The refinement of her ensembles lies in the fact that they are harmoniously completed with a flower or a precious necklace from Ostertag. And now she has added yet another charming detail—'runless' stockings manufactured for the first time in an American factory. Ardanse has the monopoly on production in Paris. All these details compete among themselves for most refined. The impression is perfect: exquisiteness combined with enchanting chic. In giving the public this magnificence, Baroness Accourti has selected beautiful young women with marvelous deportment, which is not always simple, to model the designs, and the effect has surpassed expectations.

"Among the evening gowns the most marvelous was 'Mirage' of snowy white muslin and airy laces, which was very popular. It is hard to resist 'Opium Smoke' with long muslin sleeves, falling with smooth softness. Exceptionally fine are 'Gloria' and the mysterious 'Fantaisie d'Ardanse' of black tulle stitched in white. Its clinging sleeves are embroidered from elbow to wrist with diamonds, shimmering, and are trimmed with tulle that floats like a cloud resembling the contorted shapes of Japanese trees.

"In conclusion, yet another discovery—a dress of violet pink with a veil attached to the hair with a comb with roses in the same shade. This design, marked with great taste, is cleverly called 'My Second Marriage.'"[9]

The unusual decision to make a wedding dress in violet-lilac tones, and a bold name were repeated in the design 'My Third Marriage,' shown in May 1931, which also delighted Madame de Mirecour: "The recently shown designs from Ardanse had a great success thanks to the ideas of Baroness Accourti. The last special show was intended for connoisseurs and ended with a reception that began at 10 P.M. The brilliant fashion designer appeared in a charming lace dress revealing her marvelous shoulders. The pure lines of the dress may be the fashion of the season.

"This reception for the select was given to mark the success of the House of Ardanse. The interior, decorated with rare blooms, the luxurious repast, and the lively social conversation made the fortunate guests completely forget the time.

"Would you like to hear about some of the 'small miracles' shown there? For

Drawings from the magazine L'Officiel *of designs by Ardanse, 1929.*

Фотограф Росис-Вилас, Париж

Mirecour, "there was 'Tenderness' of black tulle combined with tulle scarves of various shades of gray with a delicate nuancing of tones. This astonishing dress is simultaneously the most Parisian and the most aristocratic in the world . . . and it astonished everyone."[10]

These descriptions by Madame de Mirecour, the faithful admirer of the talent of the Baroness Accourti, show what an important role tulle played in the designs of the house of Ardanse. Working with this airy material allowed the designer to achieve her favorite effect of transparency and weightlessness. The last delighted report from *L'Art et la mode* is dated August 1931. Here it is in full:

"Ardanse is distinguished by young girls whose function is to elicit applause. They have sophisticated hairdos. The precious fabrics are so becoming to them. At first we saw modest youthful sports ensembles, then a series of evening gowns. It is impossible not to fall in love with them. They created the reputation of this totally unique house. Here is a black dress with a jacket of 'angel skin' the color of white camellia, trimmed with black karakul, that deserved the bravos it elicited. And here is an emerald green satin, enchantingly beautiful. . . . The design 'Boldness' harmoniously combines lace of a delightful cherry color with airy tulle of the same shade.

"Here is 'Fire and Flame,' a design difficult to describe, for it has so many different shades of the most lovely red tones. They all combine in a eye-pleasing silk drapery. The red tones of Ardanse seem to have been created especially for this dress, since one feels flawless taste

instance, 'Desire,' a dress of white muslin trimmed with golden 'mordore' lace; 'Hauteur'—a design of black tulle and velvet with a high waistline, decorated with a snow-white camellia. There was also an ensemble of wool in a blue stripe on ochre, called 'End of April,' with a blouse of ocher crepe de chine.

"There was 'Love of Ardanse' in black tulle. The dress was sewn with white lace on the diagonal, and the pattern resembles thin branches. And Ardanse also presented 'My Third Marriage' a dress of fiery carmine red, whose brightness was dimmed by a short cloak of amethyst crepe de chine.

"Among the original dresses that made us fall in love is 'Joy of Life' of golden yellow muslin with inserts of lace in the same shade and a floating shawl.

"In conclusion," wrote Madame de

This page and opposite: Evening dresses by Ardanse, mid-1930s. Photo by Boris Lipnitsky.

Архив автора, Париж

Библиотека декоративных искусств, Париж

Библиотека декоративных искусств, Париж

in the selected scale of colors. And here is yet another unique color in 'Roxana.' The dress is made from Ophelia tulle, the low waistline is underlined with precious ornamentation in the form of a branch, which gives the design a rare wholeness.

"And so many other designs using inserts of lace, more than can be mentioned! I will stop on just one very beautiful dress, consisting of black tulle skirt and corsage of nymph tulle. . . . This refined ensemble is successfully completed with embroidery along the edge. This is the most exquisite embroidering from the house of Batay and is called Souvenir de Malmaison. It depicts slightly faded roses in mother-of-pearl and pale pink tones. The embroidery added to the charm of the ensemble and did not go unnoticed by the connoisseurs.

Left and right: *Drawings from* Vogue *of silk cocktail dresses designed by Ardanse, 1928.*

Above: *The famous French singer Mistinguett, a client of the house of Ardanse, Paris, 1928.*

Opposite: *Nina Tverdaya, a model for Ardanse and one of the finalists of the 1930 Miss Russia contest in Paris, in a black jersey dress designed by Ardanse, 1934.*

"This detail is enough to understand that Baroness Accourti, a great artist who heads the House of Ardanse, is not afraid to cooperate with other firms if it is for the greater good."[11]

Ardanse's work with other French and American firms helped solidify the house's reputation. The house's exclusive designs, combined with jewelry and embroidery of the highest class from other houses, achieved enviable success.

By the mid-1930s, Ardanse's primary Russian competitor in Paris was Nadine Oblonsky's fashion house, which dressed the British nobility. Another competitor was the house of de Nagornoff, which advertised heavily in the 1930s.

Ardanse continued to operate into the 1940s. In the February 1937 collection an unusual design, wittily named "Wedding in an Airplane" by Baroness Accourti, garnered general accolades. The last mention of this interesting Russian fashion house in Paris was in the May 1946 issue of *Fémina*, where an Ardanse design—a summer suit with padded shoulders and raglan sleeves—is mentioned along with designs from such famous houses of the postwar period as Hermès, Carven, Jacques Griffe, and Germaine Lecomte.

In the 1940s the press illustrates Ardanse's fidelity to its style: "An Ardanse suit of crepe in the shade of blue sax with raised designs in the shape of landscapes and white people. In front the jacket closes with four large buttons of white and gilt wood. The skirt has deep, wide pleats."[12] As you can see, the Baroness Accourti retained her love for porcelain figurines forever.

The direction chosen by the house of Ardanse was highly valued by the picky Parisian arbiters of fashion, and the mistress of the house had their deserved respect.

Ardanse enjoyed a wide range of clientele. "Baroness Accourti," they wrote, "has shown designs that charmed the

Архив автора. Париж

representatives of the knowing elite. In creating wedding dresses and trousseaus for brides, she uses old family lace with tact. To ornament a cloak she uses rare furs that can be appreciated only by Russians. Thus, gradually, her creations in the highest taste found their way from her house for the elite to big foreign clients, who did not care about price and demanded her work."

Admirers of Ardanse in Paris were not only the aristocrats of the salons, but the famous stars of the Paris stage. Mistinguett, the popular singer of the

1920s who sang of love for princes, bought a famous dress called 'The Only One' for two million francs. The corset belt was made of precious stones by Ostertag jewelers. The skirt of gold lace looked like butterfly wings. The dress astonished connoisseurs with its freshness and lovely lines.

Ardanse, almost the only Russian fashion house to survive the economic crisis of 1929, continued its activities throughout the 1930s, lasted through the difficult war years, and closed only in 1946.

15

THE VALENTINA HOUSE OF FASHION

Dedicated to Valentina Sanina

Where do you wilt, milady, as you get on in years,
Years catch women in a web, cast wrinkles on their faces
Even the most gorgeous orchids droop, poor dears,
Without some aspirin in their vases.
Good thing you're not here in the Soviet Union.
Whatever would you do?

Here women are not vamps or Medusas—
*   they serve better uses,*
They sensibly get degrees, society for to please,
And become warriors of science and of labor.

Alexander Vertinsky, *Myshi* [Mice]
April 24, 1949, Moscow

The Valentina House of Fashion was established in New York in 1928 and was in business until 1957. Its founder and designer was Valentina Nikolayevna Sanina. This remarkable woman's date of birth generates legends. According to American sources, Valentina Sanina was born in Kiev on May 1, 1904. However, a more in-depth study of the Russian period of her biography reveals that 1894, if not even earlier, is the actual year of her birth.

Sanina reduced her age when she moved to the United States and stubbornly held to her self-created version all her life. Only after she died was the secret date of her birth uncovered—it was announced that she was in her nineties, a decade older than her contemporaries believed.

Valentina Sanina's life in Russia has been little studied until now. The Ukranian State Theater Museum in Kiev does not contain any records on her career there. Sanina's triumphs as a costume designer for Broadway shows are usually attributed to the power and influence of her husband, George Shlee, a well-known producer, while her fame, to a considerable degree, was attributed to her friendship with Greta Garbo, who subsequently became Shlee's lover.

Much about Sanina's life has escaped biographers. Her love affair with the famous "Russian Pierrot," Alexander Vertinsky, before she left Russia, is worth discussing. His dedication "to Valentina Sanina" appears on several editions of the sheet music of his sad

Opposite: Valentina Nikolayevna Sanina in a design from her house of Valentina, New York, 1951. Photo by Horst.

Above: An autographed photograph of Valentina Sanina, 1930s.

songs from 1918 to 1919. They include "*Buynyi veter*" [Turbulent Wind], "*Za kulisami*" [Backstage], and "*Eto vsyo, chto ot Vas ostalos*" [This Is All that Remains of You]. These songs are infatuated, sad, heart-rending ballads, pining for the trampled love that Vertinsky suffered and cherished all his life. The poems, *Myshi* [Mice], dedicated to Valentina Sanina as late as 1949 attest to this. Who was she, this enigmatic Valentina, who later became the star of fashionable New York?

Apparently, after graduating from

high school in Kiev before the revolution, Sanina took drama courses and dreamt of becoming an actress. She began acting on the Kharkov stage during the 1917–18 season. Vertinsky wrote about her:

I remember you as a young actress.
How you looked . . . Your nostrils, full
*   of fire . . .*
At times you'd play Nora, at others—
*   sad Beatrice*
Or sweet Larisa or some other
*   miss . . .*
But as a rule the act you put on was
*   for me—*
Your consummate fool.[1]

Vertinsky met Sanina in 1918 in Kharkov during the Russian civil war. At that time Kharkov was ruled by the government of the Ukrainian Hetman, and Colonel Balbachan was governor. Quite a few celebrities sparkled on the Kharkov stage: Timme, Valerskaya, Blumenthal-Tamarina, and Leontovich, who became famous in New York in the Broadway musical *Grand Hotel* after she emigrated. The fateful encounter between the singer and the actress took place in the basement of the Kharkov Artists' Club, at 6 Sumskaya Street, where there was a lively artistic cabaret, known for its bar and full program of improvisation. Vertinsky reminisced about this important meeting in detail: "Volynsky the prompter, a small man whom I knew from Kiev, took me to the bar. It was still early, about nine in the evening. There was a beautiful young woman sitting on a high stool at the bar.

"'I'd like you to meet,' he said, 'Valentina Sanina.'

"Enormous, serene blue eyes with long lashes looked at me mellowly, and she extended a slim hand with long fingers of rare beauty to me. She was very striking, this woman. She held her head as if she were wearing a heavy gold crown. She had slanting cheekbones and a beautifully curved, slightly ironic mouth."[2]

According to this description, Vertinsky met a beautiful young woman in Kharkov in 1918, and not an adolescent, which is what she would have been had she actually been born in 1904. He met a woman who could enchant, who knew what she was worth. A striking woman who loved and knew how to dress, and who subsequently made a career dressing others.

Vertinsky continues: "Besides, she looked a lot like a fluffy angora cat. Sanina lazily sucked some sort of grenadine drink through a straw, and calmly scrutinized me, before swallowing.

"I realized that I was a goner, but I wasn't about to give up without a battle. I examined her just as calmly. She was wearing a black dress buttoned up to the neck; a white crystal cross hung from a ribbon around her neck. Unfortunately, people recognized me and, in a few minutes, actors and actresses, and various other people surrounded me. They pestered me, kissed and embraced me, and asked me questions. This was the usual scene when I appeared in any public place.

"When the commotion around me died down somewhat, Sanina asked, smiling ironically:

"'Aren't you sick and tired of all this yet?'

"'Of what?'

"'Well . . . this . . . idolatry.'

"'Of course, I am,' I replied. 'I have this dream that I'll find myself an understudy.'

"She burst out laughing.

"'Poor thing!' she said. 'I feel sorry for you. Has this been going on for a long time?'

Above: *Alexander Vertinsky, the year of his love affair with Valentina Sanina, 1918.*

Opposite: *Sheet music with the song "This Is All that Remains of You" by Vertinsky dedicated to Sanina, Kharkov, 1918.*

"'Oh, yes! . . . About three years.'

"She shook her head: 'You ought to have it treated.'

"'How?'

"'I don't know. Something . . . Go to a monastery. Maybe that will help.'

"'Now, really!' I expressed surprise. 'Let's go now. The program's about to start.'

"We walked out of the bar and sat down at a small table. That's how the 'history of my illness' began."[3]

The singer continues: "I gave concerts and courted Valentina. On my nights off from concerts, I would go to see her perform in the theater, although she had bit parts.

"'They're still young. . . . Let them study some more,' Nikolai Nikolayevich [the impresario Nikolai Nikolayevich Sinelnikov] would say about the young actors and actresses. And Valentina studied and worked, trying out her powers mostly on me. I was something of a guinea pig for her.

"Sometimes she would be harsh with me, at other times very affection-

ate and, after an absurd argument, she would come to the Astrakhanka to beg my forgiveness.

"'And why is it,' I would ask suspiciously, 'that you're putting on such an air of meekness?'

"She made a martyr's face, bowed low from the waist, monk-style, and said:

"'Today is Forgiveness Sunday. You have to ask everyone to forgive you. Forgive me, in the name of Christ, if I've offended you in some way.'

"And she giggled like a madwoman.

"'God will forgive you, Ma'am,' I said.

"She was acting 'for practice.'"[4]

Valentina Sanina was a femme fatale, in the complete sense of the word, able to bewitch men and hold them in thrall. Obviously, a relationship with her was a torment for Vertinsky, and the wound took a long time to heal. Lines from Vertinsky's songs rekindling painful memories are evidence of this: "Listen, little one, may I love you gently?" or lines from the poet Alexander Blok, which the singer set to music: "You left to meet your lover, I'll put up with it, I'll endure it, I'll say nothing." It was in Kharkov that Vertinsky wrote these lines dedicated to Sanina:

This is all that remains of you—
Nothing but a sheaf of letters and a
  lock of your hair.
My heart sinks, and I'm somewhat
  blue—
Nothing remains in it for you, dear,
  not a single tear.
It was an ending so banal,
So cynical and cruel a way to part.
You told me not to bring my heart
To your bedroom door anymore.[5]

After breaking up with Valentina, Vertinsky apparently kept her love letters for a long time and was thinking about them when he wrote in 1949:

Your notes and letters now nibbled by
  mice,
How amusing now those words, unfor-
  gettable!
How close we were . . . and now how
  regrettable,

„ЭТО ВСЕ, ЧТО ОТЪ ВАСЬ ОСТАЛОСЬ"

ВАЛЕНТИНЪ САНИНОЙ.

Слова и муз. А. Н. Вертинскаго.

MARLENE DIETRICH.

That we're distant as ice
And now how grim . . .
When once you caused my head to
swim.[6]

After he returned to the Soviet Union, as he was writing his book, *Dorogoi dlinnoyu* [Taking the Long Road], Vertinsky recalled the black dress with the crystal cross, which later became the signature decoration of the house of Valentina.

The actress Anastasia Vertinskaya, the singer's daughter, said about the relationship: "Vertinsky reproached Sanina with betrayal: 'Your tin heart rolled to my feet.' Apparently, she was incapable of falling in love. She was a femme fatale, and used Vertinsky. Of course, she was a page in his biography and in his poetry."[7] Apparently, Vertinsky's romance with Sanina ended in the same year, 1918. They parted—"A parting bow at the station." Vertinsky left on tour for Odessa, Crimea, and Constantinople. They met again in New York in the 1930s, when Valentina Sanina had already become a well-known fashion designer, and Vertinsky a touring performer who was much in demand.

Valentina Sanina met her future husband, Georgii Matveyevich Shlee, at a Ukrainian train station during the civil war and married him in 1921. After ar-

Opposite: *A summer dress from the house of Valentina, c. 1934.*

Above: *Clients of the house of Valentina, from left to right: Hollywood stars Pola Negri, Marlene Dietrich, and Claudette Colbert in advertising photos from the 1920s and 30s.*

riving in Italy via Constantinople and Greece, she tried to find work in silent films. Then, after settling in Paris with her husband, she joined Nikita Baliev's La Chauve Souris cabaret troupe in 1922, playing bit parts for two seasons. Shlee and Valentina moved to New York in 1923. In New York Valentina became the mistress of a well-known Wall Street lawyer, Eustace Seligman, who sponsored Valentina's ambitions of becoming a fashion designer.

Valentina always had her own unique style of dressing, and her clothes soon began to attract attention. As Therese Duzinkiewicz-Baker, the American fashion researcher points out, Valentina was distinctive because she tried to look feminine at a time when women wanted to look like boys. George Shlee became a successful theater impresario, and the couple began to move in a circle of wealthy and famous people, affording Valentina a wonderful opportunity to "advertise" her dresses at society recep-

tions. They were long dresses with puffy sleeves and a natural waistline, not one dropped to the hips, as fashion dictated. Ignoring short, modern "boyish" haircuts, Valentina arranged her long, light hair into a bun. She provoked modish New York's interest with her rare Slavic appearance and elegant originality, and was her own best model for showing her dresses. By nature extremely artistic, she was a master of dramatic gestures that were full of expression, at times even tragedy. Valentina brought this theatrical note into her designs as well, which were always original and possessed the magnetism of the stage.

By 1925 Valentina had organized a small atelier in New York, and, after the incredible success of her designs, she opened Valentina House Incorporated, a house of fashion on the fashionable Upper East Side in 1928. Thanks to her husband's connections, her business mainly attracted the artistic elite of New York. The most famous movie and theater actresses were among her clients, and ballet and opera divas, too. According to Sanina's and Garbo's former neighbor Tatyana Varshavskaya, the house's specialty was beaded dresses, which became a hit in Hollywood.

Consistently maintaining two hundred clients, she was able to pay individual attention to each one, working in

Библиотека декоративных искусств, Париж

Архив автора, Париж

the manner of the big Parisian fashion houses. One of her favorite clients during that period was Greta Garbo. Initially a friend, then a rival, and, at the end of her life, a most vicious enemy, Garbo played an enormous role in Valentina's life and destiny. Valentina looked like a movie star and, according to accounts by her contemporaries, at first Valentina and Greta attended parties together, frequently wearing the same dresses in order to emphasize their resemblance to each other.

Dictatorial by nature, Valentina man-aged the taste of her clients and, like the house of Worth, sometimes imposed the color, shape, and finish of their clothes, changing or altering designs at the last minute. Today, studying the designs from her house that have been preserved in museums in the United States and England, you can see more than the obvious theatricality. Each of her dresses carried a definite image, each was created with "soul," and contains the signature of this remarkable fashion designer. Valentina did not copy the designs of the Parisian houses—originality,

Left: *Valentina Sanina in a design from her house of Valentina, New York, 1943.*

Above: *Greta Garbo and Valentina's husband, George Shlee, New York, 1946.*

Opposite: *Greta Garbo, at one time a client and friend of Valentina Sanina's, Hollywood, 1929.*

Библиотека школы искусств. Глазго

exploration, and, not infrequently, surprise, distinguish her cuts.

In 1933 Valentina Sanina began working as a theater costume designer, making her debut in the production of a play starring Judith Anderson. She enjoyed success in this career for many years. The American critic Brooks Atkinson wrote: "The costumes created by Valentina speak even before the actors do."

Perhaps her greatest flight as a costume designer was *The Philadelphia Story*, produced by Bob Sinclair in 1939, with Katherine Hepburn in the leading role. This play ran at the Guild Theater in New York, and became so popular that Valentina got orders for copies of Katherine Hepburn's dresses for the following five years. (The designer Adrian did the costumes for the Hollywood screen version of *The Philadelphia Story*.)

Valentina was a gifted and cultivated individual who loved Renaissance paintings. She often used details from historical costumes of various periods, linking the cultures of the past to the present. One of her most famous designs was an emerald and diamond pendant in the shape of the Maltese cross, a piece that was copied everywhere. Another of Valentina's novelties was the wide-brimmed capelin hat that came into fashion in the mid-1930s. She admired medieval clothing and introduced several elements of women's costume from that time, such as nets and drapings that cover the neck, similar to the "barbettes" worn by Catholic nuns. She also brought back the beauty and femininity of hoods, which became so poplar during World War II.

Above: *Valentina Sanina in a coat design from her house of Valentina, New York, 1943.*

Opposite: *Valentina Sanina in an evening gown design from her house of Valentina, New York, 1939. Photo by Horst.*

Архив Хофера. США

Her dresses combined velvet and silk, gold lace and chains. Often varying the shades of silk, Valentina achieved remarkable effects. Designs from Valentina's house were very expensive. Therese Duzinkiewicz-Baker states that the minimum price for a dress from Valentina was $250 in the 1930s, and had gone up to an average of $600 by the mid-1950s.

Designs from her house combined classical Greek draping, Persian and Indian motifs. An enemy of frills, flowers, and tawdry tinsel and gloss, Valentina was possibly the most original fashion designer among the Russian émigrés. In the 1940s, a time of economy and thriftiness, she created short evening gowns, which accented the shoulders minimally, in defiance of the fashionable wartime silhouette. She introduced the fashion of flat ballet shoes with ribbon ties worn with dark stockings made of viscose silk.

Valentina was often photographed wearing her designs for advertising purposes, although editors of fashion magazines advised her against it. Well-known painters, Dmitrii Dmitrievich Bouchéne in particular, painted portraits of Valentina, and she, in turn, collected their paintings, as did Garbo. She was a passionate lover of art in general and, in her apartment at 450 East 53rd Street in New York, amassed a most valuable collection of eighteenth-century furniture and bronzes, which were auctioned off by Christie's after her death in 1989.

In the 1950s the house of Valentina supplied the American fashion market with gathered blouses and pleated skirts, as well as fancy organdy cocktail dresses. These dresses had plunging necklines, which were very popular with Broadway stars and women who lived on the Upper East Side because the neckline allowed them to show off their jewelry. The only fur that Valentina acknowledged was sable; she used it for winter hats. Although she worked skillfully with wool fabrics, she nonetheless preferred natural silks, and used crepe satins, chiffons, and organdy. In 1950 Valentina launched a perfume called "My Own," which was very popular at the time. She closed down her business in 1957.

Valentina's personal life was not simple. She was a difficult person, which her longtime friend Bouchéne emphasized often in his conversations with the author. Apparently Valentina's husband, George Shlee, told him: "You understand why I'm with Greta Garbo; she's an angel compared to Valentina." To the end of her days, Valentina, who was accustomed to dominating men, could not get over the fact that her own husband preferred another woman. Garbo's very name aroused Valentina's indignation.

After her husband's death in 1971, she even invited a priest over to bless her apartment in order to exorcise the spirit of Greta Garbo, with which she had to live in the same house to the end of her days. Valentina Nikolayevna Sanina died in New York on September 14, 1989.

16

THE HITROVO HOUSE OF LINGERIE

The Russian Hitrovo House of Lingerie was established in Paris in 1924 and stayed in business through 1953. Its founder and designer was Olga Alexandrovna Hitrovo.

Changes in everyday life during World War I inevitably engendered changes in fashion. Corsets made of rigid whalebone, which had been holding in waists for 500 years, finally fell out of fashion, and a freer clothing silhouette appeared, one more suited to the new rhythm of the lives of emancipated women. These dresses were straight and had a dropped waist. At first they were long, then they were shortened almost to the knee at the command of the two great reformers of women's fashion—Chanel and the Charleston. Along with this new dress style, new undergarments appeared: a short, straight slip, a chemise worn with a tight brassiere that flattened the breasts, panties, and a garter belt. The new fashions created an immediate and unprecedented demand for new designs.

Sewing and hand-trimming underwear was a significant production for the Russian émigré houses of fashion in Paris—TAO and Annek produced exquisite underwear beginning in the early 1920s. There were, of course, also French ateliers in Paris that pursued this specialty.

The making of underwear in old Russia was traditionally attended to with special care. It was sewn from fine white cotton batiste or linen and trimmed with the finest satin-stitch hand embroi-

Архив Хитрово, Сент

Opposite: *Alisa Alanova, Russian dancer and a client of the house of Hitrovo.*

Above: *A sketch for an embroidered monogram in satin-stitch by Olga Hitrovo, 1930s.*

dery or hand-woven lace. Most often this pure and unsullied underwear was sewn by nuns, which is why it was called "monastery work" in Russia.

Colored underwear was associated with Parisian "queens of the night," and respectable ladies in Russia did not wear it. Silk underwear, which was imported into Russia in the early part of 1900s, was terribly extravagant. There were several first-class firms in Moscow and St. Petersburg producing this fine underwear, such as the famous Alchwang Brothers on Petrovka Street, and Muir and Mirrielees, a firm founded by Scots-

men that was located in Moscow between the Bolshoi and Maly Theaters. The impeccable quality of Russian underwear in the early twentieth century certainly inspired the émigrés who set up their workshops in Paris in the 1920s. Olga Hitrovo's atelier was established at this time and quickly proved itself, enjoying a wonderful reputation for the twenty years it was in existence.

The noble Hitrovo family was one of the oldest in Russia. During the second half of the fourteenth century, the family's ancestors left the Mongolian Golden Horde to resettle with the Russian Prince of Ryazan, Oleg Ioannovich. The Hitrovo ancestor named Edu-Khan, nicknamed the Very Shrewd, who is considered the founder of the Hitrovo (which means "shrewd" in Russian) line, was baptized and named Andrei. His descendants were originally called Hitrov, and then renamed Hitrovo. They served the Russian tsars loyally as honored table servers, as nobles elected to the Duma, and as district heads and governors. A veteran of the war of 1812, Nikolai Zakharovich Hitrovo married the daughter of Prince Mikhail Illarionovich Golenistchev-Koutouzov-Smolensky, which merged the family line with the Koutouzov's. In emigration, the Hitrovo family was very proud of their kinship with Marechal Koutouzov and Generalissimo Suvorov.

Olga Hitrovo was born in August 1892, as the youngest of four daughters to the noble family of the Shepelyov-Voronovichs. Her relative, Maria Lvov-

Above left and right: *Olga Hitrovo, the founder of the Hitrovo house of lingerie, from the 1920s to the 1940s.*

Left: *A window display with items from the house of Hitrovo in the Hotel Carlton, Cannes, 1930s.*

Архив автора, Париж

Архив Марии Грековой, Женева

Архив Марии Грековой, Женева

Above left: *The Hitrovo family home in Sèvres, near Paris. Photo by Alexandre Vassiliev, 1996.*

Above, top right: *Olga Hitrovo in her garden at her home in Sèvres, 1932.*

Above right: *Olga Hitrovo (far left) surrounded by members of her family on the terrace of her home in Sèvres, c. 1933.*

Overleaf for pages 320–21. Left: *An invoice for an order of lingerie from the house of Hitrovo dated October 18, 1927; right: Olga Hitrovo's sketches of women's lingerie designs trimmed with fine embroidery, c. 1932.*

Overleaf for pages 322–23: *Olga Hitrovo's sketches of designs for peignoirs, 1934–35.*

na Grekova-Zinovieva, who emigrated to Geneva, recalls: "Aunt Olya was the least attractive of the girls in the family, but the most hard-working and the smartest."[1] She loved to draw and sew from childhood, which stood her in good stead later in Paris.

After World War I broke out, Olga Alexandrovna left for the front in 1914 at the age of twenty-two to serve as a nurse, for which she was awarded the St. George Cross. In Kiev she met her future husband, Colonel Vladimir Sergeyevich Hitrovo, an elite guardsman of the Artillery Cavalry. She married him during the Revolution and was then evacu-

ated with the White Army to Kislovodsk. There she gave birth to her only son, Seryozha, on July 18, 1919. Countess Brun de Saint Hippolyte says about her subsequent fate: "Hitrovo was evacuated from the Caucasus with my parents M. S. and V. P. Trubetskoy on the ship *Hannover* to Constantinople, and spent the winter there. This made them friends for life."[2]

Olga Alexandrovna left Constantinople and, via Marseilles, managed to reach Paris, where she began working in a small, recently established house of lingerie that soon became very fashionable. There she learned from the wealthy

OLGA HITROVO
LINGERIE

::::::::::::::::::::

91 rue de Rennes

21, RUE SAINT-AUGUSTIN (OPÉRA)

PARIS 2ᴱ *VI*

Littré 2..

TÉLÉPHONE : ~~CENTRAL 88-8~~

R. C. SEINE 339.288

M ᵐᵉ *Heusemann*   D

Paris, le *18 octobre* 192*7*

19 743 744	4	combinaison jupe à 475		1900
735	1	combinaison jupe noir		600
741, 740	2	combinaisons à 475		950
745	1	combinaison blanche		450
157, 155	2	pantalons à 400		800
771	1	chemise de nuit		450
751	1	chemise de nuit		650
188 759	2	chemises - robe à 700		1400
			Total	7200
				96
		monogrammes		
				7296.

Velours daphin

clients what was in demand. Maria Nikolayevna Nenarokova, a relative of Olga Hitrovo by marriage, tells us: "They sewed underwear with lace trim at the house where Olga worked, and this was what she decided to do."[3]

Sometime about 1924, Olga Alexandrovna opened her own business at no. 21 rue Saint-Augustin, near the Grand Opera. Finding the Hitrovo business already prospering in 1927, Nenarokova recalls: "Her atelier was located in a very large apartment, consisting of a spacious foyer with a glass door, a kitchen, and two living rooms where she received her clients who, at the time, included a great many Americans."

Feminine and elegant, Hitrovo's garments stood apart due to the high quality of their embroidery on silk. Olga

Above left: *An American client of the house of Hitrovo, 1930s.*

Above right: *On the right, Mrs. Johnny Walker, the wife of the whisky manufacturer and a Hitrovo client, 1930s. Eminent clients often presented autographed photographs of themselves to the owners of fashion houses, who then displayed them in a prominent place to attract customers.*

Alexandrovna acknowledged no other fabrics. Most of her things were slips with matching peignoirs, elegant, lace-trimmed negligee ensembles for the boudoir. The most popular lingerie color in the late 1920s was pink, and later, flesh. Special sales agents supplied the atelier with the best French handmade lace, which was sewn onto the underwear by hand, naturally, on the premises. Hitrovo designs were very expensive, and she had very few French clients.

The Russian seamstresses worked in a special room, cutting and trimming the designs that Olga Alexandrovna created. Irina Vasilyevna Gerbilskaya was one of the cutters, Militsa Borisovna Zelenaya was a seamstress, and the house model was Countess Marina Rehbinder. Olga Alexandrovna's husband, Vladimir Hitrovo, was in charge of bookkeeping, and he obviously managed the business very well: their business was so prosperous that the Hitrovos bought a large piece of land on rue Massenet in Sèvres.

Nenarokova recalls: "The Hitrovos built their own spacious three-story house, with an enormous dining room and terrace, which Vladimir Sergeyevich's sister Lyuba designed. It was a 1920s structure: every room had its own washbasin, but there was only one bath. Their house was furnished like an old Russian country estate: a mahogany sideboard, overstuffed sofa and armchairs, a library and a display case with porcelain knick-knacks. Olga particularly loved and collected porcelain cups. This was a household that loved to sit

Richness And Femininity Mark Lingerie Of 1934 Fashionables

Some Negligees Sport Trains, Jackets

By BARBARA BEAUFORT
(*Associated Press Fashion Editor*)

PARIS (AP)—New lingerie for 1934 is as feminine as the frivolities worn by the former French favorites and queens.

Though crepe de chine and washable satin remain the standbys for hard everyday wear, the mode is replete with filmy mousselines, sheer georgettes, chiffons, silk organdies and laces which hint of exotic powders and perfumed boudoirs.

Olga Hitrovo, who makes the lingerie for scores of American and European brides and beauties, launches negligee and nightdress ensembles as fragile as flowers. The negligees are often fashioned of printed or plaid taffeta or satin, while the nightdresses are made of mousseline printed in the same design.

Others appear in shell pink or sky blue mousseline with sleeves and yokes of sheer tinted lace.

Negligees With Trains

The negligees themselves are often designed with trains and full loose or bishop sleeves which give a soft effect. A white taffeta model plaided in red and blue stripes goes over a white chiffon nightdress printed in the same plaid, and a ruffled jacket of white satin splashed in yellow and green flowers tops a similarly patterned white georgette nightdress. Gay flowered mousselines make other ensembles.

Nightdresses of white, pale blue and shell pink mousseline, cut on the bias to mold the figure like an evening gown, are finished with tiny ruffles of the same material or deep yokes of lace.

The lace used this season is a story in itself. Fashion has turned its back on the coffee colored weaves so widely used not long ago and substituted fine Maline or Chantilly in such soft tones as cream, mother of pearl and dawn.

On nightdresses it is often shirred, though on slips it is incrusted in flat body molding effects.

Slips Cut On Bias

Slips which are replacing the short chemise in many smart wardrobes, are cut on the same bias

*S*HEER creamy lace takes the place of the old coffee colored designs on the new 1934 lingerie. Olga Hitrovo makes this nightdress of flesh colored mousseline with a top of creamy Malines lace finished with two little garlands of lace roses. The shirred shoulder line is new this year.

for fitting lines as the nightdresses. Their seams are finished with point Turc, their hems are nothing but tiny rolls in order to give the silhouette the least possible bulk.

Flesh pink or peach crepe de chine trimmed with flat incrustations of a contrasting fabric are the favorites for everyday wear, but pale gray, light blue, white and shell pink chiffon yoked and hemmed in sheer cream lace sound a luxury note for more elaborate ensembles.

——bb——

Left and above: *Articles from American magazines and newspapers with rave reviews about the quality of the house of Hitrovo's garments, 1934–35.*

Архив Хитрово, Сеар

down to drink tea with jam. Hitrovo's mother and her nanny, whom she had brought out of Russia, lived with her. The de Witte family were their neighbors and friends, and the de Witte nanny and the Hitrovo nanny would talk to their hearts' content." Near the house, which was covered with vines, they dug a garden of more than 2,000 cubic meters and planted many roses and raspberries. Olga Alexandrovna liked to garden in her free time, and even planted beets, just as she had in Russia.

The house of Hitrovo survived the 1929 crisis and even expanded greatly in the 1930s. Lingerie fashions changed at that time—more tightly fitted silhouettes replaced straight ones. Lingerie with a satin luster became fashionable, promoted by Hollywood stars, and Olga Alexandrovna began using shiny flesh-colored satin crepes and marocain crepes. At the end of the 1930s, fine silk fabrics with tiny printed pink bouquets and a fabric with a tiny vegetable pattern, for which a special trim had to be devised, came into fashion. Nenarokova recalls: "Once Olga, overwhelmed with orders, asked me to help. I was obliged to create a fastening for a new 'vegetable' design: I sewed buttons shaped like miniature carrots, leeks and radishes."

The best Parisian magazines often published Hitrovo's designs in those years. In 1931 *Vogue* raved about her

Opposite: *An advertising photograph of a woman's nightgown from the house of Hitrovo, Paris, c. 1932.*

Above right: *An invoice for an order of lingerie from the house of Hitrovo, prepared for export, dated February 15, 1937.*

Below right: *Drawings of designs from the house of Hitrovo, 1936.*

327

work: "Madame Hitrovo creates magnificent ensembles of a nightgown, chemise/slip or drawers/panties with a petticoat of the most delicate shades: peach, petal pink, or aquamarine. She chooses washable mousseline or triple-layered voile, with insets of Alençon or Maline laces. She loves to design nightgowns either in the Louis XVI or the Directoire styles."[4] Hitrovo's lingerie had an international reputation and was in demand as an export.

An incident related by Nenarokova demonstrates how much foreign clients wanted to have lingerie from Hitrovo: "Once Olga was completing a large South American order. Somewhere in the port the case with this lingerie fell into the water. . . . The client who had ordered it wanted only Hitrovo lingerie, and reordered it. Everyone at the Paris atelier was glad, because they had this client's measurements and were very familiar with her taste."

The number of Hitrovo's clients grew with each year, and celebrities of the day ordered their lingerie from her: the Duchess D'Artille, Mrs. Arpels, Mrs. Robert Fenwick and her daughter Florence Fenwick, Madame Guerlain, the ballerina Alisa Alanova, the Marquise de Lamberty, and the wife of the

Left: *A drawing of a design from the house of Hitrovo.*

Above: *An advertisement photograph of a design for an ensemble consisting of a bodice and short pants from the house of Hitrovo, 1940s.*

Opposite: *Olga Hitrovo's sketches of designs for peignoirs and nightgowns with embroidered trim and lace inserts, early 1930s.*

328

OLGA HITROVO
LINGERIE · COUTURE

21, RUE SAINT-AUGUSTIN (OPÉRA)
    PARIS 2ᵉ

TEL

Paris, le

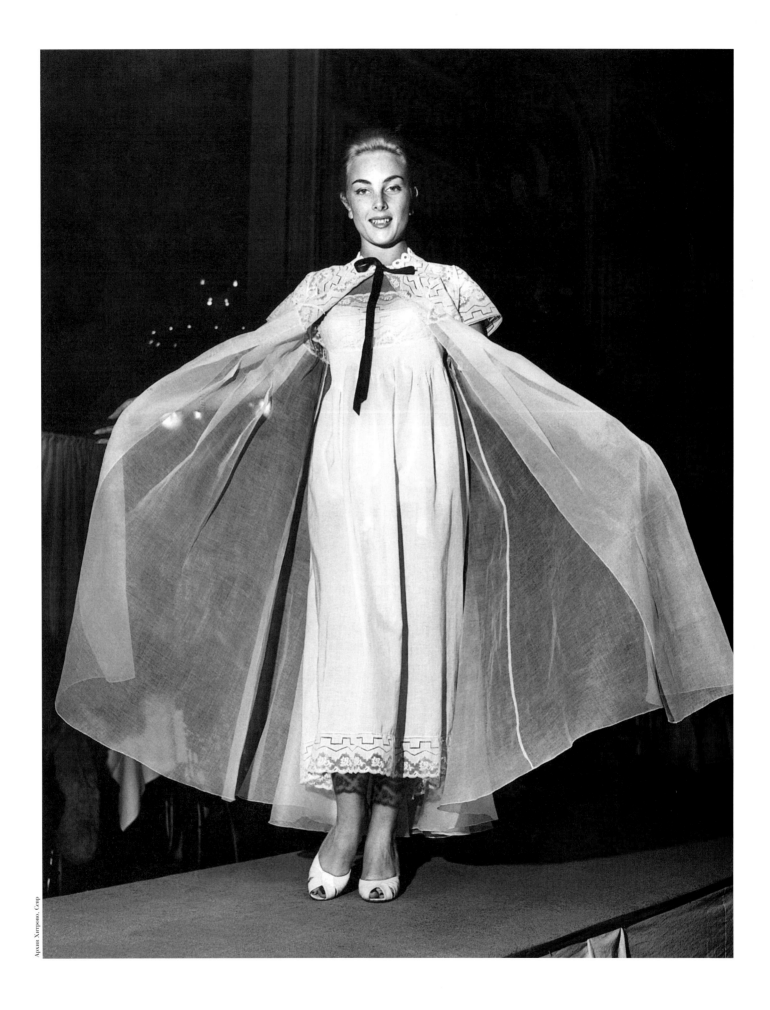

Архив Хитрово, Снр

Архив Хитрово, Сепр

Архив Хитрово, Сепр

Архив Хитрово, Сепр

Opposite and above right: *A model showing an organdy nightgown and peignoir with lace inserts during a house of Hitrovo fashion show in a hotel in Paris, early 1950s.*

Above left, top, and bottom: *Silk nightgowns with lace trim designed by the house of Hitrovo, 1953.*

331

Maharajah of Kapurtala, who lived at the Hotel Crillon on the Place de la Concorde, and to whom Hitrovo personally delivered completed orders. Another eminent client was Mrs. Johnny Walker, the wife of the whiskey producer, and among her movie-star clients was the beautiful sex symbol Rita Hayworth.

The house of Hitrovo operated in fierce competition with other Russian lingerie houses established in Paris. One was the house of Countess Alderberg, and others included the houses of Krivitzky, Tonkonogu, and Baranov, which appeared in Paris in the 1930s and whose beautifully shaped and sewn designs were also singled out by the Parisian press. Unfortunately, we lack much information about them. The house of Hitrovo remained Russian and a purely family business. Lyubov Sergeyevna Grekova, Olga's relative, sold Hitrovo designs in Cannes at the famous Hotel Carleton.

Olga Alexandrovna herself dressed simply and elegantly. She was a jovial person with a good sense of humor. One of her pet phrases was: "Everything that is pleasant in life is either sinful or harmful to one's health." However, she had a rather difficult time getting close to and interacting with people, as she had a somewhat closed nature. In her free time she loved to read memoirs and history books. Her passion was dogs, and at one time she bred and sold dachshunds; she had a small dachshund from Austria that lived with her for a long time. Sometimes relatives visited her: her sister Nadezhda Alexandrovna Shepelyova-Voronovich and nieces Olga and Duda visited from Yugoslavia, where they lived before moving to Argentina.

The house of Hitrovo remained in operation during World War II and the German Occupation. The fashion house had to be shut down in 1956 when nylon appeared on the market, a new material that forever changed the fashionable lingerie industry. Olga Alexandrovna died on October 1, 1986, at the age of ninety-four. The entire Hitrovo family is buried at the Russian cemetery Sainte-Geneviève-des-Bois.

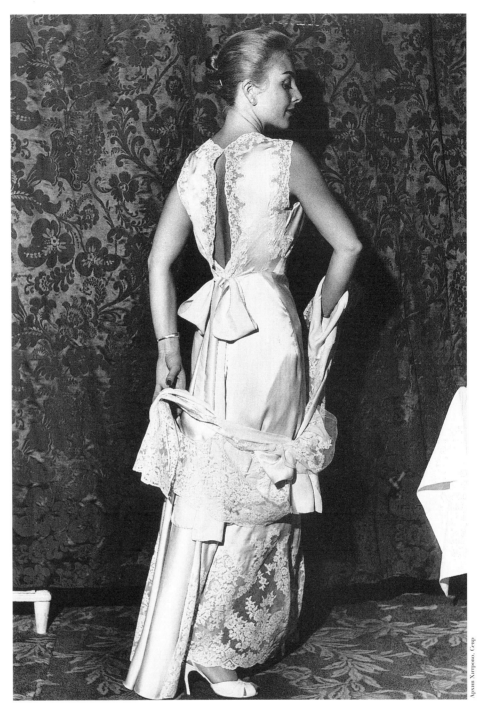

Opposite: *Rita Hayworth, a client at the house of Hitrovo. The inscription on the photograph reads, "Dear Olga Hitrovo, thank you for your beautiful things. Rita Hayworth."*

Above: *A silk morning outfit with lace bed jacket designed by the house of Hitrovo, 1950s.*

333

17

THE ADLERBERG HOUSE OF LINGERIE

The Russian Adlerberg House of Lingerie was established in Paris in the mid-1920s and remained in business until 1946. Its founder and designer was Countess Lyubov Vladimirovna Adlerberg.

Lyubov Vladimirovna was born into the family of the landowner Egorov in Voronezh on June 21, 1890. Lyubov's husband, Count Vladimir Vasilyevich Adlerberg, was a colonel in the cavalry and eighteen years her senior. The Adlerberg family was Swedish in origin and well known from the early 1700s among the landed gentry of Vermland, Sweden, who later settled in Russia along with many other Swedish aristocrats. Vladimir Fedorovich Adlerberg, an infantry general and a minister in the court of Emperor Nicholas I, was granted the hereditary title of count by an imperial edict issued on July 1, 1847. The title was later reaffirmed by three separate edicts under Alexander II and Alexander III.

The Adlerbergs were very poor when they arrived in Paris after the Bolshevik Revolution. Like other émigrés, they had to get along doing odd jobs. In the early 1920s, many Russians made handcrafted goods, sewing pillows and dolls and making handbags, beads, and lampshades. Lampshades covered in orange silk and decorated with fringe were extremely popular. This was the type of lampshade that Count Vladimir Adlerberg tried to make, but as Natalia Petrovna Bologovskaya, Countess Adlerberg's principal seamstress, recalls: "The Adler-

Архив автора, Париж

Opposite: *A detail of a batiste chemise with Valençon lace insertions and inserts of machine embroidery designed by the Alchwang Brothers, Moscow, 1900s.*

Above: *A drawing by S. Lodygin advertising the Petrograd lingerie house, Markus Zaks, in the magazine* Stolitsa i usad'ba *[Capital and Estate], 1917.*

bergs lived a very impoverished life in Paris. . . . He didn't make very good lampshades and they sold poorly."[1]

Countess Lyubov Alderberg was forced to make a living sewing. In the mid-1920s, she went to work at one of the French lingerie houses, where she mastered the technique of sewing silk lingerie, which requires painstaking con-

centration and accuracy. The countess was greatly valued at this house, and it was then that the count had the idea of opening his own fashion enterprise. As Bologovskaya recalled: "At the time, everyone who had money or connections was opening a 'maison de couture.' The Adlerbergs had very little money then, but the count had many high-level acquaintances in aristocratic society. They decided to open an atelier of high-quality silk lingerie and they rented a small apartment in the sixteenth arrondissement at no. 24 rue de Belles Feuilles." Bologovskaya described the flat as "a small foyer, a teeny-tiny kitchen, the countess's workroom, a bedroom, a small bathroom, and the count's sitting room."

Countess Adlerberg's lingerie house operated out of this apartment for about twenty years. Only Russian seamstresses worked there, either sewing at the rue de Belles Feuilles apartment or taking work home. The countess did not have enough space to receive clients at their apartment, so she used the services of so-called placing or commission agents—society ladies who were pleasantly sociable—to sell the articles to individual clients. Countess Adlerberg alone utilized about twenty-five of these ladies.

The commission agents would take the finished silk lingerie to the expensive hotels to show to wealthy clients and acquaintances, whose addresses they would often keep secret, and would receive a sizeable percentage from the fashion houses for their services. One of the agents was Nina Georgievna Pleshcheye-va, a grand-niece of the noted Russian writer, Pleschcheyev. Bologovskaya remembered her with warmth: "Life didn't work out for her: she was unattractive, and her marriage was obviously also unhappy, since her husband shot himself. She was left alone in Paris. Nina spoke excellent French, German and English and, since she had a very good clientele, worked for the Adlerbergs for many years."

The staff of seamstresses who sewed the fine silk lingerie—nightgowns, robes, and bed jackets, i.e., short coats for reading in bed—included Russian ladies from noble families, such as, for example, the embroideress Sofia Mikhailov-na Belyaeva, a graduate of Catherine's Institute for Noblewomen. Natalia Bologovskaya was the principal seamstress in the robe and bed jacket section of Countess Adlerberg's house.

Bologovskaya went to work for Countess Adlerberg in 1930. She recalled: "There was a small break in my employment as a seamstress in the early 1930s, and one lady advised me to go to the Adlerbergs. She said: 'The countess wants to open a robe and bed jacket section and she needs help.' Before this, I had worked for the big Greek house Sanmer; but the American market crashed and the Sanmer collections weren't selling anymore. So I went to the countess, who made an appointment to see me the following day. The count always wanted to meet the people who were coming to work for them, so as not to hire some stranger. The count greeted me affectionately and asked: 'What family do you come from?' I told him and

mentioned in passing that he must have known my uncle in St. Petersburg. He joyfully exclaimed: "You are Konstantin Ippolitovich Vogak's niece? What a delight! Come work with us! I will tell the countess that you're quite suitable. I'll try to see that you do well with us.'" Bologovskaya worked at Adlerberg's lingerie house for eighteen years.

It was Natalia Bologovskaya who initially shed light on the life and work of Russian émigrés in Paris for the author of this book. The reminiscences of Natalia, a marvelous raconteuse with an unusual memory, laid the foundation for this book, which has been many years in the making. Her life's path "with a needle in her hands" is fascinating and instructive. She was born in Moscow in 1900, into the family of Petr Petrovich Ivanov, an officer who was the provincial commander of Vilno. Her mother, Natalia Petrovna, soon divorced her husband and was married a second time, to von Hoyer, with whom she had one daughter, Nina (the same Nina von Hoyer discussed above in the chapter on the house of Yteb.)

Natalia Bologovskaya spent her childhood in Vilno, St. Petersburg, and Moscow. After the Revolution, she lived with her father in Yalta and Livadiya, and was then, along with so many other émigrés, evacuated from the Crimea to Constantinople. She eventually ended up in Paris by way of Salonika and Marseilles. She sewed doll dresses as a child, and was already sewing outfits for herself on the boats to Constantinople and then to France.

Natalia arrived with her father—and

Архив Натали Обержонуа, Париж

Opposite: *A silk chemise with underpants trimmed with silk ribbon and embroidered inserts, Paris, 1920s.*

Above: *Count Vladimir Adlerberg, proprietor of the Adlerberg lingerie house, Paris, 1930s.*

her dog, Lulu—at Gare de Lyon in Paris, with 100 francs between the two of them. They settled in an inexpensive hotel near the station, because Natalia wasn't able to ride on the Metro. She recalled: "I arrived in Paris in 1922. When I asked a proper-looking gentleman at the station how to get to the Russian church on rue Daru, he replied: 'Young ladies like you don't ride the Metro!' I was very grateful to this gentleman, and we settled in at a hotel near the station. Papa met many of his friends on rue Daru and told them that he needed work. The next day, having gotten a note from one of them, he went to the Gare de Lyon to wash train car windows. That first day when Papa was working at the station, I went off to the Russian Embassy to find out about work. I entered a reception room in which about ten well-dressed ladies were sitting. They were all older than I and they were all looking for some kind of work. A secretary came out: 'I have a job offer only for someone who can sew.' Total silence . . . Then I said: 'That's me!' You see, I had already sewn myself a dress in Saloniki. When I returned to the hotel and saw my father, I was horrified. He was all dirty and wet, and I found an actual louse on his shirt collar. And I said then: 'Papa, your work

Opposite: *Countess Lyubov Adlerberg, proprietress of the Adlerberg lingerie house, in a satin peignoir she designed, Paris, 1933.*

Above left: *Natalia Bologovskaya, a seamstress at the lingerie house of Adlerberg, in a summer outfit that she designed, France, late 1920s.*

Above center: *Nina von Hoyer, Natalia Bologovskaya's half-sister and a model for the house of Yteb, in a dress sewn and embroidered by Bologovskaya, Paris, late 1920s.*

Above right: *Natalia Bologovskaya with a Russian friend, France, late 1920s.*

is done! I'm the one who's going to work now. I'm going to sew!'" This was the start of the long professional road taken by the seamstress Natalia Bologovskaya, who worked unceasingly from 1922 until the late 1980s.

The next day, armed with a letter of recommendation from the Russian Embassy, Natalia went to the small fashion house, Jenny, on avenue des Gobelins in Paris. Its owner was a young Frenchwoman who had until then been a saleswoman at the well-known Lucien Lelong atelier. Natalia worked at Jenny for only six months, but she learned the most important thing: techniques for cutting and sewing fashions. Then, in the mid-1920s, working at home, she came up with a design for a cross-stitch-embroidered skirt that was a great success.

At Countess Adlerberg's lingerie atelier, Natalia's responsibility was to copy old lingerie designs, not to create new ones. She recalled: "I worked at home in Boulogne then. I had a Russian friend who made the rounds of the ateliers, buying designs from major houses at marked-down prices when the season ended, and then selling them among the Russians. She once said: 'I have an old design from Lanvin; maybe you could use it?' I took the garment to Countess Adlerberg, and she exclaimed: 'This is

Архив автора, Париж

brilliant! You couldn't come up with anything better!' The design was already five years old, so copying it would not be considered stealing. It was a pink satin dressing gown, done in real satin, not what we have now. The Lanvin design fastened at the waist with two buttons; it had two seams along the sides and a simple back. The robe had a small yoke of soft, finely machine-stitched batting. The sleeves were lantern-shaped, and I made them look like cantaloupes. When we sewed 'our' design, one of the countess's placing agents obtained an order for it. I lived for ten years and raised a daughter on that robe."

As the Adlerberg atelier copied the patterns of other houses, Bologovskaya had many stories about the designs of various ateliers: "Once Countess Adlerberg went to the Madeleine Vionnet atelier to buy one of her old nightgown designs at the seasonal clearance sale. Vionnet designed as if she were dressing antique statues. We cut open the seams on the Vionnet nightgowns, laid it out on the rug in the reception room, and saw that it was made of true geometric figures, without a single irregular line. So that there was an oblique line where there should have been an oblique one, and where there was a straight cut, the line was perfectly even. We used this pattern to sew remarkable nightgowns and dressing gowns. They were better than you can possibly imagine!"

According to Bologovskaya and her daughter's Natalia's recollections, the Adlerberg atelier did not have its own label, which makes it difficult to find its garments in the Musée de la Mode et du Costume in Paris, where the lingerie division is incredibly extensive. Advertisements for Adlerberg were still appearing in the fashion magazines in the 1930s: the house designs were primarily thin satin-stitch-embroidered silk nightgowns and robes. A stellar fate was

Above left: *Nina Koshits, a famous singer and a client of Natalia Bologovskaya's, Moscow, 1916.*

Above right: *Natalia Bologovskaya in a wool cloak of her own design, Paris, mid-1920s.*

Opposite: *Natalia Bologovskaya while she was working for the count and countess Adlerberg in the 1930s.*

Архив автора, Париж

340

awaiting one of the robes sewn by Bologovskaya: the famous French-Romanian stage actress and movie star Popesco was seen in this garment in the 1937 film *Green Camisole*, a popular sophisticated comedy by director Roger Richebé based on a script by de Flers and de Caillavet. Large-format film stills make it possible to examine this Adlerberg robe in detail.

Before she began working for the Adlerbergs, Natalia worked as a seamstress with Valya Bayanovskaya at the American house of Stein and Blaine for a month. Suppliers brought the firm samples of expensive hand-decorated fabrics, among which Natalia came across a piece of silk mousseline with an amusing cross-stitch embroidery in soft wool. This sample came in very handy a few years later. Natalia recalled: "After I sewed 'her' robe for the countess and she saw my success, she once said: 'We need a bed jacket design.' I thought about it and answered: 'Countess, I have a very good idea!' The next day I brought her that sample of embroidered mousseline: 'Countess, it's from this that I'm going to make our bed jacket.' Then I went to Rodier, the wonderful fabric store. I was on friendly terms with the porter, and he allowed me to take the elevator to the sixth floor and buy discounted fabric remnants. Once I found a roll of material similar to a woolen Orenburg shawl. It didn't cost very much because no one was buying it. I purchased this 'Orenburg' material, and the countess and I sewed our first bed jacket from it. The placing agent Pleshcheyeva took the finished garment to the Keva Institute of Beauty, where

the owner immediately purchased twelve bed jackets of our design."

Natalia had not had a single day off in her eighteen years of work at the Adlerberg atelier: the bed jackets were succeeded by robes, and the robes by more bed jackets. On one occasion, a picture of Natalia's pink dressing gown, for which the French Countess de Leusse posed, was published on the cover of the magazine *Plaisirs de France*. Countess Adlerberg once sent Natalia over to thank the Countess de Leusse for her patronage, and Natalia obtained a personal order from her. This was the golden thread that led Natalia Bologovskaya to her distinguished titled Parisian clientele.

Natalia recalled her meeting with Countess de Laise: "The countess was sitting near the fireplace, drinking coffee. . . . She began querying me as to who I was and what I did, and then asked: "Look here, dear, would you like to get some good clients from me? Can you sew beautiful peignoirs?' This was how Natalia first began sewing for the very wealthy society beauty Princess Polignac, Countess de Leusse's cousin. In addition to peignoirs, she also sewed dresses for the most eminent French aristocrats. By the late 1930s, she had twenty-five permanent clients with noble titles.

Natalia's reminiscences about the social life at the Adlerberg atelier and its visitors are also interesting. "The count did not consider me just an employee, since my uncle K. I. Vogak was a fellow-soldier at the start of his career," said Bologovskaya. "Once a year, on Lyubov Vladimirovna's name-day, tea was served

in the count's sitting room for all the employees and agents. One time, when everyone else had left, the count asked me to stay for the intimate family celebration, for 'our cup of tea,' as he put it. Among those invited was Princess Youssoupoff. I was lucky enough to sit beside Irina Alexandrovna at the table. We got to chatting during tea. 'Princess,' I said to her, 'you appear to be . . . more than anything, you look like a saint.' 'Yes,' she replied, 'many people have told me that. But, you know, I have a very odd habit. I pick up a piece of bread, and within five minutes it turns into a little devil. And there's no way to avoid it. I'm very devout, I go to church often, I behave modestly, but no matter what I take in my hands, it turns into a little devil.'"

Natalia recalled another unexpected meeting in Count Adlerberg's sitting room: "There was a knock at the door, and Grand Duke Kirill Vladimirovich entered the room. Count Adlerberg was very happy. The grand duke shook my hand, and I curtsied to him. The count addressed him: 'So, sit down, Tsar!' I felt somewhat awkward, and Kirill Vladimirovich asked: 'Volodya, why do you insult me? After all, it's not my fault that I was chosen to be a tsar.'"

The Adlerberg atelier operated throughout the war years. When the count died in 1944, Countess Lyubov Adlerberg fell into the most extreme piety. She closed down the business two years later and became an uncloistered nun, sewing cassocks for Russian priests. Countess Lyubov Vladimirovna Adlerberg died on June 9, 1963, in Auxerre, France.

Opposite: *Elvire Popesco, a well-known Romanian actress, in a house of Adlerberg gown made by Natalia Bologovskaya.*

vient de créer — *son Parfum*

Laure Belin

18

THE LAURE BELIN HOUSE OF LINGERIE

The Laure Belin House of Lingerie was established in the late 1920s in Berlin. It was moved to Paris in the early 1930s and closed down there in the early 1960s. Larissa Mikhailovna Beilin was its proprietress, and Tamara Romanovna Gamsakhourdia de Koby its designer.

The Laure Belin lingerie house became the most prosperous and long-lived of the lingerie houses founded by Russian émigrés. It belonged to the Russian Jew Larissa Beilin. She was born in 1896 in Kiev and after the Bolshevik coup fled Russia with her family and brother, who later founded the fashion house of Berlé. Like many other Russians, the family wound up in Berlin, where Larissa began with a small atelier of women's underwear.

In Berlin, Larissa Beilin met and became friends with Tamara Gamsakhourdia, another émigré from Russia and a well-known ballerina and concert performer. She was born into a circus family in 1896 in the Caucasus region, near Baku. Her father, Roman Sergeyevich Gamsakhourdia, worked in the circus all his life. As a young man, he toured Europe with a wandering circus troupe, and in Hungary the troupe happened upon a Gypsy encampment in which there was a little Hungarian girl whom the Gypsies had kidnapped. The troupe paid her ransom and took her in. She grew up wandering with the circus performers and later became the wife of Roman and the mother of four of his children, one of whom was Tamara.

Mme de KOBY, Directrice

Laure Belin

GAINES · SOUTIEN-GORGE · MAILLOTS · LINGERIE

59, RUE BOISSIÈRE PARIS   TÉL. KLÉBER 06-23
PASSY   41-94

Opposite: *An advertisement for a perfume designed by Irina Holman de Koby for the house of Laure Belin, early 1950s.*

Above: *The business card of Tamara Gamsakhourdia de Koby, the director of the house of Laure Belin.*

Tamara demonstrated dancing ability at a young age and studied in a ballet school in Tiflis in the early 1900s. From there she went to Moscow, where she got into the private school of Mikhail Mordkin, a famous soloist at the Imperial Bolshoi Theater; when she graduated, she became a soloist in Zimin's Private Opera ballet troupe. Several postcards published in 1917 with her portrait, preserved to this day in the Museum of the Bolshoi Theater in Moscow, attest to young Tamara's success.

In the pre-revolutionary period Tamara Gamsakhourdia became a well-known variety concert performer in Moscow—her name appears frequently on posters of the time. Fleeing the hunger and terror after the Revolution, Tamara managed to make it to the Crimea, where many Russian performing artists had

gathered. She used her father's money to open a ballet studio in Yalta, where a young Volunteer Army officer, Alexander Feodorovich Miroskhedzhi—her future partner in life and on the stage— was one of her students. Like Tamara, he was of Caucasian background, but adopted Demidov as his stage name. After several months of intense ballet lessons, the newly christened Alexandre Demidoff became her partner.

In 1919 the ballet duo of Gamsakhourdia-Demidoff was created and the two set off on a discovery of stages around the world. It should be noted that Russian ballet artists at that time were an incredible success in the West due to the good graces inspired by Diaghilev's popular Ballets Russes. While there may not have been very many Russian ballet troupes abroad at that time, there were more than enough duos. The most popular of them, aside from Tamara Gamsakhourdia and Alexandre Demidoff, were Alexander and Klotilda Sakharov, Alice Vronska and Konstantin Alperov, and Nina Kirsanova and Alexander Fortunato.

The first stop on the couple's long journey of wanderings was Constantinople, then they were off to Marseilles, where Tamara and Alexandre got married. However, Tamara's stepdaughter from her second marriage, Irina de Koby, recalls: "There wasn't much love in this couple." Having won deserved fame, in about 1920 they departed on a tour around the world. They danced at the Coliseum in London, the Casino

de Paris in Paris, and the Theater of Columns in Buenos Aires. The Gamsakhourdia-Demidoff's best number was *Bacchanalia*, which had been choreographed by Tamara's teacher, Mikhail Mordkin, to the music of Glinka. Apparently Demidoff, while handsome and physically strong, lacked sufficient ballet technique, so Gamsakhourdia also danced solo numbers. Photographs of her dancing a Chinese dance and a Gypsy number have come down to us.

Unfortunately, once during a performance of *Bacchanalia*, when Demidoff, in accordance with his part, dragged his partner across the stage by her hair, Tamara's back was seriously injured by a nail that a rival ballerina had deliberately driven into the stage floor. Forced temporarily to stop performing ballet, in 1927 Tamara Gamsakhourdia joined

Above: *A portrait of Tamara Gamsakhourdia by an unknown artist, 1930s.*

Above right: *Tamara Gamsakhourdia doing a Chinese dance, Berlin, end of the 1920s.*

Right: *An announcement about Tamara Gamsakhourdia's and Alexander Demidoff's tour in Germany, 1922.*

Opposite: *Demidoff and Gamsakhourdia in* Bacchanalia, *London, early 1920s.*

THE LAURE BELIN HOUSE OF LINGERIE

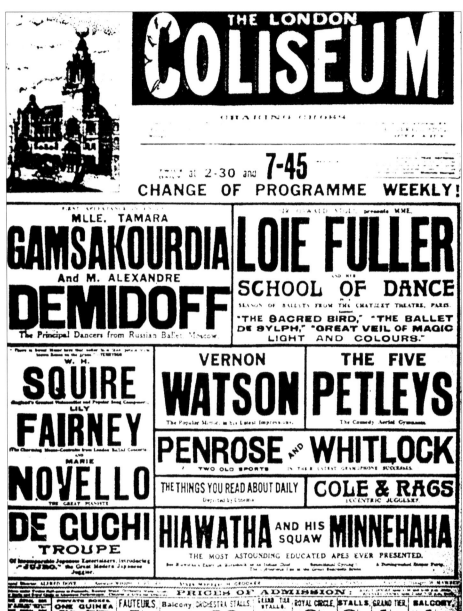

a troupe of Russian dwarfs under the direction of Nicolai Ratushev. This unique Russian émigré artistic enterprise was located in the Parisian suburb of Villemomble. The troupe of fourteen dwarfs was the hit of the Parisian Folies Bergères cabaret program during the years when there were a great many Russian performers. Tamara staged Russian, Japanese, and Dutch dances for the dwarfs and went on tour with them around the United States. It was during this time that she met the impresario of the troupe, Sergei Kobiev, a former officer in the Russian Army, who later became her second husband.

In 1931 Anna Pavlova invited Tamara to join her troupe as a soloist. The star often took good Russian ballerinas on tour with her; they danced at concerts between her solo numbers. Margarita Frohman, Nina Kirsanova, Alice Vronska, and Valentina Kachouba all toured with Pavlova at various times. Unfortunately, Tamara Gamsakhourdia's contract never materialized because of Pavlova's sudden death in The Hague on January 23, 1931. At the age of thirty-five, Tamara decided to leave the stage for good.

Larissa Beilin, the owner of the Laure Belin house of lingerie was a pretty and socially pleasant woman, but not at all a businesswoman. By nature given to enthusiasms, she was interested in vegetarianism and the teachings of the German theosophist and anthroposo-

Opposite: *Tamara Gamsakhourdia in a variety show costume with an ostrich fan, mid-1920s.*

Above left: *Demidoff and Gamsakhourdia* in Bacchanalia, *London, early 1920s.*

Above right: *London's Coliseum Theater poster, which includes Gamsakhourdia and Demidoff's performances.*

Left: *Tamara Gamsakhourdia in one of her first designs, early 1930s.*

Overleaf: *Designs from the house of Laure Belin created under Tamara Gamsakhourdia de Koby's direction, Paris, 1935–37.*

349

Архив Ирины Хельман де Кобб, Биддборо, Англия

Loure Belin

RUE BOISSIÈRE _ PARIS KLÉ 08-23

Архив автора, Париж

Архив автора, Париж

Loure Belin
59, RUE BOISSIÈRE _ PARIS KLÉ 08-23

Above left and right: *Tight-fitting bodices in a wool fabric designed by the house of Laure Belin, Paris, 1936.*

Right: *A sketch of a bodice in a checked fabric by Irina Holman de Koby for the house of Laure Belin, 1936.*

Opposite: *This underwear designed by the house of Laure Belin was worn under evening wear, 1937.*

Архив Ирина Холман де Коби, Бидборо, Англия

352

Opposite: *A lace peignoir and an at-home dress designed by the house of Laure Belin, early 1950s.*

Left and right: *Summer dresses in light wool designed by the house of Laure Belin, early 1950s.*

Below: *Tight-fitting elastic bodyshaper with garters, one of the novelties of the house of Laure Belin, early 1950s.*

phist Rudolf Steiner; after she moved to France, she immersed herself in the theories of Gourdjieff, the mystic from the Caucasus, who had his own "institute" in Fontainebleau, near Paris. Devoting far more time to studying new scientific theories than to her atelier, Beilin completely turned the management of the house of Laure Belin over to the active Tamara Gamsakhourdia (de Koby after her second marriage) in the early 1930s. Strict and energetic, Tamara was able to get things running so well that the Laure Belin house operated for more than thirty years in Paris, the capital of the fiercest competition in the fashion world.

The house of Laure Belin was located in the sixteenth arrondissement at 59 rue Boissière. Over fifty Russian women

worked there from the 1930s to the 1950s: the main cutter was Sophia Dmitrievna Garina; Oksana Sergeyevna Baikova ran the fabric warehouse; and her husband, Gleb Arkadyevich Baikov, a former Guardsman of the Izmailovsky Regiment, worked there as a chauffeur. He soon enrolled at a School of Medicine in Paris and subsequently became a good doctor—he even treated Tamara. Alexandre Miroskhedzhi-Demidoff, Tamara's former partner, built and furnished the dressing rooms with his own hands, and even his mother, Ludmila Alexandrovna, worked there as a seamstress at an advanced age. Sonya Nevedomskaya worked as the accountant, and Elizaveta Alexandrovna Solonina served as the manicurist to many distinguished clients.

355

Opposite and this page: *Silk summer dresses with bodices of bone stays designed by the house of Laure Belin, early 1950s.*

Many other Russian émigrés also found steady employment with Tamara at Laure Belin.

How did Tamara de Koby manage to become so well established that her designs were bought up by the most famous clients around the world for so many years? There were many lingerie houses and ateliers founded by Russians in Paris in the 1920s and 1930s, and each of them tried to distinguish itself in some way. Maria Viktorovna Now-itzky's house made wonderful pajamas; Olga Alexandrovna Hitrovo's house made exquisite nightgowns; Countess Lyubov Vladimirovna Adlerberg's house made superb robes, while Laure Belin specialized in corsets. Women who looked like sexless adolescents were idolized in the 1920s; in the 1930s the canon of beauty returned to the strikingly delineated womanly figure. Many of the Russian lingerie houses focused on the fashions of past seasons—widely cut designs finished with the most refined handmade trim—and thus lost their clients and were forced to close down, while Laure Belin, on the contrary, prospered.

Tamara de Koby's knowledge of ballet costume and her stage experience put her in good stead to design lingerie. Especially important to the dancer's costume are the brassiere and the bodice, which must not only fit the dancer's chest perfectly, but must also be light and comfortable when she's dancing and doing lifts and turns. These were the types of brassieres and corsets—long and tight-fitting—that were replicated at Laure Belin's in new modern fabrics and materials. From the early 1930s, Tamara used wide elastic, stretch fabrics, and zippers in the designs of corsets, girdles, and brassieres, which made them hug the body perfectly. In addition to underwear, she created sporty tight-fitting bustier-type blouses—in wool for skiing, and in silk for tennis.

Opposite: *A black lace peignoir and elastic body shaper with a slip designed by the house of Laure Belin, 1955.*

Right: *An outfit with fur trim for evening receptions designed by the house of Laure Belin, 1950.*

359

Архив Ирины Хольман де Коби, Балборо, Англия

Her bathing suits were especially elegant. All the advertising photos of the Laure Belin house that have come down to us attest to the high art of the cut.

Irina Sergeyevna de Koby, the daughter of Tamara's second husband, helped at the Laure Belin house as a fashion illustrator. She married Roger Holman, an Englishman, in 1934 and enrolled in a school of fashion illustration in Paris. Then, without breaking contact with the house of Laure Belin, she worked as an artist in the Lucille Manguin fashion house and did illustrations for the fashion magazine *Jardin des modes*. She recalls: "Using her stage experience, Tamara created a series of very successful corsets, and specialized in brassieres, bodices, girdles and beach outfits. Tamara explained her ideas to me, showed me the fabrics, and I made the drawings."[1]

Laure Belin's client book with its enthusiastic entries from clients remains intact in Irina Sergeyevna Holman de Koby's family archive. It seems there wasn't a soul in the world for whom Tamara didn't design! Among her loyal clients were the Empress Annam Nam Phuong of Vietnam, the Queen of Yugoslavia, Princesse Margaret, Jacqueline Kennedy, Begum Aga-Khan, Baroness Rothschild, Lady Deterding, Lady Sainte Just de Teulede, Russian cabaret singer Ludmila Lopato. . . . But perhaps Tamara Romanovna Gamsakhourdia de Koby's most remarkable creation at the house of Laure Belin was a corset for the incomparable Marlene Dietrich, who wore it underneath her tight, sparkling,

Left: *An outfit for at-home receptions designed by the house of Laure Belin, 1950.*

Opposite, top left: *A letter from Jacqueline Kennedy dated March 10, 1961, expressing gratitude to Tamara Gamsakhurdia de Koby.*

Opposite, top right: *Marlene Dietrich in a concert dress worn over a special corset made by Tamara Gamsakhourdia for the house of Laure Belin. The inscription on the photograph reads, "Je vous aime et je vous admire. Marlene, 1959."*

Opposite below: *The building at no. 59 rue Boissière, Paris, in which the house of Laure Belin was located. Photo by Alexandre Vassiliev, 1997.*

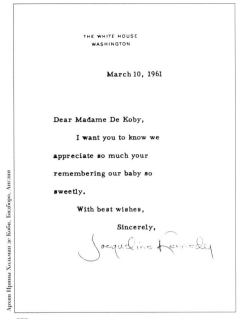

639

rhinestone-studded dresses in her concerts of the 1950s and 1960s. The inscription the great movie star made on her photograph reads: "Je vous aime et je vous admire. Marlene, 1959."

In the early 1940s, Larissa Beilin emigrated to the United States to escape the Germans, and in the 1950s the house of Laure Belin was left in Tamara de Koby's hands completely. The house's selection was expanded, and it began to create not only first-class lingerie, but also evening dresses with plunging necklines. By this time all the other fashion houses of the world, following the dictates of Christian Dior, the "hem tyrant," were dressing their clients in corsets and bustiers, as if forgetting about the fierce war that Paul Poiret had declared on corsets in the 1910s, and about Coco Chanel's knit jersey reform for emancipated women in the 1920s.

After the death of Larissa Beilin, Laure Belin was moved to New York, where it continued with some success (the New York–based Berlé, the creator of the famous delineator bra, belonged to Larissa Beilin's brother), and Tamara Romanovna Gamsakhourdia de Koby moved from Paris to Nice, where she died in 1979. She is buried in the Sainte-Geneviève-du-Bois cemetery. Before her death, this talented fashion designer visited Russia and left her archive there. The author of this book is still trying to find it.

19

RUSSIAN ÉMIGRÉ FASHION ILLUSTRATORS AND FABRIC DESIGNERS

Even in such specialized fields as fashion illustration, Russian émigrés gave the world several famous artists. Among those who emigrated before the revolution, in the 1910s, the most celebrated is Erté, who began working in fashion with Paul Poiret during the time of the Ballets Russes. Later, during the Art Deco era, Erté became famous as a fashion magazine illustrator.

During World War I Erté lived in a villa in Monte Carlo, but his fame spread worldwide. In January 1915, *Harper's Bazaar* published its first cover based on an Erté sketch, and from that point on, until 1936, the artist was a steady contributor of clothing designs and color covers to the magazine. *Harper's* publisher noted: "What would the magazine be without Erté covers?"

Together with talented French illustrators like Paul Iribe and Georges Lepape, Erté laid the aesthetic foundations for Art Deco. His graphic designs are original and inventive, and even today we are amazed by his understanding of fabric and the detail and proportion in his designs. Erté was capable of creating highly ornamented women's day and evening wear, hats, and accessories with great ease.

Erté's lifestyle was as unique as his

Opposite: *A 1926 film still from* Le P'tit Parigot *by Marcel L'Herbier. The actor is wearing a robe designed by Sonia Delaunay.*

Above: *Erté surrounded by a few of the Hollywood silent-film stars for whom he created costumes, 1925.*

work. Howard Greer, a costume designer in Hollywood, gives the following vivid account of his meeting with Erté in 1918: "Erté's villa was on the top of a hill above the Monte Carlo casino and its gardens. At the station I was met by

a fiacre. The butler, dressed in a jacket of green and white stripes with black satin sleeves, opened the door of the villa. I was led into an enormous bright room, where the only furniture was a large desk and chair placed in the very center of a black and white chessboard marble floor. The walls were hung with gray and white striped drapes that hung very high. Erté entered. He was dressed in wide pajamas trimmed in ermine. A huge Persian cat arching its back slipped around his legs. Erté's friend, the majestic Count Ouroussov, dressed in a Chinese brocade jacket with a train, followed him in.

"'Would you like to see my sketches?' Erté asked, went over to the wall, pulled a cord to open the gray and white drapes: hundreds of framed drawings hung in precise rows were revealed.

"I thought that there had never been a more productive and more refined artist than this small Russian who night and day drew exotic women with elongated eyes, swaying under the weight of furs, feathers of birds-of-paradise and pearls."[1]

At the beginning of his career in France, Erté turned to the stage. His first theater costumes were created in 1914 for the Revue de St. Cyr. While visiting Princess Tenisheva in Monte

Carlo, Erté met Sergei Diaghilev, who immediately asked him to create the costumes for the ballet *Sleeping Beauty*, since the original costumes by Bakst had been confiscated in London and sold to pay off debts. Erté recalled: "In 1922 I accepted Diaghilev's invitation to work with him with pleasure. I immediately drew two sketches, but the next day I got a telegram from the impresarios the Schubert brothers with an offer of a good contract. Not knowing what to do in this situation, I went to see Diaghilev, who told me: 'Never turn down money. I never do.'"[2]

Erté was also commissioned by Anna Pavlova to create costumes for her ballet numbers *Gavotte, Divertissement,* and *Seasons.* The path to glory was wide open. When Erté brought his relatives to France from the Soviet Union in 1923, his father, Admiral Tyrtov, admitted, "You were right to leave for Paris."

In the 1920s and 1930s Erté worked in the United States with George White's Scandals, a famous New York revue; with the Chicago opera; and on Hollywood films. Erté's influence on American film was strong. He brought the spirit of Parisian fashion ateliers, the imagination of Russian ballets, and the theatricality of variety reviews to Hollywood costumes. Erté designed costumes for such silent-film stars as May Murray, Eileen Pringle, Lillian Gish, Marion Davies, and Pauline Stark among others.

Once back in Paris in the 1930s, Erté worked for variety shows—his clients

Erté in the salon of his villa in Monte Carlo. On the walls are his graphic works, including his sketches for the covers of Harper's Bazaar, 1923.

365

Above left, center, right: *Hollywood silent-film stars in costumes designed by Erté, 1925.*

Right: *Alla Nazimova, a Russian silent-film star in Hollywood, in an Erté-inspired costume for the film* Salome, *1926.*

Opposite above: *One of Erté's covers for* Harper's Bazaar, *1926.*

Opposite below: *Erté amid journalists and actresses, Hollywood, 1925.*

366

included Josephine Baker and the popular Paris cabarets the Folies Bergères and Ba-Ta-Clan. Erté lived out his days in a spacious apartment on rue Gutenberg in the chic Paris suburb of Boulogne. He designed his interior in a unique style that combined Russian estate furniture with exotic souvenirs, such as zebra and leopard skins. A translucent wall created by a large aquarium separated the hall from the study where Erté worked at a large comfortable desk surrounded by his numerous cats, usually at night. His talented invention was a roomy bar in the shape of a shot glass, peppered with autographs of the admirers who visited him. To preserve and exhibit his drawings, Erté invented an expanding exhibit cupboard, illuminated by lamps of crocodile skin. He would often visit his neighbors, Prince and Princess Youssoupoff in Boulogne.

In 1932 Erté was invited to work for the Latvian National Opera in Riga, where he made sketches for the sets and costumes for *Faust* and *Don Pascuale*. After World War II Erté continued to work for cabarets in Paris, but he also created costumes and sets for operas. In a conversation with the author, Erté once said, "I prefer doing costumes for opera; ballet limits me."

Short, youthful, and natty, Erté was always elegant, and elegance knows no age. When Erté was almost seventy, he saw another period of fame. In the late 1960s the United States and Europe experienced a new interest in Art Deco, and half-forgotten artists were brought back from oblivion: Ukrainian Sonia Delaunay-Terk, Polish Tamara Lempicka, and Russian Erté. The triumph of period style from the 1920s and 1930s was often tied to the films of the day,

Библиотека декоративных искусств. Париж

Коллекция Тиссен-Борнемисса, Мадрид

and movies such as *Cabaret, Death on the Nile,* and *The Great Gatsby* increased the interest in the period. Erté's drawings were reprinted, his designs *Alphabet* and *Numbers* were published as postcards, and numerous lithographs were made of his works, which were particularly popular in the United States.

One of Erté's first patrons in the 1960s was the millionairess Isabel Estorick, who had a villa in Barbados with an interior design based on Erté's sketches. In Paris he was supported by the Russian nightclub owner Hélène Martini, known as "the empress of the night," who hired Erté to do the posters for her famous theater, Folies Bergères. In Martini's chateau in the north of France, Erté created magical interiors that, to this day, remain a veritable museum of his art. In 1967, The Metropolitan Museum in New York had an Erté retrospective, and books about his art appeared in Europe, America, and Japan. His drawings were used on Japanese towels, German T-shirts, and Italian dishes. Near the end of his life, Erté turned to sculpture. At the age of ninety-seven he designed costumes and sets for his last production, the Broadway musical *Stardust.* Erté is perhaps the only St. Petersburg artist who lived to see world fame and to enjoy his laurels.

Библиотека школы искусств. Глазго

Above left: *An advertisement for the boutique of Sonia Delaunay and Jacques Heim at the Exhibit of Modern Decorative and Industrial Arts, Paris, 1925.*

Above: *Sonia Delaunay's oil painting of a "simultaneous" dress, 1925.*

Left: *The shop window and entrance to the boutique of Sonia Delaunay and Jacques Heim on the Alexander III Bridge during the Exhibit of Contemporary Decorative and Industrial Arts, Paris, 1925.*

Opposite: *Beach outfits with geometric appliqués in rich tones designed by Sonia Delaunay, Paris, 1928.*

369

To the last, Erté liked traveling. He was always en route between Majorca, where he was building a summer residence, London, New York, Barbados, and Paris. During a trip to the island of Mauritius, Erté became suddenly ill and was flown by the private jet of American friends to Paris, where he died in the Cochin hospital on Easter Saturday, April 21, 1990. In the hospital, Erté made a list of guests for the memorial ceremony (including the author of this book). The funeral was at the Cathedral of Alexander Nevsky in Paris. The mahogany coffin, made from Erté's sketches, was covered with flowers sent by his faithful admirer Hélène Martini. Erté is buried in Boulogne cemetery in the family plot with his parents.[3]

Another famous designer of fabrics, clothing, and fashion accessories was Sonia Delaunay. The influence of her style and color schemes on the development of fashion in the Art Deco period is indisputable. Like Erté, her work is widely known and respected everywhere in the world except in the former Soviet Union.

Sonia Eleivna Stern was born November 14, 1885, in the small village of Gradizhsk, Poltava Province, to a large Jewish family. At the age of five she was sent to live with her maternal uncle Heinrich Terk, a wealthy St. Petersburg

lawyer, and it was then that Sonia changed her name from Stern to Terk. Her childhood in St. Petersburg was cloudless—she spent time at the family dacha in Finland and vacationed in Italy and Switzerland. Even then she was interested in figurative arts, and, in 1903, her uncle sent the young artist to Karlsruhe, Germany, to the private school of Ludwig Schmid-Reutte, where she studied for two years, without getting a classic art education—Sonia's drawing skills were always weak.

In 1905 she moved to Paris and entered the Académie de la Palette, where she studied engraving and gradually entered the circle of artist bohemia. At twenty-two she married Wilhelm Uhde, a German art critic and collector. The same year, 1908, Sonia began exhibiting her first works at the Paris gallery Notre-Dame des Champs. Her marriage

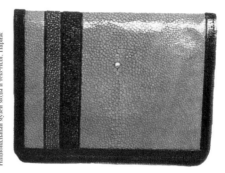

Частная коллекция, Париж

of convenience to Wilhelm lasted only two years, and after their divorce Sonia married the famous and talented French artist Robert Delaunay, the name under which she became famous. Sonia used to say about her husband, "He gave me form, and I gave him color." Her abstract art was influenced by the colors of Fauvism.

In 1911 Sonia had a son, Charles, and she made a blanket for the newborn with appliqués from colored pieces of fabric—this is how she began her first work with textiles. She called these abstract appliqués "simultaneous contrasts" and liked them so much that they became an inalienable part of her work

Opposite, top center: *A crocheted dress of colored silk that fashion historians ascribe to Sonia Delaunay, Paris, mid-1920s.*

Opposite, top right: *A woman's leather purse designed by Sonia Delaunay, Paris, mid-1920s.*

Opposite below: *A fragment of a fabric sketch by Sonia Delaunay, Paris, 1925.*

Top: *Robert Delaunay,* Portrait of Mrs. Heim in a shawl by Sonia Delaunay, *1926–27.*

Right: *A dress made from fabric designed by Sonia Delaunay, Paris, 1928.*

Библиотека декоративных искусств, Париж

372

Архив Асами Маки, Токио

Библиотека декоративных искусств, Париж

for many years. Her works of the 1910s are imbued with the atmosphere of the innovation of the period: *Electric Prisms* and *Studies of Light* are created in a rainbow scale of fractured sunlight. She worked on book illustrations, posters, and objects of applied art, and in the 1920s she created her first dresses and jackets with "simultaneous" appliqués. Sonia's works, which rejected the artistic canons and principles of the past, became the standard of new art for fabric designers of the period. Robert Delaunay wrote about her in 1923: "For Sonia, a dress or coat is part of space with specific sizes, forms, and content. She creates an organic whole in accordance with the laws that are obligatory for her art."[4]

With the start of World War I, the Delaunays moved to Madrid. Sonia loved the Spanish sun and flowers, traveled to Portugal, studied Spanish dances, and even organized a personal exhibit far afield in Stockholm. The revolution in Russia deprived Sonia Delaunay of the financial support she received from her uncle in St. Petersburg. Fortunately, the Diaghilev troupe was touring in Spain then, and Sergei Diaghilev, always ready to bring in new talent, offered Sonia work with his company. Boris Kokhno, Diaghilev's secretary, wrote: "In 1917, during a tour of the Russian Ballet in Latin America, the sets to *Cleopatra* burned, and in July 1918

Diaghilev commissioned Robert Delaunay to do new ones, and his wife, Sonia, to design new costumes for Lyubov Chernysheva and Leonid Massine, who danced the roles created by Rubinstein and Fokine."[5] These multicolored costumes were later inherited by the troupe of Colonel de Basil, which used them in the 1930s and 1940s. In 1968 the public saw Lyubov Chernysheva's costume once more, not on the stage, but at a Sotheby's auction. It was sold among other objects from the enormous inheritance of Colonel de Basil's widow, Olga Alexandrovna Morozova de Basil. The auction revived a widespread interest in Diaghilev and Delaunay.

Sonia and Robert Delaunay returned to Paris in 1921 and plunged into the cultural life. They were friends with Marc Chagall, writers Tristan Tzara and Vladimir Mayakovsky, Pierre Loti, and many others. The couple's art grew more popular and they received many commissions to design interiors of stores and apartments. At the same time, Sonia created "simultaneous" scarves, which brought her even greater fame. From 1922 to 1925 Sonia made numerous coats, shawls, and fabric samples with appliqués, and designed several fashion shows and social balls devoted to the "new art." Her talent was particularly appreciated by the Dadaists, who saw the future of fashion in her dress-

Opposite, top left: *Yurek Shabelevsky and Lyubov Chernysheva in the ballet* Cleopatra *in costumes designed by Sonia Delaunay, Paris, 1937.*

Opposite right: *Knit sweaters and dresses with bright geometric designs created under the influence of Sonia Delaunay, Longchamps, 1925.*

Above: *A drawing from the French magazine* L'Art et la mode *of sports dresses: second from left and far right are designed by Sonia Delaunay, 1928.*

Right: *A sketch of a dress by Sonia Delaunay, 1924–25.*

"poems." She told British *Vogue* in January 1966, "I think new painting began with us: we liberated it with our color."[6]

Sonia Delaunay's experiments with rectangular, spherical, and square shapes were truly revolutionary. Her works drew the interest of celebrities, such as the film star Gloria Swanson, who bought an evening coat with rectangular silk appliqués that resembled polychromatic architectural forms. The Paris journal *L'Art vivant* wrote about Delaunay's work in 1925: "These printed and embroidered fabrics follow one principle—equilibrium of volume and color. The profound feeling of marvelous rhythm is characteristic of the compositions of Madame Delaunay. There is no place here for color whims or the charms of natural beauty. Here

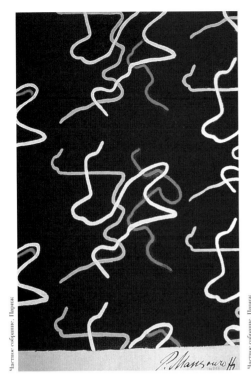

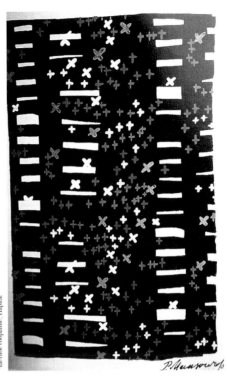

reigns abstraction, constant geometry that however it changes shape, is alive and raised to the heights of lightness by her inspiration, accompanied by the caprice of the play of her brush and the all-conquering joy of color."[7]

One of the most significant events in the life of Sonia Delaunay was her participation in the Exhibit of Contemporary Decorative and Industrial Arts in Paris in 1925. Jointly with the famous fashion and fur designer Jacques Heim, Delaunay had an exhibit of her works in a specially constructed "simultaneous boutique" on the Alexander III Bridge. Her scarves, purses, and cloaks were exhibited in a small shop window. The world fair in Paris brought enormous attention, and people started talking about her work. She began lecturing at the Sorbonne on her creative method and she was hired more frequently by theaters and film studios to do costumes. Leonid Massine, who knew the Delaunays in Madrid and had kept up relations with them, commissioned sets and costumes from them for the ballet *Perpetuum Mobile*, with music by Schubert. Sonia, an admirer of plotless ballet, agreed readily.

The atelier Sonia opened to handle the influx of orders produced numerous

Opposite, top left: Artist Pavel Mansurov in the years when he worked at the Renault automobile factory, France, 1929.

Opposite and above: Five sketches of textile designs by Pavel Mansurov, early 1930s.

Below: The Duke and Duchess of Windsor. The duke's tie is made from fabric designed by Pavel Mansurov, mid-1930s.

new designs: crocheted colored vests and dresses, scarves, bathing suits, coats, and bags. Of a common color scheme and level of abstraction, Sonia's designs were easily recognizable in cities and at spa resorts as a symbol of avant-garde fashion from the years 1925 to 1929. According to the fashion magazines of the period, Sonia's bathing suits conquered the popular beach resort of Trouville, on the English Channel. The fashion of those days, thanks to the simplicity of line, showed off the exceptionally decorative drawings on the fabric and the magnificence of the rainbow color combinations. Sonia Delaunay was, without a doubt, in the vanguard of the top fashion designers of the twentieth century, using the achievements of her paintings in her fabric designs.

Textile factories, such as Rodier and Lyon, manufactured printed fabrics with geometric designs based on Sonia's sketches. Her explorations in the area of textiles and fashion were interrupted by the economic crisis of 1929, which made anything reminiscent of the extravagant "roaring twenties" suddenly unfashionable. Sonia had to close her atelier of fashion and fabrics on Boulevard de Malesherbes, but this did not mean an end to her creativity. Continu-

ing to paint and draw, in 1932 she published in *Journal d'Heim* an article, "Artists and the Future of Fashion," which predicted the victory of prêt-à-porter. Her husband, Robert Delaunay, died in 1941, but Sonia lived until 1979, actively creating up until her death.

In the group of designers and creators who emigrated from Russia after the revolution, a special place belongs to Dmitrii Dmitriievich Bouchéne, the last surviving artist of the *Mir iskusstva* [World of Art] group.

Bouchéne was born April 26, 1893, in St. Tropez, France. He came from an ancient French family that had long been Russified. Bouchéne's ancestors left France in 1685 during the reign of Louis XIV, and the first Bouchéne reached Russia in Catherine the Great's reign. In the nineteenth century, Dmitrii Khristianovich Bouchéne served as director of Russia's corps of pages; he was the head of a large family, and his many sons joined the corps. Dmitrii Bouchéne's father, also a Dmitrii Dmitriievich, was a graduate of the corps of pages and a colonel in the tsar's army. His mother, née Alexandra Semenovna Mikhaltseva, died of consumption when Dmitrii was only two, and the doctors were sure that the

Above: *Three sketches of textile designs by Tatyana Pokrovskaya-Klepinina, 1950s.*

Below: *An illustration by Boris Grigoriev for* Harper's Bazaar, 1933.

sickly child would not survive—however, Dmitrii lived to be just two months shy of a hundred. The artist's father soon married Elena Valerianovna Gempel, a society lady and the daughter of the mayor of Warsaw. She did not wish to bring up another woman's children, and Dmitrii and his sister, Alexandra (who also lived to be one hundred years old), were taken in by their aunt, Ekaterina Dmitriievna Kuzmina-Karavayeva, née Bouchéne.

The artist told the author about his new family: "The Kuzmin-Karavayev family was very cultured. My aunt's son (my cousin) Dmitrii was married to Elizabeth Pilenko, better known as Mother Maria. Another cousin, Mikhail Kuzmin-Karavayev, was my age, and Anna Akhmatova was in love with him. The poet Nikolai Gumilev was my cousin. Their estate Slepinevo was seven *versts* [kilometers] from Boriskova, the Kuzmin-Karavayev estate."[8]

Dmitrii Bouchéne received an art education in St. Petersburg, taking evening courses at the Society for the Promotion of Artists, which he attended while still at the Imperial Gymnasium of Alexander I. Nikolai Roerich noted the young artist's talent, and presented him to his

Left: *Zinaida Serebryakova*, Portrait of Dmitrii Bouchéne, *1923.*

Right: *Sergei Ivanov*, Self-portrait, *1939.*

Below: *Three drawings by Sergei Ivanov of designs from the house of Patou for the magazine* Plaisirs de France, *1937.*

fellow members in the *Mir iskusstva* group. In 1912, during the height of the Ballets Russes, Dmitrii's parents sent him to Paris, where he studied at the Ranson Academy and met Maurice Denis and Henri Matisse. Once Matisse told the young artist: "You must not depict the object before you, but the feeling that it arouses in you."

Returning to St. Petersburg, called Petrograd during World War I, Dmitrii Bouchéne grew close to *Mir iskusstva*, particularly to Alexandre Nikolayevich

Benois, who appreciated his talent. This is when he met Sergei Ernst, an art connoisseur and esthete who became the artist's best friend for life. After the revolution, with the help of Benois, Bouchéne got a position at the State Hermitage Museum, where he worked as a junior curator in the department of fans, headed by the outstanding historian of material culture, Sergei Troinitsky. The young artist took part in three group exhibits of *Mir iskusstva* at the Anichkov Palace. Bouchéne and Ernst went abroad in

1925, on a legal leave of three months, and they never returned. Bouchéne went to Paris, via Tallinn, and with a recommendation to Anna Pavlova from her former colleagues, ballerinas at the Maryinsky Theater, he immediately began working on her costumes.

It is curious that although Erté and Bouchéne were almost the same age and had much in common—their origins in St. Petersburg, their work in the world of fashion in Paris, Anna Pavlova as a client—they did not become friends,

377

Above: Three sketches by Leon Kudin for the cover of L'Art et la mode, *1938–39.*

Below: A drawing by Leon Kudin of an evening dress for a fashion magazine, 1938.

and even avoided each other throughout their almost century-long lives.

In the 1920s Bouchéne began working in fashion, offering his designs to the biggest houses of the day, such as Nina Ricci, Jean Patou, Jeanne Lanvin, and Lucien Lelong (Princess Paley, then married to Lelong, was a distant relative of Bouchéne through the Pistolkors family). He recalled this period in his life: "I drew designs. Jeanne Lanvin was the first to buy them in Paris and even asked me to work at her house. I also worked for Lelong, Patou, and Jane Regny: they all bought my designs." His style, poetic and painterly, conveyed the image of the design, its spirit, and not just the silhouette that was the orientation for tailors. Some of his drawings from the 1920s are currently in private collections, and, in 1983 during a large sale of the artist's work, six sketches created for Lucien Lelong in the early 1930s were sold at the Drouot auction in Paris.

In 1931 Bouchéne created costumes for Alisa Alanova, a ballerina of a neo-classical bent. Three years later he designed costumes for the unique Ida Rubinstein, who received the artist in her Paris apartment lounging on pillows like Zobeide, fully believing in eternal youth and the majesty of her own tal-

ent. The rest of his work was for the opera and ballet, where he worked with such stars as Kurt Jooss, Leonid Massine, Serge Lifar, and George Balanchine and with such houses as La Scala, Amsterdam Opera, the Gulbenkian Ballet in Lisbon, and the Grand Opera de Paris. To his last day Bouchéne continued easel painting.

Among the other Russian émigré artists who worked in fashion and magazine illustration in the 1930s were Eugene Gustavovich Berman and Boris Dmitriievich Grigoriev. Eugene Berman was born November 4, 1899, in St. Petersburg to a banking family. He lost his father early and was brought up in the house of Anatoli Shaikevich, a major art collector and financier. In 1908 Eugene was sent to study in Switzerland, France, and Germany, where he first came to know the magical world of opera and began his lifelong love affair with it. Returning to Petrograd in 1914, he studied privately at the art studios of painter Pavel Naumov and architect Sergei Gruzenberg. The Bolshevik Revolution caught Berman in Petrograd and he was arrested by the Cheka; fortunately, he avoided the sad fate of so many and was released and forced to leave Russia—forever, as it turned out.

The Berman family arrived in Paris

in 1919, via Finland and then England, where the brothers Leonid and Eugene continued painting at the Ranson Academy under Maurice Denis, Eduard Vuillard, and Felix Valloton. It was during this period that the Berman brothers began their long friendship with Christian Bérard. Both Bermans became avid admirers of Diaghilev's ballets in Paris and especially of his set designers, Picasso and Derain. Exhibiting constantly with Paul Tchelichew and Christian Bérard

of fashion illustration of the prewar period.

In the second half of his life, the artist concentrated on painting and set design, working with celebrated theaters in Monte Carlo, as well as the Metropolitan Opera in New York and La Scala in Milan. Eugene Berman, a respected artist in both the new and old worlds yet totally unknown in Russia, died in Rome, at the palace of the Princess Doria Pamphili on December

in Paris, the Bermans earned a good reputation and new friends and patrons.

Frequent trips to Italy enriched Eugene's work. He began getting attention in the United States, and in 1932 he exhibited in New York, a major collector started buying his work, and he was hired by the best American magazines to do illustrations. By 1935 he was doing dozens of covers for *Vogue*, *Harper's Bazaar,* and *Town and Country.* Eugene's creations of those years resemble the fantastic compositions of Guardi and Pannini, but they also have the dreaminess of Hubert Robert and the divine exaltation of Mantegni. This amazing mixture is the essence of Berman's style, which made a significant contribution to the development

Above: *Zinaida Alexeyevna de Plagny, Kudin's wife and the founder of the Zina atelier, which manufactured painted silk scarves, Paris, late 1930s.*

Center: *Leonid Kudin during the height of his popularity in the Parisian world of fashion, 1930s.*

Below: *Leon Kudin with the artists from his fashion illustration and textile design studio, Paris, 1936.*

Архив Зинаиды де Планьи, Париж

14, 1972, surrounded by his marvelous collection of antiquities.

Boris Grigoriev came to fashion illustration as a mature and famous artist. He was born in Moscow to a merchant family on July 11, 1886. His father, Dmitrii Vasilyevich Grigoriev, was director of the Rybinsk branch of the Volga-Kama Bank, and his mother, Klara Ioghannovna Lindenberg, was a Swede from Riga, a daughter of a sea captain. Boris's childhood was spent in Rybinsk with his two brothers and a sister. Upon graduating from high school, Boris was sent to Moscow, where he passed the entrance examination for the Practical Academy of Commercial Studies. But his desire to be an artist was stronger, and in 1903 he entered the Stroganov Industrial Arts School in Mos-

Above: *A drawing of evening dresses by Leon Kudin for a fashion magazine, 1937.*

Opposite above: *A sketch by Leon Kudin for a portrait of his wife, Zinaida de Plagny, c. 1937.*

Opposite below: *Sketches of women's blouses by Irina Holman de Koby, 1938.*

cow, in the class of Dmitrii Shcherbi-novsky, his idol from his student years. There he met his future wife, Elizaveta Georgievna von Brachet, who was from a Baltic aristocratic family. Boris completed his studies at the Academy of Arts in St. Petersburg and then traveled through Europe with his young wife. In 1909 he visited Norway and later went to Paris, where he created a series of drawings called *Women*. Apparently, this was the artist's first appreciation of the beautiful lines of women's clothing.

Back in Russia, Grigoriev did illustrations for the journal *Novyi Satirikon*. Then, at an exhibit of his works, he was noticed by Alexandre Benois, which brought him close to the *Mir iskusstva* circle. He became a frequent exhibitor with the group. In wartime Petrograd, the cabaret "The Comedian's Rest" was popular, and Grigoriev, Sudeikin, and Yakovlev were famed as the creators of the set's frescoes, which are now lost. Grigoriev's series *Raseia*, later published as an album, also brought him great fame in Russia during this time. His gift for the grotesque found an outlet in his brilliant portraits of such artists as Vsevolod Meyerhold, Feodor Chaliapin, Boris Kustodiev, Velemir Khlebnikov, Mstislav Dobuzhinsky, Alexander Kerensky, and others.

Grigoriev emigrated in 1919 via Finland to Berlin. There he published several books of his illustrations and he regularly published his drawings in the Russian-language magazine *Zhar-ptitsa* [Firebird]. In 1921 he moved to Paris, where he painted several first-rate portraits of actors of the Moscow Art Theater during their European tour.

Exhibits in the United States in the 1920s brought the artist world recognition. His profound images of Russia touched the hearts of viewers during this period when everything Russian was fashionable. Grigoriev's paintings were bought by the Luxembourg Museum in Paris and by private collectors. Thanks to a flow of commissions, in

1927 he built a villa in Cagnes-sur-Mer near Nice, which he called "Borisella," a combination of his name and his wife's; their son, Kirill, lives there now. During the years 1927 and 1928 Grigoriev visited South America twice, and many of his drawings from this period are in private art collections in Chile. Grigoriev painted wonderful portraits of the members of influential and wealthy Chilean families Aguirre-Tupper and Edwards-Mackenna. Grigoriev also traveled in Argentina, Uruguay, and Brazil. The Academy of Arts in Santiago offered him a teaching position, but he gave only thirty-seven lessons. The Santiago Museum of Fine Arts has acquired four paintings from his *Breton* series.

Back in Europe, Grigoriev took up fashion illustration in the 1930s. Thanks to his international acclaim and great commercial success, several American magazines offered him work. *Harper's Bazaar* asked Grigoriev to create several illustrations with a typical "Grigorievian" line. His son, Kirill, recalled, in a conversation with the author, "When father and I went to New York, he always met with editors of fashion magazines and brought them completed fashion illustrations from Paris, which they bought."[9]

Right up to his death on November 7, 1939, in Cagnes-sur-Mer, Grigoriev continued working, despite ill health. Three years before his death he traveled through South America again, working in Colombia, Ecuador, Peru, Chile, and Brazil, and in Cuba; the vivid colors of these countries had a strong influence on the palette of his later works.

While Dmitrii Bouchéne, Eugene Berman, and Boris Grigoriev were educated and trained in Russia and came to the world of fashion illustration as mature artists, there were also Russian émigré fashion illustrators and textile artists who were educated and developed their professional mastery outside Russia.

Among the Russians who created designs for printed fabrics and fashion silhouettes, we should particularly note the talented Leonid Maximovich Kudin. He was born in Rostov-on-Don into the family of a schoolteacher. He was fascinated by drawing, and worked as a cartoonist for a local newspaper. He

emigrated with the White Army to Constantinople and then Greece, and eventually ended up in France without any means of survival. Like hundreds of other Russians, he worked at the Renault automobile plant, where the pay was low and the presence of Russian workers did not help in learning French. Around 1929, Kudin met Pavel Andreyevich Mansurov, an avant-garde artist who had just arrived from Russia, and who was close to Tatlin, Filonov, and Malevich.

Together with another Russian émigré, Okolov, who was later deported by the Germans for participating in the Resistance, Kudin started a modest atelier of

textile design on Boulevard Strasbourg-Saint-Denis in Paris. The Okolov-Kudin sketches were bought by textile factories, and Mansurov offered his sketches for fabrics, too—his geometric style was best suited to the expressions of the 1920s. Mansurov was friends with many artists of the "Russian Montparnasse," particularly Chaim Soutine. Kudin's widow, Zinaida Alexeyevna de Plagny, told the author: "Mansurov and Soutine went to Montparnasse. They were friends and they starved together. Soutine drew a still life with a herring and then they ate the herring." Mansurov also knew Sonia and Robert Delaunay, who appreciated his

textile work. However, with the new fashion for small flower ornamentation in the early 1930s, Mansurov's geometric designs became less popular, and by the mid-1930s he was better known as a designer of ties, one of which was worn by the Duke of Windsor.

In 1933 Kudin married Zinaida Alexeyevna de Plagny, who had emigrated from Moscow in 1923 and whose family had old French roots. At that time the atelier of Okolov and Leon Kudin, as he was known in Paris, was located in a twelve-room apartment on rue Louis le Grand, with business going very well. In 1937 they moved their atelier to the most prestigious fashion street in prewar Paris—rue de la Paix. There, according to Kudin's widow, they had close to fifteen employees, including several Russian émigrés. One of the fabric designers was Irina Mamontova, and Kirill Kovalevsky was in charge of selling the sketches to textile factories. Their designs were extremely successful, and Kudin's talent drew the attention of fashion designers, such as Nina and Robert Ricci, owners of the fashion house, who, in 1936, asked Kudin to draw their designs.

Kudin's graphic manner, slightly reminiscent of Christian Bérard, was very popular in the fashion magazines from 1937 to 1939, and he created several covers for *Jardin des modes* and *Mode et travaux*, which delight us to

this day with the elegance of their lines. Unfortunately, Kudin's premature death of tuberculosis in 1939 cut off his brilliant career as a fashion illustrator. After her husband's death, Zinaida Alexeyevna de Plagny continued to work in fashion, and, together with the Italian Locatelli, she maintained the Parisian atelier Zina in the 1940s, which specialized in batik scarves of parachute silk.

Other Russian textile designers active in Paris in the 1930s were Wladimir Isdebsky, from Kiev, Eugene Okolov-Subkovsky, from Krasnoiansk, and Ilia Zdanevich, from Tiflis, who designed textiles for Chanel from 1927 to 1937.

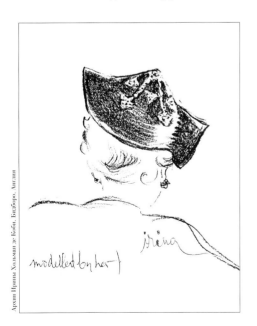

Opposite left: A sketch by Irina Holman de Koby for an evening dress, 1949.

Opposite right: A sketch by Irina Holman de Koby of an evening dress designed by the house of Lucille Manguin, 1937.

This page: Irina Holman de Koby's sketches of hats for the fashion house of Madame Kitty, which was run by her mother, Ekaterina Ionina, 1950.

Among the other fashion illustrators of the 1930s we should mention Irina Sergeyevna Holman de Koby. Graduating from lycée in Paris in 1933, she spent almost a year in England, where she met her future husband, Roger Holman. The daughter of the famous model Katyusha Ionina, Irina Holman came back to Paris and entered the School of Applied Fashion design. Possessing an unusual talent as a fashion illustrator, she first drew hat designs and then took a job with the Lucille Manguin fashion house, which was considered one of the most prestigious. Irina also drew for the magazine *Jardin des modes*, where quite a few Russians worked, and later did drawings for advertisements for the Laure Belin lingerie house, which was run by her stepmother, Tamara Gamsakhurdia de Koby.

The talented portraitist Sergei Ivanov also worked successfully as a fashion magazine illustrator in the 1930s. He was born in Moscow on December 25, 1893, and from early childhood he drew from nature and was interested in anatomical studies. In 1917 he studied at the Academy of Arts in Petrograd under Academician Osip Braz, and upon graduation emigrated, reaching France via Finland in 1922. In Paris, Ivanov won fame as a magazine illustrator and brilliant portraitist. He traveled extensively in Italy, Belgium, Holland, and Denmark and visited distant Brazil. In 1930 Ivanov began a twenty-year relationship with the Paris magazine *Illustration*, publishing travel sketches, views of French cathedrals, and fashion silhouettes. In 1937 and 1938 the magazine *Plaisirs de France* published his masterful drawings of designs from the famous Parisian fashion houses of Jean Patou, Schiaparelli, Lanvin, Molyneux, and Rochas. In 1939, van Cleef and Arpels hired him to do their advertisements in French *Vogue*. Women, whom he always adored, are attractive, seductive, and, of course, elegant in his drawings, which are precise, almost portrait-like.

Indeed, Ivanov was recognized not only as a magazine illustrator but as a portraitist. He did an entire gallery of portraits of the highest clergy of the Catholic Church: Pope Pius XI, the Bishop of Chartres, the primate of Belgium (Cardinal van Roy), the cardinal of Rio de Janeiro, and others. Government officials, politicians, diplomats and stage stars also commissioned Ivanov to paint them. His portrait subjects include Grand Duke Vladimir Kirillovich, Eleanor Roosevelt, Alexandre Benois, Edwige Feuillère, Lisette Darsonval, Serge Lifar, Yvette Chauviré, and Solange Schwartz.

Ivanov moved to the United States in 1950 and continued to work and travel in Brazil and Argentina. Back in France in the 1960s, he frequently exhibited his popular portraits and compositions. For his participation in the Salon des Artistes of 1966, Ivanov was given a gold medal by André Malraux, Minister of Culture of France. The talented artist, so little-known in his homeland, died on February 8, 1983, at the age of eighty-nine, in his Paris studio with a brush in his hand.

Opposite: *Irina Holman de Koby,*
Moonlight in the Forest, *an illustration*
for a fashion magazine. De Koby made
the dress of white satin for a formal ball.

20

RUSSIAN BEAUTIES OF THE 1920S

And into this city—the world of dreams of previous
Russian generations—with gentle tread came a
*   Russian émigré:*
In their day her mother and grandmother had dressed
at Worth, Poiret, and Beschoff-David,
but this young woman had just escaped the hell
of revolution and civil war! Quite recently she had
served as a nurse at the front with Denikin
and in British hospitals in Constantinople.

She entered the capital of women's elegance and knocked
at the doors of a luxurious maison de haute couture.
And the massive doors swung open before her,
and she conquered every heart. ...

G. Nemirovich-Danchenko,
"Plat'e, telo, dusha" [Dress, Body, Soul]
Illustrirovannaya Rossiya [Illustrated Russia]
January 23, 1932

In the 1920s there were almost a hundred Russian beauties modeling clothes in Paris, the fashion center of the world. Before these Russians arrived in France, models could not have boasted of such aristocratic manners, such élan in presenting new outfits, or such ability to converse with the clients. In those years there was a strict hierarchy in the profession. Models working in various fashion houses were divided into categories: *mannequins de cabine*, or those who were on the payroll; *mannequins vedettes*, stars, or those who came for special shows; *mannequins volantes*, flying models, that is, those hired to travel with a show abroad; and *mannequins mondaines*, society models, those who were particularly beautiful or had impressive titles and were given dresses to wear out in society.

The Russian beauties who were celebrated in Paris in the 1920s were, as a rule, recognized priestesses of elegance and taste back in pre-revolutionary Russia. The most important Paris fashion houses hired them. During the interwar years in Paris, it seemed there was not a single house that did not have Russian models. At Chanel, for example, the most popular models were Princess Mary Eristova and Gali Bajenova.

Mary Prokofievna Eristova, née Princess Schervachidze, was born October 17, 1895, in Batumi, Georgia. Her father, Prince Schervachidze, was a member of the State Duma of Russia, and Princess

Архив автора, Париж

Opposite: *Thea Bobrikova in a design from Lanvin, Paris, 1929. Photo by A. De Meyer.*

Above: *Tatyana Lishchenko, a Russian model, Paris, 1926. Photo by D'Orr.*

Mary lived in St. Petersburg from childhood. Her exotic beauty was quickly noticed. She and her sister, Princess Tamara Prokofievna Schervachidze, who later married Count Zarnekau, were constant ornaments at society events and balls. Fashion magazines such as *Stolitsa i usad'ba* often ran pictures of the young beauty. Thanks to her aristocratic origins, marvelous manners, and exceptional looks, Princess Schervachidze became a lady-in-waiting to Empress Alexandra Feodorovna.

The princess lost her father during the revolution and moved with her family to the Caucasus, where in 1919 she married Prince Gigusha Eristov. Irina Holman de Koby recalled how Princess Eristova would take her walks along the boulevards of Batumi in 1920 with "raised eyebrow and proud facial expression." At about this time the famous St. Petersburg society portraitist Savely Sorin painted Princess Eristova in a light silk dress belted beneath the bosom, with a "faux-classical shawl" over her left shoulder and a string of large pearls sparkling between her fragile fingers; unfortunately, the portrait remained in Russia. In *Zhar-ptitsa*, the Berlin magazine of the Russian émigré community, Sergei Makovsky wrote that Sorin's "beauties' hands inherited the graceful weakness of their elongated fingers from Van Dyke."[1]

In 1921 the Schervachidze-Eristov family joined the flow of émigrés to Constantinople, the first foreign city on the long refugee path. As Countess Zarnekau, Princess Eristova's niece, who now lives on the Côte d'Azur, recalls, their family was forced to look for work even in Constantinople, and her grandmother, Princess Schervachidze, took up dressmaking.

After an anxiety-fraught journey, the family reached Paris, and Mary Eristova was hired in 1925 by the head of Chanel, Prince Sergei Alexandrovich Koutouzov. Coco Chanel's turbulent af-

Архив Жака Феррана, Париж

Above left: *Princess Mary Eristova in a design by Chanel. Photo by George Hoyningen-Huene for* Vogue, *Paris, December 1928.*

Above right: *Princess Mary Eristova (Princess Schervachidze) in a court dress, Petrograd, 1914.*

Right: *Princess Mary Eristova in an ermine cloak designed by Redfern. Photo by Cecil Beaton for* Vogue, *Paris, December 1929.*

fair with Grand Duke Dmitrii Pavlovich had just ended, and Chanel continued to work with his sister, Grand Duchess Maria Pavlovna, and to employ many Russian émigrés. A fragile brunette, Mary Eristova personified the type of beauty popular in the 1920s, and her face and figure suited the Chanel style. Coco Chanel also liked the fact that she, a provincial from the Auvergne, had "real Russian princesses" working for her.

The other star at Chanel in the 1920s was Gali Bajenova, a woman with a unique and heroic life. She came from an ancient Kabardinian family of Hagondokov. Her father, General Konstantin Nikolayevich Hagondokov, commander of the second brigade of the Dikaya Division, was head of a large family: Gali (or "Elmiskhan," as she was called in Kabardinian) had four sisters and three brothers, and her mother, Elizaveta Emilyevna, née Bredova, came from a family of Polabian Slavs. Gali Hagondokova and her older sister, Nina, studied at the Smolny Institute in St. Petersburg. During World War I, Gali married Nikolai Bajenova, a graduate of the corps of pages, and she later became famous under her married name. Gali's family managed to escape from Russia, and in 1922 they settled in Paris, in the largely Russian fifteenth arrondissement.

Gali Bajenova, or as she was then called by Paris fashion magazines, "the Russian beauty Bajenova," arrived in Paris from Shanghai in 1923. On the recommendation of Prince Koutouzov, Chanel hired Bajenova, and her pho-

Библиотека декоративных искусств. Париж

Above: *Gali Bajenova when she worked as a "society model" at Chanel, Paris, 1924.*

Above left: *Gali Bajenova, "Russian blonde," Paris, late 1920s.*

Above right: *Gali Bajenova in an evening dress of panne velvet, from the house of Elmis, Paris, 1929.*

Left: *General de Gaulle and Gali Bajenova, who headed the surgical department of a mobile hospital during the war, 1944.*

Opposite above: *Ekaterina (Katyusha) Ionina in handcrafted earrings, Paris, 1924.*

Opposite below: *Katyusha Ionina during a tour of France with the collection Dames de France, Toulon, 1928.*

tographs began to appear in the very popular magazines *Fémina* and *Vogue*. A tall, slender blonde with a good figure, Bajenova was a real "society model," dressed by Chanel. Yevgeny Rogov writes: "She dressed with the same taste, and as a 'mannequin,' she dazzled with her outfits, which, perhaps, she was given in aid of advertising."[2]

We know that Bajenova worked as a saleswoman at Chanel for a while. Then, in 1928 she opened her own house of fashion, Elmis, which created embroidered evening gowns with striking decorative details and sold the perfume of Paul Poiret, who was in the decline of his brilliant career. The Elmis saleswoman was the famous Greek Princess Mourouzi from St. Petersburg, and the models were Chura Deleani and the beauty Katyusha Ionina. Bajenova's design assistant was her brother Georgy Hagondokov, who was a godson of Nicholas II. A nephew of Nicholas II, Prince Nikita Romanov, also worked there.

Bajenova's career changed abruptly when Elmis closed in 1932. For some time she did interior decoration, then, in 1934, she married Count Stanislas de Luart, a senator and the son of the Marquis de Luart. When she became the Countess de Luart, Gali converted to Catholicism and took the name Irene. During World War II the Bajenova family displayed heroism. Gali's son by her first marriage, Nikolai, fought bravely in the United States Army under the command of General Clark; Gali, now Countess Irene de Luart, joined the French Resistance and commanded the surgical department of a mobile hospital unit. With the American army, she was present at the liberation of Italy and was awarded the Légion d'Honneur by President Charles de Gaulle. As Ismail Hagondokov, a brother of this extraordinary woman, recalls, "She was a strong commander by nature." The Countess de Luart was buried with high military honors in the church of St.-Louis in Paris.

Bajenova's high school friend from Batumi, Ekaterina (Katyusha) Yevgenyevna Ionina, also became a famous model in Paris in the 1920s. She was born in Tiflis in 1896 to the family of

Архив Ирины Хольман де Коби, Бидборо, Англия.

Архив Ирины Хольман де Коби, Бидборо, Англия.

Colonel Yevgeny Apollonovich Ionin of the Imperial Army. As he advanced in his career, he became commander of the Batumi Military District.

At the age of eighteen, Katyusha was married in the Batumi cathedral to Sergei Davidovich Kobiev, an officer of the general staff, and the scion of an aristocratic family from the highlands of Georgia. In 1916 their daughter Irina was born. After the revolution Yevgeny Ionin fled from Batumi to Yalta, and from there to Constantinople. The Kobievs managed to get there, too, on a British warship. Ekaterina was convinced that her father had died while missing in action, and was overjoyed when she met him by coincidence on a trolleycar in Constantinople in 1920.

The family decided to go via Turkey to Serbia, where thousands of Russians had sought refuge. In Zemun, a suburb of Belgrade, Yevgeny opened a Russian restaurant, decorated with Caucasian and Turkish kilims, handmade rugs with no pile. Their real life as émigrés began. Unhappy in provincial Belgrade, Ekaterina left Yugoslavia with her husband in 1922 and moved to Paris. With Bajenova's help, she found work modeling at Caris, a small Russian fashion house that made designs exclusively in the popular Russian style.

At Caris, Ekaterina posed in various traditional Russian costumes, which followed the ephemeral whims of Paris fashion. Other employees at Caris included Vera and Sonya Guchkov, the daughters of the Moscow city head Nikolai Ivanovich Guchkov, who were saleswomen and who also designed beads and earrings. Katyusha worked at Caris for several months and then moved to the more prestigious and well-known Parisian fashion house Jenny, on the Champs-Elysées, which had been founded by Jenny Sacerdote in 1908. There were other Russian émigrés at Jenny, including Baroness Kira and Baroness Lelya von Medem, both of whom later became very famous models. Katyusha worked as a model at Jenny from 1923 until 1926. During this time her marriage to Sergei Kobiev came to an end.

In 1927 Katyusha began working as a model at Dames de France and traveled all over the country, doing fashion shows in Nice and Lyons. Militsa Porokhonskaya, the daughter of General Porokhonsky, a representative of the Denikin government in Batumi, and the Guchkov sisters also worked there. Of the six permanent models, only two were French. About 1930 Katyusha joined the famous Callot Soeurs fashion house, which was in business from 1888 to 1950. She was beginning to lose her marvelous figure, and, in 1933, she quit Callot Soeurs and became a saleswoman at Eric, a milliner's, where she worked with clients—her good French

Above: *Chura Deleani, a ballerina who danced in the Vronskaya Ballet, in a beaded evening dress designed by Elmis, Paris, 1931.*

Right: *Countess Marina Vorontsova, Paris, 1926. Photo by D'Orr for* Vogue.

came in handy. In 1934 she met Nikolai Vasilyevich Strakhovich, a singer with the Russian Opera, a former naval officer, and he became her second husband. Two years later she opened her own millinery shop, Madame Kitty, which lasted for almost twenty years, then closed in 1955 due to Katyusha's ill health.

Among the models in Paris in the 1920s who came from Russian high society, we must include Countess Elizaveta Nikolayevna Grabbe. She was born on December 24, 1893, into the old Baltic family Grabbe. The family had received its title in 1866 on the personal orders of Emperor Alexander II and from that time on was closely allied with the Imperial Army. Liza's father,

Count Nikolai Grabbe, was a cavalry guards officer of the Cossack Regiment, and Elizaveta's brother, Count Nikolai Nikolayevich Grabbe, was a graduate of the corps of pages.

When Countess Liza Grabbe was twenty she met Prince Sergei Sergeyevich Beloselsky-Belozersky, also of the corps of pages. He was a member of one of the most ancient princely families of Russia, going back to Rurik. Emperor Paul I decreed on February 27, 1794, that the Beloselsky princes could bear a double surname in memory of their older branch, the Belozersky princes, who died in battle on Kulikovo Field, fighting with the southern Slavs against the Turks, in 1380. The young people had met at the Grabbe family estate, Kolo-

Архив автора. Париж

Fash·1403

Архив автора. Париж
712

myaga, near St. Petersburg. They fell in love, but married only three years later, during World War I, when Prince Sergei came home to Petrograd on a two-months' leave from the front. The wedding took place in the family church of the Beloselsky-Belozersky family near their country palace on Krestovsky Island in Petrograd.

Thanks to the publication of the memoirs of Prince Beloselsky-Belozersky, we can re-create that memorable day. He wrote: "I wore my field uniform, Liza—in a traditional wedding gown. Proxy of my father was Prince Ioann Konstantinovich, ushers—officers of the Horse Guards. After a grand reception at my grandfather's home, accepting congratulations, toasts and

Above: *Olga Baklanova, an actress from the Moscow Art Theater who became a Hollywood star, Hollywood, 1929.*

Above right: *Zoe Karabanova, a silent-film star in Russia who became one of the stars of Le Chauve Souris Cabaret as an émigré, Paris, 1924. Olga Baklanova, Natalya Kowanko, and Zoe Karabanova personified the ideal of beauty of the 1920s and were well-known actresses in silent films.*

Right: *Natalya Kowanko, a silent-film actress, at her dacha, France, 1927.*

Архив автора. Париж

good whishes [sic] we left for the Niko-layevsky Railroad station where we took the Sebastopol express and went for our honeymoon to the shores of the Black-Sea, to Yalta, in Crimea, for 2-weeks of furlough from my 'sapper science.'"[3]

In Yalta the newlyweds were happy, enjoying the peaceful landscape of the Crimean shore for the last time. This idyll was interrupted when the prince returned to the front. where he encountered the February revolution, followed by the degradation and corruption of the army. The young Princess Belosel-skaya-Belozerskaya did not see her husband until November 1917, when he returned to their apartment on the Moika in Petrograd. The prince found work as an interpreter at the American Mission, since he spoke excellent English thanks to his mother, née Susan Whittier, an American. For refusing to serve in the Red Army, Sergei was arrested on August 4, 1918, along with his household and brother-in-law, and sent to the Fortress of Peter and Paul, and then removed to Kronstadt. Thanks to the efforts of Liza and family friends, after three weeks of incarceration, Sergei was miraculously spared execution (his "foreign origins" helped), which required a personal decree from Uritsky.

However, Liza's brother, Count Nikolai Grabbe, was shot by the Bolsheviks. Fleeing certain death, the couple moved to the family estate in Finland. After a brief respite, Liza and Sergei tried to get back into Russia through Tallinn and Pskov with Yudenich's army. Suffering defeat, they returned briefly to Finland and then traveled by sea via Copenhagen to England.

Liza, who knew French better than English, wanted to move to Paris, thinking that it would be easier to get her parents out of Soviet Russia from there. With the help of Poklevsky-Kozel, the Russian ambassador to Rumania, Liza had the idea to bring her family across the border to Bessarabia—but that failed, too. The couple returned to Paris, where they received the good news that Liza's parents had evacuated to Constantinople with Wrangel's army.

The young couple took a small, two-room apartment in the sixteenth arrondissement. Prince Sergei easily found work at Crédit Lyonnais thanks to his facility with languages, and Princess Liza, thanks to her impressive title and pleasant looks, got a job as a model at Chantal, then a popular house on the Champs-Elysées. Her boyish figure suited the dresses of the period, which were straight with a low waistline. Parisian fashion magazines were always publishing her photographs, especially those

Above: *Nina Polezhaeva, a beauty of the Russian émigré community, Paris, 1920s. Nina Polezhaeva was indirectly related to the kidnapping of Generals Kutepov and Miller by agents of the GPU (a precursor of the KGB) and was close to the German occupying forces in the 1940s. She vanished without a trace.*

Opposite: *Xyusha Katkova modeling a bathing costume by Lanvin, Paris, 1928.*

taken by Baron George Hoyningen-Huene, which are classics. Kira Alexandrovna Sereda, a model who knew her well, recalled, "Liza Grabbe was a marvelous 'mannequin.' She was a real lady, and it was easy working with her. A languid lady with marvelous manners."[4]

Liza soon became one of the recognized beauties of the Russian émigré

community. Vera Ippolitovna Pokrovskaya recalled: "When we were young, we would run over to the Russian church on rue Daru to admire the Russian beauties—the blond Liza Grabbe (Beloselskaya-Belozerskaya) and the brunette Tatyana Lishchenko, who was married to a dentist. Russian models were in fashion then. Liza was invited by everyone, but she didn't seem to care. She had marvelous eyes, eyes the color of translucent water."[5]

Prince Sergei's memoirs make it clear that Liza had not only won universal love and popularity in the world of fashion, but that she also made a lot of money, more than the prince. "Now we were much better off. Liza liked her work, she had almost all her relatives near-by, she could see them often and she loved Paris. But I was unhappy in my work at the bank."[6] This situation led to a family drama and separation: in 1928 Prince Sergei moved to London, where he found a job in a large shipping company. Liza did not leave her profession. The once-famous Russian model Mona Averino (née Maria Petrovna Yanova) recalled, "Liza was a very elegant woman, always wearing beautiful dresses from Chantal or Molyneux. She was very successful. She had lovely hands and eyes. . . . She was a big star at Chantal."[7]

After Chantal, Liza, who had divorced her husband, began working at the house of the Irishman Edward Molyneux, which existed from 1919 to 1950. Molyneux had a brilliant list of clients who appreciated the severity of his style and his taste in color. Pierre Balmain started out at Molyneux in 1934. In the catalogue for an exhibit of Pierre Balmain at the Musée de la Mode et du Costume in 1986, curator Guillaume Garnier wrote, "In the 1920s Paris was filled with young Russian aristocratic émigrés trying to earn their daily bread: many of them chose a career as models. They had great talent and grace, as a result of being well bred. The most vivid example is Elizabeth Grabbe, a leading model whom Pierre Balmain met at Molyneux. Liza Grabbe, who had come from Russia, retained the

This page and opposite: *Countess Liza Grabbe in designs by Chantal, where she worked as a model, Paris, 1928–29. Photo by George Hoyningen-Huene for* Vogue.

custom of bowing deeply during a show before Grand Duchess Elena Vladimirovna, who would kiss the model on the brow, following the tradition of ancient court etiquette in St. Petersburg."[8]

Although she ended her modeling career in the early 1940s, Countess Grabbe continued to work in the world of fashion. Pokrovskaya recalled, "I knew her later, when she became a salesclerk and sold dresses, in 1945–47. She was getting on in age, but we could all see the traces of her beauty, her mar-velous eyes. She lived near Passy then, around rue Raynouard. I remember her garden there. Her former husband always helped her and regularly sent money from America. When I left France for the USA I bought a jacket from her."

When Prince Sergei Beloselsky-Belozersky and Countess Grabbe divorced in 1928, he married American heiress Florence Crane from Massachusetts. The Cranes were the largest manufacturers of bathroom fixtures in the United States, and wags in the Russian

396

émigré community called Florence "Madame WC." Their marriage produced two children, Marina and Tatyana. It is to the honor of Florence Crane and Prince Beloselsky-Belozersky that they contributed mightily to the Russian community, especially helping to settle deported Russians in the United States during and after World War II.

The constellation of titled Russian beauties in the 1920s included the striking Obolensky sisters. Princesses Nina and Salomia (Mia) belonged to the thirty-second generation of the ancient princely Obolensky family, which is traced back to Rurik. Their mother was the Megrelian princess Dadiani, from whom they inherited many Caucasian traits. Baroness Yanina Arturovna von Kleist, the widow of their younger brother, Prince Alexander Alexandrovich Obolensky, who now lives in Santiago, described the Obolenksy sisters as, "[Of] average height, thin-boned and white-skinned beauties with very dark hair."[9]

Princess Nina Alexandrovna Obolenskaya was born January 14, 1898, in St. Petersburg and was the eldest child in the family of Prince Alexander Leonidovich Obolensky and Princess Salomia Nikolayevna. Their second daughter, named for her mother, but always known as Mia, was born November 13, 1902.

After fleeing the Bolsheviks, the family finally reached France. The daughters' good looks were quickly noticed and in the early 1920s both were hired as models by good fashion houses. Their first engagement was probably working for Lady Egerton at Paul Caret. In 1922 Nina married former colonel of the life guards Konstantin Vasilyevich Balashev, and, in 1923, Mia married Prince Vladimir Ivanovich Shakhovskoi, who had been in the cavalry regiment of the life guards. Although she now had two important titles, Mia did not abandon her modeling career. The two sisters next worked at the house of Chantal, where Mia became very famous and was often photographed for Parisian fashion magazines to advertise the house. Monna Averino, who knew her from work, recalled in a conversation with the author: "Princess Shakhovskaya was considered

Архив княгини Белосельской, Вашингтон

Библиотека декоративных искусств, Париж

a big star and always showed wedding dresses, which usually close a collection. Her sister, Nina Obolenskaya, was charming. I remember her at Chantal. She was cheerful, pretty, and for some reason, blinked frequently. We got along well."

The Obolensky sisters' career went into a decline in the 1930s when blondes became more popular. Both sisters later divorced their first husbands, and Mia married again, at age forty-six, to Yevgeny Vladimirovich Bolotov, formerly a captain in the sapper regiment of the life guards. Neither of the sisters had children. The pride of their family was their brother Prince Nikolai Alexandrovich. He was a priest in the Russian church, and during the war he and his wife, Vera Apollonovna Makarova, the daughter of the vice governor of Baku, worked actively with the French Resistance. They were arrested by the Germans, and Nikolai Alexandrovich was sent to Buchenwald and Vera Apollonovna was taken to Berlin, where she was tried and executed in the Berlin Pletsenz prison. In April 1945, Nikolai was liberated from the concentration camp by the American army. He was awarded the French military cross and a medal, and in 1956 the cavalry cross of the Légion d'Honneur, France's highest award. His wife was given the Légion d'Honneur posthumously.

Two charming young Russian women who worked as models in Paris in the 1920s were the sisters Baronesses Kira and Lelya von Medem, the daughters of Baroness Nina Vladimirovna von Medem, née Shlitter. A couple of years ago, Kira, who is now in her nineties and lives outside Paris, told the author: "My father, a colonel in the Erevan Regiment, told my mother that she had to sew her own clothes. Since Mama had three sisters and a family seamstress, she learned tailoring well. We were living near Tiflis then in our own house, which was called Manglis, with a big orchard. When the White Army retreated, my brother stayed in the Crimea. He was in charge of a machine gun command and defended the Crimea, and was executed by the Bolsheviks.

Архив Ирина Хохлова де Кобб, Багберо, Англия

"In Paris I first started working with mother at Kitmir for Grand Duchess Maria Pavlovna. We did embroidery for her, and then my mother became a seamstress at Yteb, where she remained as deputy chief seamstress for two years."

Lelya von Medem married Officer Leskov, the grandson of the famous writer, and had a daughter, Tatyana, who grew up to be a ballerina. From Rio de Janeiro, where she now lives, Tatyana Leskova recalls, "My mother was very beautiful and as a mannequin often went to the races, where she would be photographed. For a time she worked for Schiaparelli, but died young, and my aunt Kira, who became a second mother to me, brought me up."[10]

Kira, whose last name by marriage was Sereda, worked as a model for almost twenty years, starting about 1925. She worked at many houses: for a short time she was at Irfé with Felix and Irina

Opposite above: Princess Mia Alexandrovna Shakhovskaya in a design by Chantal, Paris, 1924.

Opposite below: Princess Shakhovskaya in a design by Chanel, Paris, 1927.

Above: Russian models in front of the Cathedral of Alexander Nevsky, Paris, 1928. From left to right: V. A. Kiseleva, V. N. Karpova, and Katyusha Ionina.

Youssoupoff, then moved to Yteb, where she worked with Princess Paley. Kira then moved on to the big Parisian fashion houses: Paul Poiret, Patou, Worth, Drecoll, Molyneux, and Chanel. She said about working with Poiret: "Paul Poiret wanted me to work for him and let me try on a dress. Then he put it on himself and started to show me how to present it."

For the fashion house Jenny, she traveled to England, Belgium, and Holland. As for her work with Chanel, Kira said, "Chanel liked me very much and apparently took pity on me. I was pregnant then and she kept me in her house until the delivery." Kira's colleagues and friends included Genya Gorlenko de Castex, Sonya Yavorskaya, Galina Gorlenko-Delwig, Tamara Varoun-Sokret, and Xenia Kuprina, the daughter of the famous writer. Kira recalled the following about Tamara Varoun-Sokret: "The very beautiful and talented Tusya worked at Godelle and then at Germaine Lecomte and Freddy. During the war she was deported by the Germans to the Ravensbruck concentration camp, which she survived miraculously and then emigrated to the U.S."

Our list of famous models of the 1920s would not be complete without a mention of Ekaterina Nikolayevna Bonnet, née Bobrikova, who worked at Lanvin from 1927 to 1934. Ekaterina (Thea) was born in 1909 to a family close to the imperial court and she was a goddaughter of Nicholas II. The famous painting by Ilya Repin, *Solemn Meeting of the State Council*, depicts several members of the Bobrikov family. As a child Thea drew dresses and daydreamed about wearing them when she grew up. She emigrated to Paris with her parents and sister, and they found a place to live near Place de Clichy.

The family needed money, so, at the age of seventeen, Thea decided to find work. She recalled: "I went to look for work through my uncle, Alexei Nikolayevich Frolov, who had been a governor in Russia. His old French tutor had become a store director in Paris. I went to him, and he said, "My little girl, I knew your mother in Russia!" and ad-

Архив Татьяны Лесовой, Рио-де-Жанейро

Архив Татьяны Лесовой, Рио-де-Жанейро

400

vised I go to a *maison de couture.* In those day the best houses were Lanvin and Vionnet. I liked the house of Vionnet very much. The owner's husband was a Russian émigré, Dmitrii Netchvolodov, a general's son, who owned a flourishing shoe enterprise, Netch and Frater. A model at Vionnet was the Russian Sonya Kolmer, the daughter of a russified Englishman, and she later married Charles Montaigne. The Islavin sisters, Marfa and Maria, also worked there. But I decided to go to Lanvin."[11]

The house of Jeanne Lanvin has been established in Paris for over a hundred years. The owner of this first-class enterprise came to Paris from Brittany at the end of the nineteenth century and she started her fashion house, specializing in dresses for young mothers and their daughters. Paul Irib, a famous illustrator, created the house's memorable emblem of a mother and daughter in an Art Deco style. In the early 1920s Lanvin's dresses were distinguished with bright Slavic-style embroidery and coral beads on a bright blue silk background. This special shade of blue became the symbol of the elegant house and is known in fashion history as "Lanvin blue."

Thea recalls, "When I came to Lan-

Opposite, far left: *Baroness Lelya von Medem at the races at Chantilly, near Paris, 1924.*

Opposite left: *Baroness Lelya von Medem in a design by Schiaparelli, Paris, 1930.*

Above: *Galina Gorlenko, Baroness Delwig, in a design by Jenny, Paris, 1929.*

Right: *Genya Gorlenko, Galina's sister, in a design by Worth, Paris, 1929. Photo by Valerie.*

Below: *Thea Bobrikova's contract with Lanvin, June 1, 1928.*

Right: *Thea Bobrikova in a dress and coat from Lanvin, Paris, 1929.*

CM 76413

Entre les soussignées :

Madame Jeanne LANVIN, agissant en sa qualité d'Administratrice déléguée de la Société Anonyme "JEANNE LANVIN" au capital de 15 Millions dont le Siège social est à PARIS, 4 Rond Point des Champs Elysées, d'une part ;

et Mademoiselle Catherine de BOBRIKOFF, demeurant à PARIS, 34 rue Nollet, mineure et autorisée, d'autre part ;

Il a été convenu et arrêté ce qui suit :

1° - Mlle C. de BOBRIKOFF s'engage à remplir les fonctions de MANNEQUIN pour une période d'UN AN qui commencera à courir le PREMIER JUIN MIL NEUF CENT VINGT HUIT pour venir à expiration le TRENTE ET UN MAI MIL NEUF CENT VINGT NEUF.

2° - Mlle C. de BOBRIKOFF recevra pour cet emploi des appointements mensuels de ONZE CENTS FRANCS (1.100) et la table.

3° - Mlle C. de BOBRIKOFF s'engage à se conformer à tous les règlements de la Maison, heures d'arrivée, de départ, etc... et à toutes les injonctions qui pourront lui être faites par la Direction.

4° - En cas de rupture du présent engagement avant son expiration et en dehors de tout cas de force majeure, les parties conviennent, en conformité de l'article 1152 du Code Civil, d'un crédit fixé forfaitairement et à titre de dommages-intérêts à la somme de DIX MILLE FRANCS (10.000).

5° - Toutes contestations seront de la compétence des Tribunaux du Département de la Seine auxquels attribution de juridiction est formellement donnée

6° - Les frais d'enregistrement seront à la charge de celle des parties qui y donnera lieu.

Fait en triple et de bonne foi,
à Paris, le 1 Juin 1928

vin I thought I would get a job as a saleswoman at 400 francs a month. But one of the staff there said, 'Why don't you apply for a job as a mannequin?' I was seventeen then and I didn't know what that was. I thought a mannequin was a dummy on which they hung dresses. Not far from our house in Paris I saw wooden dummies in a store window and I thought that was what she meant. At Lanvin they told me I would have to put on dresses in the try-on room and show them. And when they told me that models got up to 2,000 francs a month, I decided to try on a

dress. Some old woman, who was Madame Lanvin, looked at me and said, 'I'm engaging you as of Thursday.'

"I came home and told my parents that I had been hired by Lanvin. They were happy at first that I had a job and would be working, but when they learned that I was to be a mannequin, Mother got very upset. 'You're only seventeen, how can you do that? It's not decent!' And with those words she locked me in my room. But since there was nothing to eat at home, she let me out. My first contract with Lanvin of May 6, 1927, was signed by my father, Nik-

402

Архив Екатерины Бобриковой-Бонне, Париж

Above: *Thea Bobrikova in the years she worked for Lanvin, Paris, 1928.*

Right and below: *Thea Bobrikova and an unknown model wearing neo-romantic dresses by Lanvin, Paris, 1928.*

Архив Екатерины Бобриковой-Бонне, Париж

Архив Екатерины Бобриковой-Бонне, Париж

olai Nikolayevich Bobrikov, a former colonel in the life guards. Lanvin had twenty-four models then, of which four were Russian. With me there were Tatyana Alexandrovna Mordvin-Shchedrova, who later married Louis, the director of Revillon furs. There was also Nina Duvin, the sister of the singer Seversky, and Mlle. Grobnya, also Russian. The head of the modeling office at Lanvin for a time was Princess Tenisheva. When I married Nikolai Poretsky, he signed my contracts with Lanvin for a while." The dresses modeled by Thea Bobrikova were bought by Lanvin's clients, stars such as Pola Negri, Lillian Gish, and Jeannette MacDonald.

Among the Russian beauties of the interwar period, a special place is held by Lady Abdy, a statuesque blonde with bright-blue eyes, a symbol of the beauty and elegance of fashionable Paris. The author had the fortune to meet with Lady Abdy a few days before her death and to hear a detailed story about her life in the world of fashion. She was born Iya Grigoryevna de Gay in Slavyansk on August 8, 1903, into the family of Grigory Grigoryevich de Gay, the famous actor of the Imperial Alexandrinsky Theater, and the dramatic actress Anna Ivanovna Novikova. The de Gay family also gave Russia the famous artist Nikolai Nikolayevich de Gay. The family was of French origin: Iya's great-grandfather was a Frenchman who had fled to Russia during the French Revolution. Her father, Grigory Grigorye-vich, wrote about his ancestor in the book *Teatralnaya Rossiya* [Theatrical Russia] in 1928: "Taking Russian citizenship, he married a Cossack woman Korostovtseva. Their son married a Polish woman, and his grandson, my father, a pure Russian, Kareyeva. There were five children in father's family: four daughters and me, the youngest. When I was three, as a result of a family separation, Mother took us all to Switzerland and then to Paris."[12]

Grigory later returned to Russia and on the advice of his uncle, the celebrated painter, he intended to enter the Academy of Arts. But a family friend,

the great painter Ilya Repin, talked him out of it and suggested he become an actor. Iya's maternal uncle (Ivan Novikov) came from the line of the Tatar khan Novik. A landowner and balletomane, he organized a serf theater at his large estate in Samara, spending enormous amounts of money on it. Without a doubt, Iya Grigoryevna inherited the artistic talent of her ancestors, and this helped her become a standard of taste and beauty in Paris in the 1920s and 1930s.

Iya Grigoryevna was brought up as a child in her mother's family and the family of her stepfather Vuich, who was close to the court. She recalled, "My parents divorced very early, when I was five and my brother only three. In the divorce my father took my brother and Mother got me. Father lived in the art world, the world of Nikolai Niko-layevich de Gay and his close friend, Leo Tolstoy. But I knew little about that

Above: *Grigory Grigoryevich de Gay in the role of Ivan the Terrible at the Alexandrinsky Theater, St. Petersburg, 1900s.*

Below: *Lady Iya Grigoryevna Abdy, the beautiful Russian socialite in Paris. Photo by Man Ray for* Vogue, *Paris, August 1925.*

Opposite: *Lady Abdy. Photo by Arthur O'Neill for* Vogue, *Paris, March 1926.*

Библиотека декоративных искусств. Париж

atmosphere, since the Vuiches, my mother's new family, belonged at court. My stepfather served first in the cavalry regiment and then after he retired, worked as secretary to Telyakovsky in the administration of the Imperial Theaters."[13]

Iya Grigoryevna was brought up at the Pavlovsk Institute in St. Petersburg; the war found Iya and her mother in Germany, from where they made their way to Switzerland, where Iya studied at a girls' school at the Château Montchoiseinne in Lausanne. Iya recalled, "Mama sent me there to study languages and music, since I wanted to be a musician. I had musical talent. I also liked to draw and many people expected me to become an artist or actress. I had many talents."

Iya left Switzerland to move to Paris in 1921 but did not stay long. Family circumstances forced her to try to get back into Russia through Finland. It was there she met her first husband, the Dutch businessman Jongeyans. Iya recalled: "He was a businessman, the Dutch consul in St. Petersburg, and after the revolution he started a business in the Baltic countries, which were too young for business to be good and he lost all his money." Iya had a son and daughter by this unsuccessful businessman, who in the meantime had changed his name to Gaynes. Iya lived in Holland, where she vainly tried to learn stenography, and then moved to Paris hoping to better her life.

She continues, "My stepfather's

Библиотека декоративных искусств. Париж

Opposite: *Lady Abdy's exquisite toilette is completed by a famous diamond from Chaumet. Photo by George Hoyningen-Huene for* Vogue, *Paris, December 1928.*

Above and center: *Lady Abdy, the standard of elegance, in a shawl and a black velvet dress from Soeurs Callot. Artists and illustrators often drew Lady Abdy at social events and published their works in fashion magazines. These drawings are from* Vogue *magazine, Paris, 1925–26.*

Right: *Lady Abdy in a dress from Chanel.*

Библиотека декоративных искусств. Париж

Below: *A Russian actress in Hollywood, 1926.*

Right: *The Russian model Olga Pufkina in a design from Jenny on the cover of L'Officiel, July 1927. Photo by D'Orr.*

brother, Alexander Ivanovich Vuich, was secretary to Prince Oldenburg and was very concerned about me. He was a free man, a bachelor, devoted to his mother his entire life. Thanks to his connections, I got a job with the merchant Vtorov, but his business lasted only a few months before collapsing. Then I worked as a piano player. The film theaters needed accompanists, and I worked for a short time before they fired me. My husband wrote to me from Holland demanding that I go there and take our son, Georgy, whom I had left there while I looked for a job. I was desperate, since I had absolutely nothing. My

mother was in Paris then, but she took all this rather coldly, hoping that I would get myself out of this situation. But then a Russian friend—he was living like me in a hotel in Paris—said, 'You have a good figure, why don't you go to a fashion salon, you'll probably find work.' And so I went to Jacques Doucet, and then to the Champs-Elysées to the Callot Soeurs. They tried a few dresses on me and offered me a job as mannequin and a salary of 450 francs with lunch. Of course, I was happy. I needed to feed my son, whom I had taken to the country to live with a simple woman. Work at the Callot Soeurs did

not interest me, but I had to start somewhere. They made wonderful dresses and wonderful hairdos for me. One fine day a handsome young man came to Callot with a group of English people to see the collections. When he saw me, he smiled and asked if he could meet me. They were very strict at Callot and refused, telling him that in their house the girls could not be met. Two days later I was having lunch with a Russian friend in a restaurant. And, strangely enough, opposite us seated at a table was Sir Robert Abdy—the same young Englishman."

So fate brought together Iya Grigoryevna and Sir Robert Edward Abdy, fifth baronet of a wealthy aristocratic family. He fell in love with Iya at first glance and proposed soon afterward. He married her in June 1923.

"Of course," Lady Abdy recalled, "I was forced to leave the Soeurs Callot at his request. We began a hectic social life. My husband was twenty-seven, and he had just come in to his inheritance. His big passion was French antiquity. He adored bronze, furniture, tapestries, and Versailles sculptures. He was completely lost in that life, he loved to spend money, he loved beautiful things. Finally, he became so engrossed in it that he decided to make it his profession—he opened an antiques shop. I wanted to live in England, but my husband loved Paris and Versailles, which was a temple of beauty and the ideal of his life. For

Above left: *Nyusya Penyakova-Rotwand, Paris, early 1920s.*

Above center: *Model Tatyana Lishchenko in a design by Martha and Renée. Photo from* L'Officiel. *June 1929.*

Above right: *Princess Melita Tiazievna Cholokayeva, a model at Chanel, Paris, 1928.*

instance he hated Venice, considering it and its art too mercantile. He had his way, special tastes, he adored everything antique and French. Once he found a Titian and sold it to the Metropolitan Museum; he didn't keep it for us."

The marriage did not work out. Sir Robert was busy buying and selling unique antiques in France and sent Lady Abdy on a voyage around the world with a young couple, Harrison Williams, the director of General Electric, and his wife, on their yacht. Lady Abdy visited Djibouti, Ceylon, India, Burma, Malaysia, Singapore, Thailand, Indochina, China, Manchuria, and Japan, and then they took a steamship to Canada. When Lady Abdy and her friends finally returned to Paris after more than a year, Sir Abdy had left. Looking back she said, "These things happen in life! I must have stayed away too long. . . . In 1928 we divorced. I had to organize my life again. I had the reputation of being an elegant and rather original woman, and I could wear the most special dresses well."

It should be noted that Lady Abdy had received a lot of attention in Paris back in 1923 through 1925. "I met Paul Poiret right after the wedding," Lady Abdy told me. "My first dress after I married I ordered from him. It was a long velvet dress with pendants on a low waist. Poiret was interested in me at a time when no one else knew me in Paris." *Vogue* regularly printed drawings and photographic portraits of Lady Abdy in the most incredible outfits. The June 1925 issue describes Lady Abdy in a beaded, fuchsia evening dress: "Lady Abdy, one of the beauties of the foreign community in Paris, always dresses in a profoundly personal fashion. Her taste is incontrovertible and not subject to influence. She can inspire creators of women's clothing."[14]

She was photographed by the best photographers, such as George Hoyningen-Huene. Lady Abdy permitted herself to go counter to fashion, for instance in 1925 she wore her hair with a straight part in the middle at a time when fashion called for bangs, small brimless hats, open dresses, "Russian" jackets, and shawls of gold brocade. She was particularly celebrated for her jewels—an emerald set and a huge diamond solitaire from Chaumet, which she wore as a pendant. Her elegance and vivid individuality made her a welcome guest at high society balls and parties. In those years Paris preferred Russian beauties with titles. High society had accepted Grand Duchess Maria Pavlovna, Princess Irina Youssoupoff and Princess Mary Eristova, Gali Bajenova, Musya Rotwand-Muñoz, Lady Deterding, and, later, Princess Nathalie Paley. Of the enormous number of Russian beauties in Paris of those years only a few were chosen to be among the elite of high society. Lady Abdy took an active part in running charity balls in aid of Russian refugees.

Lady Abdy worked for Chanel after her divorce from her wealthy husband. In mid-1925 *Vogue* wrote about Lady Abdy advertising a coat from Chanel. Iya recalled that time: "A famous woman in Paris then was Misia Sert, and she became my great friend. Madame Sert gravitated around Chanel, who loved that. When Chanel was just starting out, Misia Sert helped her a lot. You couldn't help Chanel too much, since she was a very imperious woman who knew just what she wanted. Apparently Chanel was engrossed in her affair with the Duke of Westminster. She did not leave her house, but she did not keep an

eye on it very closely, either. And in the spring of 1929 Patou 'pushed his way out' with his collection of long, light dresses with colored designs. He had a great success then, and *le tout Paris* dressed at Patou. Madame Sert got very worried and told Chanel: 'There's a competitor raising his head.' She advised Chanel to get in some new blood, to do something new, and pay attention to Iya Abdy. Sert felt that I had talent in the art of couture."

We know that Lady Abdy's mother, Anna Ivanovna Novikova-Vuich, had a talent for fashion and owned a small house called Annek, which specialized in lingerie and accessories; Lady Abdy sketched purses for it. Chanel met Iya Abdy at dinner at Misia Sert's. Then Chanel went to Annek, run by Kamenskaya and Novikova-Vuich, to look at the things created from Lady Abdy's concepts. Iya Grigoryevna recalled, "My mother was always a very elegant woman in St. Petersburg, she always dressed in Paris, and she had excellent taste."

Chanel offered Lady Abdy a job in her store and atelier, creating new designs together and promising her a lot of money. Lady Abdy told me, "If I had known Chanel's character, I would never have gone to work for her. She was an incredibly imperious woman. I had never seen anything like it. It's quite possible that she suppressed personalities that gave in easily. When she made her designs, we discussed them together: I proposed my ideas, which she took or not. I made small things for her store—purses, which she copied from Annek. I did a lot of things at Chanel, but I remained there only one year." Lady Abdy became one of the most famous social beauties of Paris in the 1930s.

Paul Poiret had several famous Russian models working for him at various times: Kira Sereda; Xenia (Kisa) Kuprina; Lusya Bulatsel; and Countess Natalya Nikolayevna Sumarokova-Elston. Kisa Kuprina decided to become a mod-

el to help her needy parents and she worked for Paul Poiret in 1925. In her memoirs, published in 1971, she gives a complete picture of her work in a fashion house. Kuprina wrote: "I came to get a job for the first time in my life. I went up a wide marble staircase, covered with soft rugs. An impressive doorman sent me to the back door. I felt humiliated and vacillated for a long time about whether to go in or not. Then they examined me, made me walk, smile, show my legs.

"Despite my youth and shyness, they took me. And the first day, during a break, all the models gathered in the huge living room. They started to teach me to walk slowly with a haughty air, to turn, to change with the speed of light. They nicknamed me 'virgin' for my shyness."[15] Kisa complained about the low pay, but she was happy that they let her borrow Paul Poiret designs overnight.

The owner was very picky about his staff. "He made the models line up in a semicircle and examined each one with a long, heavy stare. Then, fixing on one, he would suddenly flap his hand as if chasing away a fly. That meant the girl was fired." Kisa, luckily, was not fired. She went on: "New designs were created every six months. We had to stand on a platform for hours, while the modelers draped fabrics, laces, and ribbons on us, cutting, pinning, as if we were wooden dummies. Often girls would faint from exhaustion."

Kisa was selected as one of twelve models to go to Berlin to show Poiret's designs at Die Comedie Theatre. The couturier created a special collection of coats in bright yellow and green stripes, which marked a new tendency in his work—simplicity in cut and geometry in ornament. Once, Poiret decided to show his designs at a Berlin café before the evening performance, thereby breaking the contract. He wanted to sneak away with his girls. Kisa wrote: "Gathering us all in his room, he proposed that we secretly pack our bags and slip out without paying the bill. The models rebelled: it was obvious that twelve girls dressed to catch the eyes could not slip

Opposite: *Olga Baklanova,*
film actress, Hollywood, 1928.

410

Тургеневская библиотека, Париж

Архив автора, Париж

Музей моды и костюма, Париж

412

Архив автора. Париж

Архив автора. Париж

Opposite, above left: *Xenia Kuprina in a scene from the French film* Devil in the Heart. *Photo from* Illustrirovannaya Rossiya, *1927.*

Opposite, above right: *Natalya Astakhova and Natasha Kostka-Neprzetzka, choir members of the Russian Private Opera of Maria Kuznetsova, South America, 1929.*

Opposite below: *Paul Poiret with his models on a European tour, London, 1923.*

Above: *Tatyana Alexandrovna Maslova, the winner of the Miss Russia and Miss Europe competitions, 1933.*

Right: *Nina Alexandrovna Pol, the winner of the Miss Russia competition, in Russian costume, 1932.*

out unnoticed. In the end everything was settled and we left."[16]

She met the famous French filmmaker Marcel L'Herbier when she was no longer working for Poiret, but was at a dinner party in one of his gold dresses, looking very striking. This was the start of Kisa's career in silent film—L'Herbier made five films with her, all of which were popular. Photographs of Kisa as a film star appear in French magazines of that period. Later, in 1955, when she returned to the Soviet Union, she joined the Pushkin Drama Theater in Moscow, but appeared in plays very rarely.

It was during this period of the 1920s that Countess Natalya Nikolayevna Sumarokova-Elston, née Belik, and Billi Bibikova, a soon-to-be-famous Russian model, worked for Poiret. Although Billi only worked for Poiret for a brief period in Cannes, Countess Sumarokova-Elston recalled that she was "beautiful and very sweet, it was a pleasure working with her."[17]

There were so many Russian runway models and photography models in the émigré community in Paris that, in 1926, the magazine *Illustrirovannaya Rossiya* decided to run a beauty contest to pick

413

the most beautiful girl. Originally the contest was called "Queen of the Russian Colony," then, from 1928, it was called "Miss Russia." It was considered very prestigious to participate, and the winners were elevated to the skies: their pictures were published on the cover of *Illustrirovannaya Rossiya*, made into postcards by French publishers, and they were interviewed frequently. The Russian émigré contest counted in France, and its winners were allowed to participate in the most prestigious competition of the day: "Miss Europe."

The winners of the beauty contest were known throughout the Russian diaspora. Postcards with their pictures appeared in Riga, Lvov, Harbin, and Belgrade. Not wanting to fall behind Paris, which was the recognized center of fashion, other cities where there were Russian émigré communities began electing their own "queens of the Russian colony." Competitions took place in Berlin, where several times the queen was the silent-film star Xenia Desni (Desnitskaya); in Hamburg, where Ella Marynova won the title in the summer of 1926; in New York, where the queen was ballerina Valentina Kachouba; and in Harbin, Tianjin, Shanghai, Sofia, and Belgrade, among other cities.

In 1926 the "queen of the Russian colony" in Paris was Larisa Popova with two runners-up. In 1927 the queen was nineteen-year-old Kira Sklyarova,

Архив автора, Париж

with four runners-up: Elena Medintseva, Nina Severskaya, Galya Brailovskaya, and Segda Bogdasarova. Beauty canons change from year to year and decade to decade, and the photographs of these women depict heavyish faces overloaded with makeup. Nevertheless, they met the beauty standards of those years. The fate of the winners varied: most chose to be models in fashionable houses and then got married. Galya Brailovskaya had a tragic fate. Apparently the title of runner-up won in 1927 did not bring her happiness: a few months later she shot herself at the grave of her father, the famous industrialist Brailovsky, who had died two years earlier.

Above and below: *The Miss Russia competition at the editorial offices of* Illustrirovannaya Rossiya, *1930.*

Center: *Valentina Osterman, the winner of the Miss Russia competition, 1929.*

Left: *Tatyana Maslova, the winner of the Miss Europe competition, Paris, 1933.*

Below left: *An invitation to Nina Tverdaya to participate in the Miss Russia competition from the magazine* Illustrirovannaya Rossiya, *January 20, 1930.*

Below: *Valentina Kachouba, the winner of the "Queen of the Russian Colony in New York" competition, 1929.*

ИЛЛЮСТРИРОВАННАЯ РОССIЯ

REVUE HEBDOMADAIRE
DIRECTEUR : M. MIRONOFF

RÉDACTION ET ADMINISTRATION
34, RUE DE MOSCOU, PARIS (VIII°)

TÉLÉPHONE : CENTRAL 92-26
CHÈQUES POSTAUX · PARIS 671-61

PARIS, LE **20 января** 19**30**

Милостивая Государыня

Жюри конкурса по выборамъ "Миссъ Россіи" на 1930 годъ проситъ Васъ пожаловать завтра, 21 января, къ 7 час. веч. въ редакцію "Иллюстрированной Россіи" / см. выше новый адресъ/ для предварительнаго отбора кандидатокъ. Туалетъ — по желанію.

Для участія въ окончательномъ конкурсѣ, который состоится въ воскресенье 26 января, Ваше присутствіе завтра обязательно.

Примите увѣренія въ совершенномъ почтеніи

Секретарь

Архив автора, Париж

Victory brought more problems than happiness to Valentina Konstantinovna Osterman, who won the title in 1928. It should be noted that the juries included the most famous and respected figures in the arts of the Russian community, who had been famous back in Russia. Thus, in 1928 the judges included the writer Nadezhda Teffi, the ballerina Olga Preobrazhenska, the actress Ekaterina Roshchina-Insarova, the writer Alexander Kuprin, and the critic Serge Makovsky.

The final selection took place on January 27, 1929, and the winner, Valya Osterman, came, accompanied by her older sister, to Paris from Berlin, where she lived with her family since

Архив автора, Париж

Архив автора, Париж

Above left: *Genya Dashkevich, the winner of the Miss Russia competition, 1930s.*

Below left: *Genya Dashkevich, 1930s.*

Above: *Natalya Krassovska-Leslie, a dancer in the Russian ballet of Monte Carlo and a second-place winner in the Miss Russia competition, 1935. That year the winner was Princess Asya Obolenskaya, and Serge Lifar was one of the judges.*

Opposite: *Princess Guedianova, the winner of the Miss Russia competition, 1938. Photo from the cover of* Paris-Match, *December 1938.*

MATCH

UNE RUSSIE SE MEURT
La princesse Gorodzoff
n'est plus, à Paris, qu'une
reine de beauté

2fr

HEBDOMADAIRE DE L'ACTUALITÉ MONDIALE   15 DÉCEMBRE 1938

Архив автора. Париж

417

they had left Russia in 1921. Not knowing for sure about her citizenship (understandable for an eighteen year old), Valya did not tell the magazine editors when she registered that she did not have the Russian émigré "Nansen" passport but a German one. The rules of the competition were very strict: only girls with the Russian refugee passports could participate, and not holders of

Lithuanian or Bulgarian ones, for example. As soon as the secretary of the editorial board, Khokhlov, learned about the German passport, a huge scandal erupted, and Valya Osterman, whose picture was on the cover of issue no. 195 of *Illustrirovannaya Rossiya*, was disqualified, and the crown passed to her runner-up, Irina Nikolayevna Levitskaya, holder of a "Nansen" pass-

port. *Illustrirovannaya Rossiya* published detailed accounts of the to-do.

The Miss Russia contest continued until the beginning of World War II, making a number of Russian beauties famous in the 1930s; the best-known among them were Anna Marly-Betulinskaya, Genya Dashkevich, and Marina Chalyapina. The last Miss Russia posed for *Vogue* in 1938 dressed by Chanel.

Opposite: *A Russian émigré couple on the Place de la Concorde in Paris, 1929.*

THE MODEL NATASHA
A Summer Story

I

Model Natasha,
Little *midinette*,
Rarely had a day of rest.
All day long Natasha
Was like a fish in a net:
Turn, Natasha!
Try it on, Natasha!
Walk, Natasha!
No vacations,
A bitter life,
Poor Natasha,
Work and strife.
And then—
The vicious circle broke!
The director came and spoke:
He repeated in his deep, deep voice,
"Natasha, you are now our choice:
"Off to the station in the morn,
First class to the Riviera,
South,
To Nice and Cannes,
You are now reborn
As a socialite,
A general's daughter
And you have to dress
And live among the best.

You will easily pass the test.
Here's your trunk,
Forty-three outfits
To display and show.
Wear each one once
Don't be a dunce
Don't sit on the grass
Or we'll take it out
Of your pay.
No need to cry or shout."

II

Natasha saw the sea,
The shores, the lawns,
The azure sky,
And she forgot about old Paris:
Her piece of bread and coffee
Standing in a bistro,
The bus and metro,
Five transfers,
The job,
The strict *maison*.
And when she put on her
Bathing suit
And lay down on the sunny beach,
She even forgot her role,
Her socialite speech,

Her forty-three outfits,
Her instructions, every bit.
She breathed the ozone.
Tanned, grew plump,
Lulled by the waves
Tickled by the foam.
She didn't want to go home.
And the model grew so lush
Her eyes like cornflowers
Her cheeks with peony blush,
That she was snared by
Charlie the American.

III

A telegram flew
Straight to Paris
To rue Daru:
Good-bye and thanks!
I've got another place,
And—oh—I'm engaged,
And by the way,
So you're not too upset
And to save your face,
Send the bill to me
For the outfits forty-three!

—*Valentin Goryansky, 1920s*

Архив автора. Париж

21
RUSSIAN BEAUTIES OF
THE 1930S AND 1940S

Why, maybe work in some chic maison de couture as a model.
Something like Paquin or Rollande—what's wrong with that?
You're perfectly built, and you'd make an excellent model.
You'll try on lovely dresses, you'll go to the Opera to model them . . .
It's work that is not hard and even pleasant.

Lina Izlomova, *Oblomki* [Fragments]
Paris, 1931

The world was shaken by economic and political change. Power throughout Europe was concentrated in the hands of dictators—Stalin, Hitler, Franco, and Mussolini. Political and economic factors were influencing the aesthetic norms of society. Trying to create "colonies of exemplary order," totalitarian regimes imposed new "positive" ideals of beauty. Society's new ideals of women in the 1930s as honest laborers and good mothers could not in any way resemble the decadent ideals of women in the 1920s. The great depression forced the free world to reexamine its ideals, too.

While in the freewheeling 1920s, the ideal of feminine beauty was *à la garçon*, the 1930s saw the recanonization of traditional femininity. Figures of classical proportions, Nordic faces, and long wavy hair came into fashion. Men regarded the better half of humanity with new eyes, and women took a different look at themselves. The gamine who dominated the late 1920s, who thought only of the Charleston, millionaires, and champagne, suddenly seemed profoundly flawed and socially dangerous. The extravagances of the 1920s were considered the fundamental reason for the economic crisis and the resulting dramatic political changes.

The new feminine ideal was disseminated into all strata of society by film, which had just recently developed sound. The medium's new capabilities—it could

Opposite: *Ludmila Feodoseyeva,*
a Russian fashion and photo model, in
an evening dress from Chanel, 1938.

Above: *Lidia Zelenskaya and her mother,*
Princess Melita Tazievna Cholokayeva,
models in Paris, 1927.

now express feelings and emotions not only in dry subtitles but in music, song, and dialogue—attracted numerous theatergoers. The birth of film is often connected with the Swedish actress Greta Garbo. A marvelous dramatic actress, she had extraordinary looks, both mysterious and feminine. Her influence on the public's perceptions of beauty was so profound that millions of women copied her look: thin, penciled brows, false eyelashes, and particularly light hair. This light color became firmly established, and in the 1930s women changed from brunettes to blondes overnight, and the bob haircuts and heavy bangs of the previous decade disappeared. Hair was now worn shoulder length and given permanent waves. Many Hollywood movie

stars followed the dictate of the "new face"—Marlene Dietrich, Mae West, Jean Harlow, Ginger Rogers, and Carole Lombard. The great success of their movies firmly entrenched the new type of beauty in the mass audience, forcing even the capricious Parisian fashion world to obey. Runway models, who were the most accurate reflection of the generation's views on the ideal of female beauty, also had to follow the new look.

Ateliers and fashion houses were closing down because of a lack of foreign clients. Many Russian émigrés lost work and had no chance of finding more. The faces of the famous models of the 1920s no longer seemed so appealing—that type of beauty was out of style, and the fashion houses changed their approach in selecting models. In the 1920s the determining factor often had been social position rather than merely beauty. Back then a Russian title had power, and Russian princesses and countesses had been very effective with their innate elegance, good manners, and education. However, political changes in France as well as rising unemployment caused people to look at the Russian émigrés with fresh eyes: their status changed from welcome guests with important titles into unneeded neighbors after the same piece of bread. All this was quite comically described by French playwright Jacques Deval in his play of 1933, *Tovaritch*.

Republican France not only recognized the Soviet Union but also deprived

Top: *Marlene Dietrich in costume for the film* The Red Empress, *Hollywood, 1934.*

Above: *Greta Garbo on the cover of an American film magazine in the role of Anna Karenina in the film of the same name, 1935.*

Above right: *Lidia Zelenskaya in a neo-Victorian evening dress, Paris, 1938.*

Russian émigrés, who were generally monarchist, of all privileges and support. The coolness toward Russians was also related to the murder on May 6, 1932, of French President Paul Doumer by a Russian émigré, Paul Gorgouloff. Russians in France had almost no rights; the Russian accent, which had elicited delight in the 1920s, was now laughed at; and titles seemed an unnecessary anachronism. Émigré children tried to assimilate as quickly as possible, changing their names, surnames, and interests.

The fashion for all things Russian, which had been so prevalent in Paris in the 1920s, had passed. Now all most Russians could hope for was work in the Citroen and Renault factories, or work as cab drivers, as waiters in Russian restaurants, or with the Russian ballet, which people also had begun to mock (as in the film *On Your Toes* with Vera Zorina, or in the Broadway musi-

Vera Koréne

Архив автора. Париж

these features were able to find runway work on a more or less steady basis.

According to the famous model Baroness Galina Romanova Gorlenko-Delwig, even in the 1930s up to a third of all models in Paris were Russian. Delwig recalled, "Back then every house had many models. There was even a category called 'model doubles,' that is, girls who had the same figure as the stars. The doubles were used for fittings.

"The main category in all the fashion houses was *'mannequin vedette,'* the stars for whom all the collections were sewn, who were sent abroad to show them (for instance, I went to Holland twice), were invited to shows and galas and even sent to resorts—Deauville, Monte Carlo, and Cannes."[1]

Thanks to the reminiscences of Baroness Delwig and other Russian models, we have a lot of detailed infor-

Музей театра "Принцесса Александра". Торонто

cal of the same name with Tamara Geva). Many of the celebrated models of the 1920s were married, had children, and, alas, had lost their youthful charm. However, their daughters, many of whom were born in France, took their place. They had been brought up in a Franco-Russian milieu free of the heavy baggage of sad memories that members of the older generation had carried with them from Russia. They were more receptive to new fashion and to the changes it entailed.

The new fashionable silhouette stressed female curves and elongated proportions, with draping in the neo-classical manner. The fashionable ideal of Nordic beauty resembled Slavic looks, which is why Greta Garbo played Anna Karenina, a Russian ballerina in *Grand Hotel*, and the KGB agent Ninotchka in the film of the same name. Young blondes with broad Slavic cheekbones suited a lot of fashion houses and despite the crisis, Russian women with

Above left: *Vera Koréne, a Russian actress in French films, famed for her beauty in the 1930s.*

Above right: *Anna Sten, a Russian actress who made films in Hollywood in the mid-1930s.*

mation about their work in Parisian fashion houses in the 1930s. As a rule, Russians became models by accident, on the advice of friends and neighbors. Delwig said, "These were girls who mostly came from good families, often someone knew someone else already working there. For instance, my sister [the famous model of the 1930s Genya Gorlenko, whose married name was Vicountess de Castex dropped out of the last year of Russian high school because she had to earn money, and took a job at a factory. She was very lovely, with marvelous hands, and at the factory she had to turn something. I heard that such a profession existed and suggested she become a model. Genya started working in 1926 in a small house called Carol, and then moved to Worth. And in 1927 I started at Jenny, and I had to tell them (for my sister told me how things worked) that I was working at Carol. It was very hard to start out. They would tell me, for instance, 'Show the dress!' and watch how I walked, how I turned. It was so worrying at first! The administration and the girls there were very nice to me, because I was very friendly and I was no rival, since I was always dressed worse than anyone else. Every house had one or two Russian stars: at Worth there were two—Elena and Irina Goldiev, who took part in absolutely every gala and outing. Irina was very popular. Aside from them they often took my sister Genya Gorlenko, and Tatyana Bazarova and Kira Sereda."

One of the famous models of the 1930s was Thea (Ekaterina) Bobrikova—a *mannequin vedette* at Lanvin from 1927 to 1934. The house of Jeanne Lanvin so valued her that they kept increasing her salary, which we can see from her pay stubs that she kept all these years. Thea also posed for the famous photographer Baron de Mayer. When she stopped working at Lanvin, Thea, like Gali Bajenova who opened her own fashion house, Elmis, in the 1920s, decided to start a fashion house and called it Catherine Parel (from the Western version of her first name and from the French *par elle*, "by her"). She began preparations in 1935 and opened the house on January 6, 1936; it stayed in business until 1948.

Like the big fashion houses, Catherine Parel put out two small collections a year. As many as sixty-nine people worked in the three stories of Thea and her husband's, Nikolai Poretsky's, flourishing enterprise. The mistress of the house recalled, "The embroidery was done by the house of Lessage, and I got my first cutter from the house of Ardanse, where the director was my husband's older brother. Jeanne Lanvin immediately sent her senior seamstress to check whether I was copying her designs, but once she saw my work, she relaxed. My greatest success was a dress of chiffon in a tiny pleating that was ironed out along the bottom. It sold very well, and it was my design. Some of my designs I sold to Italy. My clients were the famous Paris actresses Michelle Morgan and [singer] Lys Gauty."[2]

Catherine Parel stayed in business during the German occupation, selling on the black market. The wives of German officers were not allowed to come to Paris for their dresses, so fashion houses often made clothes for them from their measurements.

Opposite: *Nina Shatalova (Shestopalova), a dancer with* Folies Bergère, *Paris, 1932.*

Above: *Sonia Kolmer, model at the house of Vionnet, in a draped dress, Paris, 1932.*

Thea's designs were often used in fashion magazines, and in 1945 the house of Catherine Parel was written about in the magazine *L'Officiel*. In 1946 the house created several designs for the movie *Pastoral Symphony*, distinguished at the Cannes Film Festival. In an interview in *L'Exportateur Français* on November 25, 1946, Bobrikova said, "I whole-heartedly support close cooperation between film and fashion. Paris will always be the arbiter of elegance, and film is the only opportunity we have to show French fashion, of which we are so rightly proud, to the whole world."[3]

Catherine Parel suffered as a result of union conflicts and was shut down in 1948. A few Russian models worked there in the 1930s and 1940s. Among them were Valya Drugova, who was married to a Spaniard and died quite young, Olga Fride, Tamara Ponzhina, the famous Lud Feodoseyeva, and Princess Maria Meshcherskaya. Bobrikova's childhood friend, Baroness Anastasia Nolken, who had started her career at Irfé and had worked in over seven fashion houses, also worked at Catherine Parel (becoming a co-owner of the business when her husband, Semyon Margulis, became a shareholder). After she left Prince and Princess Youssoupoff at Irfé, Anastasia worked for two years as a model at Chanel, then two years at Madeleine Vionnet, then at Maggy Rouff, Germaine Lecomte, Agnes Drecoll, and Lucien Lelong. While she was at Maggy Rouff, Anastasia was invited to a party chaired by Beck de Fouquier and won first prize for elegance.

Other famous models of the period were Countess Marina Vorontsova-Dashkova (née Princess Meshtcherskaya), who worked at Schiaparelli; Inna Sergeyevna Mishchenko, who worked at the O'Rossen house of suits on Place Vendôme; Princess Maria Wolkonskaya, who showed dresses at Alix; Princess Ekaterina Makinskaya, née Princess Melikova, who advertised the designs of Agnès Drecolle; and Mary Perevoshchikova, who worked for a time at Lucien Lelong and then married a rich Frenchman (after having been Paul Getty's mistress for years).

Архив Екатерины Бобриковой Бонне, Париж

Архив автора. Париж

CATHERINE PAREL

PRIE _ _ _ _ _ _ _ _ _ _
DE BIEN VOULOIR ASSISTER A LA PRESENTATION
DE SES NOUVEAUX MODELES

22. AVENUE MONTAIGNE   TELPHONE | ELVBEES 15.50
                                   | 2 LIONES
                         VINDEUSE

Top: *Models showing designs from Catherine Parel, Paris, 1938.*

Above: *An invitation to a fashion show by Catherine Parel, Paris, late 1930s.*

Above right: *Thea Bobrikova, the owner of Catherine Parel, in a hand-pleated dress of her own design, Paris, 1937.*

Opposite top: *The traditional holiday of St. Catherine, patron saint of seamstresses, at Paquin, Paris, 1936.*

Opposite, bottom left: *Baroness Anastasia Nolken and Thea Bobrikova at a Russian restaurant, Paris, 1936.*

Opposite, bottom right: *Baroness Anastasia Nolken in a German Leconte design, Paris, 1934.*

Elena Lvovna Boulatzel-Roussel, now living in Paris, recalls, "I began working in 1928 at Paul Poiret and then moved to Madeleine Vionnet, where I remained from 1929 to 1931. At Vionnet I worked with Kira Borman, who then married Deputy Archambeault, and Sonia Colmer, the daughter of a russified Englishman who later married the owner of the fashion house of Charles Montaigne, a very wealthy Dutchman."

The Russian models of that period were friends with one another. Delwig recalled, "During lunch our Russian group gathered with sandwiches in a small, modest café on rue Cambon. We were all models, and the owner knew us, we played cards there, got letters, brought dresses we wanted to re-sell, and told all sorts of stories. It was this small, modest café, and inside—some of the most beautiful women in Paris. The absolute beauty of us all was the model at Revillon furs, Sonia Yavorskaya, but she didn't have much luck with men, her beauty was very cold and she was very demanding, men fled from her. Other habitues of the cafe were Nina Ushakova, Tatyana Bazarova, Nina Chernova, Genya Gorlenko, Irina Korsakova, Tanya Gorichevskaya, Genya Dashkevich, who later won the

Архив Марии Януюшевской, Париж

Miss Russia contest, and also the society beauty Countess Maria Chernyshova-Bezobrazova.

"Our life then was very interesting: we organized Russian parties and balls, we hired halls for this, and absolutely everyone came. We went to the Napoleon Hall, the Naval Society, and also we had a big ball of all the fashion houses on St. Catherine's day, which everyone called 'Catherinette.' The administration of our house gave these balls annually with food and drink for all the staff and with the permission of the bosses we could invite guests. To show our gratitude every atelier and we—the six who worked in one models' cabin—performed a show. We hired a coach and staged Polynesian dances. We had Tahitian costumes—short skirts of raffia, and we put paint on our skin, which we had a lot of trouble getting off later. The band was hot. We brought in a Russian saleswoman to our 'Russian' troupe: we were all Tahitian women. We were each given two tickets, and we went alone

Музей моды и костюма, Париж

Архив Екатерины Бобриковой-Бонне, Париж
772

427

Архив Елены Булацель, Париж

Below, left and right: *Lusya Boulatzel, a model at Paul Poiret, Paris, early 1930s.*

Opposite top left: *Lusya Boulatzel as a child, St. Petersburg, 1910s.*

Opposite right: *Lusya Boulatzel in a white dress (the skirt is bias-cut) from the house of Vionnet, Paris, 1932. Photo by D'Orr.*

Архив Елены Булацель, Париж

Архив Елены Булацель, Париж

L'ORA
PARIS

Архив Елены Булацель, Париж

and gave out the second to other Russians, so that the hall was filled with our countrymen. And how well Russians tipped! We treated all the maîtres d'hotel. It was a wonderful party at the Lutetia Hotel given by the house of Marie-Louise Bruyere.

One of the famous Russian stars of the 1930s who still lives outside of Paris is Maria Petrovna Averino, better known in the Parisian world of fashion by the pseudonym Mona. She began working as a model at Philippe et Gaston in 1926. Maria Petrovna recalled, "I was supporting my whole family and earning money for my parents. At that time many Russian girls, if they were young, not too thin or ugly, became models. But we had to know how . . . to wear dresses!" From Philippe et Gaston, Mona moved to the then-popular Chantal on the Champs-Elysées, where "there were tons of Russians," and Averino noted, "they adored Russians then." From Chantal, Mona moved to Chanel, and from there to Lenief, founded by Alfred Lenief, a former assistant of Paul Poiret for several years. Then she worked as the leading model at Lucien Lelong. His house was famed for its large hall for showing designs, with a stage that had a rotunda of four Ionic columns. "Lelong made a large collection for me once. I remember that I wore an ensemble of ruby color trimmed

Top: *Baroness Galina Delwig in a blouse from Hermès, Paris, 1934.*

Above: *Greta Garbo as Nina Yashenko in the film* Ninotchka, *Hollywood, 1939.*

Above right: *Baroness Galina Delwig in a summer dress with asymmetrical inserts from the house of Bruyere, Paris, 1933–34.*

Opposite: *Genya Gorlenko, a famous Parisian model of the 1930s, Paris, 1935.*

Overleaf, left and right: *Genya Gorlenko in evening dresses from Franz Breman, Paris, 1935.*

433

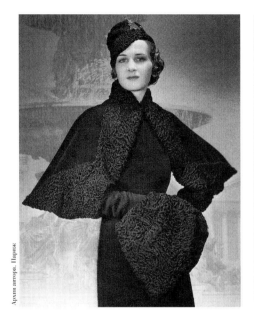

with ermine. He appreciated me as a model,"[4] Averino recalled.

In addition to the professional models, many Russian society beauties were photographed by famous photographers. This group included Princess Nathalie Paley, Lady Abdy, Lady Deterding (Lidia Pavlovna Bagrateni by her first marriage), and Nyusya Muñoz.

The life and fate and Nathalie Paley is astonishing and sad at the same time. She was born on December 5, 1905 in the Paris suburb of Boulogne-sur-Seine, in a mansion that belonged to her father, Grand Duke Paul Alexandrovich, the uncle of Emperor Nicholas II and the father of Grand Duchess Maria Pavlovna. Little Natasha was the fruit of a great passionate love between the grand duke and Olga Valerianovna Karnovich, Pistolkors by her first marriage, a well-known socialite and mother of three at the time she fell in love with the grand duke. Olga was still married to guards

officer Erik Avgustinovich Pistolkors when she gave birth to Vladimir in 1897; she got an immediate divorce, and went abroad with her lover. On October 10, 1902, Olga and the grand duke were married in Livorno. As soon as word of the morganatic marriage reached the Winter Palace, Tsar Nicholas II stripped his uncle of his military regalia and forbade his return to Russia.

Settling in France during their en-

Opposite: *Genya Gorlenko in an evening dress from Maggy Rouff, Paris, 1936.*

Top left: *Genya Gorlenko in a winter outfit trimmed in karakul designed by Maggy Rouff, Paris, 1937.*

Below left: *Russian models showing furs from Bransweig. Genya Gorlenko is on the far left, Paris, 1932.*

Above: *Genya Gorlenko in a mid-season suit from Maggy Rouff, Paris, 1935.*

Архив автора. Париж

Opposite: *Genya Dashkevich, a winner of the Miss Russia competition in the 1930s, Paris, 1936.*

Below: *Princess Nadezhda Shcherbatova in a design from Heim, Paris, 1935.*

Right: *Princess Nadezhda Shcherbatova in a design from an unknown house, Paris, mid-1930s.*

forced exile, the banished couple chose for their residence a mansion in Boulogne that had once belonged to Princess Zinaida Nikolayevna Youssoupoff. Their daughter Irina was born there on December 21, 1903. Wanting to help the marriage that had violated the laws of Russia's monarchy, the king of Bavaria gave Olga the title of Countess of Hohenfelsen. Thus, when Nathalie was born two years later, even though she could not be a Romanov, she had the Hohenfelsen title.

Countess Olga Valerianovna was a woman of rare beauty. In Paris she had her dresses made at Worth: there is a well-known photograph of her in a ball gown and a "Hungarian" fur toque (a subtle reminder of her Hungarian roots). Olga had her jewelry made at Cartier and she was known for her ability to select and to wear expensive jewelry well, knowledge she passed on to Nathalie, who later became the idol of the young

social set in Paris and one of the most beautiful women in France.

The grand duke and his wife were passionate art collectors, especially of old porcelain. Their collection was considered to be of museum quality: they had paintings by François Boucher, Jean-Baptiste Greuze, Simeon Chardin, Jean-Marc Nattier, Leopold Boilly, Perronneau, Hubert Robert, Bellotto, Francesco Guardi, Thomas Lawrence, Gerard Dow, Anthony van Dyke, and other great masters. The grand duke and his family finally returned to Russia in May, 1914, with Nicholas II's forgiveness, and moved almost all the furnishings from their Boulogne mansion to their new home in Tsarskoe

Selo, outside St. Petersburg. The architect Schmidt built them a mansion in the style of Louis XVI, made to resemble in exterior and interiors the palaces of the French aristocracy. With the beginning of World War I, the German title of Countess Hohenfelsen grated on Russian ears, and by decree of Nicholas II, Olga was permitted to call herself Princess Paley.

The Bolshevik revolution caught the grand duke's family in Tsarskoe Selo. In January, 1919, Pavel Alexandrovich was arrested and shot by the Bolsheviks at the Fortress of Peter and Paul, despite all the efforts made by the family for his release. Olga and Pavel's son, the talented young poet Prince Vladimir Paley, was exiled to Vyatka and then shot in a mine shaft in Alapayevsk with other Romanovs on the night of July 4, 1918.

Princess Paley, overwhelmed by grief and terrified by the night visits of Red Army soldiers to their house in Tsarskoe Selo, fled Russia with her small daughters. She reached Paris, where she still had the house in Boulogne, via Finland and Sweden. The hardships that the family underwent in those years are described in detail in Olga's diary, published in Paris in 1989; the life of her famous daughter, Princess Nathalie Paley, has been retold by the talented young French writer Jean Noel Liaut in a book published in 1996.

In the early years of her life as an émigré, Princess Paley took up charity work. The houses of Worth, Lelong, Revillon, and Cartier took part in the charity evenings and sales to aid Russian refugees, and one can assume that it was Princess Paley, a generous and long-time client, who prompted them to do so. In January 1922 Princess Olga Paley and her step-daughter, Grand Duchess Maria Pavlovna, gave a ball to aid Russian refugees at the Cercle interallié in Paris. In her free time, Olga visited Biarritz, an exclusive resort area where Russian aristocrats in exile met, where she acquired a small estate called Ballindux.

In 1923 Princess Irina Paley married Prince Feodor Alexandrovich Romanov, a nephew of Nicholas II, and therefore a relative by her father. She took up chari-

ty work and lived the ordinary life of a wealthy émigré. Tall and attractive Nathalie could also have found herself an enviable match among the Russian aristocrats with brilliant titles who frequented her mother's house, but she chose a different path, uniting her life with the world of fashion. We know that for a while Nathalie worked as a model at the house of Yteb. She was brought even closer to the world of Paris fashion when her half-sister, Grand Duchess Maria Pavlovna, opened Kitmir, and by the connection of her half-brother, Grand Duke Dmitrii Pavlovich, with Coco Chanel.

Princess Nathalie Paley went on to become a model at the house of Lucien Lelong, a famous couturier and a talented but vain man. Natalia Petrovna Bologovskaya, a seamstress there, said: "Following the example of Chanel, who brought in many Russian models, Lucien Lelong also hired the best Russian young lady, a real Romanov, the daughter of Grand Duke Paul Alexandrovich by a morganatic marriage. Princess Paley began as a model at Lelong; she was very good looking. Lucien Lelong was married to a charming woman then, but he got a divorce and married that real Romanov."[5]

Lucien Lelong divorced Anne-Marie Audoy on July 16,1927, and on August 10 married Nathalie Paley at the Cathedral of Alexander Nevsky on rue Daru in Paris. During their marriage, which lasted officially for ten years, Nathalie Paley became the symbol not only of the house of Lelong but also of "beauty in exile." Beginning in 1928, *Vogue* regularly published her portraits. Her beauty inspired the best photographers of the times— Baron George Hoyningen-Huene, Cecil Beaton, Horst P. Horst, Dorvin, and André Durst. Her appearance holds the

Opposite: Princess Nathalie Paley in a dress with a Pierrot collar designed by Lucien Lelong. Paris, 1933. When Princess Paley married the Parisian couturier it was considered a misalliance and newspapers wrote, in 1937, "The crown is leveled with a pair of scissors."

same mystery as Greta Garbo's face, and she was adored and imitated by many Parisian women. Mona Averino, who knew her from work at Lelong, said, "Nathalie kept her distance from the Russians who worked at the house, but she was very polite and considerate. There was something feline about her eyes."

The Lelongs were not happily married. Without a doubt, the famous fashion designer was proud of his beautiful wife, whose photographs ornamented so many magazines, but she preferred the society of her friends—brilliant and talented men who worshiped her as the personification of beauty but had no interest in physical intimacy. Among her friends were the photographers George Hoyningen-Huene, his friend Horst, the British Cecil Beaton, the talented Russian artist Paul Tchelichew, Christian Bérard, and of course, Jean Cocteau and Serge Lifar. With Cocteau and Lifar she had affairs that were tumultuous, but more platonic than passionate. It was clear that "real men" repulsed Nathalie: she perceived them as a threat to her beauty and preferred adoration and the poetry of emotions.

Princess Olga Paley, Nathalie's mother, had one more shock in store. In 1928 the Bolsheviks organized an auction in London of the best objects from her and Grand Duke Paul Alexandrovich's famous collection, which they had confiscated from their home in Tsarskoe Selo during the revolution. Porcelain, paintings, gold, silver, and the princess's furs went under the hammer. No amount of protesting and appealing to the British authorities would stop the sale. This humiliating procedure also was endured by Felix Youssoupoff. Auctions in Berlin, New York, London, and Paris were filled with confiscated objects and jewelry that the Soviet Russian government sold off without permission from its lawful owners. Such a scene was depicted in the Hollywood film *Ninotchka*, starring Greta Garbo. There, the Paris jewelers Bertlier were selling the diamonds of Grand Duchess Svana (marvelously played by Ina Claire). Of course, in real life it wasn't at all as funny as it was in the movies.

439

In 1933 Nathalie Paley became a film actress. Her looks attracted Marcel L'Herbier, who often used Russian actors. Dressed in luxurious gowns from Lucien Lelong, she was in *The Hawk* with Charles Boyer, and the following year acted in Jean de Margen's *Prince Jean*. She made three Hollywood films: *The Man from the Folies Bergère* by Roy del Rutt and Marcel Achard with Maurice Chevalier, and *Sylvia Scarlett* by George Cukor with Katherine Hepburn and Cary Grant in 1935. Back in France in 1936, she was in Marcel L'Herbier's *New Men* with Jean Marais. Nathalie Paley was very photogenic, but alas, she was not a talented actress. She usually played character parts—dizzy, eccentric, and, of course, elegant women who were not noted for their depth.

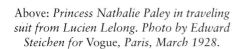

Above: *Princess Nathalie Paley in traveling suit from Lucien Lelong. Photo by Edward Steichen for* Vogue, *Paris, March 1928.*

Right: *Princess Olga Paley in a "Hungarian" ball gown from Worth and jewelry from Cartier, Paris, 1911.*

Above: *Nathalie Paley. Photo by Cecil Beaton for* Vogue, *1932.*

Above right: *Princess Irina Romanova, the sister of Nathalie Paley, in a formal dress from Worth. Photo by Arthur O'Neill for* Vogue, *Paris, 1926.*

The year of his divorce from Nathalie, whose life and career had long moved on without him, Lucien Lelong produced a new perfume called "N." Nathalie's initial? But no, in fact, it was a pun. The name was pronounced in French as "La En," which sounds just like the word *la haine*, or hatred. Natalia Petrovna Bologovskaya said about the Lelong couple: "They lived together for a time. But since Lucien Lelong was not interesting, Nathalie Paley went to

America and started a new life there."

In New York, where her stepsister, Grand Duchess Maria Pavlovna, and the famous Russian fashion designer Valentina Sanina, were living, Nathalie took a job at the popular American house of Mainbocher, which dressed the Duchess of Windsor. In 1937 Nathalie married for a second time to famous theatrical producer John Chapman Wilson. They lived in Manhattan, Connecticut, and Jamaica.

Vera Zorina (Brigitta Harvig), a Norwegian prima ballerina who was friends with Nathalie in New York, wrote in her memoirs about the dresses from Paris that Nathalie lent for a charity ball and about her friendship with another Russian émigré beauty, the Georgian Princess Mdivani, married name Sert. Lady Abdy said about Nathalie Paley, who later became the godmother of her granddaughter, "I loved her very much, and she was friendly and sweet to me, but we saw each other rarely, since we led completely different lives. Natasha Paley had her mother's face, while her sister, Duchess de Monbrison, looked like her father, the grand duke. Irina was very serious, she was interested in Berdayev and translated him into French."

Both in looks and temperament, the Paley sisters did not resemble each other—many people who knew them

Библиотека декоративных искусств. Париж

442

said so. Life on different continents must have separated them even more. In New York Nathalie was markedly eccentric. As her nephew Prince Mikhail Romanov wrote, her bedroom in Manhattan was completely covered in black satin, and the windows were tightly shut, with black curtains. Both in New York and in Paris, Nathalie spent time with the artistic elite, who bowed to her beauty. Her friends included Erich Maria Remarque, Horst, Valentina Sanina, Marlene Dietrich, Count Vladimir Adlerberg, Prince Sergei Obolensky, Fulco Santostefano della Serda, Count Verdura, and Baron Nicky de Gunzburg.

Nathalie did not return to Europe until the end of World War II, and then only briefly. On September 3, 1951, she took part in the most famous carnival of the twentieth century—given by Charles de Beistegui and held in the Venetian palazzo of Labia. Through the watercolors of Alexander Serebriakoff, the son of the famous Russian artist Zinaida Serebriakova, we can imagine the magnificent spectacle. Nathalie's fame was beginning to fade at this time, and one after another her close friends, who had adored her, passed away.

Her first husband, Lucien Lelong, died in 1958. Her second husband, John Wilson, who drank heavily, died in 1961. Left alone, she felt alienated in the rhythms of American life. Like Greta Garbo, Nathalie chose a reclusive life in her later years. She ceased all contact with the outside world, refused to see anyone, and even with her sister Irina, communicated only by telephone and mail. In her last years Nathalie Paley was half blind and drank heavily. In late 1982, she fell in the bath and broke a hip. She died later that year, on December 27, at Roosevelt Hospital in New York. Her last words were "I want to die with dignity." This incomparable Russian beauty, who never was truly happy, was buried next to her second husband, John Wilson, in New Jersey.

No matter how changeable fashion may be, not all the beauties of the 1920s were eclipsed and soon forgotten. In the 1930s and 1940s Lady Abdy continued to shine in Paris society. After her di-

vorce from Robert Abdy in 1928 she kept her title and began working at Chanel, where she was still considered the standard of elegance. Her portraits often appeared in *Vogue* and other fashion magazines in the prewar years, usually dressed by the big Paris houses, in particular Molyneux. Lady Abdy recalled, "I didn't work for Molyneux, I merely wore his dresses, which he offered me for my sorties. Many houses gave their beautiful designs to famous women. Mainbocher did that too, but I didn't work anywhere except Soeurs Callot and Chanel."[6]

Lady Abdy's fame as arbiter of elegance continued to grow. She was a frequent guest at social masquerade balls and parties given by the tireless socialite Count Cyril de Beaumont. One of Lady Abdy's most famous costumes for such an evening consisted of balloons with a seashell on her head. She recalled it in a conversation with the author: "I made the silver sea shell myself and I came up with the idea for the balloons. A sweet French milliner helped me. With her I made another of my famous costumes— a deep red dress in Italian rococo style, with a small white tricorn and crumpled and torn long calfskin gloves."

One of the most faithful photographers of Lady Abdy was George Hoyningen-Huene. Lady Abdy said, "George photographed me often and a lot. He compared me to Garbo. Once I was in Berlin and people took me for Garbo, and I couldn't have any peace for three days. I got so sick of them! They even wrote about me in the papers. The film *Mata Hari* starring Garbo was playing in Berlin then, and the naive audience even wanted me to come out on stage instead of her, but I didn't do that.

"Besides George, I was also photographed by Man Ray and Lipnitsky. Cecil Beaton not only photographed me, he also drew me. By the way, I was drawn by very many artists: André De-

Opposite: *Princess Nathalie Paley in an evening dress from Lucien Lelong. Photo by A. de Meyer for* Vogue, Paris, 1931.

rain did five portraits of me. I was also painted by Balthus, and there was a portrait of me at his exhibit at the Metropolitan Museum. In France I was painted by Leonor Fini."

Lady Abdy's life in the late 1930s and early 1940s became mysterious and incredible. At the height of the Stalin terror, in 1937, she made her very first trip to Moscow—a rather bizarre action for a Russian émigré, to say the least. Here is how she described it: "As I child I had lived in St. Petersburg and had not visited Moscow before the revolution. In 1937, not long before the start of the war, I went to Russia. My father was stricken with paralysis and suddenly recalled that he had a daughter in Paris. That was my first sight of Moscow—a very sad sight! It was winter, everything was covered in snow, and my hotel, the Metropole, was not far from the Kremlin. A drab crowd walked in the streets, and I looked out the window and saw the Kremlin all in snow. I was very sad. A Hungarian journalist asked me, 'What do you expect, that Moscow show you the bathrooms in workers' dormitories or in communal flats?' He was hinting at the poverty of Soviet people. Then I took a train to St. Petersburg. It was a beautiful road—thick fir trees in the snow, and the train, like in the old Russian times! Samovars and tea in every car. In every compartment the men were very proper looking. In mine there were three very neat men. These gentlemen always stepped out when I went to sleep and when I rose. Strange gentlemen for Soviet times!" We can merely guess who accompanied the famous foreigner on her trip through snowy Russia in 1937, why she was permitted to go there, and why they let her back out to France, where she was too well known.

In 1936, Lady Abdy, gifted and artistic by nature, had made her stage debut in the play *King Oedipus*, in an unusual costume by Chanel. She also had a starring role in *Senso* by Suvchinsky at the Folies Wagram Theater. She recalled, "There was a talented Russian then. Suvchinsky. He thought that I was theatrical and he could put on a spectacu-

443

Библиотека декоративных искусств, Париж

lar play with me. The plot of *Senso* is from the fifteenth to seventeenth centuries—the story of a father who rapes his daughter, who then kills him. It was produced lavishly, the costumes were marvelous. We were not a popular success, but the specialists adored it."

Lady Abdy never did remarry. As she put it, "After the divorce from Abdy, I could have married many times, but I kept having doubts, and then time passed. I was so good being free!" She was was financially independent—after the divorce she kept the famous diamond, over 30 carats, from Chaumet. She had other first-class jewels, too. In Paris Lady Abdy lived extravagantly and in expensive neighborhoods: first at 22 quai de Bourbon, then not far from the Ritz on Place Vendôme in an apartment furnished with exquisite taste.

She recalled, "My Paris apartments had no particular style, but only things I loved. On the quai de Bourbon my interior was more suitable to l'Ile Saint-Louis, and on Place Vendôme, where I lived just before the war, it was quite different: a long window and view of the Vendôme column. The walls had antique lacquer panels, which I bought in Peking. I liked old things, I was an avid collector. My mother and her sister Olga were collectors. They got that from their father, my grandfather. He adored art and his estate Rayok was marvelous!

Opposite: *Princess Nathalie Paley in a jacket of gray karakul from Lucien Lelong. Photo by Edward Steichen for* Vogue, *Paris, 1932.*

Top: *Princess Nathalie Paley in a hat from Reboux and a dress from Lucien Lelong. Photo by George Hoyningen-Huene for* Vogue, *Paris, 1932.*

Bottom left: *The cover of the exhibition catalogue for Paris Fashion of the 1930s at the Musée de la Mode et du Costume with a photo of Nathalie Paley, Paris, 1937.*

Bottom right: *An advertisement for three perfumes, "N," "Passionnement," and "Indiscret," from Lucien Lelong, Paris, 1939.*

So beautiful! Grandfather was an esthete just like Diaghilev. Mother collected antique Russian silver and furniture, and so did my aunt. She had, for example, a bed that had belonged to Catherine the Great. Where she got it, I don't know. Yes, they were obsessed!"

In her apartments Lady Abdy received *le tout Paris.* Among her friends were Jean Cocteau, Serge Lifar, Tatyana Riabouchinska, Princess Nadezhda Shcherbatova and Princess Ilyinskaya, Princess Nathalie Paley, Prince Felix Youssoupoff, Misia Sert, the Princes Mdivani and Meshtchersky, Nimet Eloy Bey, and many other celebrities of the 1930s.

How did Lady Abdy dress and what was the secret of her elegance? The tall, statuesque, blue-eyed blonde with great bearing and a proud face knew her worth. Possessing flawless taste, she was strict in her color selection. Retaining her legendary beauty until she was ninety-five, she told me, "For dresses I like red or light blue to match my eyes. Violet in all its shades—reddish-lilac-blue. There are shades that are hard to put into words. I am ninety-five now, and I've decided not to care about fashion any more. Everyone around me is so provincial!"

In the late 1930s Lady Abdy tied her life to an Italian, a representative of the Mussolini government, a man named Enzio. Accused of spying for Italy, she was arrested, and after the Germans occupied Paris, she was exiled to Vichy. "If that will save France, I go to Vichy," Lady Abdy said then. Her admirer was recalled to Rome and replaced with another representative. From Vichy, despite the military action, Lady Abdy made her way to England. There she was mobilized, since she was British by passport, and she served as an interpreter in the British Army. She was irreplaceable in negotiations since she spoke fluent French, Russian, and German. At the end of the war, Lady Abdy worked closely with the Soviet mission on the repatriation of Russian prisoners of war, along with a certain Colonel Letunov, with whom all the women fell in love.

Back in Paris after demobilization, Lady Abdy worked as a translator at the Pasteur Institute. But her connections with the military circles of Italy, the United States, the Soviet Union, France, and England must have made her further life in Paris impossible. Lady Abdy left France for New York on business, planning to stay away for a while. From New York, she moved to Mexico and fell in love with it. She recalled, "Mexico 'ruined' my taste—after it even Paris did not seem the same." Princess Nina Lobanova-Rostovskaya, who visited Lady Abdy in Mexico, recalled, "Her house looked like a tropical garden with Spanish colonial

furniture. Her admirer at that time was a Mexican sculptor named Mario, much, much younger than Iya, who was still very glamorous."

In Mexico Lady Abdy met and became friends with another émigré—the famous Polish artist Tamara Lempicka. Lady Abdy said about her, "Tamara was a baroness then, married to a Hungari-

Above: *Lady Abdy. Photo by George Hoyningen-Huene.*

Opposite: *Lady Abdy in a masquerade costume with balloons, which she designed, and a headdress in the shape of a seashell, made by a professional milliner. Photo by George Hoyningen-Huene for* Vogue, *Paris, 1928.*

an baron. She died there in Mexico. Before she died she asked that her ashes be scattered over the big volcano on the way to Acapulco."

She did not return to France from Mexico until the 1970s, and then she chose to live in the south, in the small town of Roquebrune, a refuge for many aristocrats. She occasionally went to Paris, where she met with Alexander Lieberman, the art director of *Vogue,* and Tatyana Yakovleva. Her son and daughter continued living in California. Lady Abdy's long life ended in a nursing home in Le Canuet, near Nice, in the autumn of 1992.

Another socialite beauty from Russia who drove prewar Paris crazy was Nyusya Penyakova, Rotwand by her first marriage and Muñoz by the second. She was born in the Ukraine in 1889 or 1890 (the exact date is not known). She was beautiful from an early age and got married in the 1910s to a Jewish banker named Casimir Lvovich Rotwand, owner of a bank in Poltava; the ceremony was held in Switzerland. At the age of 106, Nadezhda Dmitrievna Nilus, who had known Nyusya Rotwand in Petrograd in the 1910s, recalled, "Her back was extraordinarily beautiful, and she often wore clothes that revealed it. I remember her in her box at the Mariinsky Theater in 1914 with other beauties. Everyone knew her then."[7]

After moving to France during World War I and divorcing her husband, with whom she had a son, Nyusya Rotwand married once more, this time to a Spanish diplomat named Alvaro Muñoz, from a noble family related to the oldest aristocratic families of Spain. His father had been the Spanish ambassador to St. Petersburg and then to the Vatican. In the 1920s photographs of Nyusya in Rome, Biarritz, or Paris began appearing in *Vogue.* While never a model, she was celebrated as the embodiment of elegance. The society columnist of the magazine *L'Art et la mode,* Andre de Fouquer, describing a charity ball given by Princess Olga Paley in 1921 in Biarritz, could not refrain from delighted phrases: "Two gowns stood out from the multitude of others: the one worn by

Opposite: *Lady Abdy in the costume of Hamlet. Photo by Cecil Beaton for* Vogue, *Paris, September 1929.*

Below: *Lady Abdy's costume from Chanel for the play* King Oedipus, *1937.*

Right: *Lady Abdy in an evening dress. Photo by Man Ray for* Vogue, *Paris, December 1925.*

Madame Rotwand—white gauze embroidered with mother-of-pearl beads—and the one worn by Marquise de Mohernando."

Many fashion houses lent her dresses for going out, as this was their best advertising. Nyusya Rotwand was very photogenic, which was noticed immediately by master photographers George Hoyningen-Huene, Vladimir Rehbinder, and Boris Lipnitsky. Her beauty reached the apogee of fame in the 1930s: she was photographed wearing diamonds from Cartier, and at costume balls given by Count Cyril de Beaumont. She was most striking in her costume of Nefertiti, queen of Egypt, which we can admire thanks to photographs of the ball by Horst. Nyusya Rotwand-Muñoz died at

the age of forty-five, in 1936, on the eve of Spain's civil war.

Among the Russian socialite beauties who became professional photography models we must note Lidia Konstantinovna Zelenskaya, married name Rotwand (she married Nyusya Rotwand's son). Born in the Caucasus, the daughter of Georgian princess Melita Tazievna Cholokayeva, Lidia entered the world of fashion through her surroundings. Her mother spent a few months in the 1920s as a model for Chanel together with Princess Mary Eristova. Lidia had refined, regular features, a lovely figure, and very shapely legs. Such great photographers as Horst, Lipnitsky, Durst, and Dorvin began photographing her in the mid-1930s. She posed in fashions by

449

Robert Piguet and Marcelle Dormoy and, between the years 1935 and 1937, her face often appeared in *Vogue*.

Even so, primacy belongs to only one beauty among the Russian émigrés—Ludmila Leonidovna Feodoseyeva, known in the Paris fashion world as Lud. She was born April 21, 1913, in Petrograd to the family of vice-governor of Vladimir Province Leonid Alexeyevich Fedoseyev, who also held a prominent position in the Red Cross since the Russo-Japanese War, and Anastasia Matveyevna Lashina, from a family of Cossacks from Vladikavkaz. Lud's brother, her loyal confidant through her life, was born July 23, 1917. After the revolution the parents took the children first to the Crimea and then evacuated by ship to Gallipoli and Constantinople, where they were helped by the Franco-Ottoman Bank and the Red Cross. From there the family sailed to Marseilles via Greece in November 1922.

Life in foreign lands began sadly. The first year her father died. Her mother, a graduate of the Petrograd Women's Medical School, managed to find work as a dentist in Paris, but not for long. Trying to make a living, she then took jobs as a dentist in Africa. From 1928 to 1935 she worked in the French colonies of the Ivory Coast, Sudan, and Upper Volta. The children remained in France in various boarding schools, but would visit their mother in Africa during school holidays.

Above: *Nyusya Rotwand, Paris, 1932. Photo by Boris Lipnitsky.*

Left: *Nyusya Rotwand in her wedding dress after her marriage to Alvaro Muñoz, a Spanish diplomat at the Spanish embassy in the Vatican, 1930.*

Opposite: *Nyusya Rotwand in jewelry from Cartier, 1932. Photo by George Hoyningen-Huene.*

In the meantime Lud studied at the lycée and showed strong talent in philology, which gave her an opportunity to enter university to study literature. For pocket money, she worked as a delivery person, a film extra, and acted in the theater with the stage name Hedda Grane (getting good reviews). She was "discovered" by Horst one day when she brought a few dresses to the Paris *Vogue* studio, and he asked her to pose. When Conde Nast, the owner of *Vogue*, saw the photographs, he told Horst that he didn't like Lud: her nose was too upturned and it did not look serious. However, Horst continued taking her picture and then Mr. Nast fell madly in love with her and even wanted to marry her.[8]

At the age of eighteen, Lud signed her first contract on October 1, 1933, with the house of Vera Borea in Paris, which had just opened that year. The house of Countess Vera Borea, which last until 1963, was known for its sports outfits and draped evening wear. At the age of twenty-two, Lud married Marquis Lucien de Boucoiran, a music lover and the director of Citroen, who was twenty years her senior. By the mid-1930s Lud was one of the symbols of beauty, and her face appeared constantly in the leading fashion magazines and on their covers. Alexei Fedoseyev recalled, "My sister began with Patou, then switched to Chanel. She was photographed a lot for *Vogue* and *Harper's Bazaar*. Lud was constantly traveling—she worked in America, England, Italy . . . "[9]

Lud often advertised dresses for the best houses of the period. Chanel and Schiaparelli vied for her. She became

Opposite: *Lidia Zelenskaya-Rotwand, the daughter-in-law of Nyusya Rotwand. Photo from* Vogue, *Paris, June 1928.*

Top left: *Lidia Zelenskaya-Rotwand in a fur jacket from Robert Piguet, Paris, 1937.*

Top right: *Princess M. T. Cholokayeva, a model at Chanel, Paris, 1930. Photo by Boris Lipnitsky.*

Right: *Lidia Zelenskaya-Rotwand in a karakul jacket, 1937.*

Архив Александры Гайяр, Тулс

Архив Александры Гайяр, Тулс

dian soldiers in 1945. Lud's marriage to the marquis did not go well. She tried to get a divorce, but the marquis would not consent for seven years. Once she was divorced, Lud married again in 1943 to a naval engineer Pierre Gaillard-Stievenard and moved into his large apartment on quai de Passy in Paris.

In spite of the war and occupation, Lud made films. Marcel L'Herbier gave her a small part in *Honorable Catherine*. Her next film was Louis Daquin's *Madame and Death*. But her main calling was fashion. Success, perhaps too much success, accompanied all those years. After the liberation of Paris in August 1944, Lud began traveling: England, Egypt, Tunis. Her brother Alexei emigrated to Brazil in March 1947 and started an optical business. Lud was pregnant when her brother invited her to Rio de Janeiro to his wedding, and

one of the immortal images of twentieth-century fashion thanks to a photograph by Horst of her in a dress from Alix.[10] To this day many consider this draped dress to be the best creation of Parisian fashion of the twentieth century. Lud was photographed for Marcel Rochas, Lanvin, Mainbocher, Molyneux, and many others. Horst's photographs and the portraits by André Durst immortalized her enchanting and seductive image. Ubiquitous commercial advertising could not do without her, either. According to Russian model Thea Bobrikova, "Lud's face could be seen on every fence" (she was in an ad for Javel bleaching detergent).

Lud's brother, Alexei, was drafted by the French army, and at the beginning of World War II ended up in the German concentration camp Dinan, where he remained until it was liberated by Cana-

This page and opposite: *Ludmila Feodoseyeva (Lud), the best photo model of the 1930s–40s, posing in designs from various fashion houses, 1937–38.*

Overleaf, left: *Lud in a dress from Alix, Paris, 1937. Many people consider this to be the best dress of the twentieth century. Photo by Horst.*

Overleaf right: *Lud in an evening dress, 1937.*

Архив Александры Гайер. Туве

This page: Ludmila Feodoseyeva (Lud), posing in designs from various fashion houses of the late 1930s.

Opposite: Lud posing in a design from Chanel, late 1930s.

her only daughter, Alexandra Gaillard, was born in Buenos Aires. After the difficult childbirth, Lud stayed in Argentina for three months and then moved with her daughter to the United States, where she lived for two years. The marriage with Gaillard was also unhappy and she demanded a divorce. Lud's daughter wrote, "This was a difficult period for her morally. Later she admitted that she had been very depressed."[11]

Lud returned to France with her daughter in 1951 and began working for Cristobal Balenciaga. But she had nagging suspicions that the time of her fame was over and that she was no longer in fashion. Life for Lud outside the luxurious world of fashion grew very difficult. Used to extravagance, she was forced to live modestly, finding a job at the Slenderella beauty institute. In the evenings, to make more money, she sang in the chorus of the Paris opera. The daughter wrote, "An unhappy life, loneliness . . . Mother's character was purely Slavic: manic joy replaced by endless sorrow."[12]

In 1959 Lud moved to the city of Le Touquet, where she worked for five years as a clerk in the local airport. After the air-

port was shut down, she was unemployed. Four semi-starving years passed. At last she found work as head of curriculum in a private school in the town of Vaucresson, where she worked from 1968 to 1972. In 1969 and in 1972 she traveled as a tourist to Russia, which she knew only secondhand. Then Lud became director of a Russian home for the aged in Gagny, where two of the residents were the poet Irina Odoevtseva and the former famous model Princess Mary Eristova. Alexandra, Lud's daughter, who had married a Russian, lived for a time in Moscow, and Lud came to visit her in 1978 and 1981. Lud retired in 1982. It was then that she married for a third

time—finally, happily it seems—to her childhood friend Pierre de la Grandière. Lud Fedoseyeva died of cancer on December 15, 1990, in the village of Pugny-Chanenod in the French Alps.

Lud's personality is marvelously described by her daughter, "She loved to joke and made others believe her pranks. For instance, she made up a story that she had married a lion tamer. . . . Once my mother introduced me to a persistent admirer as her sixth child—that was how she got rid of him! In 1968 she hung red cloths from our balcony and shouted from it that she was on strike. A bottleneck formed in the street. And she laughed till she cried."

Архив автора, Париж

"She wasn't afraid of anything: she could get on a boat on a lake in a storm or walk alone through sordid neighborhoods in Paris. She was in love with life. She ate it up. She was the daughter of Epicurius. She loved to eat and drink and make merry. She loved to travel.

"She was direct with people, told the truth to their faces. She was born under the sign of Taurus."[13]

Another first-class model in the 1930s and 1940s was Varvara Borisovna Rapponet, born on July 10, 1911, in Kiev to the family of a military man. Her father, a colonel in the engineering corps, Boris Nikolayevich Rapponet, was the son of Countess Evdokiya Musina-Pushkina, and her mother, Magdalina Alexandrovna Feodorova, was the daughter of active state councilor and chairman of the nobility of Tver Province. Magdalina

Alexandrovna was a writer, publishing her novels under the pen name Lina Izlomova. The Rapponet family lived in Kiev on Bankovskaya Street, and at the beginning of the revolution moved to Feodosia, where Varvara's father was appointed chief of the naval base, and in 1920 the family emigrated via Turkey to Yugoslavia.

Varvara recalled, "My father was an old officer who fought Japan in 1905. During the war we spent about three

Above: Varvara Rapponet in a blue velvet suit and orange velvet beret from Schiaparelli, 1948.

Opposite: Varvara Rapponet in a gray silk evening dress, with embroidered butterflies as head ornamentation, from Schiaparelli, 1943.

years in the Crimea. The ship *General Kornilov*, commanded by my father, took us to Turkey, where we were docked at the Golden Horn in Constantinople for twenty-four hours. We children were bathed and cleaned up by Americans. The ship was overcrowded with refugees in military uniform and there were masses of officers' wives. People had taken trunks and samovars. Papa ordered them to toss all that into the sea, because the ship was listing. Mama wore a fur coat, on her finger there was a diamond ring, and in her hands, an icon. That was all we had. All our property remained in Kiev, since we thought we would be back soon. We stored all our things—carpets, furniture, and silver—in the Zemsky pawnshop, and that's the first place the Bolsheviks went.

"After Turkey we went by a French

460

ship right to Yugoslavia and landed at Dubrovnik, where we were arrested for a while. Father spoke French and German, but he did not know Serbian. He got work building roads in Montenegro, and for that reason we lived in the town of Boka Katorska. From there I walked to school in shoes with wooden soles, and then I was transferred to Polyakova's Russian high school, where I studied for about five years (1920–1925) and then went to the Kharkov Institute in Novy Bichey. The teaching staff consisted of people from the Smolny, Ekaterininsky, and Kiev institutes. Our directrice, Maria Alexeyevna Nekhludova,

Top left: *Varvara Rapponet in a ski outfit from Hermès, 1946.*

Bottom left: *St. Catherine's festivities at Schiaparelli. Third from left in the top row is Varvara Rapponet, fourth from right at the table is the future couturier Hubert de Givenchy, late 1940s.*

Above: *Varvara Rapponet in a black-and-white suit from the first Balenciaga collection, Paris, 1937. Photo by D'Orr.*

Opposite: *Varvara Rapponet in a traveling suit and coat at the Lyons train station, from Hermès, Paris, 1943. Photo by Jean-Louis Moussempes.*

Архив автора. Париж

Архив Варвара Раппонет, Монморанси

but I tried anyway, saying that I was a *mannequin volante*. They liked me at the house of Franck, which was on the Madeleine in Paris and specialized in suits, and I traveled to twenty-eight cities in France with them. But when I first came out to model the designs, my bosses panicked: I couldn't even set one foot in front of the other. They took away my dresses and gave them to other girls, but gradually I learned how to walk properly."

In 1937 the great Spanish fashion designer Cristobal Balenciaga, who had just opened his own house, hired Varvara, whom everyone called Barbara or Barbarita. A talented palm reader, Barbara foretold great success for Balenciaga and her prediction came true, as we know. In those years another Russian worked at Balenciaga—Princess Xenia Tcherbatova. Varvara recalled her debut at Balenciaga: "The house of Balenciaga had just opened. The walls were still being painted, and everyone sat on the floor. I worked there for a year. I showed suits, coats, and dresses. Some designs were sewn specially for me. His business was better than in other houses, since he made very good things that were distinguished by their color scheme and fine work."

Then the war came, and Paris was occupied. In 1941 Barbara, exhausted and hungry, ended up at Schiaparelli. There she became a real star for many years. Barbara recalled, "My husband was at war, I was very sick with peritonitis, and my entire capital consisted of 11 francs.

was from Smolny. Mother at the time was working as a nurse in the hospital of the American Red Cross, run by Zelennikov. Then my father, as an engineer, got a better job at a pyrotechnics factory in Kragujevac."[14]

Upon graduation from the institute in Novy Bichy, not far from the Hungarian border, Varvara moved back in with her parents in 1930, but she was bored in the small town. One day she decided to give it all up and move to Belgrade, the center of the Russian émigré community. There she tried to find a job while living with friends. She recounted

the rest, "In Belgrade they arranged a passport for me through friends, and in 1933 I went to France. Not alone of course, but with a young man who became my husband. He was a Russian French Legionnaire. At first I didn't have the right to work in Paris, but all my friends advised, 'You have such a good figure, you should be a model.' There were many famous Russian models then: Sonya Yavorskaya at Revillon, Billi Bibikova at Piguet, Mona Averino at Paquin and Balenciaga. I saw an ad in the paper: 'hiring models for travel.' I didn't know how to walk like a model

Архив автора, Париж

A clairvoyant in Paris told me to light a candle at St. Teresa's. As I came out of the church I headed toward Place Vendôme, I don't know why. It was opening day for Schiaparelli and they were hiring models. One of the workers there, the Swedish Irene Dana, asked me, 'Are you a model? Just look at yourself in the mirror, you're nothing but skin and bones!' I replied that I had been sick and that I used to work at Balenciaga. But then came the voice of Elsa Schiaparelli herself, 'Madame Dana, what right do you have to select models? And you, young lady, come with me! And bring me the dress that was made for Lili. They seem to be the same size.' And the miracle happened!" Schiaparelli functioned during the war, but the owner went to the United States. During the years she worked for Schiaparelli, Varvara got a new name in the fashion world—Barbara Schiap. In 1947 she married a second time, to the famous French racing driver Louis Gerard de Saint-Hilaire.

After the war Varvara took part in fashion shows and was photographed for Lanvin and Maggy Rouff. She was sent to the wedding of Grace Kelly and the Prince of Monaco on April 19, 1952, with gifts—dresses from Lanvin. She stopped working in 1956.

Aside from professional models, famous Russian actresses, and especially ballerinas, often were photographed. For instance, the prima ballerina Tamara Toumanova was the most popular and frequently photographed ballet star, and was celebrated for her incomparable beauty from the 1930s to the 1950s.

Opposite above: *Varvara Rapponet in an evening cloak of black karakul from Maggy Rouff, 1947.*

Opposite below: *Varvara Rapponet in a dress of black taffeta and hat with a veil from Schiaparelli, 1949.*

Right: *Varvara Rapponet in a pleated silk dress the color of milk chocolate, from Schiaparelli, 1952.*

Архив Варвары Раппонет, Монморанси

sional stage. At age nine she could do thirty-two fouettées and appeared in the ballet *Jeanne's Fan* at the Grand Opéra de Paris. She began her professional career at the age of thirteen in the troupe of the Ballets Russes de Monte Carlo, directed by Colonel de Basil, where she had been recommended by George Balanchine. Tamara was dubbed "baby ballerina," a term that was used for two other talented dancers—Irina Baronova, a student of Preobrazhenska, and Tatyana Riabouchinska, a student of Kchessinska.

Her talent and grace were combined with rare beauty. Beginning in 1932, Tamara Toumanova was the most photographed Russian ballerina. People raved about her and called her "the black pearl of Russian ballet." She had great success in *Choreartum* and *Symphonie fantasque*, as well as leading roles in Massine's *Tricorne* and in Fokine's ballets *Carnaval*, *Le Spectre de la Rose*, and *Petrouchka*. Alexandra Danilova, a Diaghilev ballerina who knew Tamara on and off stage, recalled, "Toumanova's beauty was her greatest stage attribute."[15]

Tamara was born March 2, 1919, in a train, stuck in the snows of Siberia. She was the daughter of army engineer Vladimir Khazidovich-Boretsky and Yevgenia, an Armenian woman. Tamara's parents fled Russia to China, and then made their way to France via Harbin, Shanghai, and Cairo. Tamara was a gifted child and began dancing at an early age in Egypt. In Paris this talented and lovely child attended the famous ballet studio of Olga Osipovna Preobrazhenska, who suggested she change her name from Khazidovich-Boretskaya to Toumanova.

Displaying rare ballet talent at Madame Preo's studio, Tamara very quickly began appearing on the profes-

Opposite: *Tamara Toumanova, a ballerina from the de Basil company, in a zebra cloak, 1940. Photo by Horst.*

Above: *Tamara Toumanova in a stage costume, Monte Carlo, 1932.*

Right: *Tamara Toumanova in a dress from the American fashion house Tripori. Photo by Rawlings for British* Vogue, *1942.*

DANCE

DECEMBER 1937   PAUL R. MILTON, Editor   25c

IRINA BARONOVA
BALLET GOES NATIVE   BACK TO THE PEOPLE!
By George Balanchine   By Rolf de Maré
DANCE INTERNATIONAL 1900-1937
The Magazine for All the Dance Profession

Her exotic, semi-Caucasian beauty made her the most brilliant of all the Russian émigré ballet stars. Dressed in fashionable clothing, she was photographed by Horst and Man Ray, her portraits were printed by *Vogue*, and fashion magazines vied for her interviews, which were overseen by her vigilant mother, whom her friends jokingly called "ballet mother." Toumanova's makeup, hair, and stage costumes were flawless. Varvara Karinska, costumer for the Balanchine troupe, created a Dying Swan costume for Toumanova, in which she shone in Fokine's miniature. A friend and colleague in de Basil's company, George Zoritch, recalled, "Tamara had flawless beauty in life and on the stage. Her technique was incomparable, dynamic, and left an unforget-

Above: *A cover of* Dance *magazine with a photo of Irina Baronova, December 1937.*

Above right: *Nina Verchinina and Tamara Toumanova, ballerinas from the de Basile company, United States, 1937.*

Opposite above: *Tamara Grigoryeva, a ballerina from the de Basil company, Buenos Aires, 1944.*

Opposite below: *Tamara Gevergeyeva (Tamar Giva), a Broadway musical star. Photo by Horst for British* Vogue, *New York 1938.*

table impression with its magnetism, one that lasted a long time."

In 1939 Tamara made her Broadway debut in the musical *Stars in Your Eyes*, and then returned to the ballet stage. World War II found Toumanova in the United States, where she obtained American citizenship. In 1943 Toumanova made her first feature film, *Days of Glory*, with Gregory Peck, and married

the director of the film, Casey Robertson. Moving to Beverly Hills, Tamara often left her husband with her father while she went on tour around the world, accompanied by her mother and her dog.

In the 1950s Tamara made three more feature films: *Tonight We Sing* (1953), *Deep in my Heart* (1954), and *Invitation to the Dance* (1955), and also danced triumphantly on European stages. The audiences of the Grand Opéra applauded her in Serge Lifar's *Phèdre*. The critics were not always generous to Toumanova, but the halls were packed. The magic of her name attracted hundreds, thousands of viewers thirsting to see the queen of Russian ballet.

After divorcing Casey Robertson, who could not tolerate the "Russian style" of her life, she went on tour in Latin America with ballet stars Andrei Ukhtomsky, Roman Jasinsky, and Oleg Briansky. In 1966 she was in Hitchcock's film *Torn Curtain* starring Julie Andrews, Lilia Kedrova, and Paul Newman. Tamara's film career ended with Billy Wilder's *Private Life of Sherlock Holmes* in 1969. She retained her extraordinary beauty to the end, even after she left her artistic career to live reclu-

sively with her mother in a house on Elm Drive in Beverly Hills.

There were quite a few other beauties among the Russian ballerinas: Tatyana Riabouchinska, Irina Baranova, who made films (for example, *Dorian*), and Natalya Krassovska, who won second place in the Miss Russia competition in the 1930s in Paris. Nina Verchinina and Tamara Grigorieva were outstanding beauties in the de Basil company.

After World War II, the fashion for Russian émigré beauties faded. The victory of the Soviet army and the massive repatriation of some émigrés to the Soviet Union created a situation that made being a Russian émigré unpopular. The whirlwind of those postwar years nevertheless brought two new Russian models to the top; Princess

Tatyana Kropotkina and Alla Ilchun became stars in the newly opened house of Christian Dior in 1947. The former worked for Dior at the very beginning of the house's existence, and the latter— a slender beauty with a Eurasian appearance—remained a *vedette* of the house for almost twenty years.

Born in Harbin, Alla was the daughter of the soprano opera singer Tatyana Mikhailovna Ilchun and a railroad man from Alma-Ata, Yevgeny (Guankhala) Ilchun. When she moved to Paris she went to Dior with a friend who was applying for a job as model. The friend was rejected right away, but Dior himself noticed Alla. She told me, "Waiting for my friend in the vestibule, I noticed that the curtains in the try-on cabins kept being opened and curious eyes were looking me over from head to toe. At last I got sick of the glances and the waiting, and I decided to look for my lost friend. And then some woman told me that Christian Dior wanted to see me. I agreed reluctantly. They took me to a cabin, whisked off my dress, combed my hair over to one side like a big pancake, colored my mouth with red lipstick, put on a new dress and strangely uncomfortable stiletto heels, and led me downstairs, where a whole team of house painters in white coats were working away. Well, I thought, they've dressed me up like a monkey and brought me to the house painters. They brought me and they took me away, and I didn't see Dior there. But then the same woman said, 'Mademoiselle, you are hired.'"[16]

One of Alla's great successes was showing the "Junon" dress in 1948. The matching outfit, "Venus," was worn by Princess Kropotkina. Dior called the ar-

guments between the two models "Russia at war with China," a reference to Alla's Oriental eyes, which, incidentally, made her world-famous. Before Alla, there were no Eurasian models in high fashion—Alla was the trailblazer. Her slanting eyes not only delighted millions of women, but inspired them to lengthen their own eyes with eyeliner, a look that became popular in the 1950s. Alla recalled her work at Dior, "Dior adored me and forgave me all kinds of mischief and

Архив Аллы Илчун, Париж

tricks. He was a second father to me and he let me wear his dresses for evenings out. I was very nasty—for instance, I would shake sneezing powder under the nose of clients or pinch other models with my toes during try-ons."[17]

Alla traveled around the world with fashion shows. She was a close friend of Dior and his assistant Yves Saint Laurent, and she remained with the house for "three regimes," as she called it: she worked there when Marc Bohan ran the house, too. Other houses also engaged her, including the house of Princess Irina Galitzine. Alla maintained her slim figure throughout her life: at the start of her career she had a 47-centimeter waist and at the end of her life it was 49 centimeters.

In the 1950s and 1960s there were occasional echoes of the former glory of Russian fashion houses. In California the fashion house Marusia opened, specializing in evening and formal dresses, run by Princess Toumanova (no relation to Tamara). In Rome Princess Irina Galitzine began her work with great success; she popularized palazzo pants. In the 1950s there were also the Laure Belin and Hitrovo houses of lingerie and the fashion house of Oleg Cassini. But the period of greatest activity of the Russian émigrés in fashion was over.

The end of the Cold War and the fall of the Berlin Wall brought hundreds of models from Eastern Europe, especially Russia, to the fashion markets of Europe and America. Today, once again, there isn't a single fashion house or modeling agency without young Russian beauties. But the history of their lives and careers is for the future. Let this book be a gift to the memory of those first fashion designers and arbiters, who upon finding themselves in exile, far from Russia, used their stubborn work, talent, and beauty to make the world take notice.

Above: *Alla Ilchun in a coat from Christian Dior, Paris, 1951.*

Opposite: *Alla Ilchun in a silk walking outfit from Lanvin, 1956.*

Музей моды и костюма. Париж

Notes

1 THE BALLETS RUSSES AND RUSSIAN FASHION

1. Tenisheva, M. K. *Vpechatleniya moei zhizni* [My Life's Impressions]. Leningrad, 1991, pp. 246.
2. Ibid., p. 247.
3. Ibid., p. 247.
4. Lifar, S. M. *Diagilev*. Moscow, 1994, p. 142.
5. Ibid., p. 144.
6. Ibid., p. 147.
7. Haskell, Arnold (with Nouvel Walter). *Diaghileff: His Artistic and Private Life*. New York, 1935, p. 157.
8. Lifar, S. M., op cit., p. 195.
9. Haskell, Arnold, op. cit., p. 158.
10. Lifar, S. M., op. cit., p. 196.
11. Poiret, Paul, *En habillant l'epoque* [About Dressing An Era]. Paris, 1930, pp. 57–58.
12. Ibid., p. 10.
13. Lieven, Peter, Prince. *The Birth of the Ballets-Russes*, London, 1936, pp. 117–118.
14. Quoted in *Russkaya Mysl'*. Paris, November 4-8, 1993, p. 10.
15. Quoted in MacDonald, Nesta. *Diaghilev Observed*. London, 1975, p. 41.
16. Poiret, Paul, op. cit., p. 106.
17. Quoted in *Russkaya Mysl'*. Paris, October 28–November 4, 1993, p. 10.
18. Vassiliev, A. A. "Volshebnik Erte" [The Magician Erté] *Russkaya Mysl'*. Paris, November 27, 1987, p. 13.
19. Dandre, Victor. *Anna Pavlova*. London, 1935, p. 216.
20. Conversation A. A. Vassiliev had with A. F. Vronska. Lausanne, April 1990.
21. Conversation A. A. Vassiliev had with N. Kirsanova. Belgrade, August 1987.
22. Conversation A. A. Vassiliev had with V. P. Kachouba. Madrid, February 1996.
23. See *Art, gout, beauté* [Art, Taste, Beauty]. 1921, No. 14, p. 12.
24. Quoted in *Gazette du bon ton* [Gazette of Good Taste]. Paris, April 1923, p. 204.

2 RUSSIAN FASHION DURING WORLD WAR I AND THE GREAT EXODUS

1. *Zhurnal dlia khoziaek* [Magazine for Housewives]. 1915, No. 24, p. 11.
2. *Zhurnal dlia zhenshchin* [Magazine for Women]. 1915, No. 24, p. 10.
3. *Stolitsa i usad'ba* [Capital and Estate]. 1917, No. 74, p. 15.
4. Ibid., 1916, No. 60-61, p. 14.
5. Ibid.
6. *Zhurnal dlia khoziaek*. 1915, No. 2, p. 9.
7. Teffi, N. A. *Vospominaniya* [Memoirs]. Paris, 1932, pp. 73–74.
8. Ibid., p. 9.
9. Ibid., pp. 11-12.
10. Ibid., p. 152.
11. Ibid., p. 19.
12. Ibid., p. 178.
13. Ibid., p. 265.

3 RUSSIAN CONSTANTINOPLE

1. Rogov, Ye. *Skitalets po nevole. Chast' II* [Unwilling Wanderer, Part II]. San Francisco, 1970, p. 1.
2. Quoted in *Zhar-ptitsa* [Firebird]. Berlin, 1922, No. 8, p. 26.
3. Ibid.
4. Dogorukov, P. D. *Velikaya Razrukha* [The Great Collapse]. Madrid, 1964, p. 10.
5. Vertinsky, A. *Zapiski russkogo P'ero* [The Notes of a Russian Pierrot]. New York, 1982, p. 13.
6. *Na proshchan'ye* [In Parting]. Istanbul, 1924, p. 57.
7. *Russkiye na Bosfore* [Russians on the Bosphorus]. Istanbul, 1928, p. 47.
8. Isheyev, P.P. *Oskolki proshlogo. Vospominaniya 1889–1959* [Fragments of the Past: Memoirs 1889-1959]. New York, 1959. p. 138.

9. *Teatr i zhizn'* [Theater and Life]. Berlin. 1922, No. 8, p. 16.
10. Conversation A. A. Vassiliev had with Ye. Gordienko. Istanbul, April 1989.
11. *Teatr i zhizn'* [Theater and Life]. Berlin. 1922, No. 8, p. 16.
12. Ibid., No. 7, p. 16.
13. Ibid.
14. *Na proshchan'ye*, p. 93.
15. Conversation A. A. Vassiliev had with V. Yu. Clodt von Jurgensburg. Istanbul, April 1989.
16. Vertinsky, A., op cit., p. 13.
17. *Russkiye na Bosfore*, p. 56.
18. Vertinsky, A., op cit., p. 16.
19. *Russkiye na Bosfore*, p. 56.
20. *Histoire de l'industrie et du commerce en France. Vol. II*. [The History of Industry and Commerce in France: Vol II]. Paris, 1926, p. 134.
21. Vertinsky, A., op cit., p. 16.
22. Quoted in *Istanbullu kim*, Istanbul, 1991, p. 79.
23. Dolgorukov, I.D., op cit., p. 206-207.
24. Ibid., p. 219.

4 RUSSIAN BERLIN

1. *Zhar-ptitsa* [Firebird]. Berlin, 1921, No. 3, p. 2.
2. Tikanova, N. *Devushka v sinem* [The Girl in Blue]. Moscow, 1992, p. 50.
3. *Zhar-ptitsa*. Berlin, 1921, No. 3, p. 2.
4. *Teatr i zhizn'* [Theater and Life]. Berlin. 1922, No. 10, p. 14.
5. Ibid., p. 13.
6. Ibid., p. 14.
7. Leonidov, L. *Rampa i zhizn'* [Footlights and Life]. Paris, 1955, p. 175.
8. Gzovskaya, O. *Puti i pereput'ya* [Paths and Crossroads]. Moscow, 1976, p. 160.
9. Kuznetsov, S. *Sbornik statei* [Collected Essays]. Moscow, 1927, p. 14.
10. Quoted in Knipper, V. *Pora gallyutsinatsii* [The Time of Hallucinations]. Moscow, 1995, pp. 288-289.
11. Beriozoff, N. *Zhizn' i balet* [Life and Ballet]. London, 1983, p. 109-110.
12. Quoted in Baroness Lempicka, Kizette de, *Passion by Design*. New York, p. 123.

5 RUSSIAN HARBIN

1. Quoted in *Politekhnik*. Anniversary issue. Sidney, 1979, p. 101.
2. Ibid., p. 102.
3. Ibid., p. 79.
4. Ibid., p. 10.
5. Ibid., p. 235.
6. Conversation A. A. Vassiliev had with N. A. Davidenko. Harbin, January 1993.
7. Zhemchuzhnaya, Z. *Puti izgnaniya. Vospominaniya* [Paths of Exile. Memoirs]. New Jersey, 1987, p. 181.
8. Letter dated October 26, 1994 to A. A. Vassiliev from N. Briansky in Allambie, Australia.
9. Ibid.
10. Conversation A. A. Vassiliev had with F. Pisarsky. Hong Kong, March 1995. Further statements by F. Pisarsky are quoted from the tape of this conversation.
11. Letter dated September 23, 1996 to A. A. Vassiliev from O. S. Koreneva in Sidney. The author wishes express his gratitude to his correspondent, a historian of Harbin and publisher of the magazine *Politekhnik*, for the information she so generously shared with him.
12. Conversation A. A. Vassiliev had with G. Achair-Dobrotvorskaya. Queensland, Australia, July 1996.
13. Quoted in *Politekhnik*, p. 224.
14. Ibid., p. 233.
15. Letter dated September 23, 1996 to A. A. Vassiliev from O. S. Koreneva in Sidney.

16. *Rubezh* [Borderline]. Harbin, 1930.
17. *Sovremennaya zhenshchina* [Modern Woman]. Shanghai, March 1937, p. 2.

6 Russian Émigré Handicrafts

1. *Fémina.* March 1, 1921, p. 48.
2. Damanskaya, A. F. *Miranda.* New York, 1953, p. 10.
3. *L'Art et la mode* [Art and Fashion]. May 3, 1924.
4. Conversation A. A. Vassiliev had with I. S. Mishchenko. Paris, April 1991.
5. Teffi, N. A. *Gorodok* [The Little Town]. Paris, 1927, pp. 59–60.
6. Quoted in *Harper's Bazaar,* Moscow, 1996, No. 3, p. 10.
7. Conversation A. A. Vassiliev had with Lady Abdy. Le Cannet, near Nice, August 1992.
8. Wakhevitch, George. *L'Envers des decors* [The Reverse of Decor]. Paris, 1977, p. 52.
9. *L'Art vivant* [Living Art], 1927, No. 3, p. 37.
10. Marevna. *Memoirs d'une nomade* [Memoirs of a Nomad]. Paris, 1979, p. 300.
11. *Krasnaya Nov'* [Red Virgin Soil], 1933, No. 2, p. 170.
12. Ibid.

7 The Kitmir House of Embroidery

1. Skott, Staffan. *Romanovy* [The Romanovs]. Yekaterinburg, 1993, p. 171.
2. Quoted in Youssoupoff, Felix Prince. *Pered izgnaniem* [Before Exile]. Moscow, 1993, p. 235.
3. Marie de Russie [Maria of Russia]. *Une princesse en exil* [A Grand Duchess in Exile]. Paris, 1933, p. 20.
4. Ibid., p. 35.
5. Ibid., p. 38.
6. Ibid., p. 68-69.
7. Ibid., p. 87.
8. Ibid., p. 95.
9. See *Vogue,* Paris. January 15, 1922, p. 24.
10. Quoted in Roux, Edmond Charles. *Le temps Chanel* [The Time of Chanel]. Paris, 1979, p. 24.
11. Marie de Russie, op. cit., p. 176.
12. Ibid., p. 202.
13. Ibid., p. 205.
14. Conversation A. A. Vassiliev had with K. S. Sereda. Montmorency, July 1994.
15. Conversation A. A. Vassiliev had with R. M. Dobuzhinsky. Paris, May 1991.
16. Quoted in Etherilton-Smith, Meredith. *Patou.* London, 1982, p. 36.
17. Marie de Russie, op. cit., p. 206.
18. Strizhenova, T.K. *Iz istorii sovetskogo kostyuma* [From the History of Soviet Costume]. Moscow, 1972, p. 62.
19. Letter dated November 30, 1992 to A. A. Vassiliev from M. V. Kireeff in Buenos Aires.

8 The Emergence of Russian Fashion and Fashion Houses in Paris

1. *Vogue.* Paris, December 15, 1922, p. 37.
2. Mosolov, A. A. *Pri dvore poslednego imperatora* [In the Court of the Last Emperor]. St. Petersburg, 1922, p. 194.
3. *Vogue.* London, January 1, 1920, p. 22.
4. Zeeler, V. *Russkie vo Frantsii* [The Russians in France]. Paris, 1946, p. 10.
5. See Gorboff, Maria. *La Russie-Fantome* [Phantom Russia]. Paris, 1995, p. 7.
6. *Fémina,* March 1, 1921, p. 48.
7. This outfit from the House of Princess Ouroussow was discovered by the author in the Musée de la Mode et du Costume thanks to the kind assistance of the curator Valerie Guillaume.
8. *Histoire de l'industrie et du commerce en France,* p. 132.
9. Ibid.
10. Ibid., p. 126.
11. Ibid.
12. *Art, gout, beauté.* 1922, No. 17, p. 19.
13. Conversation A. A. Vassiliev had with V. I. Kachouba. Madrid, February 1996.

14. Conversation A. A. Vassiliev had with F. M. Zelinskaya. Moscow, August 1990.
15. *Harper's Bazaar.* Paris, February 1, 1928, p. 58.

9 The Paul Caret House of Fashion

1. *Histoire de l'industrie et du commerce en France,* p. 131.
2. *Vogue.* Paris, April 1, 1924, p. 125.
3. Ibid., September, 1924, p. 72.
4. Ibid., April 1, 1924, p. 48.
5. Ibid., February 1, 1928, p. 48.

10 The TAO House of Fashion

1. Conversation A. A. Vassiliev had with M. A. Yanushevskaya. Paris, April 1991. Further statements by M. A. Yanushevskaya are quoted from the tape of this conversation.
2. Dogorukov, P. D. *Velikaya Razrukha* [The Great Collapse], p. 212.

11 Yteb House of Fashion

1. Quoted in Ewing, William A. *The Photographic Art of Hoyningen-Huene.* London, 1991, p. 4.
2. Ibid., pp. 4-5.
3. Quoted in *Histoire de l'industrie et du commerce en France,* p. 129.
4. Ibid.
5. Conversation A. A. Vassiliev had with Ye. S. von Tiesenhausen. Paris, 1990.
6. Ibid.
7. *Vogue.* Paris, May 1, 1927, pp. 48-52.
8. Ibid., February 1, 1928, p. 70.
9. The reminiscences of Baroness Nina von Hoyer were written down by her son Graham McCartney during the 1970s. He kindly made the text available to A. A. Vassiliev in 1992. Further statements by Nina von Hoyer are based on this unpublished manuscript.
10. *Vogue.* Paris, March 1, 1929, p. 21.
11. Ibid., May 1, 1931, p. 48.

12 The Fashion House of Irfé

1. Youssoupoff, Felix Prince. *Pered izgnaniem* [Before Exile]. Moscow, 1993, p. 68.
2. Ibid.
3. Ibid.
4. Ibid., pp. 118-119.
5. Erté. *Things I Remember: An Autobiography.* London, 1975, p. 56.
6. Ibid., pp. 56-57.
7. Metternich, Tatiana. *Memoirs.* Paris, 1991, p. 71.
8. *Histoire de l'industrie et du commerce en France,* p. 137.
9. Youssoupoff, Felix. *Memoirs.* Paris, 1990, p. 296.
10. Metternich, Tatiana, op. cit., p. 71.
11. *Vogue.* Paris, February 1, 1926, p. 46.
12. Marevna. *Memoirs d'une nomade* [Memoirs of a Nomad]. Paris, 1979, pp. 281-282.
13. Conversation A. A. Vassiliev had with A. V. von Nolken. Paris, August 1995.
14. Conversation A. A. Vassiliev had with V. P. Kachouba. Madrid, February 1996.
15. Conversation A. A. Vassiliev had with A. D. Danilova. New York, August 1996.
16. Conversation A. A. Vassiliev had with Lady Abdy. Le Cannet near Nice, August 1992.
17. Youssoupoff, Felix, op. cit., p. 345.
18. Ibid., p. 346

13 The Bery House of Fashion

1. Kchessinska, M. K. *Vospominaniya* [Memoirs]. Moscow, 1992, p. 131.
2. Krymov, V. *Kak khorosho zhili v Peterburge* [How Well They Lived in St. Petersburg]. Berlin, 1923, p. 102.
3. Youssoupoff, Felix Prince. *Pered izgnaniem,* p. 205.
4. *Vogue.* Paris, April 1, 1924 p. 48.
5. *Histoire de l'industrie et du commerce en France,* p. 135.
6. Conversation A. A. Vassiliev had with V. V. Pyatakova.

Montmorency, May 1991. Further statements by V. V. Pyatakova are quoted from the tape of this conversation.

7. Conversation A. A. Vassiliev had with N. A. Offenstadt. Paris, September 1992.

14 ARDANSE HOUSE OF FASHION

1. Conversation A. A. Vassiliev had with Ye. N. Bobrikova-Bonnet. Paris, March 1992.
2. *Histoire de l'industrie et du commerce en France,* p. 126.
3. *L'Art et la mode* [Art and Fashion]. Paris, September 1, 1928, p. 153.
4. Ibid., March 23, 1929, p. 153.
5. Ibid., February 20, 1930, p. 100.
6. Ibid., August 20, 1930, p. 53.
7. Ibid.
8. Conversation A. A. Vassiliev had with N. V. Tverdaya. Paris, April 1997.
9. *L'Art et la mode.* Paris, February 31, 1928, p. 100.
10. Ibid., May 20, 1931, p. 100.
11. Ibid., August 20, 1931, p. 53.
12. *Fémina.* Paris, May 1946, p. 139.

15 THE VALENTINA HOUSE OF FASHION

1. Vertinsky, A. *Dorogoi dlinnoyu . . .* [Taking the Long Road . . .]. Moscow, 1991, p. 349.
2. Ibid., p. 113.
3. Ibid., p. 113–114.
4. Ibid., p. 114.
5. Ibid., p. 287–288.
6. Ibid., p. 349.
7. Conversation A. A. Vassiliev had with A. A. Vertinskaya. Paris, December 1996.

16 THE HITROVO HOUSE OF LINGERIE

1. Conversation A. A. Vassiliev had with M. Grekova-Zinovieva. Geneva, September 1996.
2. Conversation A. A. Vassiliev had with Countess P. V. de Saint Hipolyte. Paris, 1994.
3. Conversation A. A. Vassiliev had with M. N. Nenarokova. Paris, May 1996. Other statements by M. N. Nenarokova are quoted from the tape of this conversation.
4. *Vogue.* Paris, May 1, 1931, p. 10.

17 THE ADLERBERG HOUSE OF LINGERIE

1. Conversation A. A. Vassiliev had with N. P Bologovskaya. Paris, December 1986. Further statements by N. P. Bologov-skaya are quoted from the tape of this conversation.

18 THE LAURE BELIN HOUSE OF LINGERIE

1. Letter dated June 19, 1996 to A. A. Vassiliev from I. S. Holman de Koby. Other statements by I. S. Holman de Koby are quoted from the tape of this conversation.

19 RUSSIAN ÉMIGRÉ FASHION ILLUSTRATORS AND FABRIC DESIGNERS

1. *Costume Designers of Hollywood.* New York 1975, p. 10.
2. Vassiliev, A. A. "Volshebnik Erte" [The Magician Erté], *Russkaya mysl'.* Paris, November 27, 1987, p. 10.
3. There was no interest in Erté in the Soviet Union during his lifetime. Thanks to A. A. Vassiliev, who was a friend of his, Soviet television filmed Erté at his home in the late 1980s, but later found the documentary lacking in value and erased the tape.
4. Quoted in Jacques Damase. *Sonia Delaunay, Fashion and Fabrics.* No date. p. 63.
5. Kochno, Boris. *Diaghilev and the Ballets Russes.* New York, 1970.
6. *Vogue.* London, January 1996, p. 78.
7. *L'Art vivant* [Living Art], 1925, No. 4, p. 6.
8. Conversation A. A. Vassiliev had with D. D. Bouchéne. Paris, May 1989. Further statements by D. D. Bouchéne are quoted from the tape of this conversation.
9. Conversation A. A. Vassiliev had with K. B. Grigoriev. Cagnes-sur-Mer near Nice, 1996.

20 RUSSIAN BEAUTIES OF THE 1920S

1. *Zhar-ptitsa* [Firebird]. Berlin, 1922, No. 8, p. 26.
2. Rogov, Ye. *Skitalets po nevole. Chast' II* [Unwilling Wanderer, Part II], p. 8.
3. Beloselsky-Belozersky, S. S. Prince. *Memoirs.* Paris, 1994, p. 50.
4. Conversation A. A. Vassiliev had with K. A. Sereda. Montmorency, July 1994. Further statements by K. A. Sereda are quoted from the tape of this conversation.
5. Conversation A. A. Vassiliev had with V. I. Pokrovskaya. La Faviere near Le Lavandou, July 1992. Further statements by V. I. Pokrovskaya are quoted from the tape of this conversation.
6. Beloselsky-Belozersky, S. S. Prince, op. cit., p. 10.
7. Conversation A. A. Vassiliev had with M. P. Yanova (Averino). Paris, May 1993. Further statements by M. P. Averino are quoted from the tape of this conversation.
8. Balmain, Pierre. *40 Annees de creation.* Paris, 1985, p. 29.
9. Conversation A. A. Vassiliev had with Ya. A. Obolenskaya. Santiago, August 1992.
10. Conversation A. A. Vassiliev had with T. Leskova. Montmorency, August 1995.
11. Conversation A. A. Vassiliev had with Ye. N. Bobrikova-Bonnet. Paris, March 1992.
12. de Gay, G. G. *Teatral'naya Rossiya* [Theatrical Russia]. Leningrad, 1928, p. 283.
13. Conversation A. A. Vassiliev had with Lady Abdy. Le Cannet near Nice, August 1992. Further statements by Lady Abdy are quoted from the tape of this conversation.
14. *Vogue.* Paris, June, 1925, p. 10.
15. Kuprina, K. A. *Kuprin—moi otets* [Kuprin, My Father]. Moscow, 1971, p. 191.
16. Ibid., p. 192.
17. Letter dated March 21, 1992 to A. A. Vassiliev from Countess N. N. Sumarokova-Elston in London.

21 RUSSIAN BEAUTIES OF THE 1930S AND 1940S

1. Conversation A. A. Vassiliev had with G. R. Gorlenko-Delwig. Chaville near Paris, 1987.
2. Conversation A. A. Vassiliev had with Ye. N. Bobrikova-Bonnet. Paris, March 1992.
3. *L'Exportateur Francais* [The French Exporter]. November 25, 1946, p. 22.
4. Conversation A. A. Vassiliev had with M. P. Yanova (Averino). Paris, May 1992.
5. Conversation A. A. Vassiliev had with N. P. Bologovskaya. Paris, 1986.
6. Conversation A. A. Vassiliev had with Lady Abdy. Le Cannet near Nice, August 1992. Further statements by Lady Abdy are quoted from the tape of this conversation.
7. Conversation A. A. Vassiliev had with N. D. Nilus. Gagny near Paris, May 1991.
8. See Castle, Charles. *Model Girl.* London, 1977, p. 22.
9. Telephone conversation A. A. Vassiliev had with A. L. Feodoseyev in Rio de Janeiro in September 1993.
10. Germaine Barton (her real name), the proprietress of the Alix house of fashion, renamed it the house of Madame Gres in 1941. The name was based on the French name of her husband, the Russian emigre-artist, Serge Cherevkov, from the letters of his first name read from right to left.
11. Letter by fax dated January 5, 1997 to A. A. Vassiliev from A. Gayard in Le Touquet.
12. Letter dated September 10, 1993 to A. A. Vassiliev from A. Gayard in Le Barelle, France.
13. Letter by fax dated January 5, 1997 to A. A. Vassiliev from A. Gayard in Le Touquet.
14. Conversation A. A. Vassiliev had with V. B. Rapponet. Montmorency, July 1991. Further statements by V. B. Rapponet are quoted from the tape of this conversation.
15. Letter from A. D. Danilova to A. A. Vassiliev in 1996.
16. Vassiliev, A. A. "Christian Dior, bulavochnyi tiran" [Christian Dior, The Hemline Tyrant] *Russkaya Mysl'.* Paris, November 24, 1987, p. 13.
17. Conversation A. A. Vassiliev had with A. Ilchun. Paris, April 1987.

INDEX

PHOTO CREDITS

Chapter 1
Author's collection, Paris; Art Theater Museum, Moscow; author's collection, Paris; Musée Grand Opéra, Paris; Sotheby's, Monaco; Valentina Kachouba collection, Madrid; Valentina Kachouba collection, Madrid; author's collection, Paris; author's collection, Paris; author's collection, Paris; Cartier, Paris; La Cambre Library, Brussels; Valentina Kachouba collection, Madrid; Musée des Arts Decoratifs, Paris; author's collection, Paris; Valentina Kachouba collection, Paris; private collection, Paris; Bibliothèque des Arts Decoratifs, Paris; Paul Poiret collection, Paris; private collection, Paris; author's collection, Paris; Glasgow School of the Arts Library, Scotland; National Library, Santiago; National Library, Santiago; Carol Mann collection, Paris; Musée de la Mode et du Costume, Paris; San Telmo Market, Buenos Aires; Museum of Art, Indianapolis; National Library, Santiago; The National Gallery of Victoria, Melbourne; private collection, Paris; Svetlana Samsonow collection, Paris; author's collection, Paris; National Library, Santiago; author's collection, Paris; Bibliothèque des Arts Decoratifs, Paris; author's collection, Paris; author's collection, Paris; La Cambre Library, Brussels; author's collection, Paris; National Library, Santiago; Mikael Dilon collection, London; author's collection, Paris; author's collection, Paris; National Library, Santiago; Theater Museum, London; Bibliothèque des Arts Decoratifs, Paris; Nina Tikanova collection, Paris; author's collection, Paris; author's collection, Paris; National Library, Santiago; Olga Stark-Kononovich collection, Montmorency.

Chapter 2
Author's collection, Paris; author's collection, Paris; author's collection, Paris; author's collection, Paris; author's collection, Paris; author's collection, Paris; author's collection, Paris; author's collection, Paris; author's collection, Paris; author's collection, Paris; author's collection, Paris; author's collection, Paris; author's collection, Paris; author's collection, Paris; author's collection, Paris; author's collection, Paris; author's collection, Paris; Bibliothèque des Arts Decoratifs, Paris; author's collection, Paris; author's collection, Paris; author's collection, Paris; author's collection, Paris; National Gallery of Georgia, Tbilisi; author's collection, Paris; author's collection, Paris; author's collection, Paris; author's collection, Paris; author's collection, Paris; author's collection, Paris; author's collection, Paris; author's collection, Paris; author's collection, Paris; author's collection, Paris; author's collection, Paris; author's collection, Paris; author's collection, Paris; Kissel-Zagoriansky workshop, Moscow; author's collection, Paris; Andrey Korliakov collection, Paris; author's collection, Paris; private collection, Chile; author's collection, Paris; author's collection, Paris.

Chapter 3
National Library, Ankara; author's collection, Paris; author's collection, Paris; author's collection, Paris; author's collection, Paris; author's collection, Paris; author's collection, Paris; author's collection, Paris; author's collection, Paris; author's collection, Paris; National Library, Ankara; author's collection, Paris; author's collection, Paris; National Library, Ankara; National Library, Ankara; National Library, Ankara; National Library, Ankara; National Library, Ankara; private collection, Istanbul; National Library, Ankara; National Library, Ankara; National Library, Ankara; author's collection, Lithuania; National Library, Ankara; author's collection, Lithuania; National Library, Ankara; author's collection, Paris; House-Museum of Ataturk, Ankara; National Library, Ankara; author's collection, Paris; La Cambre Library, Brussels; La Cambre Library, Brussels; National Library, Ankara; National Library, Ankara; National Library, Ankara; author's collection, Paris; author's collection, Paris.

Chapter 4
Author's collection, Paris; author's collection, Paris; author's collection, Paris; Micheline Solomoniks collection, Paris; author's collection, Paris; author's collection, Paris; National Library, Santiago; author's collection, Paris; private collection, Moscow; author's collection, Paris; Vita Sevrikova collection, Moscow; author's collection, Paris; author's collection, Paris; author's collection, Paris; Alice Vronska collection, Lausanne; Micheline Solomoniks collection, Paris; author's collection, Paris; author's collection, Paris; Swetlana Beriozova collection, London; author's collection, Paris; author's collection, Paris; author's collection, Paris; author's collection, Paris; author's collection, Paris; author's collection, Paris; Irina Holman de Koby collection, England; author's collection, Paris; Bibliothèque Tourgeneff, Paris; author's collection, Paris; author's collection, Paris; author's collection, Paris; Andrey Korliakov collection, Paris; author's collection, Paris; author's collection, Paris; author's collection, Paris; author's collection, Paris; author's collection, Paris; author's collection, Paris; author's collection, Paris; author's collection, Paris; Musée de la Mode et du Costume, Paris; author's collection, Paris; author's collection, Paris; author's collection, Paris; author's collection, Paris; author's collection, Paris.

Chapter 5
Hkapa Library, Hong Kong; University Library, Harbin; author's collection, Paris; author's collection, Paris; author's collection, Paris; author's collection, Paris; author's collection, Paris; author's collection, Paris; Nikolas Briansky collection, Australia; Nikolas Briansky collection, Australia; author's collection, Paris; Hkapa Library, Hong Kong; University Library, Harbin; University Library, Harbin; University Library, Harbin; University Library, Harbin; Hkapa Library, Hong Kong; Hkapa Library, Hong Kong; University Library, Harbin; University Library, Harbin; University Library, Harbin; Nikolas Briansky collection, Australia; author's collection, Paris; author's collection, Paris; Asami Maki collection, Tokyo; author's collection, Paris; Shemansky, U.S.; author's collection, Paris; author's collection, Paris; Nikolas Briansky collection, Australia; author's collection, Paris; Hkapa Library, Hong Kong; author's collection, Paris; author's collection, Paris; University Library, Harbin; University Library, Harbin; University Library, Harbin; University Library, Harbin; University Library, Harbin.

Chapter 6
Holman de Koby collection, England; Bibliothèque Tourgeneff, Paris; author's collection, Paris; Michel Baibabaeff collection, Paris; author's collection, Paris; author's collection, Paris; Bibliothèque Tourgeneff, Paris; author's collection, Paris; author's collection, Paris; Bibliothèque Tourgeneff, Paris; author's collection, Paris; Andrey Korliakov's collection, Paris; author's collection, Paris; author's collection, Paris; author's collection, Paris; author's collection, Paris; National Library, Santiago; San Telmo Flea Market, Buenos Aires; author's collection, Paris; author's collection, Paris; National Gallery, Santiago; Bibliothèque Art Deco, Paris; author's collection, Paris; author's collection, Paris; La Cambre Library, Brussels; author's collection, Paris; National Library, Santiago; Musée de la Mode et du Costume, Paris; National Library, Santiago; Musée de la Mode et du Costume, Paris; National Library, Santiago; Bibliothèque Art Deco, Paris; Mishchenko colleciton, Paris; author's collection, Paris; Bibliothèque Tourgeneff, Paris; author's collection, Paris; Bibliothèque Tourgeneff, Paris; author's collection, Paris; La Cambre Library, Brussels; La Cambre Library, Brussels; Holman de Koby collection, England.

Chapter 7
Author's collection, Paris; Bibliothèque Art Deco, Paris; Jacques Ferrand collection, France; Jacques Ferrand collection, France; Bibliothèque Tourgeneff, Paris; Jacques Ferrand collection, France; Countess de Beaugourdon collection, Paris; Bibliothèque Art Deco, Paris; Bibliothèque Art Deco, Paris; private collection, Paris; Bibliothèque Art Deco, Paris; La Cambre Library, Brussels; author's collection, Lithuania; Bibliothèque Art Deco, Paris; Museum of Art, Cincinatti; UFAC, Paris; Bibliothèque Art Deco, Paris; La Cambre Library, Brussels; Bibliothèque Art Deco, Paris; Bibliothèque Tourgeneff, Paris; National Library, Santiago; La Cambre Library, Brussels; La Cambre Library, Brussels; Bibliothèque Art Deco, Paris; Bibliothèque Tourgeneff, Paris; Bibliothèque Art Deco, Paris; author's collection, Paris; author's collection, Paris; Bibliothèque Art Deco, Paris; author's collection, Paris; author's collection, Paris; author's collection, Paris; Bibliothèque Art Deco, Paris; Bibliothèque Art Deco, Paris; Bibliothèque Art Deco, Paris; La Cambre Library, Brussels; Bibliothèque Tourgeneff, Paris; Bibliothèque Tourgeneff, Paris; Bibliothèque Art Deco, Paris; author's collection, Paris; Bibliothèque Art Deco, Paris; Bibliothèque Art Deco, Paris; UFAC, Paris; author's collection, Paris; author's collection, Paris; author's collection, Paris.

Chapter 8
Bibliothèque Art Deco, Paris; author's collection, Paris; National Portrait Gallery, London; State Historical Museum, Moscow; author's collection, Paris; State Russian Museum, St. Petersburg; Galina Panova collection, Jerusalem; author's collection, Paris; Elena Shreter collection, Santiago; National Library, Santiago; author's collection, Paris; Bibliothèque Art Deco, Paris; National Library, Santiago; Art Theater Museum, Moscow; National Library, Santiago; author's collection, Paris; La Cambre Library, Brussels; private collection, Paris; author's collection, Paris; La Cambre Library, Brussels; National Library, Santiago; Glasgow School of Art Library, Scotland; La Cambre Library, Brussels; Bibliothèque Art Deco, Paris; Musée de la Mode et du Costume, Paris; Musée de la Mode et du Costume, Paris; La Cambre Library, Brussels; Musée de la Mode et du Costume, Paris; author's collection, Paris; National Library, Santiago; Musée de la Mode et du Costume, Paris; author's collection, Paris; Bibliothèque Art Deco, Paris; author's collection, Paris; author's collection, Paris; Countess Soumarokova-Elston collection, London; Bibliothèque Art Deco, Paris; La Cambre Library, Brussels; La Cambre Library, Brussels; author's collection, Paris; La Cambre Library, Brussels; La Cambre Library, Brussels; Musée de la Mode et du Costume, Paris; Bibliothèque Art Deco, Paris; Musée de la Mode et du Costume, Paris; Musée de la Mode et du Costume, Paris; UFAC, Paris; author's collection, Paris; Bibliothèque Art Deco, Paris; Victoria and Albert Museum, London; Victoria and Albert Museum, London; private collection, Paris; Bibliothèque Art Deco, Paris; La Cambre Library, Brussels; La Cambre Library, Brussels; author's collection, Paris; La Cambre Library, Brussels; author's collection, Paris; Bibliothèque Art Deco, Paris; La Cambre Library, Brussels; Zelinskaya collection, Moscow; author's collection, Paris; La Cambre Library, Brussels; author's collection, Paris; author's collection, Paris; author's collection, Paris; private collection, Paris; author's collection, Paris; author's collection, Paris; Bibliothèque Tourgeneff, Paris; author's collection, Paris; La Cambre Library, Brussels; Bibliothèque Art Deco, Paris; author's collection, Paris; Kachouba collection, Madrid; Bibliothèque Art Deco, Paris; author's collection, Paris; Bibliothèque Art Deco, Paris; author's collection, Paris; author's collection, Paris; Bibliothèque Art Deco, Paris; La Cambre Library, Brussels; La Cambre Library, Brussels; Bibliothèque Art Deco, Paris; La Cambre Library, Brussels; Bibliothèque Art Deco, Paris; La Cambre Library, Brussels; Bibliothèque Art Deco, Paris; Bibliothèque Art Deco, Paris.

Chapter 9
Author's collection, Paris; Bibliothèque Art Deco, Paris; La Cambre Library, Brussels; Bibliothèque Art Deco, Paris; Bibliothèque Art Deco, Paris; Bibliothèque Art Deco, Paris; Bibliothèque Art Deco, Paris; Bibliothèque Art Deco, Paris; Bibliothèque Art Deco, Paris; Bibliothèque Art Deco, Paris; La Cambre Library, Brussels; Bibliothèque Art Deco, Paris; Bibliothèque Art Deco, Paris; author's collection, Paris.

Chapter 10
National Library, Santiago; author's collection, Paris; Prince Troubetskoy collection, U.S.; Prince Troubetskoy collection, U.S.; Janovskevskaya collection, Paris; National Library, Santiago; Bibliothèque Art Deco, Paris; Prince Troubetskoy collection, U.S.;

Prince Troubetskoy collection, U.S.; La Cambre Library, Brussels; Prince Troubetskoy collection, U.S.; author's collection, Paris; author's collection, Paris.

Chapter 11
Bibliothéque Art Deco, Paris; Bibliothéque Art Deco, Paris; Bibliothéque Art Deco, Paris; La Cambre Library, Brussels; Bibliothéque Art Deco, Paris; Bibliothéque Art Deco, Paris; La Cambre Library, Brussels; Bibliothéque Art Deco, Paris; Bibliothéque Art Deco, Paris; Bibliothéque Art Deco, Paris; Bibliothéque Art Deco, Paris; Bibliothéque Art Deco, Paris; Bibliothéque Art Deco, Paris; Bibliothéque Art Deco, Paris; Natalie Auberjonis collection, Neuilly; Bibliothéque Art Deco, Paris; Bibliothéque Art Deco, Paris; Bibliothéque Art Deco, Paris; Bibliothéque Art Deco, Paris; Olga Wienand collection, England; Bibliothéque Art Deco, Paris; Bibliothéque Art Deco, Paris; La Cambre Library, Brussels; La Cambre Library, Brussels; Bibliothéque Art Deco, Paris; Bibliothéque Art Deco, Paris; Bibliothéque Art Deco, Paris; La Cambre Library, Brussels; Bibliothéque Art Deco, Paris; Bibliothéque Art Deco, Paris; La Cambre Library, Brussels; Graham McCartney collection, London; La Cambre Library, Brussels; Grey MacCartney collection, London; La Cambre Library, Brussels; Grey MacCartney collection, London; Bibliothéque Art Deco, Paris; Bibliothéque Art Deco, Paris; Bibliothéque Art Deco, Paris; Bibliothéque Art Deco, Paris; Bibliothéque Art Deco, Paris; Bibliothéque Art Deco, Paris; Bibliothéque Art Deco, Paris; Bibliothéque Art Deco, Paris; Bibliothéque Art Deco, Paris; La Cambre Library, Brussels; Bibliothéque Art Deco, Paris; Bibliothéque Art Deco, Paris; La Cambre Library, Brussels; Glasgow School of Art Library, Scotland; Bibliothéque Art Deco, Paris; Bibliothéque Art Deco, Paris; Bibliothéque Art Deco, Paris; author's collection, Paris; author's collection, Paris.

Chapter 12
Xenia Sfiris collection, Athens; Bibliothéque Art Deco, Paris; Hermitage Museum, St. Petersburg; State Russian Museum, St. Petersburg; State Historical Museum, Moscow; author's collection, Paris; Zenia Sfiris collection, Athens; Bibliothéque Art Deco, Paris; Bibliothéque Art Deco, Paris; Bibliothéque Tourgeneff, Paris; Bibliothéque Tourgeneff, Paris; Bibliothéque Tourgeneff, Paris; Bibliothéque Tourgeneff, Paris; Bibliothéque Art Deco, Paris; La Cambre Library, Brussels; Princess Obolenskaya collection, Washington, D.C.; Bibliothéque Art Deco, Paris; Bibliothéque Art Deco, Paris; La Cambre Library, Brussels; Bibliothéque Art Deco, Paris; Bibliothéque Art Deco, Paris; Bibliothéque Art Deco, Paris; Bibliothéque Art Deco, Paris; Bibliothéque Art Deco, Paris; Bibliothéque Art Deco, Paris; La Cambre Library, Brussels; La Cambre Library, Brussels; La Cambre Library, Brussels; Nolken-Margoulis collection, Paris; Xenia Sfiris collection, Athens; Xenia Sfiris collection, Athens; Xenia Sfiris collection, Athens; author's collection, Paris; author's collection, Paris.

Chapter 13
Andrey Korliakov collection, Paris; author's collection, Paris; State Theater Museum, St. Petersburg; State Theater Museum, St. Petersburg; State Theater Museum, St. Petersburg; State Theater Museum, St. Petersburg; State Theater Museum, St. Petersburg; Asami Maki collection, Tokyo; private collection, U.S.; Bibliothéque Art Deco, Paris; Bibliothéque Art Deco, Paris; La Cambre Library, Brussels; Jacques Ferrand collection, Paris; author's collection, Paris; author's collection, Paris.

Chapter 14
Author's collection, Paris; Constantin Zuravlev collection, Moscow; author's collection, Paris; La Cambre Library, Brussels; La Cambre Library, Brussels; Bibliothéque Art Deco, Paris; Bibliothéque Art Deco, Paris; Roger-Viollet, Paris; Roger-Viollet, Paris; Bibliothéque Art Deco, Paris; author's collection, Paris; Bibliothéque Art Deco, Paris; author's collection, Paris.

Chapter 15
Bibliothéque Art Deco, Paris; Christie's, New York; author's collection, Paris; author's collection, Paris; Historical Society, Chicago; author's collection, Paris; author's collection, Paris; author's collection, Paris; Bibliothéque Art Deco, Paris; private collection, New York; private collection, Lithuania; Glasgow School of Art Library, Scotland; Bouchéne collection, Paris.

Chapter 16
Hitrovo collection, Sevres; Hitrovo collection, Sevres; Maria Grekova collection, Geneva; Maria Grekova collection, Geneva; Maria Grekova collection, Geneva; Maria Grekova collection, Geneva; author's collection, Paris; Maria Grekova collection, Geneva; Maria Grekova collection, Geneva; Hitrovo collection, Sevres; Maria Grekova collection, Sevres; Hitrovo collection, Sevres.

Chapter 17
Author's collection, Paris; author's collection, Paris; author's collection, Paris; Natalie Auberjonois collection, Neuilly; Natalie Auberjonois collection, Neuilly; author's collection, Paris; author's collection, Paris; author's collection, Paris; author's collection, Paris; author's collection, Paris; Natalie Auberjonois collection, Neuilly; author's collection, Paris.

Chapter 18
Holman de Koby collection, England; author's collection, Paris; Holman de Koby collection, England; Holman de Koby collection, England; author's collection, Paris; author's collection, Paris; Holman de Koby collection, England; author's collection, Paris; Holman de Koby collection, England; Holman de Koby collection, England; Holman de Koby collection, England; Holman de Koby collection, England; author's collection, Paris; Holman de Koby collection, England; author's collection, Paris; author's collection, Paris; author's collection, Paris; author's collection, Paris; Holman de Koby collection, England; author's collection, Paris; Holman de Koby collection, England; Holman de Koby collection, England; Holman de Koby collection, England; Holman de Koby collection, England; Holman de Koby collection, England; Holman de Koby collection, England; Holman de Koby collection, England; Holman de Koby collection, England; Holman de Koby collection, England; author's collection, Paris.

Chapter 19
Bibliothéque Art Deco, Paris; Glasgow School of Arts Library, Scotland; Glasgow School of Arts Library, Scotland; Glasgow School of Arts Library, Scotland; Glasgow School of Arts Library, Scotland; Glasgow School of Arts Library, Scotland; Glasgow School of Arts Library, Scotland; Glasgow School of Arts Library, Scotland; Glasgow School of Arts Library, Scotland; Glasgow School of Arts Library, Scotland; Bibliothéque Art Deco, Paris; Tyssen-Bornemitla Museum, Madrid; Glasgow School of Arts Library, Scotland; Glasgow School of Arts Library, Scotland; Glasgow School of Arts Library, Scotland; author's collection, Paris; UFAC, Paris; private collection, Paris; Bibliothéque Art Deco, Paris; Asami Maki collection, Tokyo; Bibliothéque Art Deco, Paris; La Cambre Library, Brussels; private collection, Paris; private collection, Paris; private collection, France; private collection, France; private collection, France; private collection, France; private collection, Paris; private collection, France; Andrè Prokovsky collection, Tourette-sur-Loup; Andrè Prokovsky collection, Tourette-sur-Loup; Grigorian collection, Cagnes-sur-Mer; Andrè Prokovsky collection, Tourette-sur-Loup; State Russian Museum, St. Petersburg; National Library, Santiago; National Library, Santiago; private collection, Paris; National Library, Santiago; Zinaida de Plagny collection, Paris; Zinaida de Plagny collection, Paris; Zinaida de Plagny collection, Paris; Zinaida de Plagny collection, Paris; Zinaida de Plagny collection, Paris; Zinaida de Plagny collection, Paris; Zinaida de Plagny collection, Paris; Zinaida de Plagny collection, Paris; Holman de Koby collection, Paris; Holman de Koby collection, Paris; Holman de Koby collection, Paris; Holman de Koby collection, Paris; Holman de Koby collection, Paris; Holman de Koby collection, Paris; Holman de Koby collection, Paris.

Chapter 20
Bobrikova-Bonnet collection, Paris; author's collection, Paris; Bibliothéque Art Deco, Paris; Jacques Ferrand collection, France; Bibliothéque Art Deco, Paris; Bibliothéque Art Deco, Paris; Hagondokoff collection, Paris; Hagondokoff collection, Paris; Hagondokoff collection, Paris; Holman de Koby collection, Paris; Holman de Koby collection, Paris; Hagondokoff collection, Paris; Bibliothéque Art Deco, Paris; author's collection, Paris; author's collection, Paris; author's collection, Paris; Michel Baibabaeff collection, Paris; Bibliothéque Art Deco, Paris; Bibliothéque Art Deco, Paris; Bibliothéque Art Deco, Paris; Bibliothéque Art Deco, Paris; Princess Obolensky collection, Washington, D.C.; Holman de Koby collection, England; Tatiana Leskova collection, Rio de Janeiro; Tatiana Leskova collection, Rio de Janeiro; Musée de la Mode et du Costume, Paris; author's collection, Paris; Bobrikova-Bonnet collection, Paris; Bobrikova-Bonnet collection, Paris; Bobrikova-Bonnet collection, Paris; Bobrikova-Bonnet collection, Paris; Bobrikova-Bonnet collection, Paris; Bibliothéque Art Deco, Paris; author's collection, Paris; Bibliothéque Art Deco, Paris; Bibliothéque Art Deco, Paris; Bibliothéque Art Deco, Paris; Bibliothéque Art Deco, Paris; Bibliothéque Art Deco, Paris; author's collection, Paris; Bibliothéque Art Deco, Paris; Rotwand collection, Paris; Bibliothéque Art Deco, Paris; Rotwand collection, Paris; Art Theater Museum, Moscow; Bibliothéque Tourgeneff, Paris; Musée de la Mode et du Costume, Paris; author's collection, Paris; author's collection, Paris; author's collection, Paris; Tverdy collection, Paris; Tverdy collection, Paris; author's collection, Paris; author's collection, Paris; Kachouba collection, Madrid; author's collection, Paris; author's collection, Paris; author's collection, Paris; Bibliothéque Art Deco, Paris; author's collection, Paris.

Chapter 21
Alexandra Gaillard collection, Le Touquet; Lidia Rotwand collection, Paris; Glasgow School of Art Library, Scotland; Lidia Rotwand collection, Paris; author's collection, Paris; Princess Alexandra Theater collection, Toronto; Olga Stark collection, Montmorency; Bibliothéque Art Deco, Paris; Bobrikova-Bonnes collection, Paris; Bobrikova-Bonnes collection, Paris; author's collection, Paris; Yanouchevsky collection, Paris; Bobrikova-Bonnes collection, Paris; Musée de la Mode et du Costume, Paris; Boulatzel-Roussel collection, Paris; Boulatzel-Roussel collection, Paris; Boulatzel-Roussel collection, Paris; Boulatzel-Roussel collection, Paris; Musée de la Mode et du Costume, Paris; Bibliothéque Art Deco, Paris; Musée de la Mode et du Costume, Paris; author's collection, Paris; author's collection, Paris; author's collection, Paris; author's collection, Paris; author's collection, Paris; author's collection, Paris; author's collection, Paris; author's collection, Paris; Bibliothéque Art Deco, Paris; Count Stenbock-Fermor collection, Neuilly; Musée de la Mode et du Costume, Paris; Bibliothéque Art Deco, Paris; Cartier Foundation, Paris; Bibliothéque Art Deco, Paris; Bibliothéque Art Deco, Paris; Bibliothéque Art Deco, Paris; Bibliothéque Art Deco, Paris; Bibliothéque Art Deco, Paris; Musée de la Mode et du Costume, Paris; Bibliothéque Art Deco, Paris; Bibliothéque Art Deco, Paris; Bibliothéque Art Deco, Paris; Bibliothéque Art Deco, Paris; Druot Auctions, Paris; Bibliothéque Art Deco, Paris; Lidia Rotwand collection, Paris; Lidia Rotwand collection, Paris; Bibliothéque Art Deco, Paris; Bibliothéque Art Deco, Paris; Lidia Rotwand collection, Paris; Lidia Rotwand collection, Paris; Lidia Rotwand collection, Paris; Alexandra Gaillard collection, Le Touquet; Alexandra Gaillard collection, Le Touquet; Alexandra Gaillard collection, Le Touquet; Bibliothéque Art Deco, Paris; Alexandra Gaillard collection, Le Touquet; Alexandra Gaillard collection, Le Touquet; Alexandra Gaillard collection, Le Touquet; Alexandra Gaillard collection, Le Touquet; author's collection, Paris; Rapponet collection, Montmorency; author's collection, Paris; Rapponet collection, Montmorency; author's collection, Paris; author's collection, Paris; Rapponet collection, Montmorency; author's collection, Paris; Rapponet collection, Montmorency; Bibliothéque Art Deco, Paris; Asami Maki collection, Tokyo; National Library, Santiago; Asami Maki collection, Tokyo; Nina Verchinina collection, Rio de Janeiro; National Library, Santiago; author's collection, Paris; Ilchun collection, Paris; Musée de la Mode et du Costume, Paris.